Costa Rica
a travel survival kit

Rob Rachowiecki

Costa Rica – a travel survival kit

1st edition

Published by
  Lonely Planet Publications Pty Ltd (ACN 005 607 983)
  PO Box 617, Hawthorn, Vic 3122, Australia
  Lonely Planet Publications, Inc
  PO Box 2001A, Berkeley, CA 94702, USA

Printed by
  Colorcraft Ltd, Hong Kong

Photographs by
  Robert Harrison (RH)
  Richard Laval (RL)
  Patricia Payson (PP)
  Rob Rachowiecki (RR)
  Ronald Todd (RT)

  Front cover: Poison Arrow Frog (RL)

Published
  September 1991

National Library of Australia Cataloguing in Publication Data

Rachowiecki, Rob, 1954–
  Costa Rica – a travel survival kit.

  Includes index.
  ISBN 0 86442 106 0.

  1. Costa Rica – Description and travel – 1981 –
  I. Title.

919.7286045

text & maps © Lonely Planet 1991
photos © photographers as indicated 1991

Rob Rachowiecki

Rob was born in London and became an avid traveller while still a teenager. He spent most of the 1980s in Latin America, travelling, teaching English, visiting National Parks, and working for *Wilderness Travel*, an adventure travel company. His first visits to Costa Rica in 1980-81 led to his co-authorship, with Hilary Bradt, of *Backpacking in Mexico & Central America*, Bradt Publications. He is the author of Lonely Planet's travel survival kits for *Ecuador* and *Peru* and he has contributed to Lonely Planet's *South America on a shoestring* and *Central America on a shoestring*. Rob found Costa Rica to be an ideal country for combining his particular interests of bird watching and natural history, visiting wilderness areas, and conservation. When not travelling, he lives in Arizona where he is a graduate student in biology and helps his wife, Cathy, raise their daughters, three-year-old Julia and one-year-old Alison. His dream is to sail around the world some day.

Dedication

This book is for my Alison June, who showed me a rabbit in the desert yesterday.

From the Author

Many people helped me in the conception, research, and writing of this book. In the US, Bill Abbott of Wilderness Travel arranged transportation and touring. In Costa Rica, Michael Kaye of Costa Rica Expeditions and his family invited me on a memorable private Pacuare river running trip and provided much help and information. Amos Bien of Rara Avis not only showed me his rainforest preservation project, but also provided a wealth of conservation background. Wolf Bissinger of the Gavilán Lodge took me on a fascinating river excursion up to and along Costa Rica's border with Nicaragua, affording me a look at a rarely visited part of the world. Richard Laval of the Monteverde Conservation League told me much about Costa Rica in general and the Monteverde Cloud Forest in particular. Terry Moore in Golfito helped with local transportation

problems. Don Montague of the South American Explorers Club in Denver allowed me access to a pile of very useful trip reports. The Costa Rica National Tourist Bureau allowed me to photocopy transport information and answered many questions. I also thank many park and reserve rangers throughout Costa Rica who cheerfully answered my questions, without realising that I was researching this book.

My mother-in-law, Pat Payson, joined me for three weeks of travel in Costa Rica and was a cheerful and interested companion, even during rainforest mud slogs. My old friend, Jeff Eldred, travelled in Costa Rica with me a decade ago and those unforgettable early trips provided a good reference point for seeing changes in the country over the years. Various travellers provided information during conversations in bars and bus stations throughout the country.

Whilst I was writing this book, Shawn McLaughlin helped me with computer problems. Back home, my in-laws were helpful beyond the bounds of familial duty. Pat Payson baby sat frequently to provide me with more computer time; Richard Payson attractively landscaped the bare earth of our new back yard; and John Payson did a number of essential projects around the house. My dear wife, Cathy, allowed me to spend long undisturbed hours writing in my room – I couldn't have done it without you.

From the Publisher

This book was edited by Hugh Finlay, proofed by Peter Turner and Sue Mitra. Peter Turner saw the book through production and Sharon Wertheim indexed.

The maps were drawn by Trudi Canavan, Greg Herriman, Graham Imeson and Chris Lee Ack with corrections by Ann Jeffree. Chris Lee Ack did the design, illustrations and layout, while Ann Jeffree designed the cover and colour pages.

A Warning & a Request

Things change – prices go up, schedules change, good places go bad and bad places go bankrupt – nothing stays the same. So if you find things better or worse, recently opened or long since closed, please write and tell us and help make the next edition better!

Your letters will be used to help update future editions and, where possible, important changes will also be included as a Stop Press section in reprints.

All information is greatly appreciated and the best letters will receive a free copy of the next edition, or any other Lonely Planet book of your choice.

Contents

Map Legend

BOUNDARIES

▬ ‧ ▬ ‧ ▬ ‧ ▬	.... International Boundary
▬ ‧‧ ▬ ‧‧ ▬	.... Internal Boundary
++++++++++++++	.... National Park or Reserve
‒ ‒ ‒ ‒ ‒ ‒ ‒	.... The Equator
· · · · · · · · · · · · · · · ·	.... The Tropics

SYMBOLS

◉	NEW DELHI	.... National Capital
●	BOMBAY	.... Provincial or State Capital
●	Pune	.... Major Town
●	Borsi	.... Minor Town
■		.... Places to Stay
▼		.... Places to Eat
≙		.... Post Office
✈		.... Airport
i		.... Tourist Information
⊖		.... Bus Station or Terminal
66		.... Highway Route Number
☪ † ‡		...... Mosque, Church, Cathedral
∴		.... Temple or Ruin
✚		.... Hospital
❊		.... Lookout
⚑		.... Camping Area
⊓		.... Picnic Area
⌂		.... Hut or Chalet
▲		.... Mountain or Hill
		.... Railway Station
		.... Road Bridge
		.... Railway Bridge
		.... Road Tunnel
		.... Railway Tunnel
		.... Escarpment or Cliff
		.... Pass
		.... Ancient or Historic Wall

ROUTES

▬▬▬▬▬▬	.... Major Road or Highway
‒ ‒ ‒ ‒ ‒ ‒ ‒	.... Unsealed Major Road
▬▬▬▬▬	.... Sealed Road
‒ ‒ ‒ ‒ ‒ ‒	..... Unsealed Road or Track
═════════	.... City Street
+++++++++++++++++	.... Railway
▬●▬	.... Subway
· · · · · · · · · · · · · · ·	.... Walking Track
‒ ‒ ‒ ‒ ‒ ‒	.... Ferry Route
++++++++++++++	.... Cable Car or Chair Lift

HYDROGRAPHIC FEATURES

	.... River or Creek
	.... Intermittent Stream
	.... Lake, Intermittent Lake
	.... Coast Line
	.... Spring
	.... Waterfall
	.... Swamp
	.... Salt Lake or Reef
	.... Glacier

OTHER FEATURES

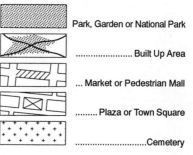

	Park, Garden or National Park
	.... Built Up Area
	... Market or Pedestrian Mall
	.... Plaza or Town Square
	.... Cemetery

Note: not all symbols displayed above appear in this book

Introduction

Travellers today are turning increasingly towards the tropics as an exciting, adventurous and exotic destination. Of the many attractive tropical countries to choose from, Costa Rica stands out as one of the most delightful in the world. There are not only tropical rainforests and beautiful beaches but also some surprises – active volcanoes and windswept mountaintops. So although Costa Rica is a small country, a large variety of tropical habitats are found within it – and they are protected by the best developed conservation programme in Latin America.

Costa Rica is famous for its enlightened approach to conservation. About 27% of the country is protected in one form or another and over 11% is found in the national park system. This means that the traveller who wishes to do so can experience the tropics in

a natural way. The variety and density of wildlife in the preserved areas attracts people whose dream is to see monkeys, sloths, caiman, sea turtles, and exotic birds in their natural habitat. And see them they will! Many other animals can be seen and, with some luck, such rare animals as jaguars, tapirs, and harpy eagles may be glimpsed.

With both a Pacific and Caribbean coast, there is no shortage of beaches in Costa Rica. Some have been developed for tourism while others are remote and rarely visited. For a relaxing seaside vacation, you can stay in a luxurious hotel or you can camp – the choice is yours. And wherever you stay, you can be sure of finding a preserved area nearby where you will find monkeys in the trees by the ocean's edge.

An active volcano is surely one of the most

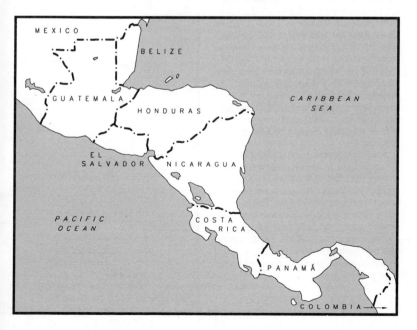

dramatic of natural sights and few visitors to Costa Rica can resist the opportunity to peer into the crater of a smoking giant. Whether you want to take a guided bus tour to a volcanic summit or whether you prefer to hike up through the rainforest and camp out amidst a landscape of boiling mudpools and steaming vents, you will find the information you need within the pages of this book.

Apart from hiking and camping in rainforests, mountains, and beaches, the adventurous traveller will find the opportunity to snorkel on tropical reefs, surf the best waves in Central America, or raft some of the most thrilling white water in the tropics. Pristine rivers tumble down the lower slopes of the mountains and the river banks are clothed with curtains of rainforest – a truly unique white-water experience. Those liking to fish will find the rivers and lakes offer a beautiful setting for their sport, and the ocean fishing is amongst the best in the world.

In addition to this natural beauty and outdoor excitement, there is the added attraction of a country which has long had the most stable political climate in Latin America. Costa Rica has had democratic elections since the 19th century and is one of the most peaceful nations in the world. Since the 1948 civil war, the armed forces have been abolished and Costa Rica has avoided the despotic dictatorships, frequent military coups, terrorism, and internal strife that have torn apart other countries in the region. Costa Rica is the safest country to visit in Latin America.

Not only is it safe, but it is friendly. Costa Ricans delight in showing off their lovely country to visitors and wherever you go you will find the locals to be a constant source of help, smiles, and information. The transportation system is inexpensive and covers the whole country, so Costa Rica is both one of the most beautiful and one of the easiest tropical countries to travel in. This book will show you where and how to go – no matter what your budget.

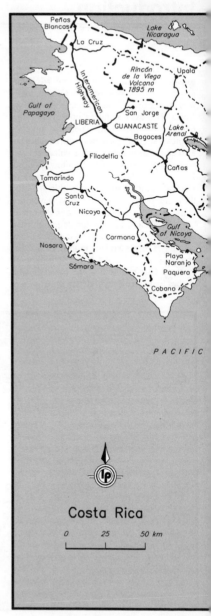

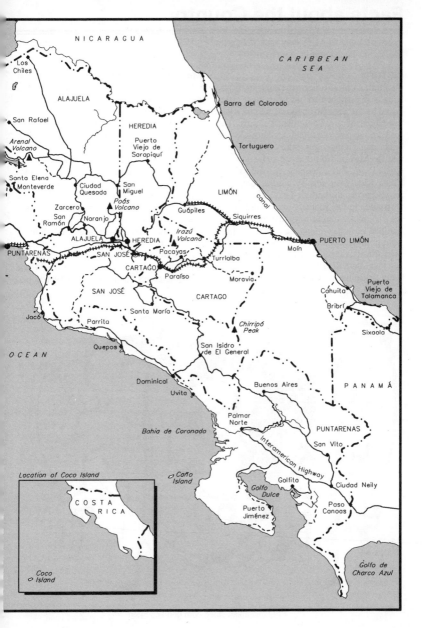

Facts about the Country

HISTORY

Of all the Central American countries, Costa Rica is the one which has been most influenced by the Spanish conquest, and there are few signs of pre-Columbian cultures. The well known Mexican and northern Central American civilisations, such as the Aztecs and the Mayas, did not reach as far south as Costa Rica. Those peoples who did exist in Costa Rica were few in number and relatively poorly organised. They offered little resistance to the Spanish, left us little in the way of ancient archaeological monuments, and had no written language. Many indigenous populations were wiped out by diseases after the arrival of Europeans. This is not to say that Costa Rica's pre-Columbian peoples were uncivilised. A visit to San José's Jade Museum or Pre-Columbian Gold Museum will awe the visitor. The Jade Museum has the world's largest collection of pre-Columbian jade – and most of it comes from the Costa Rican area. The Gold Museum has approximately 2000 pieces on display. Unfortunately, little is known about the cultures which produced these treasures.

The major archaeological site in Costa Rica is the Guayabo National Monument which is about 85 km east of San José, the capital. This area is currently under investigation and is thought to have been inhabited from about 500 BC to 1400 AD. Streets, aqueducts and causeways may be seen, though most of the buildings have collapsed and have not yet been restored. Gold and stone artefacts have been discovered and

Pre-Columbian stone corn grinding table

archaeologists believe Guayabo was an important religious and cultural centre, although minor compared to Aztec, Inca or Maya sites.

Spanish Conquest

Because of the lack of a large and rich Indian empire at the time of the arrival of the Spaniards, the conquest of Costa Rica is euphemistically called a 'settlement' by some writers. In reality, the Spanish arrival was accompanied by diseases to which the Indians had no resistance and they died of sickness as much as by the sword. Although the Indians did try to fight the Spanish, the small numbers of natives were unable to stop the ever larger groups of Spaniards who arrived every few years attempting to colonise the land.

The first arrival was Christopher Columbus himself, who landed near present-day Puerto Limón on 18 September 1502 during his fourth (and last) voyage to the Americas. He was treated well by the coastal Indians during his stay of 17 days and he noted that some of the natives wore gold decorations. Because of this, the area was dubbed 'costa rica' (the rich coast) by the Spaniards who imagined that there must be a rich empire lying further inland.

Spanish King Ferdinand appointed Diego de Nicuesa as governor of the region and sent him to colonise it in 1506. This time the Indians did not provide a friendly welcome – perhaps they had become aware of the deadly diseases which accompanied the Europeans. The colonisers were hampered by the jungle, tropical diseases and the small bands of Indians who used guerrilla tactics to fight off the invaders. About half the colonisers died and the rest returned home, unsuccessful.

Further expeditions followed. The most successful, from the Spaniards' point of view, was a 1522 expedition to the Gulf of Nicoya area led by Gil González Dávila. Although the expedition claimed to have converted tens of thousands of Indians to Catholicism and returned home with a hoard of gold and other treasures, they were unable to form a permanent colony and many expedition members died of hunger and disease.

By the 1560s, the Spanish had unsuccessfully attempted colonisation several more times. By this time the Indian resistance, such as it was, had been worn down. Many Indians had died or were dying of disease and others had simply moved on to more inhospitable terrain.

In 1562 Juan Vásquez de Coronado arrived as governor and decided that the best place to found a colony was in the central highlands. This was an unusual move because the Spanish were a seafaring people and had naturally tried to colonise the coastal areas where they could build ports and maintain a contact with Spain. This proved problematical because the coastal areas were more prone to disease. When Coronado founded Cartago in 1563, his followers found a healthy climate and fertile volcanic soil and thus the colony survived.

Cartago was quite different from Spanish colonies in other parts of the New World. There were few Indians and so the Spanish did not have a huge workforce available, nor were they able to intermarry with the Indians to form the *mestizo* culture prevalent in many other parts of Latin America. The imagined riches of Costa Rica turned out to be very little and were soon plundered. The small highland colony soon became removed from the mainstream of Spanish influence.

For the next century and a half the colony remained a forgotten backwater, isolated from the coast and major trading routes. It survived only by dint of hard work and the generosity and friendliness which have become the hallmarks of the contemporary Costa Rican character.

Eventually, in the 1700s, the colony began to spread and change. Settlements became established throughout the fertile central highlands (now known as the *meseta central*). Heredia was founded in 1717, San José in 1737, and Alajuela in 1782, although at the time of their founding the cities had different names. Much of Cartago was destroyed in an eruption of Irazú Volcano in 1723 but the survivors rebuilt the town. This expansion reflected slow growth from within Costa Rica, but the colony remained one of the poorest and most isolated in the Spanish empire.

Independence

Central America became independent from Spain on 15 September 1821, although Costa Rica was not aware of this situation until at least a month later. It briefly became part of the Mexican empire, then a state within the Central American United Provinces. The first head of state to be elected was Juan Mora Fernández, who governed from 1824 to 1833. During his time in office, coffee (introduced in 1808 from Cuba) began to be exported in modest amounts.

The rest of the 19th century saw a steady increase in coffee exports and this turned Costa Rica from an extremely poor and struggling country to a more successful and worldly one. Inevitably, some of the coffee growers became relatively rich and a class structure began to emerge. In 1849, a successful coffee grower, Juan Rafael Mora, became president and governed for 10 years.

Mora's presidency is remembered both for economic and cultural growth, and for a somewhat bizarre military incident which has earned a place in every Costa Rican child's history books. In June 1855, the American filibuster William Walker arrived in Nicaragua with the aim of conquering Central America and converting it into slaving territory, then using the slaves to build a Nicaraguan canal to join the Atlantic and Pacific. Walker defeated the Nicaraguans and marched for Costa Rica, which he entered more or less unopposed, reaching a hacienda at Santa Rosa (now a national park in north-western Costa Rica).

Costa Rica had no army, and so Mora organised 9000 civilians to gather what arms they could and march north in February 1856. In a short but determined battle, the Costa Ricans defeated Walker who retreated to Rivas in Nicaragua, followed by the victorious Costa Ricans. Walker and his soldiers made a stand in a wooden fort and Juan Santamaría, a drummer boy from Alajuela,

volunteered to torch the building, thus forcing Walker to flee. Santamaría was killed in this action and is now remembered as one of Costa Rica's favourite national heroes.

Despite his defeat, Walker returned unsuccessfully to Central America several more times before finally being shot in Honduras in 1860. Meanwhile, Mora lost favour in his country – he was thought to have brought back cholera with his army which caused a massive epidemic in Costa Rica. He was deposed in 1859, led a coup in 1860, failed, and was executed in the same year as Walker.

Democracy

The next three decades were characterised by power struggles among members of the coffee-growing elite. In 1889, the first democratic elections were held, with the poor *campesinos* as well as the rich coffee growers able to vote, although women and Blacks had not yet received that right.

Democracy has been a hallmark of Costa Rican politics since then, and there have been few lapses. One was between 1917 and 1919 when the Minister of War, Frederico Tinoco, overthrew the democratically elected president and formed a dictatorship. This ended in Tinoco's exile after opposition from both the rest of Costa Rica and the US government.

In 1940, Rafael Angel Calderón Guardia became president. His presidency was marked by reforms which were supported by the poor but criticised by the rich. These reforms included workers' rights to organise, minimum wages and social security. To further widen his power base, Calderón allied himself, strangely, with both the Catholic church and the communist party to form the United Christian Socialist Party. This further alienated him from the conservatives, the intellectuals and the upper classes.

Calderón was succeeded in 1944 by the United Christian Socialist Teodoro Picado who was a supporter of Calderón's policies, but the conservative opposition claimed the elections were a fraud. In 1948, Calderón again ran for the presidency against Otilio Ulate. The election was won by Ulate but

Calderón claimed fraud because some of the ballots had been destroyed. Picado's government did not recognise Ulate's victory and the tense situation escalated into civil war.

Calderón and Picado were opposed by José (Pepe) Figueres Ferrer. After several weeks of civil warfare over 2000 people had been killed, and Figueres emerged victorious. He took over an interim government and in 1949 handed over the presidency to Otilio Ulate of the National Liberation Party.

This year marked the formation of the Costa Rican constitution which is still in effect. Women and Blacks received the vote, the army was abolished, presidents were not allowed to run for successive terms, and a neutral electoral tribunal was established to guarantee free and fair elections. All citizens over the age of 18 are required to vote in elections held every four years.

Although there are over a dozen political parties, since 1949 either the United Christian Socialists or the National Liberation Party have always been elected, usually alternating every four years. Figueres has continued to be popular, and was returned to two more terms of office (in 1954 and 1970). Another famous National Liberation Party president was Oscar Arias, who governed from 1986 to 1990. For his work in attempting to spread peace from Costa Rica to all of Central America, Arias received the Nobel Peace Prize in 1987.

The United Christian Socialists have continued to be the favoured party of the poor and working classes and Calderón's son, Rafael Angel Calderón Fournier, has played a large role in that party, running for president three times. After two losses, he was finally elected president in 1990, succeeding Oscar Arias.

GEOGRAPHY

Costa Rica is bordered to the north by Nicaragua, to the north-east by the Caribbean Sea, to the south-east by Panama, and to the west and south-west by the Pacific Ocean. It lies completely within the tropics between latitudes 11°13'N and 8°N, and longitudes 82°33'W and 85°58'W. In addition, Costa Rica claims the island of Coco (25 sq km) at about 5°30'N and 87°05'W.

Geographically, Costa Rica is an extremely varied country despite its tiny size, which at 50,700 sq km is almost half the size of the state of Kentucky in the USA, two-thirds the size of Scotland, or three-quarters the size of Tasmania in Australia.

A series of volcanic mountain chains runs from the Nicaraguan border in the north-west to the Panamanian border in the south-east, thus splitting the country in two. The more south-easterly mountains tend to be both higher and geologically older. The highlands reach 3820 metres at the Chirripó Volcano, and changing altitudes play an important part in determining geographical variation. Many different ecological habitats are found corresponding with altitudinal changes up the mountains.

In the centre of the highlands lies a plain called the meseta central, which is surrounded by mountains. It is this central plain, between about 1000 and 1500 metres high, which contains four of Costa Rica's five largest cities, including San José, the capital. Over half of the population lives in this plain, which contains fertile volcanic soils. Most of the mountains are volcanoes, some of which are still active.

On either side of the volcanic central highlands lie coastal lowlands which differ greatly in character. The smooth Caribbean coastline is 212 km long and is characterised by year-round rain, mangroves, swamps, an intracoastal waterway, sandy beaches and small tides. The Pacific coast is much more rugged and rocky. The tortuous coastline is 1016 km long, with various gulfs and peninsulas. It is bordered by tropical dry forests, which receive almost no rain for several months each year, as well as by mangroves, swamps and beaches. Tidal variation is quite large and there are many offshore islands.

The two most important peninsulas are the Nicoya, separated from the mainland by a gulf of the same name, and the Osa, separated from the mainland by the Golfo Dulce. The Nicoya Peninsula is hilly, dry and dusty, and is known for its cattle farming and beach resorts. The Osa Peninsula contains the Corcovado National Park, one of the country's protected rainforests.

FLORA & FAUNA

Costa Rica is a small country, but its range of habitats gives it an incredibly rich diversity of flora and fauna. This biodiversity attracts nature lovers from all over the world.

Birds

The primary attractions for many naturalists are the birds, of which some 850 species have been recorded. This is far more species than found in any one of the continents of North America, Australia or Europe.

It is not only the biodiversity which makes Costa Rica attractive to the birder (bird-watcher). The birds are spectacular, and, if you know where to go, surprisingly easy to see. A favourite destination of birders is the Monteverde Cloud Forest. Here, based in comfortable hotel accommodation, you can see birds such as the resplendent quetzal, perhaps one of the most dazzling birds of the tropical rainforest.

A member of the trogon family, the male resplendent quetzal lives up to its name with

Hummingbird

a glittering green plumage set off by a crimson belly, and white tail feathers contrasting with bright green tail coverts streaming over 60 cm beyond the bird's body. The head feathers stick out in a spiky green helmet through which the yellow bill peeks coyly. The male tries to impress the female by almost vertical display flights during which the long tail coverts flutter sensuously. A glimpse of this bird is the highlight of many a birder's trip to Costa Rica.

A walk through the cloud forest is often made eerie by the penetrating whistles and ventriloqual 'bonk!' calls of the three-wattled bellbird, a member of the cotinga family. The haunting notes sound so loud that they can easily be heard half a km away. Spotting this large, chestnut-brown bird, with its pure white head and neck decorated with three black worm-like wattles, is another matter. They call from display perches at the tops of the highest trees and are heard more often than seen.

For many visitors the hummingbirds are the most delightful birds to observe. Over 50 species have been recorded in Costa Rica, and their beauty is matched by extravagant names, such as purple-throated mountain gem, white-crested coquette, and red-footed plumeleteer, to name a few. Hummingbirds

Blue and Gold Macaw

can beat their wings up to 80 times a second, thus producing the typical hum for which they are named. This exceptionally rapid beat also enables them to hover in place when feeding on nectar, or even to fly backwards. The energy needed to keep these tiny birds flying is high, and species living in the mountains have evolved an amazing strategy to survive a cold night. They go into a state of torpor, which is like a nightly hibernation, by lowering their body temperature by between 17°C and 28°C, depending on the species, thus lowering their metabolism drastically.

Other exciting birds include brightly coloured scarlet macaws and 15 other parrot species; six different toucans, with their incredibly large and hollow bills; the huge and very rare harpy eagle, which is capable of snatching monkeys and sloths off branches as it flies past; and a large array of other tropical birds such as flycatchers (75 species), tanagers (45 species), antbirds (29 species) and cotingas (19 species).

Mammals

Mammals, too, are fairly well represented with over 200 species recorded in the country. Visitors to national parks and other protected areas are likely to see one or more of the four monkeys found in Costa Rica – the howler, spider, white-faced capuchin and squirrel monkeys. The male howler monkeys are heard as often as they are seen; their eerie vocalisations carry long distances and have been likened to a baby crying or the wind moaning through the trees. Many visitors are unable to believe they are hearing a monkey when they first hear the mournful sound.

Other tropical specialities include two species of sloths. The three-toed is quite often sighted because it is diurnal, whereas the two-toed sloth is nocturnal and is therefore rarely seen. Sloths are often found hanging motionless from tree limbs, or seen progressing at a painfully slow speed along a branch towards a particularly succulent bunch of leaves, which are their primary food source. Leaf digestion takes several days and sloths defecate about once a week.

Sloths are most fastidious with their toilet habits, always climbing down from their tree to deposit their weekly bowel movement on the ground. Biologists do not know why sloths do this; one suggested hypothesis is that by consistently defecating at the base of a particular tree, the sloths provide a natural fertiliser which increases the quality of the leaves of that tree, thus improving the sloth's diet.

There are three anteater species, of which the tamandua is the most commonly seen by visitors, while the giant and silky anteaters are glimpsed only occasionally.

Other likely mammal sightings include armadillos, agoutis (large rodents), peccaries (wild pigs), kinkajous, raccoons, skunks, otters, foxes, squirrels and bats. Other exotic mammals such as ocelots, jaguars and tapirs are rarely seen, but the chance of seeing one of these rare species in the wild makes any trip to a national park an exciting one.

Insects

At least 35,000 species of insects have been recorded in Costa Rica, and many thousands remain undiscovered. Among the first insects that the visitor to the tropics notices are the butterflies. One source claims that Costa Rica has 10% of all the butterfly species in the world; another states that hundreds of butterfly species remain to be discovered here; a third reports that over 3000 species of butterflies and moths are recorded from one national park alone (Santa Rosa).

Perhaps the most dazzling butterflies are the morphos. With their 15 cm wingspans and electric-blue upper wings, they lazily flap and glide along tropical rivers in a shimmering display. When they land, however, their wings close and only the brown underwings are visible. In an instant they have changed from outrageous display to modest camouflage.

Camouflage plays an important part in the lives of many insects. Some resting butterflies look exactly like green or brown leaves, while others look like the scaly bark of the tree on which they are resting. Caterpillars are often masters of disguise. Some species mimic twigs, another is capable of constricting certain muscles to make itself look like the head of a viper, and yet another species looks so much like a bird dropping that it rarely gets attacked by predators.

Any walk through a tropical forest will almost invariably allow the observer to study many different types of ants. Among my favourites are the *Atta* leaf-cutter ants, which can be seen marching in columns along the forest floor, carrying pieces of leaves like little parasols above their heads. The leaf segments are taken into the underground colony and there they are allowed to rot down into a mulch. The ants tend their mulch gardens carefully, and allow a certain species of fungus to grow there. The bodies of the fungus are then used to feed the colony, which can exceed a million ants.

Other insects are so tiny as to be barely visible, yet their lifestyles are no less esoteric. The hummingbird flower mites are barely half a mm in length, and live in flowers visited by hummingbirds. When the flowers are visited by the hummers, the mites scuttle up into the bird's nostrils and use this novel form of air transport to disperse themselves to other plants. Smaller still are mites which live on the proboscis of the morpho butterflies.

From the largest to the smallest insects, there is a world of wonder in the tropical forests.

Other Animals

Amphibians and reptiles form a fascinating part of the Costa Rican fauna. The approximately 150 species of amphibians include specimens such as tree frogs which spend their entire life cycle in trees. These remarkable creatures have solved the problem of where to lay their eggs by doing so into the water trapped in cup-like plants called bromeliads, which live high up in the forest canopy.

Dendrobatids, better known by their colloquial name of poison-arrow frogs, have also been well studied. They are among the most brightly coloured of frogs; some are

Red-eyed tree frog

bright red with black dots, others red with blue legs, and still others are bright green with black markings. Several Costa Rican species have skin glands exuding toxins which can cause paralysis and death in many animals, including humans. It is well known that dendrobatids have long been used by Latin American forest Indians to provide a poison with which to dip the tips of their hunting arrows. It should be mentioned that the toxins are most effective when introduced into the blood stream (as with arrows) but have little effect when a frog is casually touched.

A toad which many people see is the so-called marine toad, which is actually found both on the coast and inland up to a height of 2000 metres. It is frequently seen in the evenings around human habitations in rural areas and is unmistakable because of its size. It is the largest lowland toad in tropical America and specimens reaching 20 cm long and weighing up to 1.2 kg have been recorded – that is one big toad!

Snakes make up over half of the 200-plus species of reptiles found in Costa Rica. They are much talked about but seldom seen – they usually slither away into the undergrowth when people approach, and only a lucky few visitors are able to catch sight of one. Perhaps the most feared is the fer-de-lance, which is very poisonous and sometimes fatal to humans. It often lives in overgrown, brushy fields. Agricultural workers clearing these fields are the most frequent victims; tourists get bitten very rarely.

More frequently seen reptiles include the common *Ameiva* lizards, which have a white stripe running down their backs. The bright green basilisk lizards are seen on or near water and the males are noted for the huge crests running the length of their head, body and tail, giving them the appearance of a small dinosaur. They can reach almost a metre in length and are nicknamed Jesus Christ lizards for their ability to literally run across water when they are disturbed.

Larger reptiles which attract visitors to coastal national parks such as Tortuguero on the Caribbean or Santa Rosa on the Pacific include turtles and crocodiles (or caymans). There are 14 species of turtles, some of which are marine and others freshwater.

Marine turtles reproduce by climbing up sandy beaches to lay their eggs, and this can be a spectacular sight. The largest marine turtles are the leatherbacks, with a carapace (shell) up to 1.6 metres long and an average weight of a stunning 360 kg. Watching this giant come lumbering out of the sea is a memorable experience. The olive ridleys are much smaller, but practise synchronous nesting when tens of thousands of females may emerge out of the sea on a single night – another unforgettable sight.

Other sea creatures are found by snorkellers and divers visiting offshore islands and coral reefs. Spectacularly coloured tropical fish, starfish, sea urchins, sea anemones and other species await those travellers willing to venture below the surface of the sea.

Plants

The floral biodiversity is also high; some 9000 species of vascular plants have been described and more are being added to the list every year. Orchids alone account for

some 1500 species, and about 900 tree species have been recorded.

The tropical forest is very different from the temperate forests that many North Americans or Europeans may be used to. Temperate forests, such as the coniferous forests of the far north or the deciduous woodlands of milder regions, tend to have little variety. It is pines, pines and more pines, or endless tracts of oaks, beech and birch.

Tropical forests, on the other hand, have great variety. If you stand in one spot and look around, you'll see scores of different species of trees, but often have to walk several hundred metres to find another example of any particular species.

This incredible variety generates biodiversity in the animals which live within the forests. There are several dozen species of fig trees in Costa Rica, for example, and the fruit of each species is the home of one particular wasp species. The wasp benefits by obtaining food and protection; when it flies to another fig tree, the fig benefits because the wasp carries pollen on its body. Many trees and plants of the forest provide fruit, seeds or nectar for insects, birds and bats. They rely upon these visitors to carry pollen across several hundred metres of forest to fertilise another member of the appropriate plant species.

These complex inter-relationships and high biodiversity are among the reasons why biologists and conservationists are calling for a halt to the destruction of tropical forests. It is a sobering thought that three-quarters of Costa Rica was forested in the late 1940s; by the late 1980s, barely a quarter of the country remained covered by forest. To try and control this deforestation and protect its wildlife, Costa Rica has instigated the most progressive national parks system in the New World.

National Parks

The national parks system began in the 1960s and now there are 34 national parks, wildlife refuges, biological reserves, monuments and recreation areas in Costa Rica.

These comprise about 11% of the total land area and more are being planned, notably in the Arenal Volcano area. In addition there are claims of various buffer zones and forest reserves which boost the total area of protected land to about 27%. These buffer zones still allow farming, logging and other exploitation, however, and so the environment is not totally protected.

As well as the national parks system there are about twenty privately owned lodges, reserves and haciendas which are set up to protect the land, and these are well worth visiting.

Ecologists use a system called Holdridge Life Zones, presented by L R Holdridge in 1947, which classifies the type of vegetation to be found in a given area by analysing climatic data such as temperature, rainfall and its variation throughout the year. This data is combined with latitudinal regions and altitudinal belts to give approximately 116 'life zones' on earth. Twelve tropical life zones are found in Costa Rica, and are named according to forest type and altitude. Thus there are dry, moist, wet and rain forests in tropical, premontane, lower montane, montane and subalpine areas.

Within a life zone several types of habitat may occur. Much of Santa Rosa National Park, for example, is tropical dry forest, but types of vegetation within this zone include deciduous forest, evergreen forest, mangrove swamp and littoral woodland. Thus Costa Rica has a huge variety of habitats, each with particular associations of plants and animals, and an attempt has been made to protect them all.

With so much to offer the wildlife enthusiast, it is small wonder that ecotourism is growing in Costa Rica. Two-thirds of foreign travellers visit one or more nature destinations; one-third come specifically to see Costa Rica's wildlife.

Up to date information about the national parks system can be obtained from the public information office in the Parque Bolívar Zoo in San José. It is open from 8 to 11.30 am and 12.30 to 3.30 pm from Tuesdays to Fridays and can be reached by phone at 335673 or 335284, if you speak Spanish. They have some maps and brochures. The national wildlife refuges are administered by the National Wildlife Directorate, which works with the National Parks Service. For information about these refuges call 338112 or 219533.

Most national parks and wildlife refuges provide basic camping facilities and some may be able to provide food and accommodation in ranger stations or park headquarters. This has to be arranged beforehand and can be done by telephoning 334160 or 334070. The staff at these numbers are in radio contact with all national parks and wildlife refuges and can make arrangements. Again, it helps if you speak Spanish. Some of the parks have telephones, and their numbers are given in the appropriate sections.

Most national parks can be entered without permits, but a few of the biological reserves do require a permit which can be obtained by applying to the public information office. The entrance fee to most parks is US$1.10, and a further US$0.55 is charged if you intend to camp overnight.

The latest National Parks Service project (under the auspices of the Ministry of Natural Resources, Energy and Mines) is to link geographically close groups of national parks and reserves, private preserves, and national forests into regional conservation units (RCUs). Carefully managed agricultural land will help create buffer zones to protect the more critical areas. Wildlife corridors will be used to enable wildlife to range over larger areas. These areas have been dubbed 'megaparks' by local conservationists, and it is anticipated that they will eventually cover 27% of Costa Rica's land area.

The result will have two major implications. First, larger areas of wildlife habitats will be protected in blocks, allowing greater numbers of species and individuals to exist. Second, the administration of the national parks will be delegated to regional offices, allowing a more appropriate management approach for each particular area.

The individual parks will retain their present names, but the regional conservation units may be a reality by the time you read this.

Conservation

The loss of key habitats, particularly tropical forests, is a problem which has become significantly more pressing in recent years. Deforestation is happening at such a rate that most of the world's tropical forests will have disappeared by early in the 21st century; loss of other habitats is a less publicised but equally pressing concern. With this in mind, two important questions arise: why are habitats such as the tropical rainforests so important, and what can be done to prevent their loss?

Much of Costa Rica's remaining natural vegetation is tropical forest and there are many reasons why this particular habitat is important. Roughly half of the two million known species on earth live in tropical rainforests such as that found in the Corcovado National Park. Scientists predict that millions more plant and animal species remain to be discovered, principally in the world's remaining rainforests, which have the greatest biodiversity of all the habitats known on the planet. This incredible array of plants and animals cannot exist unless the rainforest that they inhabit is protected – deforestation will result not only in the loss of the rainforest but in countless extinctions as well.

The value of tropical plants is more than in simply providing habitat and food for animals; it is more than the aesthetic value of the plants themselves. Many types of medicines have been extracted from forest trees, shrubs and flowers. These range from anaesthetics to antibiotics, from contraceptives to cures for heart diseases, malaria and various other illnesses. Many medicinal uses of plants are known only to the indigenous inhabitants of the forest. Other pharmaceutical treasures remain locked up in tropical forests, unknown to anybody. They may never be discovered if the forests are destroyed.

A number of Costa Rica's crops are monocultures which suffer from a lack of genetic diversity. In other words, all the plants are almost identical because agriculturalists have bred strains which are high yielding, easy to harvest, good tasting, etc. If these monocultures are attacked by a new disease or pest epidemic they could be wiped out because the resistant strains may have been bred out of the population. Plants such as bananas (an important part of Costa Rica's economy) are found in the wild in tropical forests and so in the event of an epidemic scientists could look for disease-resistant wild strains to breed into the commercially raised crops. Deforestation leads not only to species extinction, but also to loss of the genetic diversity which may help species adapt to a changing world.

Whilst biodiversity for aesthetic, medicinal and genetic reasons may be important to us, it is even more important to the local indigenous peoples who still survive in tropical rainforests. In Costa Rica there are Bribri Indian groups still living in the rainforest in a more or less traditional manner. A few remaining Cabecar Indians still practice shifting agriculture, hunting and gathering. Over 60% of Costa Rica's remaining Indian people are protected in the new La Amistad Biosphere Reserve which comprises two national parks and a host of indigenous and biological reserves in the Talamanca region on the Costa Rica-Panama border. Various international agencies, notably Conservation International, are working with the Costa Rican authorities to protect this area and the cultural and anthropological treasures within.

Rainforests are important on a global scale because they moderate global climatic patterns. Scientists have recently determined that destruction of the rainforests is a major contributing factor to global warming which would lead to disastrous changes to our world. These changes include melting of ice caps causing rising ocean levels and flooding of major coastal cities, many of which are only a scant few metres above present sea level. Global warming would also make many of the world's 'breadbasket' regions unsuitable for crop production.

All these are good reasons why the rainforest and other habitats should be preserved and protected, but the reality of the economic importance of forest exploitation by the developing nations which own tropical forests must also be considered. It is undeniably true that the clearing of the rainforest provides resources in the way of timber, pasture and possible mineral wealth, but this is a short-sighted view.

The long-term importance of the rainforest both from a global view and as a resource of biodiversity, genetic variation and pharmaceutical wealth is becoming recognised both by the countries that contain forest as well as the other nations of the world which will be affected by destruction of these rainforests. Efforts are now underway to show that the economic value of the standing rainforest is greater than the wealth realised by deforestation.

One important way of making the tropical forest an economically productive resource without cutting it down is by protecting it in national parks and preserves and making it accessible to visitors. This type of ecotourism is becoming increasingly important for the economy of Costa Rica and other nations with similar natural resources. More people are likely to visit Costa Rica to see monkeys in the forest than to see cows on pasture. The visitors spend money on hotels, transport, tours, food and souvenirs. In addition, many people who spend time in the tropics gain a better understanding of the natural beauty within the forests, and the importance of preserving them. The result is that when the visitors return home they become goodwill ambassadors for tropical forests.

Other innovative projects for sustainable development of tropical forests are being developed. Many of these developments are occurring on private reserves such as Monteverde or Rara Avis. Here individuals not connected with the government are showing how forests can be preserved and yield a higher economic return than if they were cut down for a one-time sale of lumber and then the land turned into low yield pasture.

Monteverde is particularly interested in educating children worldwide. It has created the Children's Rainforest programme which preserves rainforest and promotes education of children both in Costa Rica and throughout the world. They have also begun the Monteverde Conservation League (MCL) which works towards protecting existing forest by promoting environmentally responsible use of surrounding lands. The MCL works with farmers to increase their productivity and thereby remove pressures on further farm expansion into forested areas. It promotes reforestation in regions where it is possible to plant seedlings as a future economic resource and for prevention of soil erosion.

Rara Avis is a private preserve with two lodges set in pristine rainforest with superb bird-watching. In addition to ecotourism, Rara Avis is developing sustainable use of the surrounding rainforest by harvesting seeds from valuable ornamental plants growing in the area, by harvesting aerial roots of philodendron plants for use as wicker in local furniture manufacture, and by developing farms of such forest animals as pacas, which are considered a delicacy in Central America. In other parts of the region iguana farms are being created, and these reptiles are another forest delicacy.

Selective logging is also possible. Trees in the tropical forests are very diverse and tend not to grow in stands but as mixed crops of hundreds of species. Clearcutting the rainforest leads to the waste of over 90% of the timber. Selective logging of a few of the most valuable species, carefully managed, can create a long term financial reward that surpasses the value of the clearcut forest, and yet leave much of the rainforest intact.

On a governmental and international level, Costa Rica is a leader in conservation. The national parks system is the best developed in Latin America, although it was set up only just in time. Had the system not been implemented, Costa Rica would undoubtedly have lost all its tropical forests by the end of the century. The National Parks Foundation and the Neotropical Foundation are two agencies working hand in hand in preserving the national parks.

The Costa Rican authorities have been particularly progressive in working towards conservation of their natural areas. Various international agencies such as Conservation International, The Nature Conservancy, Natural Resources Defense Council and the World Wildlife Fund (WWF) have provided much needed expertise and economic support. They have also developed programmes such as the 'debt for nature' swaps whereby parts of Costa Rica's national debt are exchanged in return for preserving crucial habitat areas.

Most of these organisations rely on support from the public. Even large entities such as the WWF receive the bulk of their income not from government agencies or corporate contributions, but from individual members. In 1989, for example, fully 69% of the WWF's revenue came from its individual members worldwide. The Nature Conservancy reports that 78.7% of its 1990 revenue came from individual members. The vital work of these and other agencies requires every assistance possible. If you visit Costa Rica and would like to help conserve it, please obtain further information from, and contribute whatever you can to, the following organisations:

Fundación de Parques Nacionales
    Apartado 236, 1002 San José, Costa Rica
Fundación Neotropica
    Apartado 236, 1002 San José, Costa Rica
Monteverde Conservation League
    Apartado 10165, 1000 San José, Costa Rica
The Children's Rainforest
    PO Box 936, Lewiston, Maine 04240, USA
    The Old Rectory, Market Deeping, Peterborough
    PE6 8DA, UK
    Barnens Regnskog, PL 4471, Hagadal, S-13700
    Vasterhaninge, Sweden
Rara Avis
    Apartado 8105, 1000 San José, Costa Rica
Conservation International
    1015 18th St NW, Suite 1000, Washington DC
    20036, USA
The Nature Conservancy – Latin America Division
    1815 North Lynn St, Arlington, VA 22209, USA

World Wildlife Fund
    1250 Twenty-Fourth St, NW, Washington DC
    20037, USA
Natural Resources Defence Council
    40 West 20th St, New York, NY 10011, USA
Rainforest Alliance
    295 Madison Ave, Suite 1804, New York, NY
    10017, USA

GOVERNMENT

Government is based on the Constitution of 7 November 1949 (as described in the History section). The president wields executive power, assisted by two vice presidents and a cabinet of 17 ministers. Elections are held every four years and an incumbent cannot be re-elected.

The country is divided into the seven provinces of San José, Alajuela, Cartago, Heredia, Guanacaste, Puntarenas, and Limón. Each province has a governor who is appointed by the president. The provinces are divided into 81 *cantons* (counties) and subdivided into 415 districts. For about every 30,000 people in each province, a deputy is elected every four years to the Legislative Assembly, or Congress, which totals 57 deputies in all. This is where much of the power of government lies.

The Legislative Assembly appoints 17 Supreme Court judges for minimum terms of eight years, and these judges select judges for the lower courts. The idea behind these three power structures is to prevent any one person or group from having too much control, thus ensuring a real democracy. There is also an Electoral Tribunal which is a special government branch responsible for supervising elections and ensuring that the electoral process is fair and democratic.

There is no army in Costa Rica. Instead, there is a 5000-strong Civil Guard, which is a form of police force. There are also rural and municipal police forces.

Although there are about a dozen political parties, only two have come to power since 1949; the National Liberation Party and the United Christian Socialists. The latter have been in power since 1990 under the presidency of Rafael Angel Calderón Fournier.

The vote is mandatory for all citizens over

18. An up-to-date and validated electoral card must be carried by all Costa Ricans as identification and is needed for anything from opening a bank account to getting a job.

ECONOMY

Until the middle of the 19th century, Costa Rica was a very poor country with an economy based on subsistence agriculture. Then the introduction of coffee began to provide a product suitable for export. This was followed by bananas and today these two crops continue to generate the most foreign income for the country.

The Central Bank of Costa Rica gives the following figures for five major sources of foreign currency. These figures represent an average for the period 1986 to 1988.

Coffee	US$341.8 million
Bananas	US$235.2 million
Tourism	US$144.6 million
Beef	US$ 60.8 million
Sugar	US$ 15.3 million

Coffee harvesting

Inflation for the same period ran at 16.4%, which is less than half of what it was between 1981 and 1985, but is much higher than in the 1960s and 1970s. The national debt is about US$5 billion. The standard of living is the second highest in Central America (after Panama).

Recent economic news indicates that as Costa Rica enters the 1990s, non-traditional export items such as ornamental plants and flowers, textiles, electrical components and other industries are beginning to rival the traditional big four exports (coffee, bananas, beef and sugar). Total exports reached US$1.29 billion in the 1988-89 financial year.

With its lack of armed forces and its commitment to peace, Costa Rica is able to spend its money in ways that many travellers find surprising. For example, 23.5% of the national budget in a recent year was spent on education.

POPULATION

As of July 1989 the population of Costa Rica was 2,922,372, of which just over 50.5% are male. About 60% of the people live in the highlands and the annual population growth rate is 2.5%. Literacy is over 90% – among the best in Latin America.

The population broken down into provinces is as follows:

San José	1,068,206
Alajuela	519,351
Cartago	328,259
Heredia	235,700
Guanacaste	234,962
Puntarenas	326,163
Limón	209,731

The population density is about 58 people per sq km, the third highest in Central America, after El Salvador and Guatemala. This is about 25% of the population density of the United Kingdom, but over twice as high as the United States.

PEOPLE

The vast majority of the people are White,

mainly of Spanish descent. Less than 2% of the population is Black. They live mostly in the Caribbean province of Limón and trace their ancestry to either the early days of slavery in Costa Rica or to the immigration of labour forces from Jamaica to build the railways and work the banana plantations in the late 1800s. As with other Caribbean Blacks, many of them speak a dated and rather quaint form of English. They were actively discriminated against in the early 1900s, not being allowed to even spend a night in the highlands, but since the 1949 constitution they have had equal rights.

A small number of Indians remain, making up much less than 1% of the population. Precise figures are difficult to obtain and estimates vary from 5000 to 20,000. Many of these have integrated to the extent that they are more or less indistinguishable from other Costa Ricans. Small populations of culturally distinct tribes include the Bribri from the Talamanca area near the southeastern coast and Panamanian border, and the Borucas in the southern Pacific coastal areas.

The people call themselves *ticos* or *ticas* (male and female). I find them to be the most friendly, polite and helpful people I have met. Visitors are constantly surprised at the warmth of the Costa Rican people.

CULTURE

Because of the overwhelmingly European population there is very little indigenous cultural influence. And because the country was a poor subsistence agricultural nation until the middle of the 19th century, cultural activities have only really blossomed in the last 100 years.

Costa Rica is famous for its natural beauty and friendly people, not for its culture. Ticos consider San José to be the cultural centre of the country, and it is here that the most important museums are found. It is also the centre of a thriving acting community, and theatre is one of the favourite cultural activities in Costa Rica.

The most famous theatre in the country is the National Theatre, built between 1890 and 1897. The story goes that a noted European opera company featuring the talented singer Adelina Patti was on a Latin American tour but declined to perform in Costa Rica for lack of a suitable hall. Immediately, the coffee elite put a special cultural tax on coffee exports to enable a world class theatre to be built.

The National Theatre in the heart of San José is now the venue for plays, opera, performances by the National Symphony, ballet, poetry readings and other cultural events. It also is an architectural work in its own right and is a landmark in any city tour of San José.

RELIGION

This can be summed up in one word, Catholicism. About 90% of the population is Roman Catholic, at least in principle. In practice, many people tend to go to church only at the time of birth, marriage and death, but they consider themselves Catholics nevertheless. Religious processions on holy days are generally less fervent or colourful than those found in other Latin American countries. Holy Week (the week before Easter) is a national holiday and everything, including buses, stops operating at lunch time on Maundy Thursday and doesn't start up till Holy Saturday.

Other religious views are permitted – after all, Costa Rica is Latin America's most democratic country. The Blacks on the Caribbean coast tend to be Protestants, and most other denominations have a church in or around San José. There is a small Jewish community with a B'Nai Israel church and a synagogue, and there's a sprinkling of people holding oriental or Asian beliefs.

LANGUAGE

Spanish is the official language and is the main language for the traveller. English is understood in the better hotels, airline offices and tourist agencies, as well as along much of the Caribbean coast.

If you don't speak Spanish, take heart. It is an easy language to learn. Courses are available in San José (see under the San José section) or you can study books, records and tapes before your trip. These study aids are often available for free from many public libraries or you might want to consider taking an evening or college course. Once you have learned the basics, you'll find it possible to travel all over Latin America because, apart from Brazil which is Portuguese-speaking, most of the countries use Spanish.

Spanish is easy to learn for several reasons. First, it uses Roman script, and secondly, with few exceptions, it is spoken as it is written, and vice versa. Imagine trying to explain to someone learning English that there are seven different ways of pronouncing 'ough'. This isn't a problem in Spanish. Thirdly, many words are similar enough to English that you can figure them out by guesswork. Instituto Geográfico Nacional means the National Geographical Institute, for example.

Even if you don't have time to take a course, at least bring a phrasebook and dictionary. Don't dispense with the dictionary, because the phrasebook limits you to asking where the bus station is and won't help you translate the local newspaper. My favourite dictionary is the paperback University of Chicago *Spanish-English, English-Spanish Dictionary*. It's small enough to travel with, yet has many more entries than most pocket dictionaries and also contains words used in Latin America but not in Spain.

Although the Spanish alphabet looks like the English one, it is in fact different. '*Ch*' is considered a separate letter, for example, so *champú* (which simply means 'shampoo') will be listed in a dictionary after all the words beginning with just '*c*'. Similarly, '*ll*' is a separate letter, so *llave* (key) is listed after all the words beginning with a single '*l*'. The letter '*ñ*' is listed after the ordinary '*n*'. Vowels with an accent are accented for stress and are not considered separate letters.

Pronunciation is generally more straightforward than it is in English, and if you say a word the way it looks like it should be said, the chances are that it will be close enough to be understood. You will get better with

practice of course. A few notable exceptions are '*ll*' which is always pronounced 'y' as in 'yacht', the '*j*' which is pronounced 'h' as in 'happy', and the '*h*' which isn't pronounced at all. Thus the phrase *hojas en la calle* (leaves in the street) would be pronounced 'o-has en la ka-yea'. Finally, the letter '*ñ*' is pronounced as the 'ny' sound in 'canyon'.

Grammar

Articles, adjectives and demonstrative pronouns must agree with the noun in both gender and number. Nouns ending in 'a' are generally feminine and the corresponding articles are *la* (singular) and *las* (plural). Those ending in 'o' are usually masculine and require the articles *el* (singular) and *los* (plural).

There are, however, hundreds of exceptions to these guidelines which can only be memorised or deduced by the meaning of the word. Plurals are formed by adding *s* to words ending in a vowel and *es* to those ending in a consonant.

In addition to using all the familiar English tenses, Spanish also uses the imperfect tense and two subjunctive tenses (past and present). Tenses are formed either by adding a myriad of endings to the root verb or preceding the participle form by some variation of the verb *haber* (to have/to exist).

There are verb endings for first, second and third person singular and plural. Second person singular and plural are divided into formal and familiar modes. If that's not enough, there are three types of verbs – those ending in *ar*, *er* and *ir* – which are all conjugated differently. There are also a whole slough of stem-changing rules and irregularities which must be memorised. This sounds a lot more complicated than it really is – you'll be surprised how quickly you'll pick it up!

Common courtesies

good morning	*buenos días*
good afternoon (or good evening)	*buenas tardes*
yes	*sí*

no   *no*
hello   *hola*
See you later   *Hasta luego*
How are you?   *Cómo estás?* (familiar) or
                  Cómo está? (formal)
please   *por favor*
thank you   *gracias*
It's a pleasure   *Con mucho gusto*

Some Useful Phrases

Do you speak Spanish?
   Habla usted castellano?
Where do you come from?
   De donde es usted?
What time is it?
   Qué hora tiene?
Don't you have smaller change?
   No tiene sencillo?
Do you understand? (casual)
   Me entiende?
I don't understand
   No entiendo
Where can I change money/travellers'
cheques?
   *Donde se cambia dinero/cheques de
   viajeros?*
Where is the ... ?
   Donde está el/la ... ?
How much is this?
   There are fortunately several variations on
   this well-worn phrase:
   *A cómo?, Cuanto cuesta esto?, Cuanto
   vale esto?*
too expensive
   muy caro
cheaper
   más barato
I'll take it
   Lo llevo
The bill please
   La cuenta por favor
to the right
   a la derecha
to the left
   a la izquierda
continue straight ahead
   siga derecho
more or less
   más o menos

when?
   cuando?
how?
   cómo?
How's that again?
   Cómo?
where?
   donde?
What time does the next plane/bus/train
leave for ... ?
   *A qué hora sale el próximo avión/bús/tren
   para ... ?*
where from?
   de donde?
around there
   por allá
around here
   por aquí
It's hot/cold
   Hace calor/frío

Some Useful Words

airport   *aeropuerto*
bank   *banco*
block   *cuadra, cien metros*
bus station/stop   *terminal/parada de
                     autobuses*
cathedral/church   *catedral, iglesia*
city   *ciudad*
downhill   *para abajo*
exchange house   *casa de cambio*
friend   *amigo/a*
here   *aquí*
husband/wife   *marido/esposa*
mother/father   *madre/padre*
people   *la gente*
police   *policía*
post office   *correo*
rain   *lluvia*
there   *allí, allá*
town square   *plaza* or *parque*
train station   *estación de trenes*
uphill   *para arriba*
wind   *viento*

Time & Dates

What time is it?
   Qué hora es? or *Qué horas son?*
It is one o'clock
   Es la una

It is two o'clock
  Son las dos
midnight
  medianoche
noon
  mediodía
in the afternoon
  de la tarde
in the morning
  de la mañana
at night
  de la noche
half past two
  dos y media
quarter past two
  dos y cuarto
two twenty-five
  dos con veinticinco minutos
twenty to two
  veinte para las dos

Sunday	*domingo*
Monday	*lunes*
Tuesday	*martes*
Wednesday	*miércoles*
Thursday	*jueves*
Friday	*viernes*
Saturday	*sábado*

spring
  la primavera
summer (the December to April dry season)
  el verano
winter (the May to December wet season)
  el invierno

today	*hoy*
tomorrow	*mañana*
yesterday	*ayer*

Numbers

1	*uno, una*
2	*dos*
3	*tres*
4	*cuatro*
5	*cinco*
6	*seis*
7	*siete*
8	*ocho*
9	*nueve*

10	*diez*
11	*once*
12	*doce*
13	*trece*
14	*catorce*
15	*quince*
16	*dieciseis*
17	*diecisiete*
18	*dieciocho*
19	*diecinueve*
20	*veinte*
21	*veintiuno*
30	*treinta*
40	*cuarenta*
50	*cincuenta*
60	*sesenta*
70	*setenta*
80	*ochenta*
90	*noventa*
100	*cien(to)*
101	*ciento uno*
200	*doscientos*
201	*doscientos uno*
300	*trescientos*
400	*cuatrocientos*
500	*quinientos*
600	*seiscientos*
700	*setecientos*
800	*ochocientos*
900	*novecientos*
1000	*mil*
100,000	*cien mil*
1,000,000	*un millón*

Costa Rican Terms

The following colloquialisms and slang are mainly used only in Costa Rica.

Adios!
  Hi! (used when passing a friend in the street, or anyone in remote rural areas; also means 'farewell' but only when leaving for a long time)
bomba
  petrol (gas) station
buena nota
  OK, excellent (literally 'good note')
Hay campo?
  Is there space? (on a bus)

cien metros
one city block
maje
buddy (used by young men to close friends)
mi amor
my love (used by both sexes as a friendly form of address)
pulpería
corner grocery store
pura vida
super, far out (literally 'pure life', can be used as an expression of approval or even as a greeting)
salado
too bad, tough luck
soda
cafe or lunch counter
Upe!
Anybody home? (used mainly in the countryside at people's houses, instead of knocking)
vos
you (informal, equivalent to 'tu')

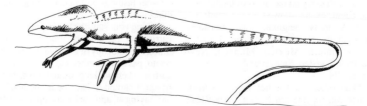

Facts for the Visitor

VISAS

Citizens of the USA and Canada do not need a passport; they can buy a 30-day tourist card for US$3 at the airline ticket counter on their way to Costa Rica, or at a Costa Rican consulate. To obtain a tourist card, American and Canadian travellers must show a birth certificate or voter registration card, a picture identification (such as a driver's licence), and their airline ticket.

I recommend, however, that American and Canadian citizens travel with a passport, as this enables them to enter for 90 days. In addition, a passport (with a photograph) makes money exchange a lot more straightforward than with a tourist card (no photograph).

All other nationalities require at least a passport to enter Costa Rica. American citizens with passports were formerly allowed only 30 days. This was changed in late 1989, and some reference sources may still be quoting the old rules.

There are three entry levels for passport holders. The first level requires passport only and allows entry for 90 days; the second level requires passport only and allows entry for 30 days; the third level requires both a passport and a visa and allows entry for 30 days.

Passport carrying nationals of the following countries are allowed 90 days with no visa: Argentina, Austria, Canada, Colombia, Denmark, Finland, France, Holland, Israel, Italy, Japan, Luxembourg, Norway, Panama, Rumania, South Korea, Spain, United Kingdom, United States, Germany and Yugoslavia.

Passport carrying nationals of the following countries are allowed 30 days with no visa: Australia, Belgium, Brazil, Ecuador, Guatemala, Honduras, Iceland, Ireland, Liechtenstein, Mexico, Monaco, New Zealand, Sweden, Switzerland, Vatican and Venezuela.

Most other nationalities require a visa, which can be obtained from a Costa Rican consulate for US$20. Some nationalities are restricted by so-called political problems and may have difficulty in obtaining a visa for tourism. These have included Nicaragua and most communist countries, but with the 1990 election of Violeta Chamorro in Nicaragua and the general political upheaval in Eastern Europe, this may change in the near future. Recent reports indicate that travellers arriving from Nicaragua need to have malaria tablets with them. In the past, overland travellers who had spent more than a few days travelling through Nicaragua were hassled by Costa Rican border authorities and sometimes refused entry if they appeared 'pro-Sandinista'. This has probably changed since the electoral defeat of the Sandinistas in 1990.

Costa Rican entry requirements change frequently and so it is worth checking at a consulate before your trip. Travellers officially need an exit ticket out of the country before they are allowed to enter, although this is not always asked for. Most airlines will not let you board their planes unless you have a return or onward ticket, or an MCO. Sometimes a show of cash is required, US$300 to US$400 per month should be sufficient. The easiest way for overland travellers to solve the onward ticket requirement is by buying a ticket from the TICA bus company which has offices in both Managua (Nicaragua) and Panama City. Your best source of up-to-date information is from other overland travellers. Costa Ricans are very sensitive to appearances; putting on your most presentable clothes and avoiding unusual fashions will make entrance procedures easier.

During your stay, the law requires that you carry your passport or tourist card at all times. A photocopy of the pages bearing your photo, passport number and entry stamp will suffice when walking around town, but the passport should at least be in the hotel you are staying at, and not locked up in San José.

Visa Extensions

Extending your stay beyond the authorised 30 or 90 days is a time consuming hassle. It is easier to simply leave the country for 72 hours or more and then re-enter. If you cannot or do not wish to do this, then go to the Migración office on Calle 21, between Avenidas 6 & 8 in San José. It is open from 8.30 am to 3.30 pm from Monday to Friday and they will inform you of current procedures.

At time of writing, requirements for extending your stay include presenting three passport sized photos, a ticket out of the country, sufficient funds to support yourself, and maybe a blood test (to prove you don't have AIDS). Get the blood test at the Ministerio de Salud (Ministry of Health) on Calle 16, between Avenidas 6 & 8 in San José, between 7.30 am and 4 pm, Monday to Friday. Allow about four working days for the blood test, and a further three days at Migración. A few dollars are charged in fees. In the past, documents showing that you didn't owe taxes, that you hadn't fathered or given birth to a child, and that you didn't owe child support in Costa Rica were required. These are no longer necessary, but the situation changes regularly. Check with Migración before you decide whether to stay, leave or visit another country for 72 hours.

If you overstay your 30 or 90 day stay without obtaining an extension, you will not be allowed to leave the country without an exit visa, and these are available from Migración. They require the usual exit ticket, as well as a statement from the Tribunales de Justicia on Calle 17, between Avenidas 6 & 8 in San José, stating that you aren't leaving any dependents in the country. You pay a fine of US$4 per month of overstay, plus a US$12 fee if you leave by air, US$40 if you leave by land. The exit visa is valid for 30 days, so you can legally stay that long on top of whatever time you've already been there.

Children (under 18) of all nationalities are special cases. They are not allowed to stay for more than 30 days unless *both* parents request permission from the National Child Protection Agency (Patronato Nacional de la Infancia, on Calle 19 at Avenida 6 in San José) for the child to leave. Permission will not be granted to just one parent or guardian. If a child is planning a stay of more than 30 days and will not be travelling with both parents, it is necessary for the non-accompanying parent (or parents) to get a notarised permit from the Costa Rican consulate in the child's home country.

All this talk of red tape and bureaucracy may have put you off the idea of travelling in Costa Rica entirely. Remember, however, that if you stay less than 30 days there is no problem at all. If you stay from 30 to 90 days and are entitled to do so, there is no problem either. And if you want to stay longer, a few days in Panama or Nicaragua may be easier than dealing with extensions. Finally, good travel agents are used to dealing with the red tape and will help you obtain the necessary extensions for a fee.

Working Holidays

It is difficult, but not impossible, to find work in Costa Rica. The most likely source of paid employment is as an English teacher in language institutes in San José, and they advertise courses in the local newspapers. Word of mouth from other travellers is another way of finding out about this kind of work. Writers can occasionally sell work to the English language weekly, the *Tico Times*. Naturalists or river guides may be able to find work with the private lodges or adventure travel operators. Don't expect to make more than survival wages from these jobs, and don't arrive in Costa Rica expecting to get a job easily and immediately.

Getting a bona fide job requires a work permit which, as you can gather from the preceding section on extending your stay, is a bureaucratic, time consuming, and difficult process.

Volunteer work in nature preserves or national parks is sometimes possible. Volunteers usually provide their own transportation to Costa Rica, sometimes have to pay for living expenses, but can experience natural areas more intimately.

If you are interested in working in the

national parks, try writing to the Asociación Voluntarias de Parques Nacionales, Apartado 10104, 1000 San José for more information and an application. Allow several months.

The Monteverde Cloud Forest Reserve sometimes accepts volunteers, both for outdoor work, like trail maintenance and patrol, and indoor office work. Write to Monteverde at Apartado 8-3870, 1000 San José for more information.

Other Visas

Nicaragua Australians and New Zealanders travelling to Nicaragua require visas, as do many Europeans except those from the UK, Belgium, Denmark, Finland, Holland, Norway, Spain, Sweden and Switzerland.

Visas reportedly require 24 hours to process. Canadians and USA citizens do not require Nicaraguan visas.

Panama Travellers to Panama require visas if they hold passports from the USA, Japan, Canada, Australia and many European nations except the UK, Germany, Spain and Switzerland.

Visas cost anything up to US$20, depending on your nationality. Check with the appropriate embassy as visas are not normally obtainable at the border crossings. Regulations and lists of countries requiring visas can and do change frequently.

Foreign Embassies in Costa Rica

The following countries have embassies or consulates in the San José area. Addresses change frequently, particularly those of the smallest embassies, so call ahead to confirm locations and get directions. Embassies tend to be open in the mornings more often than the afternoons.

Argentina
    Avenida 6, Calle 21 & 25 (☎ 213438)
Austria
    Avenida 2, Calle 2 & 4 (☎ 232822)
Belgium
    Avenida 3, Calle 35 & 37, Los Yoses (☎ 256255)
Belize
    Curridabat (☎ 539626)

Bolivia
    Avenida 2, Calle 19 & 21 (☎ 336244)
Brazil
    Calle 4, Avenida Central & 1 (☎ 234325, 331544)
Britain
    Paseo Colón, Calle 38 & 40 (☎ 215566)
Canada
    Calle 3, Avenida Central & 1 (☎ 230446)
Chile
    Barrio Dent (☎ 244243)
Colombia
    Avenida 5, Calle 5 (☎ 210725)
Denmark
    Sabana Este (☎ 221307, 316283)
Ecuador
    Avenida 2, Calle 19 & 21 (☎ 236281)
El Salvador
    Avenida 10, Calle 33 & 35, Los Yoses (☎ 249034)
Finland
    Paseo Colón, Calle 38 & 40 (☎ 570210)
France
    Curridabat Rd (☎ 250733)
Germany
    Rohrmoser (☎ 325533)
Guatemala
    (☎ 228991)
Holland
    Avenida 8, Calle 37, Los Yoses (☎ 340949)
Honduras
    (☎ 222145)
Israel
    Calle 2, Avenida 2 & 4 (☎ 216011)
Italy
    Calle 29, Avenida 8 & 10, Los Yoses (☎ 252087, 342326)
Japan
    Rohrmoser (☎ 321255)
Mexico
    Avenida 7, Calle 13 & 15 (☎ 225528)
Nicaragua
    Avenida Central, Calle 25 & 27 (☎ 333479)
Norway
    Paseo Colón, Calle 38 & 40 (☎ 571414)
Panama
    San Pedro (☎ 253401)
Paraguay
    Los Yoses (☎ 252802)
Peru
    Los Yoses (☎ 259145)
Spain
    Calle 32, Paseo Colón (☎ 221933)
Sweden
    La Uruca (☎ 328549)
Switzerland
    Paseo Colón, Calle 38 & 40 (☎ 330052, 214829)
Uruguay
    Calle 2, Avenida 1 (☎ 232512)

Arenal Volcano (RR)

Top: Banana plantation (RR)
Left: Romelio Campos at Oro Verde, Río Sarapiquí (PP)
Right: Colonists, Río Sarapiquí area (RR)

USA
    Pavas (☎ 203939)
Venezuela
    Los Yoses (☎ 258810, 251335)

CUSTOMS

From the point of view of import of duty-free items like alcohol and tobacco, Costa Rica is less restrictive than many countries. You are allowed 500 cigarettes or 500 gram of tobacco, and three litres of wine or spirits.

Camera gear, binoculars and camping, snorkelling or other sporting equipment are readily allowed into the country. Officially, you are limited to six rolls of film but this is rarely checked or enforced. Generally, if you are bringing in items for personal use, there's no problem. If you are trying to bring in new items which you want to sell, you may be asked to pay duty. Don't ask me how they know the difference!

MONEY

Currency

The Costa Rican currency is the *colón*, plural *colones*, named after Cristóbal Colón, which is the Spanish version of Christopher Columbus. Colones are normally written ¢.

Exchange Rates

The value of the colón has been dropping steadily against the US dollar for years. Sometimes the exchange rate will remain stable for some months, at other times there is a gradual downward increase, and at other times there is a fairly sudden drop in value.

So as the prices quoted in this book aren't rendered totally obsolete due to inflation, all are expressed in US dollars.

US$1 = 125 colones
UK£1 = 275 colones

Changing Money

It is difficult to change currencies other than US dollars in Costa Rica. You can change most major currencies in the capital, but out of San José, forget it. Bring US dollars if you plan to do any travelling outside the capital. Travellers' cheques are usually exchanged at one or two colones lower than the rate for cash, so plan accordingly.

There are three places to change money: in the better hotels and travel agencies; in banks; and on the street.

Hotels & Travel Agencies Hotels and travel agencies often give the same rate as the banks, and are much faster and more convenient. One drawback to using these is that usually only guests and customers can use their services, although some places will serve outsiders – it's worth trying. Another drawback is that they have limited cash resources and sometimes don't have enough colones.

Banks Banks tend to be slow in changing money and the process can take an hour or more. Often you have to stand in one line to have your transaction approved, then in a second line to actually get your money. Some banks won't take travellers' cheques, others will take only certain kinds. American Express is usually good; I don't recommend First National Citibank cheques because they took over a year to reimburse me when I had some of their cheques stolen in South America.

Banking hours are from 9 am to 3 pm, Mondays to Fridays. Banco Nacional and Banco de Costa Rica are usually the best choices for foreign exchange. Their main branches in San José are often open for longer hours for foreign exchange (Banco Nacional, Avenida 3, between Calle 2 & 4; Banco de Costa Rica, Avenida Central, between Calles 4 & 6; Avenida 1 at Calle 7).

The San José airport bank is open from 6.30 am to 6 pm Monday to Friday and from 7 am to 1 pm on weekends and holidays. This bank is often the most efficient place to change money.

Always carry your passport when changing money. Several travellers have reported that they have been asked for proof of purchase of travellers' cheques when exchanging. This has never happened to me, but you might want to carry a copy of your receipt.

On the Streets Changing money on the streets is technically illegal, but there are so many people doing it that obviously the authorities are turning a blind eye at present. The area to find street changers is around the Banco Central at Avenida Central and Calle 2 in San José. You can get from about 2% to 10% more than in a bank, depending on whether you have travellers' cheques or cash, how much you want to change, and how well you can bargain. US dollars are the only currency that street changers are seriously interested in.

Bear in mind that street changing is illegal, and the present blind eye may not be in effect when you arrive – ask other travellers. Also remember that street changing may result in your getting cheated, so always count your money carefully before handing over your dollars. Many travellers prefer to change money legally at a slightly lower rate to avoid any hassle.

Outside of San José, money changing in major hotels is OK, but only banks in main towns and moneychangers at the land borders can be relied upon to change money. If visiting small towns, always change plenty of money beforehand. Also bring small bills, as changing large colones bills can be difficult in rural areas.

It is possible to change excess colones back into dollars (up to US$50) at the main banks and at the airport, but you may need to show your passport, ticket out of the country, and the original exchange receipts.

Credit Cards

Holders of credit cards can buy colones (but not US dollars) in banks, although this is subject to change as dollars have been available in the past.

Credit cards can also be used at the more expensive hotels, restaurants, travel and car rental agencies, and stores. Visa and Mastercard are both widely accepted, you are charged at the normal bank rates, and commissions are low.

American Express cardholders can buy American Express travellers' cheques in US dollars. The office is at Calle 1, between Avenidas Central & 1, in San José.

Transferring Money

If you need money sent to you from home, you'll find the main branches of several banks in San José will accept cash transfers but charge a commission. Shop around for the best deal.

Costs

Costa Rica is not as cheap as many other Central or South American countries, although budget travellers will find that it is much cheaper than, say, the USA or Europe. Generally speaking, San José is more expensive than the rest of the country, the dry season (December to April) is the high season and thus more expensive, and imported goods are expensive.

Travellers on a tight budget will find the cheapest hotels start at about US$2 per person for a box with a bed. Fairly decent hotels with private bathrooms, hot water and maybe air-con cost around US$5 to US$16 per person. First class hotels can reach US$100 for a single room but there are plenty of good ones for about US$40.

Meals cost from about US$2 to US$20, depending on the quality of the restaurant. Budget travellers should stick to the cheaper set lunches offered in many restaurants, which usually cost a little over US$1. Cafés or lunch counters, called *sodas*, are cheap places for meals. Beer costs from US$0.70 to US$2 depending on how fancy the restaurant or bar is. Cinemas charge about US$1.50.

Public transport is quite cheap, with the longest bus journeys from San José (to the Panamanian or Nicaraguan borders) costing about US$6. Internal air fares are also cheap, with the dearest being about US$17 (except for chartered flights which are more expensive). A taxi, particularly when you're in a group, isn't expensive and usually costs US$1 to US$2 for short rides. Car rental is expensive, however – figure on US$250 per week as a minimum for the cheapest cars.

A budget traveller economising hard can get by on US$10 per day. If you want some basic comforts, such as rooms with private baths, meals other than set meals, and occasional flights, expect to pay about US$20 per day. Travellers wanting to be very comfortable can spend from US$40 to over US$100 per day. Tours can cost upwards of US$100 per day, but you do get first class accommodation and services.

Travelling hard, eating well, staying in rooms with a private bath, writing an average of one letter each day to friends or family, buying a daily newspaper, seeing a movie once in a while, and drinking a couple of beers with dinner most nights sounds expensive – almost decadent – to the 'purist' budget traveller. I did that for several weeks while researching this book, and averaged about US$20 a day. (I also spent some time driving a rental car as well as taking an expensive tour of some of the more remote national parks, so I covered various levels of expense.)

I sometimes meet travellers who spend most of their time worrying how to make every penny stretch further. It seems to me that they spend more time looking at their finances than looking at the places they're visiting. Of course many travellers are on a grand tour of Latin America and want to make their money last, but you can get so burned out on squalid hotels and bad food that the grand tour becomes an endurance test. I'd rather spend six months travelling comfortably and enjoyably than a full year of strain and sacrifice.

Tipping

Most restaurants automatically add 10% tax and 10% tip to the bill. Cheaper restaurants might not do this. Tipping above the included amount is not necessary, but adding a few percent for excellent service is OK. Tipping bellboys in the better hotels costs about US$0.25 per bag. Tip hairdressers about 10% of the bill. Taxi drivers are not normally tipped.

On guided tours, tip the guide about US$2 per person per day (more if the group is very small, less or nothing if the guide doesn't meet your expectations).

CLIMATE & WHEN TO GO

In common with many tropical countries, Costa Rica experiences two seasons, the wet and the dry, rather than the four seasons that people living in temperate regions are used to. The dry season is generally from about late December to April and this is called *verano* (or summer) by Costa Ricans. The rest of the year tends to be wet, and is called *invierno* (or winter).

The Caribbean coastal region tends to be wet all the year round. The dry season is characterised by fewer rainy days and spells of fine weather sometimes lasting a week or more. In the highlands, the dry season really is dry, with only one or two rainy days per month. It can, however, rain for up to 20 days per month in the wet season. The north and central Pacific coastal regions have similar rain patterns to the highlands, whilst the southern Pacific coast can experience rain year round, though less so in the dry season.

Temperature varies little from season to season and the main influencing factor is altitude. San José, at 1150 metres, has a climate which the locals refer to as 'eternal spring'. Lows average a mild 15°C year round whilst highs are a pleasant 26°C. The coasts are much hotter with the Caribbean averaging 21°C at night and over 30°C during the day; the Pacific is 2°C or 3°C warmer.

When to Go

In general, visitors are told that the late December to mid-April dry season is the best time to visit Costa Rica. During this time beach resorts tend to be busy and often full at weekends and holidays, especially Easter week which is booked months ahead. School children take their main vacations from December to February.

From late April, when the rains start, many of the dirt roads in the backcountry require 4WD vehicles (which can be rented). However, travel in the wet season also means smaller crowds and lower hotel prices. Bring your umbrella and take advantage of it! I have travelled in Costa Rica in both seasons, and have thoroughly enjoyed myself at both times.

WHAT TO BRING

As an inveterate traveller and guidebook writer, I've naturally read many guidebooks. I always find the What to Bring section depressing, as I'm always told to bring as little as possible; I look around at my huge backpack, my two beat-up duffel bags bursting at the seams, and I wonder sadly where I went wrong. I enjoy camping, so I carry tent and sleeping bag. I'm an avid bird-watcher, and I'd feel naked without my binoculars and field guides. And of course I want to photograph the scenery and birds, which adds a camera, lenses, tripod and other paraphernalia. In addition, I enjoy relaxing just as much as travelling so I always have at least two books to read as well as all my indispensable guides and maps. Luckily, I'm not a music addict so I'm able to live without a guitar, a portable tape player or a shortwave radio.

It appears that I'm not the only one afflicted with the kitchen-sink disease. In Latin America alone, I've met an Australian surfer who travelled the length of the Pacific coast with his board looking for the world's longest left-handed wave; a Black man from Chicago who travelled with a pair of three-foot-high bongo drums; an Italian with a saxophone (a memorable night in San José when those two got together); a Danish journalist with a portable typewriter; a French freak with a ghetto blaster and (by my count) 32 tapes; and an American woman with several hundred weavings which she was planning on selling. All of these were budget travellers staying for at least 1½ months and using public transport.

After confessing to the amount of stuff I travel with, I can't very well give the time-honoured advice of 'travel as lightly as possible.' I suggest you bring anything that is important to you; if you're interested in photography, you'll only curse every time you see a good shot if you haven't brought your telephoto lens, and if you're a musician you won't enjoy the trip if you constantly worry about how out of practice your fingers are getting.

A good idea once you're in San José is to divide your gear into two piles. One is what you need for the next section of your trip, the rest you can stash in the storage room at your hotel (most hotels have one). Costa Rica is a small country so you can use San José as a base and divide your travelling into, say, coastal, highland and jungle portions, easily returning to the capital between sections and picking up the gear you need for the next.

There's no denying, however, that travelling light is much less of a hassle, so don't bring things you can do without. Travelling on buses and trains is bound to make you slightly grubby, so bring one change of dark clothes that don't show the dirt, rather than seven changes of smart clothes for a six-week trip. Many people go overboard with changes of clothes, but one change to wash and the other to wear is the best idea. Of course, bring extra socks and underwear. Bring clothes that wash and dry easily. (Jeans take forever to dry.)

The highlands can be cool, so bring a wind-proof jacket and a warm layer to wear underneath. A hat is indispensable; it'll keep you warm when it's cold, shade your eyes when it's sunny, and keep your head dry when it rains (a great deal!). A collapsible umbrella is great protection against sun and rain as well, particularly during the rainy season. Rainwear in tropical rainforest often makes you sweat, so an umbrella is the preferred choice of many travellers.

You can buy clothes of almost any size if you need them, but shoes in large sizes are difficult to find. I have size 12 feet (don't laugh, they're not that big!) and I can't buy footwear in Costa Rica unless I have it specially made. This is also true of most Latin countries, so bring a spare pair of shoes if you're planning a long multi-country trip. Also, if planning a trip to the rainforest, bear in mind that it will often be muddy even during the dry season, and very wet at other times, so bring a pair of shoes that you are prepared to get wet and muddy over and over again. Rubber boots are popular with the locals and are easily available in small and medium sizes in Costa Rica. Long sleeves and pants are recommended for both sun and insect protection in the tropics. Shorts and skirts are fine on the beaches but less useful in the rainforests.

I believe clothing is a personal thing and what works for one person is unsuitable for another. Therefore I don't provide an exhaustive clothing list. The following is a checklist of small items you will find useful and will probably need:

pocket torch (flashlight) with spare bulb and batteries
travel alarm clock
Swiss Army-style pocket knife
sewing & repairs kit (dental floss makes excellent, strong and colourless emergency thread)
a few metres of cord (also useful for clothesline and spare shoelaces)
sunglasses
plastic bags
soap and dish, shampoo, tooth brush and paste, shaving gear, towel
toilet paper (rarely found in cheaper hotels and restaurants)
ear plugs to aid sleeping in noisy hotels
suntan lotion (strong blocking lotions are hard to find and expensive in Costa Rica)
insect repellent (containing a high percentage of Deet)
address book, notebook, pens & pencils
paperback book (easily exchanged with other travellers when you've finished)
water bottle
first-aid kit (see Health section)
prescription medicines

Optional items:

camera and film (expensive in Costa Rica)
binoculars and field guides
Spanish-English dictionary
small padlock
large folding nylon bag to leave things in storage
snorkelling gear

Tampons are available in Costa Rica but imported items are heavily taxed so women may want to bring their own. If you use contraceptives you'll also find them available in the major cities, but again, if you use a preferred brand or method, you should bring it from home.

You need something to carry everything around in. A backpack is recommended because carrying your baggage on your back is less exhausting than carrying it in your hands. On the other hand, it's often more difficult to get at things inside a pack, so

National Tourist Bureau

Tourist Bureau logos

some travellers prefer a duffel bag with a full-length zip.

Whichever you choose, ensure that it is a good, strong piece of luggage, or you'll find that you spend much of your trip replacing zips, straps and buckles. Hard travelling is notoriously hard on your luggage, and if you bring a backpack, I suggest one with an internal frame. External frames snag on bus doors, luggage racks and airline baggage belts, and are prone to getting twisted, cracked or broken.

TOURIST OFFICES
Local Offices
In San José, the ICT answers questions (in English!) and provides maps at their public information office on the Plaza de la Cultura at Calle 5 and Avenida Central. They also have an information centre at the airport.

In other towns, there is sometimes a locally run information centre. These are mentioned in the text, where appropriate.

Overseas Reps
Roughly 30% of all foreign visitors to Costa Rica come from the USA, and therefore there are two Costa Rican National Tourist Bureaus in that country. Call or write for brochures or information:

Costa Rican National Tourist Bureau
1101 Brickel Ave, BIV Tower, Suite 801, Miami, FL 33131 (☎ (305) 358 2150 or toll-free (800) 327 7033)
3540 Wilshire Boulevard, Suite 707, Los Angeles, CA 90010 (☎ (213) 382 8080 or toll-free (800) 762 5909)

Citizens of other countries can ask the local Costa Rican consulate for tourist information. Or write to Instituto Costarricense de Turismo (ICT), Apartado 777, San José, Costa Rica.

Other
The South American Explorers Club (☎ (303) 320 0388) is at 1510 York Street, Denver, CO 80206, USA. Founded in 1977, the club functions as an information centre for travellers, adventurers, scientific expeditions, etc. They have club houses in Lima, Peru and Quito, Ecuador. Although the club has focused on South America, they have recently expanded to provide information for travellers to Central America as well.

The club has an extensive library of books, maps, and trip reports left by other travellers. Many maps and books are for sale. The club is an entirely membership supported, non-profit organisation. Membership costs US$25 and lasts for four quarterly issues of their excellent and informative *South American Explorer* magazine. Members can make use of the club houses (if heading on to Peru or Ecuador) as well as the extensive information facilities available by mail before they go.

BUSINESS HOURS & HOLIDAYS
Business Hours
Banks are open from 9 am to 3 pm Monday to Friday, with a few exceptions.

Government offices are supposedly open from 8 am to 4 pm, Monday to Friday, but often close for lunch between about 11.30 am and 1 pm.

Stores are open from 8 am to 6 or 7 pm, Monday to Saturday but a two-hour lunch break is not uncommon.

Holidays

National holidays are taken seriously in Costa Rica, and banks, public offices, and many stores close. There are no buses at all on the Thursday afternoon and Friday before Easter and many businesses are closed for the entire week before Easter. Beach hotels are usually booked weeks ahead for this week. Public transport tends to be tight on all holidays and the days immediately preceding or following them, so think ahead.

1 January
New Year's Day
19 March
Saint Joseph's Day (patron saint of San José)
March or April
Holy Week (moveable, the Thursday and Friday before Easter)
11 April
Juan Santamaría's Day (national hero at Battle of Rivas against William Walker in 1856)
1 May
Labor Day
29 June
Saint Peter & Saint Paul's Day
25 July
Guanacaste Day (annexation of Guanacaste Province, formerly part of Nicaragua)
2 August
Virgin of Los Angeles Day (patron saint of Costa Rica)
15 August
Mothers' Day (coincides with Catholic feast of the assumption)
15 September
Independence Day
12 October
Columbus Day (discovery of America, locally called *Día de la Raza*)
8 December
Immaculate Conception
25 December
Christmas Day

In addition, various towns have celebrations for their own particular day. The week between Christmas and New Year's Day tends to be an unofficial holiday, especially in San José.

POST & TELECOMMUNICATIONS
Postal Rates

The better hotels provide stamps for your letters and postcards, otherwise go to the main post office in each town.

Postcards and letters to the USA are about US$0.19 and US$0.21 respectively, and a little more to Europe or Australia. Parcels can also be mailed from the post office, but tend to be rather expensive.

Receiving Mail

Sometimes embassies will hold mail for you, but some embassies refuse to do so and will return it to the sender. You can also have mail sent care of a hotel or travel agency, but it's liable to get lost or delayed.

The best way to receive mail is at the central post office of whichever town you are staying in. San José is the most efficient, and letters usually arrive within a week from North America, a little longer from more distant places.

If you have mail sent to the post office, remember that the mail is filed alphabetically; so if it's addressed to John Gillis Payson it could well be filed under 'G' or 'J' instead of the correct 'P'. For San José it should be addressed to John PAYSON, Lista de Correos, Correos Central, San José, Costa Rica. Ask your correspondents to clearly print your last name and avoid appending witticisms such as 'World Traveller Extraordinaire' to your name. Post offices charge about US$0.10 per letter received.

Avoid having parcels sent to you, as they are held in customs and cannot be retrieved until you have paid a duty usually equivalent to the value of the gift plus the value of the mailing cost combined. This is true of even small packages like a cassette tape or book.

Telephones

Local Calls There are over 300,000 telephones in Costa Rica, which is the highest per capita number of phones in any Latin American country. Public telephones are found all over Costa Rica and are signed with a telephone symbol. They accept coins of 2, 5 and 10 colones.

Telephone numbers in Costa Rica consist of six digits and you can call anywhere in the country from a public booth. There are no area codes. Calls are generally inexpensive, with a three minute call anywhere never costing more than US$0.50. Of course operator assisted calls from hotels may be more expensive.

In remote areas of the country, look for the telephone symbol in even the most unlikely places. I was heading north on the Río Sarapiquí towards the Nicaraguan border in a motorised dugout canoe when I spied a telephone symbol on a post by the river. Sure enough, there was a tiny general store and a radio telephone. Calls could be put through to San José in a minute or two. These radio telephones require an operator (in this case it was the store assistant) and there is a meter. You pay whatever the meter charges for the call.

International Calls Calling internationally is quite straightforward. For collect (reverse charge) calls, dial 116 on any public phone to get an English-speaking international operator. The party you call can ring you back at the public telephone. Only countries with reciprocal agreements with Costa Rica will accept collect calls. These include the USA and many other countries.

If you want to pay for the call, however, you should go through an operator-assisted public telephone facility or a hotel, because trying to pay for an international call with 10 colón coins can be difficult. In San José, Radiográfica on Avenida 5, between Calles 1 & 3, will put international calls through from 7 am to 10 pm daily. There is also an international phone facility in the airport. Both these places have direct phones to an AT&T operator in the USA which you can use if you have an AT&T calling card.

Costs of calls per minute from Costa Rica are approximately US$2 to US$3 to North America (depending on area code), US$3 to US$4 to Europe, and US$5 to Australia.

Cheaper rates apply from 8 pm to 7 am and during weekends.

To call Costa Rica from abroad, use the international code (506) before the six digit Costa Rican telephone number.

Telegraph, Telex & FAX
Main post offices usually have telegraph facilities. Radiográfica in San José also has telex and FAX machines. They will also accept and hold telex and FAX messages.

TIME
Costa Rica is six hours behind Greenwich Mean Time, which means that Costa Rica time is equivalent to Central Time in North America. There is no daylight savings time.

ELECTRICITY
Costa Rica uses 110 volts, 60 cycles, AC.

LAUNDRY
There are almost no self-service laundry machines in Costa Rica, although I did find a couple of expensive ones in San José which charged close to US$4 a load to wash and dry. This means that you have to find someone to wash your clothes for you or wash them yourself.

Many hotels will have someone to do your laundry; this can cost very little in the cheaper hotels (about a dollar for a full change of clothes). The major problem is that you might not see your clothes again for two or three days, particularly if it is raining and they can't be dried. Better hotels charge more but have driers.

If you wash the clothes yourself, ask the hotel staff where to do this. Most hotels have a huge cement sink (called a *pila*) and scrubbing board which is much easier to use than a bathroom washbasin. Often there is a well-like section next to the scrubbing board and it is full of clean water. Don't dunk your clothes in this water to soak or rinse them as it is often used as an emergency water supply in the case of water failure. Use a bowl or bucket to scoop water out instead, or run water from a tap.

WEIGHTS & MEASURES

Costa Rica uses the metric system. For those travellers who still use miles, ounces, bushels, leagues, rods, roods, magnums, stones and other quaint and arcane expressions, there is a metric conversion table at the back of this book.

BOOKS & MAPS
Regional Travel Guides

South American Handbook (Trade & Travel Publications, Bath, England). This was first published in 1924 and has been updated every year since. In 1991, for the first time, this well known book was issued in three separate volumes, one of which was the *Mexico & Central American Handbook*. Its section on Costa Rica is limited to some 57 pages out of almost 700. Nevertheless, it remains a useful source of travel information, particularly for travellers doing a grand tour of Central America.

Central America on a Shoestring (due in 1992 from Lonely Planet, Australia). This book is written for the traveller on a tight budget, and again is useful for someone visiting several Central American countries. Both these guides have much background as well as travel information and both are recommended.

Costa Rica Travel Guides

At my last count, there were four travel guidebooks dealing exclusively with Costa Rica. All provide general background and travel information. All are good and have been well received. The editions I read are listed here but more recent editions may be available by the time you read this.

The New Key to Costa Rica by Beatrice Blake and Anne Becher (Publications in English, San José, Costa Rica, 9th ed 1990) is the oldest guide and updated every year or two. It is the only Costa Rican travel guide actually published in the country and hence is easily available in San José. Its emphasis is living and travelling in Costa Rica.

The Costa Rica Traveller by Ellen Searby (Windham Bay Press, Juneau, Alaska, 2nd ed 1988, updated 1989) has an emphasis on hotel listings.

Costa Rica by Paul Glassman (Passport Press, Champlain, New York, 1989) has an emphasis on general travel.

Costa Rica: A Natural Destination by Ree Strange Sheck (John Muir Publications, Santa Fe, New Mexico, 1990) has an emphasis on visiting and staying in the national parks and private reserves.

Nature & Wildlife

Several very useful books have been published for the many people coming to Costa Rica to observe wildlife, visit national parks, and enjoy the outdoors. All of the following are recommended.

Costa Rica National Parks by Mario Boza (Incafo, Madrid, Hardbound 1988, Softbound 1989) is published in conjunction with the National Parks Foundation and the Neotropical Foundation, both of Costa Rica. The hardbound version is a beautifully photographed coffee-table book with bilingual (Spanish-English) text describing the national parks; the softbound version is half the size but also has good photos and interesting text. Both books are available in San José. As of 1990, conservationist Mario Boza will be Vice-Minister of Natural Resources.

Costa Rican Natural History by Daniel H Janzen with 174 contributors (University of Chicago Press, 1983) is an excellent, if weighty (almost two kg and over 800 large pages!), introduction for the biologist.

Tropical Nature by Adrian Forsyth & Ken Miyata (Scribner's & Sons, New York, 1984). I recommend this entertaining and readable book for the layperson interested in biology, particularly of the rainforest. Forsyth is also the author of a children's book *Journey Through a Tropical Jungle* (Simon & Schuster, New York, 1988).

A Naturalist in Costa Rica (University of Florida Press, Gainesville, 1971) and *A Naturalist on a Tropical Farm* (University of California Press, Berkeley, 1980) both by Alexander F Skutch. They are slightly dated but still excellent.

A Neotropical Companion by John C Kricher (Princeton University Press, 1989). This book is sub-titled 'An Introduction to the Animals, Plants, and Ecosystems of the New World Tropics'.

In the Rainforest by Catherine Caulfield (University of Chicago Press, 1986). Another good choice, it emphasises the problems of the loss of the rainforest.

Life Above the Jungle Floor by Donald Perry (Simon & Schuster, New York, 1986). Donald Perry, whose Automated Web for Canopy Exploration can be seen and used at Rara Avis Rainforest Preserve, is the author of this fascinating book.

The Enchanted Canopy by Andrew W Mitchell (Macmillan, New York, 1986). Another very good book.

Rainforests – A Guide to Research and Tourist Facilities at Selected Tropical Forest Sites in Central and South America by James L Castner (Fekine Press, Gainesville, Florida, 1990). This is a good source book particularly for those people wishing to visit rainforests in a variety of neotropical countries. Thirty nine sites in seven countries are described and much useful background is referred to.

Field Guides

A Guide to the Birds of Costa Rica by F Gary Stiles and Alexander F Skutch (Cornell University Press, 1989). Bird-watchers will need this excellent and thorough book.

Neotropical Rainforest Mammals – A Field Guide by Louise H Emmons (University of Chicago Press, 1990). This excellent new book is detailed and portable, with almost 300 mammal species described and illustrated. Although some of the mammals included are found only in other neotropical countries, most of Costa Rica's mammals, and certainly all the rainforest inhabitants, are found within the book's pages.

The Butterflies of Costa Rica and Their Natural History by Philip J DeVries (Princeton University Press, 1987). A detailed guide for lepidopterists.

The Sea Turtles of Santa Rosa National Park by Stephen E Cornelius (Fundación de Parques Nacionales, San José, 1986). Descriptions of the four species found in Costa Rica.

Adventure Travel

Backpacking in Mexico & Central America by Hilary Bradt et al (Bradt Publications, Chalfont St Peter, UK, 3rd ed due 1992).

The Rivers of Costa Rica: A Canoeing, Kayaking, and Rafting Guide by Michael W Mayfield & Rafael E Gallo (Menasha Ridge Press, Alabama, 1988). Just the ticket for river runners.

People & Politics

The Costa Ricans by Richard Biesanz et al (Prentice-Hall, Englewood Hills, New Jersey, 1987). This is a book with a historical perspective on politics and social change in Costa Rica.

What Happen: A Folk History of Costa Rica's Talamanca Coast (Ecodesarollos, San José, 1977) and *Wa'apin Man* (Editorial Costa Rica, 1986). These two books are written by former Peace Corps volunteer Paula Palmer and cover the people of the south Caribbean coast of Costa Rica. Look for these last two in San José.

Bookshops

There is a large variety of books about Costa Rica. Many are available outside of Costa Rica in good bookshops specialising in travel and wildlife. There are a few bookshops in San José which carry some titles, especially those published in Costa Rica. These bookshops are listed under San José. Bookshops outside of San José rarely carry books of interest to the traveller.

Maps

If you want a good map of Costa Rica before you go, the best is the very detailed map drawn by Kevin Healey, an Australian cartographer who has made the best maps of Latin America I've seen. His *Costa Rica* (1990) map is a single 1:500,000 sheet with a 1:250,000 *Environs of San José* inset, and provides road, rail, topography, national park and private reserve information. It is published by and available from International Travel Map Productions (ITM), PO Box 2290, Vancouver, British Columbia, V6B 3W5, Canada. In Europe write to Bradt Publications, 41 Nortoft Road, Chalfont St Peter, Bucks, SL9 0LA, England.

Once you arrive in Costa Rica, there are several choices. The Costa Rican National Tourist Bureau publishes three useful maps, all of which are free but also subject to availability. The maps are a 1:10,000 *Centre of San José Map*, a 1:200,000 *San José Area Map*, and a 1:1,000,000 *Costa Rica Road Map*.

The Instituto Geográfico de Costa Rica publishes four kinds of maps which can be bought at the Geographical Institute in San José, or in major bookstores in the capital. There is a single sheet 1:500,000 map of Costa Rica, which is very good but not as detailed as the ITM map. There is a nine-sheet 1:200,000 map covering the country in detail. Most of the country is covered with 1:50,000 scale topographical maps (useful for hiking and backpacking), and some of the cities and urban areas are covered by a variety of 1:10,000 and 1:5000 maps. All these maps provide physical as well as political detail and are well produced.

MEDIA
Newspapers & Magazines

The best local daily newspapers are *La Nación* and *La República*. An English language newspaper published every Friday is the *Tico Times*. It costs about US$0.25 and is a useful source of information about cultural and newsworthy events in San José in particular and the country in general. It is available at news-stands throughout the city. There is an annual tourism edition published each October.

Major bookstores in San José carry some North American and other newspapers (two or three days late) as well as magazines such as *Time* or *Newsweek*.

Radio & Television

There are six local TV stations and many of the better hotels also receive cable TV from the USA. There are many AM/FM radio stations. If you have a portable shortwave radio you can listen to, among many others, the BBC World Service, Voice of America or Radio Moscow.

HEALTH

It's true that most people travelling for any length of time in Latin America are likely to have an occasional mild stomach upset. It's also true that if you take the appropriate precautions before, during and after your trip, it's unlikely that you will become seriously ill. In a decade of living and travelling in Latin America, I'm happy to report that I've picked up no major illnesses. Of all Latin American countries, Costa Rica has among the highest standards of health care and hygiene, so you are unlikely to get seriously ill.

Vaccinations

The Costa Rican authorities do not, at present, require anyone to have an up-to-date international vaccination card to enter the country, though you should make sure that your vaccinations are up to date. Pregnant women should consult with their doctor before taking any vaccinations.

Travel Insurance

However fit and healthy you are, *do* take out medical insurance, preferably one with provisions for flying you home in the event of a medical emergency. Even if you don't get sick, you might be involved in an accident.

First-Aid Kit

How large or small your first-aid kit should be depends on your knowledge of first-aid procedures, where and how far off the beaten track you are going, how long you will need the kit for, and how many people will be sharing it. The following is a suggested checklist which you should amend as you require.

antiseptic cream
antihistamine or other anti-itch cream for insect bites
aspirin

Pepto Bismol and/or Lomotil for diarrhoea
antibiotics such as ampicillin and tetracycline
throat lozenges
ear and eye drops
antacid tablets
motion-sickness medication
alcohol swabs
water purification tablets
lip salve
anti-fungal powder
thermometer in a case
surgical tape, assorted sticky plasters (band-aids),
    gauze, bandages, butterfly closures
scissors
first-aid booklet

A convenient way of carrying your first-aid kit so that it doesn't get crushed is in a small plastic container with a sealing lid.

Water & Food
You can drink tap water in San José and the major towns, though it is worth boiling or purifying it in out of the way places. The lowlands are the most likely places to find unsafe drinking water. Ask if in doubt. Commercially available water purification tablets and a water bottle are the easiest method. Bottled mineral water, soft drinks and beer are readily available alternatives.

Uncooked foods (such as salads) are best avoided unless they can be peeled.

Health Precautions
Several things must be thought about before leaving home. If you wear prescription glasses, make sure you have a spare pair and a copy of the prescription. The tropical sun is strong, so you may want to have a prescription pair of sunglasses made.

Also buy sunblock lotion, as it is hard to find and expensive in Costa Rica. A minimum sunblocking factor of 15 is recommended; higher if you are fair or burn easily.

Ensure that you have an adequate supply of the prescription medicines you use on a regular basis. If you haven't had a dental examination for a long time, you should have one rather than risk a dental problem in Costa Rica.

Diarrhoea
The drastic change in diet experienced by travellers means that they are often susceptible to minor stomach ailments, such as diarrhoea. After you've been travelling in Latin America for a while you seem to build up some sort of immunity. If this is your first trip to Latin America, take heart. Costa Rica is one of the healthiest countries in Latin America. Many people get minor stomach problems, but a simple non-prescription medicine such as Pepto Bismol usually takes care of the discomfort quickly.

Dysentery
If your diarrhoea continues for several days and is accompanied by nausea, severe abdominal pain and fever, and you find blood in your stools, it's likely that you have contracted dysentery. Although travellers may suffer from an occasional bout of diarrhoea, dysentery is fortunately not very common. There are two types: amoebic and bacillary. It is not always obvious which kind you have. Although bacillary responds well to antibiotics, amoebic – which is rarer – involves more complex treatment. If you contract dysentery, you should seek medical advice.

Hepatitis
Hepatitis A is caused by ingesting contaminated food or water. Salads, uncooked or unpeeled fruit, and unboiled drinks are the worst offenders. Infection risks are minimised by using bottled drinks except in major towns or where you know the water has been purified, washing your own salads with purified water, and paying scrupulous attention to your toilet habits.

If you get the disease you'll know it. Your skin and especially the whites of your eyes turn yellow, and you feel so tired that it literally takes all your effort to go to the toilet. There is no cure except rest. If you're lucky, you'll be on your feet in a couple of weeks; if you're not, expect to stay in bed for a couple of months.

Research is currently underway to find a 100% effective prophylactic; meanwhile you can get a gamma globulin shot as close to departure as possible. Although it is not 100% effective, your chances of getting hepatitis A are minimised. The shot should be repeated every six months, although some authorities recommend more frequent shots.

The incidence of hepatitis A is low in Costa Rica, so many travellers opt not to take gamma globulin shots.

Malaria

Malarial mosquitoes aren't a problem in the highlands but some cases of malaria have recently been reported in the lowlands, particularly the south Caribbean coastal area near the Panamanian border. If you plan on visiting the lowlands, you should purchase anti-malarial pills in advance because they should be taken from two weeks before until six weeks after your visit. Dosage and frequency of administration varies from brand to brand, so check this carefully.

Chloroquine (known as Aralen in Costa Rica) is recommended for short term protection. The usual dose is 500 mg once a week. Long term use of chloroquine *may* cause side effects and travellers planning a long trip into the lowlands should discuss this risk against the value of protection with their doctor. Pregnant women are at a higher risk when taking anti-malarials. Fansidar is now known to cause sometimes fatal side effects and this drug should be used only under medical supervision.

People who are going to spend a great deal of time in tropical lowlands and prefer not to take anti-malarial pills on a semi-permanent basis should remember that malarial mosquitoes bite mostly at night. You should wear long-sleeved shirts and long trousers from dusk till dawn, use frequent applications of an insect repellent, and sleep under a mosquito net. Sleeping under a fan is also effective; mosquitoes don't like wind. A woman traveller suggests that getting changed or dressed for dinner is not a good idea in mosquito-prone areas, because dusk is a particularly bad time for mosquitoes and that dressy skirt does nothing to keep the

insects away. Keep the long pants and bug repellent on!

The most effective ingredient in insect repellents is diethyl-metatoluamide, also known as 'Deet'. You should buy repellent with 90% or more of this ingredient; many brands, including those available in Costa Rica, contain less than 15%. I find that the rub-on lotions are the most effective, and sprays are good for spraying clothes, especially at the neck, wrist, waist and ankle openings. Bear in mind that deet is strong stuff – it is toxic to children and shouldn't be used on their skin. 'Skin So Soft' made by Avon has insect repellent properties and is not toxic – get the oil, not the lotion. Deet dissolves plastic, so keep it off plastic lenses, etc.

Mosquito spirals (coils) can be bought in Costa Rican pharmacies (ask for *espirales*). They work like incense sticks and are fairly effective at keeping mosquitoes away.

Insect Problems

Insect repellents go a long way in preventing bites, but if you do get bitten, avoid scratching. Unfortunately this is easier said than done.

To alleviate itching, try applying hydrocortisone cream, calamine lotion, some other kind of anti-itch cream, or soaking in baking soda. Scratching will quickly open bites and cause them to become infected. Skin infections are slow to heal in the heat of the tropics and all infected bites as well as cuts and grazes should be kept scrupulously clean, treated with antiseptic creams, and covered with dressings on a daily basis.

Another insect problem is infestation with lice (including crabs) and scabies. Lice or crabs crawl around in your body hair and make you itch. To get rid of them, wash with a shampoo which contains benzene hexachloride, or shave the affected area. To avoid being re-infected, wash all your clothes and bedding in hot water and the shampoo. It's probably best to just throw away your underwear if you had body lice or crabs. Lice thrive on body warmth; these beasties lurking in clothes will die in about 72 hours if the clothing isn't worn.

Chiggers are mites which burrow into your skin and cause it to become red and itchy. The recommended prevention is to sprinkle sulphur powder on socks, shoes and lower legs when walking through grass.

Scorpions and spiders can give severely painful – but rarely fatal – stings or bites. A common way to get bitten is to put on your clothes and shoes in the morning without checking them first. Develop the habit of shaking out your clothing before putting it on, especially in the lowlands. Check your bedding before going to sleep. Don't walk barefoot, and look where you place your hands when reaching to a shelf or branch. It's extremely unlikely that you will get stung, so don't worry too much about it.

Snakebite

This is also extremely unlikely. Should you be bitten, the snake may be a non-venomous one. In any event, follow this procedure: first, try to kill the offending creature for identification. Second, don't try the slash-and-suck routine. One of the world's deadliest snakes is the fer-de-lance, and it has

Fer-de-lance snake

an anti-coagulating agent in its venom. If you're bitten by a fer-de-lance, your blood coagulates twice as slowly as the average haemophiliac's and so slashing at the wound with a razor is a good way to help you bleed to death. The slash-and-suck routine does work in some cases, but this should be done only by someone who knows what they are doing. Third, get the victim to a doctor as soon as possible. Fourth, keep calm and reassure the victim. Even the deadly fer-de-lance only succeeds in killing a small percentage of its victims. Fifth, while reassuring and evacuating the victim, apply a tourniquet just above the bite if it is on a limb. Release pressure for 90 seconds every 10 minutes, and make sure that the tourniquet is never so tight that you can't slide a finger underneath it. If circulation is cut off completely, worse damage will result.

In Australia, where they have a fair amount of snake bite experience, a new method of treatment is now recommended. This is to simply immobilise the limb where the bite took place and bandage it tightly (but not like a tourniquet) and completely. Then with the minimum of disturbance, particularly of the bound limb, get the victim to medical attention. Hospitals and clinics throughout the country stock antivenin.

Altitude Sickness

This occurs when you ascend to high altitude quickly, for example if you fly into the highlands. This is not a problem in San José (1150 metres) which is not high enough to cause altitude problems.

If you are planning on driving up one of the volcanoes such as Poás (2704 metres) or Irazú (3432 metres) you may experience some shortness of breath and headache. Overnight stays are not allowed on these volcanoes, so you will be able to descend quickly if you feel unwell. Heading south from San José on the Interamerican Highway, the road crosses the continental divide at 3335 metres, 95 km south of the capital. Again, you will probably be going down again before you get sick.

If you are planning a climb of Chirripó

(3819 metres, the highest mountain in Costa Rica and south Central America) you may experience much more severe symptoms, including vomiting, fatigue, insomnia, loss of appetite, a rapid pulse and irregular (or Cheyne-Stokes) breathing during sleep.

The best thing you can do to avoid altitude sickness is to climb gradually. Consider taking two days for the Chirripó ascent rather than one. If you feel sick, the best treatment is rest, deep breathing, an adequate fluid intake and a mild pain killer such as Tylenol to alleviate headaches. If symptoms are very severe, the only effective cure is to descend to a lower elevation.

Heat & Sun

The heat and humidity of the coastal tropics make you sweat profusely and can also make you feel apathetic. It is important to maintain a high fluid intake and to ensure that your food is well salted. If fluids lost through perspiration are not replaced, heat exhaustion and cramps may result. The feeling of apathy that some people experience usually fades after a week or two.

If you're arriving in the tropics with a great desire to improve your tan, you've certainly come to the right place. The tropical sun will not only improve your tan, it will also burn you to a crisp. I know several travellers who have enjoyed themselves in the sun for an afternoon, and then spent the next couple of days with severe sunburn. An effective way of immobilising yourself is to cover yourself with suntan lotion, walk down to the beach, remove your shoes and badly burn your feet, which you forgot to put lotion on and which are especially untanned.

The power of the tropical sun cannot be overemphasised. Don't spoil your trip by trying to tan too quickly; use strong suntan lotion frequently and put it on all exposed skin. Wearing a wide-brimmed sun hat is also a good idea.

Medical Attention

If you've taken the precautions mentioned in the previous sections you can look forward to a generally healthy trip. Should something

go wrong, however, you can get good medical advice and treatment in the major cities.

The social security hospitals provide free emergency services to everyone, including foreigners. The main one in San José is the Hospital San Juan de Dios (☎ 220166) on Calle 14 at Avenida Central. Private clinics are also available and are listed under San José and other main towns. Emergency phone numbers worth knowing are the Red Cross (Cruz Roja) at 215818 for ambulances in the San José area, and San José Paramedics (☎ 118, no coin needed). Outside of San José, call the Guardia at 127.

Most prescription drugs are available in Costa Rica, some of which are sold over the counter. For minor ailments and illnesses, pharmacists will often advise and prescribe for you.

Medical care is generally less expensive than it is in most Western countries, although the standards are high. Costa Rica is recently experiencing a boom in cosmetic and plastic surgery. Foreigners come here specifically for these non-essential medical procedures at lower cost than at home.

WOMEN TRAVELLERS

Generally, women travellers find Costa Rica safe and pleasant to visit.

Women are traditionally respected in Costa Rica (Mother's Day is a national holiday!) and recently women have made gains in the workplace. A woman vice-president (Victoria Garrón) was elected in 1986 and women routinely occupy roles in the political, legal, scientific and medical fields; professions which used to be overpoweringly dominated by men.

This is not to say that machismo is a thing of the past. On the contrary, it is very much alive and practised. Costa Rican men generally consider *gringas* to have looser morals and to be easier 'conquests' than ticas. They will often make flirtatious comments to single women, both local and foreign. Women travelling with another woman are not exempt from this attention; women travelling with men are less likely to receive attention.

Comments are rarely blatantly rude; the usual thing is a smiling '*Mi amor*' or an appreciative hiss. The best way to deal with this is to do what the ticas do – ignore the comments completely and not look at the man making them.

Women travellers will meet pleasant and friendly Costa Rican men. It is worth remembering, though, that gentle seduction is a sport, a challenge, even a way of life for many Costa Rican men, particularly in San José. Men may conveniently forget to mention that they are married, and declarations of undying love mean little in this Catholic society where divorce is frowned upon. Women who firmly resist unwanted verbal advances from men are normally treated with respect.

Costa Ricans are generally quite conservative, and that applies to dress. Travellers are advised to follow suit to avoid calling unnecessary attention to themselves. Neither men nor women wear shorts in the highlands – though shorts are fine in the beach resorts.

DANGERS & ANNOYANCES
Theft

Although rip-offs are a fact of life when travelling anywhere, you'll find Costa Rica is less prone to theft than many countries. You should, nevertheless, take some simple precautions to avoid being robbed.

Armed robbery is very rare but sneak theft is more common, and you should remember that crowded places are the haunts of pickpockets – places such as badly lit bus stations or bustling streets.

Thieves look for easy targets. Tourists who carry a wallet or passport in a hip pocket are asking for trouble. Leave your wallet at home; it's an easy mark for a pickpocket. Carrying a roll of bills loosely wadded under a handkerchief in your front pocket is as safe a way as any of carrying your daily spending money. The rest should be hidden. Always use at least an inside pocket or preferably a body pouch, money belt or leg pouch to protect your money and passport.

You should carry the greater proportion of your money in the form of travellers' cheques. These can be refunded if lost or stolen. Some airlines will also reissue your ticket if it is lost. You have to give them details such as where and when you got it, the ticket number and which flight was involved. Sometimes a reissuing fee (about US$20) is charged, but that's much better than buying a new ticket.

It is a good idea to carry an emergency packet somewhere separate from all your other valuables. This emergency packet could be sewn into a jacket (don't lose the jacket!) or even carried in your shoe. It should contain a photocopy of the important pages of your passport in case it is lost or stolen. On the back of the photocopy you should list important numbers such as all your travellers' cheques serial numbers, airline ticket numbers and credit card or bank account numbers. Also keep one high-denomination bill in with this emergency stash. You will probably never have to use it, but it's a good idea not to put all your eggs into one basket.

Take out travellers' insurance if you're carrying really valuable gear such as a good camera. But don't get paranoid; Costa Rica is a safe country.

If you are robbed, you should get a police report as soon as possible. This is a requirement for any insurance claims, although it is unlikely that the police will be able to recover the property.

Swimming Safety

The tourist brochures with their enticing photographs of tropical paradises do not mention that approximately 200 drownings a year occur on Costa Rican beaches. Of these, an estimated 80% are caused by rip-tides.

A rip-tide is a strong current which pulls the swimmer out to sea. It can occur in waist deep water. It is most important to remember that rip-tides will pull you *out but not under*. Many deaths are caused by panicked swimmers struggling to the point of exhaustion.

If you are caught in a rip-tide, float, do not

struggle. Let the rip-tide carry you out beyond the breakers. If you swim, do so parallel to the beach, not directly back in. You are very unlikely to be able to swim against a rip-tide and will only exhaust yourself. When you are carried out beyond the breakers, you will find that the rip-tide will dissipate – it won't carry you out for miles. Then you can swim back in to shore. Swim in at a 45° angle to the shore to avoid being caught by the current again.

If you feel a rip-tide whilst you are wading, try to come back in sideways, thus offering less body surface to the current. Also remember to walk parallel to the beach if you cannot make headway, so that you can get out of the rip-tide. Some rip-tides are permanent, others come and go or move along a beach. Beaches with a reputation for rips are Playa Bonita near Limón; the area at the entrance of Cahuita National Park; Playa Doña Ana and Playa Barranca near Puntarenas; Playa Espadilla at Manuel Antonio National Park.

FILM & PHOTOGRAPHY

Definitely bring everything you'll need. Camera gear is expensive in Costa Rica and film choice is limited. Film is often kept in hot storage cabinets and is sometimes outdated, so if you do buy any in Costa Rica, check the expiry date.

Don't have film developed in Costa Rica if you can help it, as processing is not very good. On the other hand, carrying around exposed film for months is asking for washed-out results. It is best to send it home as soon after it's exposed as possible. You'll often meet people heading back to whichever continent you're from and they can usually be persuaded to do you this favour, particularly if you offer to take them out to dinner. I always buy either process-paid film or prepaid film mailers so I can place the exposed film in the mailer and not worry about the costs. The last thing you want to do on your return from a trip is worry about how you're going to find the money to develop a few dozen rolls of film.

Tropical shadows are very strong and come out almost black on photographs. Often a bright but hazy day makes for better photographs than a very sunny one. Photography in open shade or using fill-in flash will help. The best time for shooting is when the sun is low – the first and last two hours of the day. If you are heading into the rainforest you will need high-speed film, flash, a tripod, or a combination of these if you want to take photographs within the jungle. The amount of light penetrating the layers of vegetation is surprisingly very low.

The Costa Rican people make wonderful subjects for photos. However, most people resent having a camera thrust in their face. Ask for permission with a smile or a joke and if this is refused (rarely) don't become offended. Be aware and sensitive of people's feelings – it is not worth upsetting someone to get your photograph.

The international airport in San José has a vicious X-ray machine. My film came home with a greyish cast to it, and two friends who were there later reported the same thing. Carry all your film on separately.

ACTIVITIES

San José is the cultural centre, with good restaurants, the National Theatre, symphony, music and dance performances, cinemas, art galleries, museums and shopping centres. But it is away from the capital that many of Costa Rica's greatest attractions are to be found.

Without a doubt, Costa Rica's conservationist attitude and activity is the most developed in Latin America. The wonderful array of national parks and private preserves and their attendant wildlife and scenery draw travellers from all over the world. With 34 national park areas, and about a score of private preserves, visitors can enjoy an intimate look at habitats and environments ranging from tropical rainforest to highland *páramo*, from beautiful beaches to active volcanoes, and from white-water rivers to mountain ranges. The wildlife and vegetation is magnificent and accessible. No wonder that most visitors travel to at least one park or preserve, and that the primary focus of many trips is natural history, especially bird-watching, which is some of the best in the world.

Outdoor enthusiasts will also find much to their liking. From running some of the best white water in Central America to just relaxing on palm-fringed beaches; from backpacking through the rainforest to horse riding to camping on mountain tops; from record-breaking, deep-sea sport-fishing to snorkelling to world class surfing; many adventures are possible.

The more sedentary visitor can enjoy leisurely drives through the pretty countryside, perhaps visiting a coffee *finca* (farm) or villages known for handicrafts. An all-day train ride from the highlands to the Caribbean coast is another popular activity, as are luxurious lunch or dinner cruises on elegant boats in the Gulf of Nicoya on the Pacific coast.

ACCOMMODATION
Hotels
There is great variety and no shortage of places to stay in Costa Rica. It is rare to arrive in a town and not be able to find somewhere to sleep, but during Easter week or weekends in the dry season the beach hotels can be full. Indeed, most beach hotels are booked several weeks in advance for Easter week. Hotel accommodation can also be tight if there is a special event going on in a particular town. Private lodges and expensive hotels in remote areas should always be reserved in advance.

Sometimes it's a little difficult to find single rooms, and you may get a room with two or even three beds. In most cases, though, you are only charged for one bed unless the hotel is full. Couples sharing one bed *(cama matrimonial)* are sometimes charged less than two people sharing a two-bed room.

Look around the hotel if possible. The same prices are often charged for rooms of widely differing quality. Even in the US$3 a night cheapies it's worth looking around. If you get shown into a horrible airless box with just a bed and a bare light bulb, you can

ask to see a better room without giving offence. You'll often be amazed at the results. I recommend that you ask to see a room before you rent it, particularly in the cheapest hotels.

Bathroom facilities are rarely what you may be used to at home. The cheapest hotels don't always have hot water. Even if they do, it might not work or it may only be turned on at certain hours of the day.

Another intriguing device you should know about is the electric shower. This consists of a single cold-water shower head hooked up to an electric heating element which is switched on when you want a hot (more likely tepid) shower. Don't touch anything metal while you're in the shower or you may discover what an electric shock feels like. The power is never high enough to actually throw you across the room, but it's unpleasant nevertheless. I managed to shock myself by simply picking up the soap which I had balanced on a horizontal water pipe.

Flushing a toilet in the cheaper hotels creates another hazard – overflow. Putting toilet paper into the bowl seems to clog up the system, so a waste receptacle is often provided for the paper. This may not seem particularly sanitary, but it is much better than clogged bowls and water on the floor. A well-run hotel, even if it is cheap, will ensure that the receptacle is emptied and the toilet cleaned every day.

Most hotels will give you a key to lock your room, and theft from your hotel room is not as frequent as it is in some other countries. Nevertheless, carrying your own padlock is a good idea if you plan on staying in the cheaper hotels. Once in a while you'll find that a room doesn't look very secure – perhaps there's a window that doesn't close or the wall doesn't come to the ceiling and can be climbed over. It's worth finding another room. This is another reason why it's good to look at a room before you rent it.

You should never leave valuables lying around the room; it's just too tempting for a maid who makes US$3 a day for her work. Money and passport should be in a secure body pouch; other valuables can usually be kept in the hotel strongbox, although some cheaper hotels might not want to take this responsibility.

Hotel Categories Hotels listed as 'bottom end' are certainly the cheapest, but not necessarily the worst. Although they are usually quite basic, with just a bed and four walls, they can nevertheless be well looked after, very clean, and amazing value for money. They are often good places to meet other budget travellers, both Costa Rican and foreign.

Prices in this section begin at about US$2 per person and go up to US$10 for a double room. Every town has hotels in this price range. Although you'll usually have to use communal bathrooms in the cheapest hotels, you can sometimes find rooms with a private bathroom for as little as US$5 double.

Hotels in the 'middle' category usually cost from about US$10 to US$40 for a double room, but are not always better than the best hotels in the bottom price range. On the whole, however, you can find some very decent hotels here. Even if you're travelling on a budget, there may be occasions when you feel like indulging in comparative luxury for a day or two.

'Top-end' hotels are over US$40 double and can go to over US$100 a double in San José and in the beach resorts. The prices and services compare favourably with international standards.

Youth Hostels & Camping

There is a small youth hostel system, and the charge for a night in a hostel is about US$5. The main hostel is in San José and they have further information about other hostels.

There are rarely campsites in the towns; the constant availability of cheap hotels makes town campsites redundant. Cheap camping facilities are available in many of the national parks.

FOOD

If you're on a tight budget, food is the most important part of your expenses. You can stay in rock-bottom hotels, travel by bus, and never consider buying a souvenir, but you've got to eat well. This doesn't mean expensively, but it does mean that you want to avoid spending half your trip sitting on the toilet.

The worst culprits for making you sick are salads and unpeeled fruit. With the fruit, stick to bananas, oranges, pineapples and other fruit that you can peel yourself. With unpeeled fruit or salads, wash them yourself in water which you can trust (see Health section). It can be a lot of fun getting a group of you together and heading out to the market to buy salad vegies and preparing a huge salad.

As long as you take heed of the salad warning, you'll find plenty of good things to eat at reasonable prices. You certainly don't have to eat at a fancy restaurant; their kitchen facilities may not be as clean as their white tablecloths. A good sign for any restaurant is if the locals eat there – restaurants aren't empty if the food is delicious and healthy.

If you're on a tight budget eat the set meal offered in most restaurants at lunch time – it's usually filling and cheap. Also try the cheap luncheon counters called *sodas*. There are also reasonably priced Chinese and Italian restaurants in most towns.

Most restaurants serve *bistek* (beef), *pollo* (chicken) and *pescado* (fish) dishes. Vegetarians should note that *carne* literally means meat, but in Costa Rica tends to refer to beef. Chicken, *puerco* (pork) and *chivo* (goat) isn't necessarily included, so be specific if you want something without any meat. Many visitors from North America, used to spicy Mexican food capable of burning out taste buds, mistakenly assume that Costa Rican food is very spicy too. Generally, it's tasty rather than spicy hot.

Costa Rican specialities include:

Gallo Pinto, literally 'spotted rooster', is a mixture of rice and black beans that is traditionally served for breakfast, sometimes with *natilla* (sour cream) or *huevos fritos/revueltos* (fried/scrambled eggs). This dish is lightly spiced with herbs and is filling and tasty.

Tortillas are either Mexican style corn pancakes or omelettes, depending on what kind of meal you're having.

Casado is a set meal which is usually filling and economical. It contains *arroz* (rice), *frijoles* (black beans), *platano* (fried plantain), beef, chopped *repollo* (cabbage), and maybe an egg or an avocado.

Olla de carne is a beef and vegetable soup containing vegetables such as potatoes, plantains, corn, squash and a local tuber called *yuca*.

Palmitos are hearts of palm, usually served in a salad with vinegar dressing, whilst *pejibaye* is a rather starchy tasting palm fruit also eaten as a salad.

Arroz con pollo is a basic dish of rice and chicken.

Elote is corn, served boiled on the cob *(elote cocinado)*, or roasted on the cob *(elote asado)*.

Traditional desserts *(postres)* include:

Mazamorra is a pudding made from corn starch.

Queque seco is simply pound cake.

Dulce de leche is milk and sugar boiled to make a thick syrup which may be used in a layered cake called *torta chilena*.

Cajeta is similar to dulce de leche, but thicker still, like a fudge.

Flan is a cold caramel custard.

The following are snacks, often obtained in *sodas*:

Arreglados are little puff pastries stuffed with beef, chicken or cheese.

Enchiladas are heavier pastries stuffed with potatoes and cheese and maybe meat.

Empanadas are Chilean style turnovers stuffed with meat or cheese and raisins.

Pupusas are El Salvadoran style fried corn and cheese cakes.

Gallos are tortilla sandwiches containing meat, beans or cheese.

Ceviche is seafood marinated with lemon, onion, garlic, sweet red peppers and coriander. It can be made with *corvina* (a white sea bass), or occasionally *langostinos* (shrimps), or even *conchas* (shellfish).

Patacones are a coastal speciality, especially on the Caribbean side, and consist of slices of plantain deep fried like French fried potatoes. Delicious.

Tamales are boiled cornmeal pasties, usually wrapped in a banana leaf (you don't eat the leaf). At Christmas they traditionally come stuffed with chicken or pork, at other times of year they may come stuffed with corn and wrapped in a corn leaf. *Tamales asado* are sweet cornmeal cakes.

DRINKS
Nonalcoholic Drinks

Coffee is traditionally served very strong and mixed with hot milk to taste, but increasingly fewer establishments serve it this way. As far as I am concerned, this is just as well, because the hot milk tends to form a skin which I find quite unappetising. I much prefer it strong, tasty and black. Tea (including herb tea) is also available. Milk is pasteurised and safe to drink.

The usual brands of soft drinks are available, although many people prefer *refrescos* which are fruit drinks made either *con agua* (with water) or *con leche* (with milk). Possible fruit drinks to try are mango, papaya, *piña* (pineapple), *sandía* (water melon), *melón* (cantaloupe), *mora* (blackberry), *zanahoria* (carrot), *cebada* (barley) or *tamarindo* (a slightly tart but refreshing drink made from the fruit of the tamarind tree).

Pipas are green coconuts which have a hole macheted into the top of them and a straw stuck in so you can drink the coconut 'milk' – a slightly bitter but refreshing and filling drink.

Agua dulce is simply boiled water mixed with brown sugar, and *horchata* is a cornmeal drink flavoured with cinnamon.

Alcohol

Costa Ricans like to drink, though they don't like drunks. Most restaurants serve a good variety of alcoholic drinks. Imported drinks are expensive, local ones are quite cheap.

Many bars traditionally serve *bocas*, also known as *boquitas*. These are little savoury side dishes such as black beans, ceviche, chicken stew, potato chips and sausages and are designed to make your drink more pleasurable – maybe you'll have another one! If you had several rounds, you could eat enough bocas to make a very light meal. Many of the cheaper bars have free bocas, some charge a small amount extra for them, and some don't have them at all.

There are five brands of local beer. Pilsen and Imperial are both good, popular beers; I personally prefer the Imperial. Tropical is a

THINGS TO BUY
Coffee
Coffee is excellent and cheap; many visitors bring a kg of freshly roasted coffee beans back home. Gift stores sell expensive elegantly wrapped packages of coffee beans for export but savvy travellers will go to the market and buy coffee direct from the coffee stalls, or from ordinary grocery stores. If a kg seems like too much, you can buy as little as 250 grams without any problem.

Handicrafts
The things to buy are wood and leather items, which are very well made and inexpensive. Wood items include salad bowls, plates, carving boards and other useful kitchen utensils, jewellery boxes, and a variety of carvings and ornaments. Furniture is also made, but is hard to bring home and having it shipped is expensive. Leatherwork includes the usual wallets and purses, hand bags and brief cases, and is usually cheaper than at home.

Interesting wood/leather combinations are the rocking chairs seen in many tourist lodges and better hotels in the country. Because of their leather seats and backs, they can be folded for transport and are usually packed two to a carton. If you're not bringing too much else back, you could check a pair of them in your airline baggage.

There are plenty of excellent souvenir shops in San José, but if you want the best prices, you should go to the village of Sarchí where many souvenirs are made, especially woodwork, and you can watch artisans at work. Sarchí is the centre for making the colourfully painted replicas of the ox carts (carretas) that were traditionally used for hauling produce and people in the countryside – and still are in some remote regions. These ox carts are, as much as anything else, a typical souvenir peculiar to Costa Rica. They come in all sizes from table-top models to nearly life size replicas which double as drinks cabinets. They all fold down for transport.

Ceramics and jewellery are also popular souvenirs. Some ceramics are replicas of

low calorie 'lite' beer, not available everywhere. Bavaria has a gold foil around the cap and is a little more expensive than the first two, though I can't say it's much better. Also, a local version of Heineken is made, which costs about the same as Bavaria. Other beers are imported and expensive.

Local beers cost from about US$0.60 in the very cheapest bars to about US$1 in average bars and restaurants and almost US$2 in some of the fancy tourist lodges, restaurants, hotels and resorts.

Local Costa Rican wines are cheap, taste cheap, and provide a memorable hangover. Good imported wines are available but are expensive.

Sugarcane is grown in Costa Rica and so liquor made from this is cheap. The cheapest is *guaro* which is the local firewater, drunk by the shot. Also inexpensive and good is local rum, usually drunk as a *cuba libre* (rum & coke). Local vodka and gin isn't bad, but whisky is not as good. Expensive imported liquors are available, as are imported liqueurs. One locally made liqueur is Café Rica which, predictably, is based on coffee and tastes rather like the better known Mexican Kahlua.

pre-Columbian artefacts. Colourful posters and T-shirts with wildlife, national park and ecological themes are also very popular, attractive and reasonably priced. Some of the profits of those produced by Editorial Heliconia go towards conservation organisations in Costa Rica. Indian handicrafts from Guatemala and Panama are also available.

Getting There & Away

There are three ways of getting to Costa Rica: air, land and sea. However, very few people use the ocean route because it is less convenient and usually more expensive than flying.

AIR

Juan Santamaría International Airport is 17 km outside of San José and is where international flights to Costa Rica arrive. The airport in Liberia, 217 km north-west of San José on the Interamerican Highway, is the back-up international airport but is rarely used. There are plans to expand the facilities at the Liberia airport and it may begin to take more international arrivals, particularly those on beach charter vacations.

Cheap Tickets

The ordinary tourist or economy-class fare is not the most economical way to go. It is convenient, however, because it enables you to fly on the next plane out and your ticket is valid for 12 months. If you want to economise further, there are several options. Students and those under 26 can get discounts with most airlines.

Airline Deals Whatever age you are, if you can purchase your ticket well in advance and stay a minimum length of time, you can buy a ticket which is usually about 30% or 40% cheaper than the full economy fare. These are often called APEX, excursion or promotional fares depending on the country you are flying from and the rules and fare structures that apply there.

Normally the following restrictions apply. You must purchase your ticket at least 21 days (sometimes more) in advance and you must stay away a minimum period (about 14 days on average) and return within 180 days (sometimes less, for example passengers from the USA must return within 30 days). Individual airlines have different requirements and these change from time to time.

Most of these tickets do not allow stopovers and there are extra charges if you change your dates of travel or destinations. These tickets are often sold out well in advance of departure so try to book early.

Stand-by fares are another possibility from some countries, such as the USA. Some airlines will let you travel at the last minute if they have available seats just before the flight. These stand-by fares cost less than an economy fare but are not usually as cheap as other discounted tickets.

Bucket Shops The cheapest way to go is via the so-called 'bucket shops', which are allowed to sell discounted tickets to help airlines fill their flights. These tickets are usually the cheapest of all, particularly in the low seasons, but they often sell out fast and you may be limited to only a few available dates.

While discounted tickets, economy and student flights are available direct from the airlines or from a travel agency (there is no extra charge for any of these flights if you buy them from an agent rather than direct from the airline), discount bucket shop tickets are available only from the bucket shops themselves. Most of them are good and reputable companies. However, once in a while a fly-by-night operator comes along and takes your money for a super-cheap flight and gives you an invalid or unusable ticket, so check what you are buying carefully before handing over your money.

Bucket shops often advertise in newspapers and travel oriented magazines; there is much competition and a variety of fares and schedules are available. Fares to Latin America have traditionally been relatively expensive, but bucket shops have recently been able to offer increasingly economical fares.

Courier Flights If you are travelling with minimal luggage, you can fly to Costa Rica as a 'courier', especially from the USA. Couriers are hired by companies who need to have packages delivered to Costa Rica (and other countries) and will give the courier exceptionally cheap tickets in return for using his or her baggage allowance. You can bring carry-on luggage only. These are legitimate operations – all baggage that you are to deliver is completely legal. More details are given in the To/From the USA section below.

Other Considerations It is worth bearing in mind that round-trip fares are always much cheaper than two one-way tickets. They are also cheaper than 'open jaws' fares – an 'open jaws' ticket enables you to fly into one city (say San José) and leave via another (say Panama City).

If, because of a late flight (but not a rescheduled one) you lose a connection or are forced to stay overnight the carrier is responsible for providing you with help in making the earliest possible connection and paying for a room in a hotel of their choice. They should also provide you with meal vouchers. If you are seriously delayed on an international flight, ask for these services.

To/From the USA

Generally speaking, the USA does not have as strong a bucket shop tradition as Europe or Asia, so it's a little harder getting cheap flights from the USA to Latin America. Sometimes the Sunday travel sections in the major newspapers (the *Los Angeles Times* on the west coast and the *New York Times* on the east coast) advertise cheap fares to South America, although these are sometimes no cheaper than the APEX fares with one of the several airlines serving Costa Rica.

One travel agency which can often find you the best deal to Costa Rica (and anywhere else in the world) is Council Travel Services which is affiliated with the Council on International Educational Exchange (CIEE). You can find their addresses and telephone numbers in the telephone directories of Berkeley, La Jolla, Long Beach, Los Angeles, San Diego and San Francisco (all

in California), Amherst, Boston and Cambridge (in Massachusetts), New York City, Portland (Oregon), Providence (Rhode Island), Austin (Texas), Phoenix (Arizona), Seattle (Washington) and other cities.

Major departure cities from the USA to Costa Rica include Los Angeles, Houston, New Orleans, Miami and New York. The airlines are geared to providing cheap fares for visitors staying 30 days or less. Sample prices for round-trip tickets valid for up to 30 days are US$648 from Los Angeles, US$368 from New Orleans, Houston or Dallas, and US$336 from Miami. If you want to stay more than 30 days you end up paying about US$200 more per ticket.

The national Costa Rican airline is Lacsa and they fly from the USA to Costa Rica and other Central American countries. The cheapest fares are often with Lacsa and other Central American airlines such as Taca (of El Salvador), Sahsa (of Honduras) and Aviateca (of Guatemala).

Because Houston, New Orleans and Miami are roughly north of the Central American republics, they make good gateway cities to Costa Rica. On my last visit to Costa Rica I flew from Houston with Taca and returned with Aviateca. Southbound we stopped at Belize City and changed planes at San Salvador; northbound we stopped at Managua and changed planes at Guatemala City. It was a good opportunity to see some of Central America from the air and it was fun hopping from country to country.

The following airlines (with telephone numbers) currently serve Costa Rica from the USA:

airline	tel
Lacsa	(800) 225 2272
Taca	(800) 535 8780
Sahsa	(800) 327 1225
	(416) 675 2007 (Canada)
Mexicana	(800) 531 7921 or 7923
American	(800) 433 7300
Pan Am	(800) 221 1111

Courier Flights Courier travel is another possibility. Trans-Air System (☎ (305) 592 1771) in Miami recently required couriers for flights from New York and Miami to San José. Round trip tickets cost US$260 and were good for 30 days. Travel Unlimited (PO Box 1058, Allston, MA 02134) publishes monthly listings of courier and cheap flights to Costa Rica and many other countries. A one-year subscription costs US$15.

Package Deals American companies that may be able to provide reasonable package fares to Costa Rica, usually in combination with hotel stays, include:

American Tours & Travel
    1218 Third Ave, Suite 2207, Seattle, WA 98101 (☎ (206) 623 8850, (800) 553 2513)
González Travel
    4508 Academy Drive, Metairie, LA 70003 (☎ (504) 885 4058)
Preferred Adventures
    West Water St, Suite 300, Saint Paul, MN 55107 (☎ (612) 222 8131)
Worldwide Holidays
    7800 Red Rd, Suite 112, South Miami, FL 33143 (☎ (305) 665 0841, (800) 327 9854)

To/From Canada

Canadians will find that various companies arrange cheap winter getaway charters to Costa Rica. Often these include several days of hotel accommodation in San José and/or a beach resort, but nevertheless represent good value for money if the hotels happen to be what you want. You may be able to arrange a charter that provides a few days in San José and then some free days in the middle of your trip.

Possible companies to contact are: Fiesta Holidays (☎ (416) 498 5566) in Toronto, Fiesta West (☎ (604) 688 1102) out of Vancouver, and Go Travel (☎ (514) 735 4526) out of Montreal.

To/From Europe

Bucket shops generally provide the cheapest fares from Europe to Latin America. Fares from London, where the competition is fiercest, are often cheaper than from other European cities and there are also more bucket shops.

Bucket shops advertise in the classifieds of newspapers ranging from the *Times* to *Time Out*. I have heard consistently good reports about Journey Latin America (☎ (081) 747 3108), 16 Devonshire Rd, Chiswick, London W4 2HD. They specialise in cheap fares to the entire continent as well as arranging itineraries for both independent and escorted travel. They will make arrangements for you over the phone.

Another reputable budget travel agency is Trailfinders (☎ (071) 938 3366), 42-48 Earl's Court Rd, London W8 6EJ. The useful travel newspaper *Trailfinder* is available from them for free. Typical round-trip fares from London are about UK£520 to UK£720. The variation in fares depends on how long you want to stay (longer stays are more expensive), which airline you choose, and when you travel.

The cheapest airfare from London that I could find at time of writing was UK£522 with Avianca during their low season from 1 January to 30 April and 1 October to 30 November. High season fares were UK£630 from 1 July to 30 September and 1 December to 30 December. The rest of the year, fares were UK£567. Other airlines had different low or high seasons, but usually the northern summer and around Christmas time are high seasons.

Some airlines from Europe will take you to Miami where you connect with other airlines for flights to Costa Rica. Two airlines which fly direct to San José (with stops in the Caribbean) are KLM from Holland and Iberia from Spain. Note that fares, routes and low/high seasons change frequently and that the best information is to be had from travel professionals.

Courier flights are also possible from Europe. Look in the classifieds of Sunday newspapers.

European agents selling cheap flights to Central America from outside the UK include: Sindbad Travel, 3 Schoffelgasse, Zurich 8025, Switzerland; and Uniclam, 63 Rue Monsieur Le Prince, Paris 75006, France.

The cheap British agencies will sell tickets to other European nationals but you often have to pick them up in person in London (or have them mailed to a UK address).

To/From Australia

There is no real choice of routes between Australia and Latin America and there are certainly no bargain fares available. Your best bet is to fly to the USA west coast and from there either fly to Costa Rica or make your way overland through Mexico and Central America.

The one-way fare from Australia to Los Angeles or San Francisco is A$1013, the return fare again varies with season – from A$1446 in the low season to A$1786 in the shoulder and A$1966 in the high. Check the ads in the travel pages of papers like the Melbourne *Age* or the *Sydney Morning Herald*.

To/From Asia

There is also very little choice of direct flights between Asia and Latin America apart from Japan, and there certainly won't be any bargains there. The cheapest way is to fly to the USA west coast and connect from there.

LAND
Overland through Mexico & Central America

If you live in North or Central America, it is possible to travel overland. The nearest American town to San José is Brownsville, Texas, on the Mexican border. From there it is about 4000 km by road to San José, half of which is crossing Mexico and the rest is through Guatemala, Honduras, Nicaragua and Costa Rica. It is possible to travel through El Salvador, but remember that country is currently in a state of civil war and it is therefore safer to travel directly from Guatemala to Honduras.

A series of public buses will take you all the way from the USA to San José. Bus travel is slow, cramped, but cheap. See *Central America on a Shoestring*, (Lonely Planet, Australia, due 1992) or *The Mexico & Central American Handbook*, (Trade & Travel Publications, Bath, England, editions annually) for details of bus travel and places

to stay en route. When you add all the costs of bus tickets plus food and hotels, even if you travel 2nd class and sleep in the cheapest hotels, you'll pay as much as the airfare. You will, however, see and experience far more of course.

It is also possible to drive your own car, but the costs of insurance, fuel, border permits, food and accommodation will be much higher than an airline ticket. Many people opt for flying down and renting a car when they arrive in San José. If you want to drive all the way the American Automobile Association will give you details of obtaining international insurance, permits, carnets, etc.

It is worth noting that the Interamerican Highway continues as far south as Panama, then peters out in the Darien Gap, an area of roadless rainforest. It is not possible to drive on to South America and vehicles must be shipped or air freighted.

To/From Nicaragua There is a couple of crossing points between Nicaragua and Costa Rica.

Via Peñas Blancas The main border post is at Peñas Blancas in Costa Rica. It is a border post, not a town, and so there is nowhere to stay.

The border is open from 8 am to 5 pm daily on the Costa Rican side, but only till 4 pm on the Nicaraguan side. Lunch is from 12 noon to 1 pm. It is four km between the Costa Rican and Nicaraguan immigration offices – minibuses are available for about US$1 and there are taxis.

Moneychangers at the Costa Rican post give good rates for US cash dollars but travellers' cheques receive worse rates in the border bank. Both Costa Rican colones and Nicaraguan cordobas are freely available. Excess cordobas or colones can also be sold but usually at a small loss. Try to arrive with as little local money as possible. The best place to sell cordobas is with the moneychangers at the Nicaraguan border post.

The first (or last) Nicaraguan city of any

size is Rivas, 37 km north of the border, and it has several cheap hotels. There are four or five buses a day from the border to Rivas – get to the border by early afternoon to make sure you get on a bus.

Many nationalities do not need a visa for Nicaragua, but regulations have changed frequently, so check with the embassy in San José if you plan on travelling overland into Nicaragua.

There is a decent restaurant in the Costa Rican border building. There is also a Costa Rican tourist information office, and bus tickets can be bought for buses to San José at 10.30 am and 3 pm, and for Liberia at 12.30 pm. If coming from Nicaragua, you'll find no buses and nowhere to stay after 3 pm, though a taxi could be found. Try to arrive early.

Sometimes a ticket out of Costa Rica is asked for – if you don't have one you can buy a bus ticket back into Nicaragua from next to the tourist information office. This is accepted by the Costa Rican authorities, who are generally helpful as long as your documents are in order.

International travellers between San José and Managua (or vice versa) on Sirca or TICA bus will find that the bus will wait for all passengers to be processed. This is time consuming, and delays of up to eight hours have been reported (though two or three hours is more likely). To avoid the crowds, you could take local buses to the border, a taxi or minibus to the other border, and then continue on another bus – but cross as early as possible. Several travellers have reported that luggage placed on the roofs of buses in Nicaragua has been pilfered, sometimes when only a bus employee has been allowed on the roof. Stolen objects are often mundane items like deodorant or clothes. If you can't lock your luggage, try wrapping it in a large sack with a lock on that. Primitive – but it deters pilferers. Carry luggage aboard the bus if possible.

Via Los Chiles Officially, there is a border crossing here, but travellers who are not Nicaraguan or Costa Rican will probably not be allowed through.

A very rough road (4WD essential, or walk) takes you the 14 km from Los Chiles to the Nicaraguan town of San Carlos, on the south-eastern corner of Lake Nicaragua at the beginning of the Río San Juan. Boats on the Río Frío could go from Los Chiles to San Carlos, but the border crossing would be even more problematical, if not illegal.

San Carlos has a couple of extremely basic pensións and regular boat service several times a week to Granada, a major Nicaraguan town on the north-western corner of Lake Nicaragua. When I was in San Carlos, I could not obtain permission to cross into Costa Rica and had to return across Lake Nicaragua to the Interamerican Highway and come down the normal way via Peñas Blancas. Since the 1990 election of Violeta Chamorro as President of Nicaragua, the border crossing may be somewhat more relaxed – make local enquiry.

To/From Panama There is also a couple of crossings between Costa Rica and Panama.

Via Paso Canoas This crossing is on the Interamerican Highway, and is the most frequently used entry and exit point with Panama.

Although border hours used to be 7 am to 5 pm, these days it is open 24 hours, but there's not much point in arriving after dark because buses leave during daylight hours only.

If you are entering Panama, you may need a visa or tourist card. Nationalities requiring visas include US, Canadian and Australian visitors; British and many European visitors do not. Regulations are subject to change, however, so you should check at the Panamanian consulate in San José about current requirements. Visas are not obtainable at the border. Tourist cards are officially available but the immigration office on the border has been known to run out, so get your visa or tourist card in advance if you need one.

Once in Panama, there is a Panamanian bus terminal in front of the border crossing post. The nearest town of any size and with decent hotels is David, about 1½ hours away by bus. There are buses every hour or two throughout the day and the last one leaves the border at 7 pm. If you want to go on to Panama City, you can either fly or catch a bus from David – the last departure is at 5 pm and takes about seven hours.

If you are entering Costa Rica, you may require a ticket out of the country, although this is not always asked for. If you don't have one, buy a TRACOPA bus ticket in David for David to Paso Canoas and return; this is acceptable to the Costa Rican authorities. Apparently, you can't buy just the Paso Canoas to David section at the border. There is a Costa Rican consulate in David, as well as in Panama City.

Most nationalities require only a passport and exit ticket to enter Costa Rica. See the Facts for the Visitor chapter for more details about this. The border crossing either way is generally straightforward if your documents are in order.

Via Sixaola/Guabito This crossing is on the Caribbean coast. The continuation of Sixaola on the Panamanian side is called Guabito. There are no banks, but stores in Guabito will accept colones, balboas or US dollars. The border is open from 7 to 11 am and 1 to 5 pm, and there are reports that the border guards are not always there from Friday to Sunday. There are frequent minibuses from near the border crossing to Changuinola, 16 km into Panama.

In Changuinola, there is a bank and an airport, with daily flights to David. There is a hotel near the airport which charges about US$15 for a double.

From Changuinola, a daily train and several buses go the 30 km to Almirante, where there are cheaper hotels. From Almirante, there are early morning boats several times a week to Bocas del Toro, where there are pleasant beaches and reasonable hotels. There are no roads beyond Almirante. From Bocas del Toro, there are several boats a week to Chiriquí Grande (hotels) from where there is a road to David

and the rest of Panama. There is a Costa Rican consulate in David.

People who have travelled this way say that the Bocas del Toro area is attractive and worth seeing, but be prepared for delays. Almirante is the first (or last) place in Panama with a selection of reasonably priced accommodation.

SEA
Several cruise lines make stops in Costa Rican ports and enable passengers to make a quick foray into the country. Most cruises are, however, geared to shipboard life and ocean travel, and so passengers can expect no more than a brief glimpse of Costa Rica – perhaps a day or so.

Freighters also arrive in Costa Rica but most are for cargo only. A few may accept a small number of passengers.

TOURS
There are scores of tour operators in North America and Europe which run tours to Costa Rica. It is beyond the scope of this book to list them all (I know of 33 tour operators running Costa Rica tours from California alone!). Typical tours combine nature and adventure. One or several national parks and preserves are usually visited, with overnight accommodation in comfortable lodges and hotels. Other activities may include river running, snorkelling, deep-sea or freshwater fishing, horse riding, sailing, a railway trip, and plain touring of the countryside.

Tours in Costa Rica tend to be first class and expensive, and costs are generally well over US$100 per person per day, plus airfare to San José. Tours usually provide a guide, accommodation, all transport and some meals. If you are shopping for a tour you'll obviously be interested in the itinerary. In addition you should check on what kind of guide is provided. Is the guide fluent in English? What are the guide's particular interests and qualifications? Will they accompany you throughout the trip or will there be different guides for different portions? Other questions to consider are: How big will the tour group be? How many meals are included? What accommodation is used? Can you talk to past clients?

The advantages of a tour are that you have everything taken care of from the time you arrive till the time you leave. You don't have to worry about speaking Spanish, figuring out itineraries, finding bus stations, haggling with cab drivers, locating hotels with available rooms and translating restaurant menus. Tours are often preferred by people who have a short vacation period and enough money to be able to afford being taken care of. People on tours have activities scheduled for every day of their trip and don't need to spend time figuring out what to do and how to do it once they get to San José.

Those people with more time may prefer the adventure of arranging their travels for themselves – that's what this book is for! I have travelled to Costa Rica on guided tours, with a friend on public transport, alone, and by hired car. All methods are quite feasible

and only you can decide which is best for you.

Tour operators often advertise in magazines which deal with travel, natural history, the outdoors, or culture. Thumb through a few magazines in your local library to get an idea of what's available. It is not essential to book your tour in advance, however. There are plenty of tour operators in San José who will provide you with a variety of travel opportunities once you get there.

For more information on tours around Costa Rica, see the Getting Around chapter.

LEAVING COSTA RICA
There is a US$6 departure tax on international flights from San José. This is payable in US dollars cash or colones at the current exchange rate.

There is no departure tax when leaving overland.

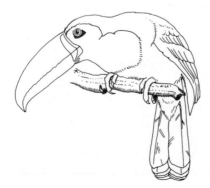

Getting Around

The population distribution of Costa Rica dictates how its public transport works. Roughly one quarter of the country's almost three million inhabitants live in the greater San José area, and roughly two thirds live in the Meseta Central, one of the most densely populated regions in Central America. This means that there are a lot of roads and buses in the centre of the country. As you go further afield, there are generally fewer roads and less public transport.

To get to most regions you have to start from San José, which is the main centre for public transport. It is often easier to go to one region, then return to San José to find transport to another area.

The majority of Costa Ricans do not own cars. Therefore public transport is quite well developed and you can get buses or trains to almost any part of the country. Remote or small towns may be served by only one bus a day, but you can get there.

AIR

The local airline is SANSA (Servicios Aereos Nacionales, SA – not to be confused with the Honduran airline Sahsa). They fly from the domestic terminal of Juan Santamaría Airport, 17 km from the centre of San José. Services are with small twin-engined DC3s and similar aircraft. Demand for seats is high, so try to book as far in advance as possible. Because the aircraft are small, baggage allowance is limited to 12 kg. SANSA flies between San José and Golfito,

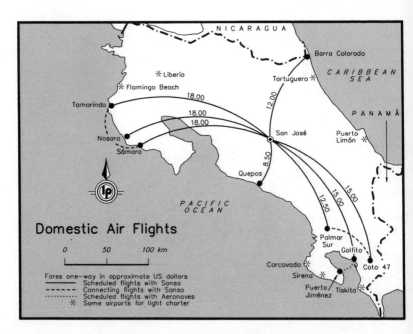

Domestic Air Flights

Fares one—way in approximate US dollars
——— Scheduled flights with Sansa
– – – Connecting flights with Sansa
·········· Scheduled flights with Aeronaves
✳ Some airports for light charter

Quepos, Nosara, Palmar, Coto 47, Tamarindo, Sámara and Barra Colorado.

Closer to the centre of San José, at Pavas, is Tobías Bolaños Airport which caters to small single and twin-engined aircraft. These will fly you to just about anywhere in the country where there is an airport. Fares are about US$120 per hour and it takes the best part of an hour to fly to most coastal destinations. You also have to pay for the return flight, unless you can co-ordinate with the company to fly you out on a day when they are picking somebody else up. Luggage space is very limited. Many towns which have an airport will have light aircraft available for charter; those which are of particular interest to the traveller are mentioned in the text.

You can arrange flights directly by going to Tobías Bolaños Airport or you can look under Taxis Aereos in the yellow pages for the four or five companies that charter aircraft. Many tour agencies will charter planes for you if you are taking one of their tours.

BUS

Buses depart from San José for just about anywhere in the country. There is no central bus terminal. Some bus companies leave from what used to be the old Coca Cola bottling plant in San José – the area is still known as 'La Coca Cola'. Other companies leave from their own offices. Still others leave from bus stops in the street, and others leave from a street corner without even a bus stop. The addresses or street intersections of bus companies are given under the appropriate city; the tourist bureau also has an up-to-date listing of bus departure points and the destinations they serve.

The larger companies with offices and buses going to major destinations will allow you to buy a ticket in advance. The smaller companies with just a bus stop expect you to queue for the next bus, but normally there is room for everyone. The exception is the days before and after a major holiday, especially Easter, when buses are ridiculously full. I have resorted to hitch-hiking in these cases. Friday nights and Saturday mornings out of

San José can be very crowded, as can Sunday afternoons and evenings coming back, so try to avoid those if possible.

If this all seems a little chaotic, take heart. Costa Ricans are used to the system and know where many buses leave from – just ask. The people are known for their friendliness, and you'll soon find out what you need to know.

Fares are generally cheap, with the longest and most expensive run out of San José costing under US$6. (The exceptions are the international buses going to Managua or Panama City from San José.)

Long distance buses are of two types, *directo* and *normal* (or *corriente*). The direct buses are faster and more expensive. Travellers on a budget can save as much as a third of the direct bus fare by taking a normal bus which stops on demand at various intermediate points and usually takes an hour or two longer.

Roads are narrow and winding and sometimes gravel or dirt; buses are rather old and so comfort is not one of the things that the bus journeys are known for, particularly to smaller and more remote destinations which are served by battered old Bluebird school buses. But they get you there. Trips longer than four hours have a rest stop, and no trips take longer than about nine hours. Luggage space is limited, so I suggest breaking your Costa Rican stay into sections and leaving what you don't need in San José. A small bag is certainly much easier to travel with.

TRAIN

The railway lines in Costa Rica run from San José to Puntarenas on the Pacific coast, and from San José to Puerto Limón on the Caribbean coast.

The Puerto Limón train journey is the most famous and popular in Costa Rica. The train carriages have uncomfortable bench seats and can get rather crowded, but the journey is generally safe although you should watch for pickpockets in the crowds. Vendors come round with snacks and drinks, but you might want to bring some of your own food if you suffer from a sensitive stomach. (I found the food to be tasty and good, but the standards of hygiene of a vendor with a basket full of empanadas cannot be guaranteed.) Carry toilet paper with you and don't expect the toilet facilities to be up to much. Try to get on the train as early as you can to stake out your seat. Check the windows nearby – some are permanently closed, others permanently opened, and others so badly marked that you can't see much through them. Despite these minor drawbacks, the trip is a fun one. Enjoy it.

If the idea of spending eight hours on the train from San José to Limón seems too much, there are two alternatives. One is to just make part of the journey by train and continue or return by bus. The major towns visited along the way are Cartago, Turrialba and Siquirres, all of which have frequent buses back to San José and, in the case of Siquirres, on to Limón. Siquirres and Turrialba both have hotels. The best views are to be had on the right of the train heading down to Limón and the prettiest section is that between Turrialba and Siquirres.

The second alternative is to ride the so-called 'jungle train' which is a more comfortable carriage used by tour companies. They charge about US$65 for the trip, provide lunch and a bilingual guide, have a bus to return you to San José from Siquirres, and stop off to visit a banana plantation along the way. One company which has been recommended for this tour is Swiss Travel Service (☎ 314055) with offices in several of the major hotels.

Many travellers find this ride to be a great way to spend the day and see some of the back country Costa Rica. The railway passes through country villages which are not served by road and the arrival of the train is the major daily occurrence. Children use the train to get to school, small-time farmers haul crops for sale, and vendors climb on to sell you locally made goodies. The scenery is spectacular at times, particularly when the tracks parallel the Río Reventazón as it drops from 1300 metres above sea level at Turrialba to less than 100 metres at Siquirres. Coffee plantations and small towns are seen,

lush and exotic vegetation brushes by the windows, and everywhere there is a backdrop of rolling hills and mountains. The last section is flat, going through banana plantations. Thousands of workers lost their lives to yellow fever and malaria when this section was being built in the 1870s. The entire line was completed in 1890 and created the first permanent year-round link between San José and the Caribbean coast, thus improving export facilities and expanding the economy.

TAXI

It may come as a surprise to most people that taxis are considered to be a form of public transport outside of urban areas. Taxis can be hired by the hour, the half day or the day. Meters are not used on long trips so you arrange the fare with the driver beforehand.

There are various occasions when you may want to consider using a taxi. Visiting some of the national parks is not possible by public transport. Your alternatives are taking a tour, renting a car, hitching a ride, walking or cycling, or taking a taxi. The round trip from San José to Poás Volcano, for example, is about 110 km. An all-day excursion allowing a couple of hours at the volcano and photo stops along the way costs about US$40, depending on the taxi driver and your bargaining ability. That's not a bad deal, and actually fairly cheap if you share your cab with other travellers.

When you are out in the country, you may want to take a taxi to a remote destination on a bad road. During the rainy season 4WD may be required. Many taxis are 4WD jeeps and can get you almost anywhere.

CAR

Few people drive to Costa Rica in their own car, though it is possible. Renting a car upon arrival, on the other hand, is something which many travellers do for part of their trip.

Rental

There are plenty of car rental agencies in San José, but few in other cities. Many agencies

Top: Jaguar (RL)
Bottom: Morpho blue butterfly (RL)

Top: Miskito Indian fisherman, Río San Juan (RR)
Left: White-faced monkey (RR)
Right: Poison arrow frog (RT)

also have offices at Juan Santamaría International Airport.

Car rental is popular because it gets you to places where you can't go by public transport. It also gives you the freedom to travel when you want, and to stop wherever you like. Because buses to remote areas are not very frequent, you can cover more ground in a shorter time in a car.

Car rental is not all that cheap. There are small discounts available if you rent by the week, but expect to pay at least US$250 per week for the smallest car with no air-con. This includes insurance and unlimited mileage (or *kilometraje*, as they call it). If you plan on driving 500 km or more in a week, you should get unlimited km; less than that and you'll save by paying a daily base rate plus the per km charge. The insurance accounts for about US$10 per day of your cost; don't try to economise by not taking out insurance as your policy at home will not be valid in Costa Rica in case of an accident or theft of the car.

If you want more than a sub-compact car without air-con, expect to pay about US$350 to US$400 for a compact or mid-sized car with air-con, and about US$450 to US$500 for a van or 4WD jeep. All rates are per week, including free km and insurance.

For travel during the rainy season many rental agencies insist that you rent a 4WD vehicle if you are going to places where you need to drive on dirt roads – the Nicoya Peninsula, for example. But the rainy season is also the low season and discounted rates may apply.

Many of the major car rental companies like Avis, Budget, Dollar, Hertz or National have offices worldwide, so you can rent a car in advance from home. Normally, you need to book a car at least 14 days in advance and often the rate when booked at home is a little cheaper than it is in San José. However, I did talk to one driver who booked at home and then was charged a hefty 'pick-up' fee when he arrived in San José. Make sure you clearly understand your agreement with the rental company before paying.

To hire a car you need a valid driver's licence, a major credit card and your passport. Your driver's licence from home is acceptable for up to three months if you are a tourist; you don't need an international driving permit. The minimum age for car rental is 21, though many car rental companies won't rent to drivers under 25. If you don't have a major credit card some companies may allow you to make a cash deposit of about US$700.

The price of petrol is currently about US$0.33 per litre (US$1.25 per US gallon), although this is down on previous years, when it was as high as US$2 per gallon.

When you rent a car, carefully inspect it for minor dents and scratches, missing radio antennae or hubcaps, and anything else which makes the car look less than brand new. These damages must be noted on your rental agreement, otherwise you may be charged for them when you return the car. The insurance won't cover it, because there's a deductible deposit of from US$500 to US$700, depending on the company.

Rental cars have special licence plates and it is immediately obvious to everyone that you are driving a rental car. There have been many instances of theft from rental cars. You should never leave valuables in sight when you are out of the car, and you should remove luggage from the trunk (boot) when checking into a hotel overnight. Many hotels will provide parking areas for cars. It is better to park the car in a guarded parking lot than on the street.

Road Safety

San José is notorious for its narrow streets, complicated one-way system, heavy traffic and thefts from cars. I certainly would not recommend driving a rental car around San José, except to get out of the city.

Once out of San José, the roads vary from barely passable to very good. But even the good ones can suffer from landslides and thick fog, and so you should always be prepared for the unexpected. Most roads are single lane and very winding, so defensive driving is recommended.

There are some roads which have a reputation for being especially dangerous. The Cerro de la Muerte area on the Interamerican Highway between Cartago and San Isidro del General is the highest section of the Interamerican and suffers from frequent landslides and dense fog at any time of day or night. (I once drove this section with visibility down to under 10 metres.) The busy San José to Puntarenas road is steep, narrow and tortuously winding, but local drivers familiar with the road drive it very fast. The new road from San José to Guápiles goes through Braulio Carrillo National Park and is subject to landslides and heavy fog, especially later in the day. The stretch of Interamerican Highway from Palmar Norte to Buenos Aires is subject to frequent rockfall and landslides.

If you should be involved in an accident you should not move the cars until the police get there. Injured people should not be taken from the scene until the Red Cross ambulance arrives. Try to make a note or sketch of what happened, and don't make statements except to authorised people. Telephone the Red Cross at 215818, the transit police at 227150 or 278030, or away from towns call the Guardia de Asistencia Rural at 127. Patrol cars can be called on 117 and emergency rescue units on 118.

Because of difficult driving conditions, there are speed limits of 80 km/h on all primary roads and 60 km/h or less on secondary roads. Traffic police use radar and speed limits are enforced. If you are given a ticket, you have to pay the fine at a bank; instructions are given on the ticket. If you don't pay the fine, your name is forwarded to the immigration authorities and it is not unheard of for people to be refused boarding at the airport if they have outstanding traffic tickets.

You can also get a traffic ticket for not wearing a seat belt. All rental cars have seat belts. It is not legal to enter an intersection unless you can also leave it, and it is not legal to make a right turn on a red light unless a white arrow painted on the road indicates that a turn is permitted. At unmarked intersections, yield to the car on your right.

Driving in Costa Rica is on the right, and passing is allowed only on the left.

Many foreign drivers complain that the roads are inadequately signed. This is often true, so try to get hold of a decent road map and ask locals if you are not sure. They are nearly always able and willing to help.

BICYCLE

All the warnings under the Road Safety section apply here – but even more so. There are no bike lanes and traffic can be hazardous on the narrow, steep, winding roads. Cycling is a possibility, however, and long distance cyclists report that locals tend to be very friendly towards them. It is possible to cycle all the way from the USA or you can fly down with your bicycle as luggage. Check with airlines for regulations – often a bicycle will be carried free of charge if it is properly packed and doesn't exceed luggage size and weight requirements.

Those planning a bicycle trip might want to read *Latin America on a Bicycle* by J P Panet (Passport Press, Champlain, New York, 1987) which includes a chapter on cycling through Costa Rica.

Bicycle touring is just beginning in Costa Rica. A company called Mountain Biking Costa Rica (a division of Ríos Tropicales & Horizontes, ☎ 550914) will rent mountain bikes at US$5 per hour and organises biking tours which includes bikes, overnight accommodation, food, a support vehicle and a guide. The cost for a three-day trip (two days of actual cycling) is about US$275 per person.

HITCHING

Frequent buses on the main roads mean that hitching is not frequently done, though it is by no means impossible. It is more common on minor rural roads. Don't simply stand there with your thumb out. Vehicles may pass only a few times per hour and you should try and wave them down in a friendly fashion. (Watch how the locals do it.) Tell the driver where you're going, ask if there's any room, could they give you a ride as you've been waiting for ages and there's no bus or all the buses are full and you really need to get to wherever you're going ... Obviously, speaking Spanish and being relaxed and friendly go a long way to getting a ride in this way.

Sometimes hitching is the only way out of town during holiday weekends when all buses come through already full to overflowing. If you get a ride, offer to pay for it when you arrive: *Cuanto le debo?* (How much do I owe you?) is the standard way of doing this. Often, your offer will be waved aside; sometimes you'll be asked to help with petrol money.

Single women do hitch sometimes and I haven't yet heard a negative story about it, in Costa Rica at least. Ticos are generally helpful and friendly. Nevertheless, discretion is urged. Try to talk to the occupants of the car and get an idea if they seem OK; don't get into the car if you don't feel comfortable; try to hitch from somewhere (a petrol station, store, restaurant, police post) where you can retreat to if you don't like the look of your prospective ride. Hitching with a companion is a good idea.

BOAT

There are various passenger and car ferries in operation. Two cheap ferries operate out of Puntarenas across the Gulf of Nicoya. One is a huge car ferry which leaves twice a day for Playa Naranjo, a two-hour trip. The other is a small passenger ferry which crosses to Paquera twice a day, taking about three hours. Buses meet the ferry at Paquera to transport you onwards into the Nicoya Peninsula. Complete details are given under the appropriate towns.

There is also a car ferry operating across the mouth of the Río Tempisque which cuts two or three hours off the road trip to the Nicoya Peninsula – if you can time your ferry crossing just right.

A daily passenger ferry links Golfito with Puerto Jiménez in the Osa Peninsula; a trip taking about 1½ hours. Puerto Jiménez is the nearest town of any size to Corcovado National Park.

Other boat trips can be made, but these are tours rather than rides on scheduled ferries. These include canal boats up the inland waterway from Moín (near Limón) to Tortuguero National Park and Barro del Colorado National Wildlife Refuge. Dugouts can be hired at Puerto Viejo de Sarapiquí up the Río Sarapiquí to the Río San Juan, which forms much of the Costa Rica/Nicaragua border. Relations with Nicaragua have improved since the 1990 electoral defeat of the Sandinistas, and it is now possible to travel along the border down the Río San Juan as far as its mouth, and then down into the Barro del Colorado National Wildlife Refuge. This is not a regularly scheduled trip but can be arranged – see under Puerto Viejo de Sarapiquí for further information.

For adventurous types, river running down the Ríos Pacuare, Chirripó, Reventazón, Corobici and Sarapiquí for one or more days is one option – see under Tours in this chapter for further information. Fishing trips on Lake Arenal or offshore is another. One-day sailing trips in the Gulf of Nicoya can be booked on the yacht *Calypso* with travel agents in San José.

LOCAL TRANSPORT
To/From the Airport

Taxis from Juan Santamaría International Airport will take you into San José, 17 km away, for US$10. Alajuela, five km away, can be reached by taxi for about US$3.

Buses from Alajuela to San José pass the airport several times an hour from about 5 am to 9 pm and often have room for passengers; the fare is about US$0.30.

Bus

Local buses serve urban and suburban areas, but services and routes can be difficult to figure out. Many towns are small enough that getting around on foot is easy enough. Some local bus details are given under the major town sections.

Local people are usually very helpful, and this includes bus drivers, who will often be able to tell you where to wait for a particular bus.

Taxi

In San José, taxis have meters, called *marías*, but these are rarely used, particularly for foreigners. Outside of San José, taxis don't have meters and so fares are agreed upon in advance. San José drivers will often overcharge tourists, particularly if they are standing outside fancy hotels and don't speak Spanish. It is worth walking a block or two away from fancy hotels and asking locals how much a fare should be. Bargaining is acceptable, especially in San José, though you'll generally find that outside of the capital taxi drivers are less likely to grossly overcharge you.

Within San José, a short ride should cost a dollar or less. A ride across town will be between US$1 and US$2. Rates are comparable in other parts of the country. Taxi cabs are red and have a small sticker in the windshield identifying them as a 'TAXI'.

TOURS
Travel & Tour Agencies in San José

There are scores, if not hundreds, of travel agencies in San José. I have attempted to include as wide a variety of agencies as possible and I have listed the San José addresses of some of the wilderness lodges described in detail elsewhere in this book.

Many companies specialise in nature tours, with visits to the national parks and wilderness lodges. They can provide entire guided itineraries with English-speaking guides and private transport to any part of the country, especially the nature destinations. Many of these nature tour companies also specialise in adventure tourism such as river rafting.

Almost all agencies also provide services such as day trips around the Central Valley, San José city tours, hotel reservations, and airport transfers.

Prices vary depending on the services you require. Two people wishing to travel with a private English-speaking guide and a private vehicle will obviously pay a lot more than two people who are prepared to join a group or can understand a Spanish-speaking guide.

Among the longest running (since 1978) and biggest nature/adventure tour companies is Costa Rica Expeditions(☎ 570766) at Calle Central, Avenida 3. Some of their guides are well qualified naturalists or ornithologists. They specialise in natural history tours, particularly to Tortuguero National Park and Monteverde (where they have their own luxurious lodges), in river rafting and kayaking trips, and in fishing trips. The standards of services are excellent and the trips are priced accordingly. The mailing address is Apartado 6941, San José, but you often can get a faster response from their USA address at Department 235, PO Box 025216, Miami, FL 33102-5216, USA.

Another recommended nature tour company is Horizontes (☎ 222022) Apartado 1780, 1002 San José. Apart from standard trips to national parks, they also organise walking and cycling excursions. Their street address is on the 2nd floor of the Edificio Cristal, Avenida 1, Calle 1 & 3, San José.

Costa Rican Sun Tours (☎ 553418, 553518) is at Avenida 7, Calle 3 & 5. They do the normal nature tours and fishing trips and, in addition, operate the Arenal Volcano Observatory (from where fishing trips on Lake Arenal can also be undertaken) and Tiskita Lodge. Sun Tours' mailing address is Apartado 1195, 1250 Escazú, Costa Rica.

Several other companies specialise in nature tours and have been recommended. They include Tikal (☎ 232811) at Avenida 2, Calle 7, or write to Apartado 6398, 1000 San José. Tikal also runs diving tours from April to November and surfing tours from January to July.

Geotur (☎ 341867; Apartado 469Y, 1011 San José) specialises in Carara Biological Reserve and Braulio Carrillo National Park tours.

Los Caminos de la Selva (Jungle Tours) (☎ 553486) on Calle 38, Avenida 5 & 7, do camping and hiking trips, and a tree-planting tour where you learn about the ecological value of native trees and get to plant a tree of your choice. Write to them at Apartado 2413, 1000 San José.

Also recommended are Cosmos Tours (☎

333466) at Avenida 9, Calle 1 & 3; or write to Apartado 298, 1000 San José.

Companies specialising in river rafting include the following, and all are recommended. Ríos Tropicales (336455) Paseo Colón, Calle 22 & 24, has both river rafting and kayaking trips, and sea kayaking expeditions. They also arrange cruises to Cocos Island National Park from December to April. Write to Apartado 472, 1200 Pavas, Costa Rica. There's also Aventuras Naturales (☎ 253939) at Avenida Central, Calle 33 & 35, or write to Apartado 7528, 1000 San José; or finally check out Costa Rica Expeditions (see earlier in this section).

Other possibilities include horse riding in the countryside around San José offered by Finca Obladi Oblada (☎ 491179) daily except Sunday from January to September. Write to Apartado 1, 6100 Cantón Mora, Ciudad Colón, Costa Rica.

One of the most famous boat trips is an all-day yacht cruise through the Gulf of Nicoya to Tortuga Island with excellent food and good swimming opportunities. The longest running of these cruises is on the *Calypso* (☎ 333617; Apartado 6941, 1000 San José). Bay Island Cruises (☎ 312898; Apartado 145, 1007 San José) also does this cruise.

There are other cruises along the Caribbean canals to Tortuguero. These usually involve one or two nights at lodges in either Tortuguero or Barro Colorado national parks, and can be combined with train, bus, or airplane returns, wildlife watching, and fishing trips, depending on your time and budget. Apart from Costa Rica Expeditions, companies running Caribbean canal cruises include Cotur (also known as Miss Caribe) (☎ 330155) Paseo Colón, Calle 34 & 36 (mail to Apartado 26, 1017 San José); and Mitur (also known as Ilan Ilan) (☎ 552031), Paseo Colón, Calle 20 & 22 (mail to Apartado 91, 1150 San José).

Several agencies have been recommended for general travel and tour arrangements. They can arrange city tours, book you into beach resort hotels, sell you standard day trips, as well as arrange more exotic tours.

Swiss Travel (☎ 314055) has offices in several of the best hotels including the Corobici (main office), Amstel, Balmoral, Irazú and Sheraton. Swiss Travel introduced the 'jungle train', which runs from San José to Siquirres and provides bilingual guides, lunch, and a banana plantation tour. Write to Apartado 7-1970, 1000 San José.

Also recommended is TAM (☎ 235111) at Calle Central, Avenida Central & 1. They are also the American Express agent and have been recommended for international airline ticketing. Write to Apartado 1864, 1000 San José.

Most of the tours offered by the above are not budget-priced, although they are not very expensive by Western standards. Travellers on a budget may want to try Interviajes (☎ 334457; Apartado 296, Heredia 3000, Costa Rica). They offer some of the lowest priced tours, though they're still not dirt cheap. If you are on a very tight budget, many places can be visited most cheaply on your own.

Another source of cheap tours is the domestic airline SANSA (☎ 226561) Calle 24, Paseo Colón & Avenida 1. They offer inexpensive beach vacations including air, hotel and transfer, and some meals for four days and three nights for US$100 to US$130 per person.

Wilderness Lodges Many of the wilderness lodges have addresses in San José where you can get information and make reservations. These are usually very exciting and recommended destinations to those interested in seeing wilderness from the comfort of a well run lodge, but they are beyond the finances of most travellers on a tight budget. Expect to pay in the order of US$45 to US$100 per person per day, all inclusive. Note that cheaper places, which don't have San José addresses, are mentioned further on in the book. Lodges include:

Arenal Volcano Observatory
    Apartado 1195, 1250 Escazú (☎ 553418, 553518)
El Gavilán Lodge
    Apartado 445, 2010, San José (☎ 536540)

La Selva Biological Station
Organization for Tropical Studies, Apartado 676, 2050 San Pedro (☎ 366696)
Los Inocentes
Apartado 1370, 3000 Heredia (☎ 395484)
Marenco Biological Station
Apartado 4025, 1000 San José (☎ 211594)
Monteverde Lodge
Apartado 6941, San José (☎ 570766) or Department 235, PO Box 025216, Miami, FL 33102-5216, USA
Rancho Naturalista
Apartado 364, 1002 San José (☎ 398036)

Rara Avis
Apartado 8105, 1000 San José (☎ 530844)
Robert & Catherine Wilson Botanical Garden
Organization for Tropical Studies, Apartado 676, 2050 San Pedro (☎ 366696)
Tiskita Biological Reserve
Apartado 1195, 1250 Escazú (☎ 553418, 553518)
Tortuga Lodge
Apartado 6941, San José (☎ 570766) or Department 235, PO Box 025216, Miami, FL 33102-5216, USA

San José

For the traveller who arrives at the Costa Rican capital overland through other Central American nations, as I first did in 1980, San José comes as something of a surprise. Compared to other capitals of the region, it is more cosmopolitan, even North Americanised. There are department stores and shopping malls, fast-food chain restaurants and blue jeans. There are almost no Indians and no Indian markets, as there are in Guatemala, for example.

It takes a day or two to start getting the real tico feeling of the city. Perhaps the first sign of being in Costa Rica is the friendliness of the people. Asking someone the way will often result in a smile and a genuine attempt to help you out – a refreshing change from many other capital cities.

Although the city was founded in 1737, little remains of the colonial era. Indeed, until the National Theatre was built in the 1890s, San José was a small and largely forgotten city. Today, the capital boasts several excellent museums, good restaurants, and a fine climate which are the main attractions for visitors. Because Costa Rica's public transport and road system radiates from San José, the capital is often used as a base from which to visit the many attractions of the country.

The population of the city itself is around 290,000 but the surrounding suburbs boost the number to about 800,000 and the population of the whole province is just over one million, or a little over a third of the country. Inhabitants of San José are sometimes referred to as *joséfinos*.

Costa Rica was hit by a powerful earthquake in April 1991. The epicentre was south of Puerto Limón, which was the city most seriously affected by the disaster, but San José was also badly shaken by the quake. The building housing the tourist office and the Pre-Columbian Gold Museum, as well as the neighbouring National Theatre, all on the Plaza of Culture, were damaged and closed.

The situation is not expected to return to normal before some time in 1992. Despite this, travellers to the country were still being welcomed and, apart from some delays in travel to the Caribbean region, getting around the country didn't present any major problems.

Orientation

The city stands at an elevation of 1150 metres and is set in a wide and fertile valley which is known as the Valle Central throughout Costa Rica.

The city centre, where most visitors spend much of their time, is arranged in a grid. All the streets are numbered in a logical fashion, and it is important to learn the system because all street directions and addresses rely on this grid system.

The streets running east to west are *avenidas* whilst the streets running north to south are *calles*. Avenida Central runs east-west through the middle of the city; avenidas north of Avenida Central are odd-numbered, with Avenida 1 running parallel and one block north of Avenida Central, followed by Avenida 3 and so on. The avenidas south of Avenida Central are even-numbered.

Similarly, Calle Central runs north-south through the heart of downtown, and calles east of Calle Central are odd-numbered and calles west of Calle Central are even-numbered.

If you ask a passerby for directions, you'll probably be told to go seven blocks west and four blocks north ('*Siete cuadras al oeste y quatro cuadras al norte*'). Often, 100 metres is used to mean a city block, and so you may be told '*Setecientos metros al oeste y quatrocientos metros al norte*'. This does not literally mean 700 metres west and 400 metres north; it refers to city blocks. *Cinquenta metros* (50 metres) means half a block.

Street addresses in San José are rarely given by the building number (although building numbers do exist). Instead, the nearest street intersection is given. Thus the address of the Tourist Information Office is Calle 5, Avenidas Central y 2. This means it is on Calle 5, between Avenida Central & Avenida 2 (*y* means 'and' in Spanish). This is often abbreviated in telephone directories or other literature to C5, A Ctl/2, or occasionally C5, A 0/2, with 0 replacing the Central.

This system is also used in many other Costa Rican towns, so it's worth getting to know.

Note that Avenida Central becomes Paseo Colón west of Calle 14. The building on the north side of Paseo Colón, Calles 38 & 40, is known as Centro Colón and is a local landmark.

Many ticos use local landmarks to give directions, or even addresses in smaller towns. Thus an address may be 200 metres south and 150 metres east of a church, a radio station, a restaurant, or even a *pulpería* (corner grocery store). Sometimes, the landmark may no longer exist, but because it has been used for so long, its position is known by all the locals. A good example is La Coca Cola, which is a bus terminal in San José where a Coca Cola bottling plant used to be for many years. Everyone knows this, except for the first time visitor! This can get confusing, but persevere. The friendly ticos will usually help you out. Note that taxi drivers especially like to know the landmark address. One driver once told me that he didn't understand where I was going until I couched my destination in terms of landmarks!

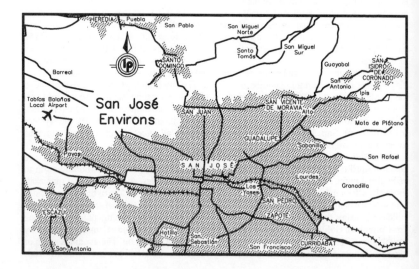

Information

The friendliness of the Costa Ricans has already been mentioned – but it really is one of the outstanding features of this country. The local people can often be your best sources of information.

Tourist Offices The main tourist office is known as the ICT, or Instituto Costarricense de Turismo (☎ 221090), and is on the east side of the Plaza de la Cultura, in the basement of the Gold Museum, on Calle 5 between Avenidas Central & 2. Hours are 9 am to 5 pm from Monday to Friday and 9 am to 1 pm on Saturday (although they were recently closed on Saturday). There is normally an English speaking person on duty. In addition to answering your questions, they can provide excellent and free San José and Costa Rica road maps published by the ICT. A useful ICT publication (in English) is the free *Costa Rica Tourist Information Guide* published annually.

There is also an ICT office at the airport which is open for longer hours, though I find that when I arrive loaded down with luggage and tired from a flight, I have little inclination to search for tourist information. ICT's main office is marked on some maps at Avenida 4, Calles 5 & 7, but this is an administrative office rather than the tourist information office.

Money The Banco Lyon, a branch of Lloyds, at Calle 2, Avenida Central & 1, is reasonably efficient, friendly, has some English speaking staff, and changes travellers' cheques in Canadian dollars and major European currencies at official rates.

The better hotels have exchange windows for their guests.

A few banks are open longer than normal hours. The Banco Nacional de Costa Rica at Avenida 1, Calle 7, is open from 8 am to 6 pm from Monday to Friday. The bank at the airport is open from 6.30 am to 6 pm from Monday to Friday, and from 7 am to 1 pm on weekends and holidays.

Credit cards are widely accepted and you can use them to buy colones in banks (see the Money section in Facts for the Visitor).

The American Express office is at Calle 1, between Avenidas Central & 1. American Express cardholders can buy US dollars travellers' cheques.

Post Office The Central Post Office is on Calle 2, Avenida 1 & 3. Hours are 7 am to 6 pm from Monday to Friday and 7 am to 12 noon on Saturday. The better hotels have mail boxes and sell stamps. Most people use the Central Post Office to mail their letters; I couldn't find any other mail boxes in central San José.

You can receive mail addressed to you c/o Lista Correos, Correos Central, San José, Costa Rica. They are very strict about whom they give mail to. You must produce identification (usually your passport) before they will even look for your mail. They will not give mail to friends or family members; you must get it in person. There is a US$0.10 fee per piece of mail received.

Telecommunications You can make local calls (to anywhere in Costa Rica) from public telephone booths, which accept 2, 5 and 10 colón coins.

You can make international calls from public telephone booths by dialling 116 which connects you to an international operator, who will normally speak English. Collect (reverse charge) and telephone credit card calls can be made in this way.

To make international calls which you pay for, go to Radiográfica at Avenida 5, Calle 1 & 3. They are open from 7 am to 10 pm daily. The better hotels will put international calls through from their switchboards, but these are more expensive.

Radiográfica also provides telex and FAX services.

Telephone directories are available in hotels and at Radiográfica. There are none in the public telephone booths.

Foreign Embassies Many countries have diplomatic representation in San José. See the Facts for the Visitor chapter for a full list.

Immigration Office The office for visa extensions or exit visas is on Calle 21, Avenidas 6 & 8. It is open from 8 am to 4 pm from Monday to Friday.

National Parks Service The public information office (☎ 335284) of the National Parks Service (Servicio de Parques Nacionales) is within the grounds of the Simón Bolívar Zoo. Maps, brochures, permits, posters and information are available. Office hours are 8 am to 12.20 pm and 1.05 to 3.30 pm from Tuesday to Friday, although I've found that the lunch hour may often be extended or changed.

There is also a National Parks Service radio communications office (☎ 334160, 335473) which maintains radio contact with many of the outlying national parks which do not have regular telephone service. Call to arrange for overnight accommodation, meals, and other services provided by the rangers in many parks. (It helps if you speak Spanish). The National Parks Service has its headquarters at Calle 25, Avenida 8 & 10.

Bookshops Four bookstores are particularly noteworthy. The Bookshop on Avenida 1, Calle 1 & 3, has the best selection of books in English (including Lonely Planet guides) but they charge twice the US price. They also have a good selection of magazines and newspapers in English.

Lehmann's on Avenida Central, Calles 1 & 3, has some books, magazines, and newspapers in English and a good selection of Costa Rican maps in the map department upstairs.

Librería Universal on Avenida Central, Calles Central & 1, also has maps and is one of the biggest bookstores in Costa Rica, but it has few books in English and tends to be crowded.

The Librería Italiana/Francesa on Calle 3, Avenida Central & 1, has, as it names implies, books in Italian and French, as well as in English.

English language magazines, newspapers, and some books are also available in the gift shops of the international airport and several of the top end hotels.

Medical Services The most centrally located (free) hospital is Hospital San Juan de Dios (☎ 220166) at Paseo Colón, Calle 14.

The clinics with the best reputations include the Clínica Americana (☎ 221010) and the Clínica Bíblica (☎ 236422) both on Avenida 14, Calle Central & 1. Both have some English speaking staff and are open 24 hours for emergencies. They will carry out laboratory tests (stool, urine, blood samples, etc) and recommend specialists if necessary.

There are plenty of pharmacies in San José. The Farmacia Rex, Calle 5, Avenidas 5 & 7, has been recommended as being helpful and having English and French speaking pharmacists.

For an ambulance, call the Red Cross (☎ 215818).

Spanish Courses There are some excellent Spanish language schools in San José, but they are not particularly cheap. Tuition is usually intensive, with class sizes from two to five per teacher and individual tuition available. Classes are usually for several hours every week day. Most students are encouraged to stay with a Costa Rican family to immerse themselves in the language. Family homestays are arranged by the schools, as are the necessary visa extensions. Costs range from about US$300 to US$700 per month without family homestays, and an extra US$300 with homestays. Cheaper classes usually involve larger group sizes and/or fewer hours. Shorter and longer courses are available.

Most language schools advertise in the *Tico Times* every week. If you want to arrange classes in advance, write to or call the following selection (arranged alphabetically) for details. The first address given is the mailing address; the second address is the street or suburb where the school is, but addresses can change so telephone before heading over to a particular school.

American Institute for Language & Culture
Apartado 200, 1001 San José (☎ 254313)
San Pedro suburb
Centro Cultural Costarricense-Norteamericano
Apartado 1489, San José (☎ 259433)
Calle 37, Avenida 1 & 5
Centro Lingüístico Conversa
Apartado 17, Centro Colón, San José (☎ 217649)
Paseo Colón, Calle 38 & 40
Forester Instituto Internacional
Apartado 6945, 1000 San José (☎ 253155; in the
USA (619) 792 5693)
75 metres south of the Automercado, Los Yoses
Instituto de Lengua Española
Apartado 100, 2350 San José (☎ 269222)
San Francisco suburb
Instituto Latinoamericano de Idiomas (ILISA)
Apartado 1001, 2050 San Pedro, Costa Rica
(☎ 252495; in the USA (818) 843 1226)
San Pedro suburb
Instituto Universal de Idiomas
Apartado 219, 2120 San José (☎ 570441)
Third floor, Edificio Victoria, Avenida 3, Calle 3
& 5
Intensa
Apartado 8110, 1000 San José (☎ 256009; in the
USA (414) 278 0631)
Calle 33, Avenida 5 & 7, Barrio Escalante
Lisa Tec
Apartado 228, San Antonio de Belen, Costa Rica
(☎ 392255)
Cariari Country Club, 10 km north-west of
downtown San José

Laundry There are very few laundromats in
San José (or, indeed, in Costa Rica). Two
which I found are: Betamatic, Avenida 2,
Calle 47, Los Yoses, open 7 am to 12.30 pm
and 1.30 to 4.30 pm from Monday to Saturday. The charge is US$3.50 per machine load
to wash & dry, self service, or US$1.20 a kg
if you drop it off and they do it for you.
Nearby is Lavamatic, Avenida 2, Calle 43 &
45, where it's US$3 per machine load for
cold and US$4 for hot water wash & dry, self
service.

Travel & Tour Agencies There are scores, if
not hundreds, of travel agencies in San José.
See the Getting Around chapter for full
details of tours and operators.

Jade Museum

(Museo de Jade) This is perhaps Costa Rica's
most famous museum. It houses the world's

largest collection of American jade and hundreds of pieces are on display. Many pieces
are mounted with a backlight so that the
exquisite translucent quality of this gem-
stone can be fully appreciated. There are also
archaeological exhibits of ceramics, stone-
work and gold arranged by cultural regions.

The museum (☎ 235800, ext 2581) is on
the 11th floor of the Instituto Nacional de
Seguros at Calle 9, Avenida 7. It is open from
9 am to 3 pm, Monday to Friday, and admission is free.

There is a good view of the city from the
11th floor vantage point – bring your camera.
An interesting metal building is seen to the
south-west. It was designed in France and
shipped over in prefabricated sections. It is
now a school.

Note that 'jade' is written the same but is
pronounced 'ha-day' in Spanish.

National Museum

(Museo Nacional) This is housed in the Bellavista Fortress, the old army headquarters.
The museum shows Costa Rican archaeol-
ogy, some jade and gold, colonial furniture
and costumes, colonial and religious art, and
historical exhibits. Some pieces are labelled
in English as well as Spanish. There is a
small garden with cannons, and some of the
walls are pockmarked with bullet holes from
the 1948 civil war.

The museum (☎ 571433) is on Calle 17,
Avenida Central & 2. Opening hours are
from 9 am to 5 pm from Tuesday to Sunday;
admission is US$0.25; and there is a gift
shop here.

The Pre-Columbian Gold Museum

(Museo del Oro Precolombino) This
museum houses a dazzling collection of pre-
Columbian gold pieces and is well worth
seeing. There is also a small numismatic
(money) museum and a display of Costa
Rican Art.

The museum (☎ 230528) is in the basement of the Plaza de la Cultura complex on
Calle 5, Avenida Central & 2, under the
tourist information office. It is owned by the
Banco Central, is open from 10 am to 5 pm

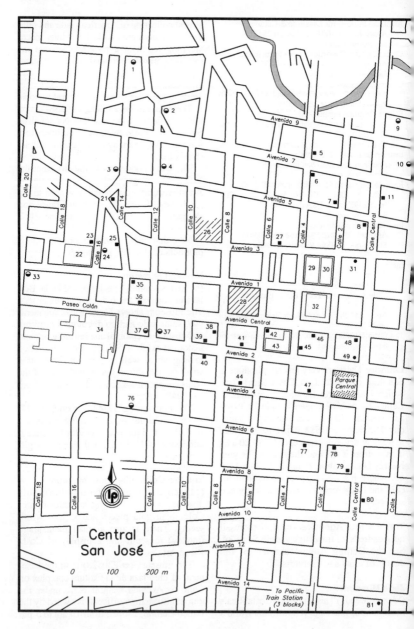

Central
San José

0   100   200 m

To Pacific
Train Station
(3 blocks)

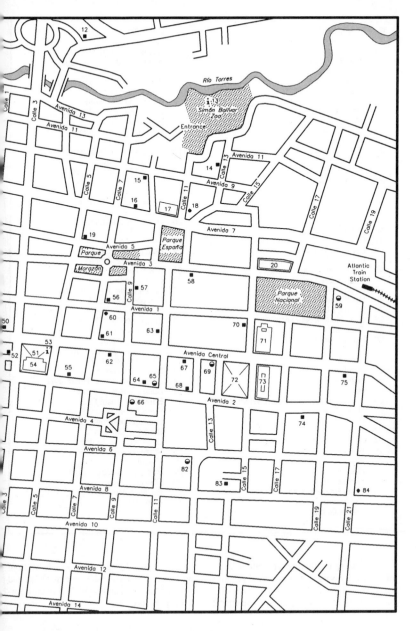

Río Torres

Simón Bolívar
Zoo

Entrance

Parque
España

Parque
Morazón

Parque
Nacional

Atlantic
Train
Station

Avenida 13
Avenida 11
Avenida 11
Avenida 9
Avenida 7
Avenida 5
Avenida 3
Avenida 1
Avenida Central
Avenida 2
Avenida 4
Avenida 6
Avenida 8
Avenida 10
Avenida 12
Avenida 14

Calle 1
Calle 3
Calle 5
Calle 7
Calle 9
Calle 11
Calle 13
Calle 15
Calle 17
Calle 19
Calle 21

Parque

■ PLACES TO STAY

5 Hotel Marlyn
6 Hotel América
7 Hotel Rialto
8 Hotel Europa
11 Pensión Otoya
12 Hotel Bougainvillea
14 Hotel L'Ambiance
15 Hotel Don Carlos
16 Hotel Astoria
19 Aurola Holiday Inn
21 Hotel Cocorí
23 Hotel Musoc
25 Hotel Boruca
27 Hotel Central
35 Hotel Roma
36 Hotel Alameda
38 Hotel Johnson
39 Hotel Generaleño
40 Hotel Talamanca
41 Gran Hotel Centroamericano
42 Hotel Diplomat
44 Hotel Doral
45 Hotel Royal Dutch
46 Hotel Plaza
47 Hotel Park
48 Hotel Royal Garden
50 Hotel La Gran Via
52 Gran Hotel Costa Rica
55 Ticalinda 1
56 Hotel Amstel
57 Costa Rica Inn
58 Hotel Morazán
61 Hotel Balmoral
62 Hotel Presidente
63 Hotel Asia
64 Hotel Avenida 2; Pensión Salamanca
67 Hotel Galilea
68 Hotel Nicaragua
70 Apartotel Lamm
74 Apartotel San José
75 Hotel Bellavista
77 Hotel Fortuna
78 Hotel Príncipe
79 Hotel Boston
80 Hotel Ritz; Pensión Centro Continental
83 Peace Center

OTHER

1 Buses to Tilarán
2 Buses to Puntarenas, Guápiles, Río Frío
3 Buses to Nicoya, Sámara, Tamarindo, Coto Brus
4 Buses to Monteverde
9 Buses to Cahuita, Sixaola
10 Buses to Heredia
13 National Parks Information Office
17 Jade Museum
18 Casa Amarilla (Yellow House)
20 National Library
21 Buses to Nicaraguan Border & Upala
22 Coca Cola Bus Terminal
23 Buses to San Isidro de El General
24 Bus To Cañas
25 Liberia Bus Terminal
26 Borbón Market
28 Central Market
29 Banco Nacional
30 Central Post Office
31 Costa Rica Expeditions
32 Banco Central
33 Buses to Nicoya & Beaches
34 San Juan de Dios Hospital
37 Buses to Alajuela (2 locations)
43 Banco de Costa Rica
49 Melico Salazar Theatre
51 Plaza of Culture
53 Tourism Information Office & Gold Museum
54 National Theatre
55 La Esmeralda Bar/Restaurant
59 Buses to Puerto Limón
60 Banco de Costa Rica
65 Sirca (International Buses)
66 Tica Bus (International)
69 Buses to Cartago
71 Legislative Assembly
72 Plaza de la Democracia
73 National Museum
76 Buses to Escazú
81 Clínica Biblica
82 Buses to Turrialba
84 Immigration

from Tuesday to Sunday, and admission is free. Security is tight, however, and you must leave your bags at the door and show your passport to get in. Free bilingual (Spanish & English) guided tours are available at 2 pm on Tuesday and Thursday, and at 11 am and 3 pm on Saturday and Sunday. Ask the door-keeper about these.

Costa Rican Art Museum

(Museo de Arte Costarricense) This art museum contains a collection of local paintings and sculpture from the 19th and 20th centuries. There are also changing shows of local artists.

The museum (☎ 227155) is in Sabana Park, which used to be San José's airport. The collection is housed in the old control tower just off Calle 42, Paseo Colón & Avenida 2. Hours are 10 am to 5 pm, Tuesday to Sunday; entrance is US$0.50, but free on Sunday.

National Contemporary Art Gallery

(Galería Nacional de Arte Contemporaneo) This art gallery houses changing shows of working Costa Rican artists. It is next to the National Library on Avenida 15, Calle 3 & 5. Hours are 10 am to 1 pm, and 1.45 to 5 pm Monday to Saturday; admission is free.

The Serpentarium

(Serpentario) The Serpentarium is an unusual collection of snakes (as well as poison-arrow frogs) housed in the centre of San José. Anyone interested in reptile or amphibian identification will benefit from a visit to this live exhibition of many of Costa Rica's exotic species. A bilingual biologist is available to explain the collection and there is a small gift shop. The serpentarium (☎ 554210) is on Avenida 1, Calle 9 & 11, and is open from 10 am to 7 pm daily; admission is US$1.

Natural History Museum

(Museo de Ciencias Naturales) This is in Colegio (High School) La Salle near the south-west corner of Sabana Park. Basically it is a collection of stuffed animals and mounted butterflies, and is a resource to those wishing to identify some of the species they may see in the wild.

The museum (☎ 321306) is open 7.30 am to 3 pm on weekdays and 8 am to 12 noon on Saturday (recent reports are that it's closed on Monday – call ahead); admission is US$0.25. Most cab drivers know the Colegio La Salle and charge less than US$2

to get there. A Sabana-Estadio or Sabana-Cementario city bus from the Parque Central will take you there for a few cents – ask the driver to let you know where the museum is.

Entomology Museum

(Museo de Entomología) The Entomology Museum is a fine collection of insects curated by the Universidad (University) de Costa Rica. It is claimed that this is the only insect museum of any size in Central America – I don't know if that's true but the collection is certainly extensive and many splendid and exotic insects can be seen. You should call the museum ahead of time (☎ 255555, ext 318) or ask at the tourist office for opening hours, as they often change. The latest word is 1 to 5 pm on weekdays, and admission is free; ring the bell to gain admission.

Surprisingly, this museum is housed in the Facultad de Artes Musicales (Musical Arts Faculty) of the Departamento de Bellas Artes (Fine Arts Department) of the University. There are signs on campus, or ask. A cab to the University (in San Pedro) costs about US$2 or take a San Pedro bus along Avenida 2 from Calle 5.

Simón Bolívar Zoo

(Parque Zoológico Simón Bolívar) This small national zoo is in the Simón Bolívar Park, hence its name. Many of Costa Rica's animals are to be seen, along with a small sprinkling of foreign exotics. Unfortunately, as in many Latin American countries, the cages are small, although not as bad as in some zoos I've seen. The zoo is popular with joséfinos at weekends. The gate is at Avenida 11, Calle 7 & 9 (go north on Calle 7 and east on Avenida 11 to get there). Hours are from 8.30 am to 3.30 pm from Tuesday to Friday, 9 am to 4 pm on weekends, closed Monday; admission is US$0.30.

The public information office of the National Parks Service is within the grounds of the zoo (see the Information section for details).

Costa Rican Post & Philately Museum

(Museo Postal, Telegráfico, y Filatélico de Costa Rica) This museum (☎ 239766, ext 269) is in the Central Post Office, 1st floor, at Calle 2, Avenida 1 & 3. Hours are 8 am to 4 pm on Monday to Friday; admission is free.

Criminological Museum

(Museo Criminologico) The stated objective of the Criminological Museum (☎ 230666, ext 2378) is the prevention of crime through the presentation of exhibits of criminal acts. I plead guilty to not personally visiting this museum, which is in the Supreme Court of Justice, Avenida 6, Calle 17 & 19, open from 1 to 5 pm on Monday, Wednesday and Friday.

National Theatre

(Teatro Nacional) This is considered San José's most impressive public building. Built in the 1890s, the National Theatre is the centre of Costa Rican culture. The outside is not particularly impressive, with statues of Beethoven and Calderón de la Barca (a 17th century Spanish dramatist) flanking the entrance, and a columned facade.

Inside, there are some paintings of Costa Rica, of which the most famous is a huge canvas showing coffee harvesting and export, painted in Italy in the late 19th century and reproduced on the 5 colón note. (This note is now out of circulation, but can sometimes be obtained in banks). The marble staircases, gilded ceilings and parquet floors of local hardwoods are worth seeing.

There are regular performances in the National Theatre and this is the best way to see the inside of the building. Otherwise, it is open from 10 am to 12 pm and 2 to 6 pm from Monday to Friday and costs US$1.10 to visit. There is a pleasant coffee shop to the left of the lobby with changing shows of local artists, good coffee and a quiet atmosphere to write postcards. It is open when the theatre is open.

National Liquor Factory

(Fabrica Nacional de Licores) The National Liquor Factory (☎ 236244) was founded by President Juan Rafael Mora in 1856. There are guided tours and tasting sessions available at 4 pm from Monday to Friday. The factory is at Avenida 7, Calle 13 & 15.

Central Market

(Mercado Central) This is interesting to visit if you've never been to a Latin American market, although a little tame compared to the markets of many other countries. Nevertheless, it is crowded and bustling, and has a variety of produce for sale.

The Central Market is at Avenida Central & 1, Calle 6 & 8. A block away is the similar Mercado Borbón, at Avenida 3 and Calle 8. Beware of pickpockets in these areas.

National Park

(Parque Nacional) The pleasant and shady National Park is between Avenida 1 & 3, Calle 15 & 19. It has two statues of note. In the centre of the park is the National Monument showing the Central American nations driving out William Walker. Opposite the south-west corner is a statue of national hero, Juan Santamaría.

Important buildings surrounding the National Park include the Legislative Assembly (or Congress Building) to the south, the National Library to the north, and the National Liquor Factory to the north-west.

Park of Spain

(Parque España) This small park seems to have some of the tallest trees in San José. It is a riot of birdsong just before sunset, and a riot of colour on Sundays when there is an outdoor art market. The park is between Avenida 3 & 7, Calle 9 & 11.

To the north of the park is the INS building, housing the Jade Museum, and fronted by a huge statue of 'The Family'. To the west is the famous iron building (now a school), to the east is the Liquor Factory, and to the north-east is the Casa Amarilla (Yellow House) which is Costa Rica's Ministry of Foreign Affairs.

Morazán Park

(Parque Morazán) This park covers four city blocks and is quartered by busy streets, Avenida 3 and Calle 7. At the intersection of these streets is a dome-roofed structure, the so-called Temple of Music. The north-east quarter of the park has a small Japanese garden and is of interest to parents with small children as there is a playground here.

Plaza of Culture

(Plaza de la Cultura) This plaza is not particularly prepossesing in itself, but it is the site of the National Theatre, Gold Museum and tourist information office. In addition, the western side of the plaza is an open-air market of arts and crafts – it gets very busy just before Christmas and around other holidays. Young people hang out here and check out what everyone else is doing.

Central Park

(Parque Central) The Central Park is between Avenida 2 & 4, Calle Central & 2. These streets are very busy (especially Avenida 2) and the park is known as the place to catch many of the local city buses. To the east is the fairly modern and not very interesting Metropolitan Cathedral. To the north is the well-known Melico Salazar Theatre and the Soda Palace Bar, which is a plain but very popular 24 hour *soda* restaurant and bar.

Tours

The following is a list of the most popular tours offered in, around, and out of San José. Approximate prices per person are given, but look around for occasional bargains such as two people for the price of one.

Day tours normally include lunch and pick up and return from your San José hotel, multi-day tours normally include overnight accommodation, meals and transport. Guides, usually bilingual in English, accompany most tours.

For a full list of tour operators, see the Getting Around chapter.

Half-day city tour; US$14 to US$16

Half-day tours to one of the following: Irazú Volcano; Poás Volcano; Ox-cart factory at Sarchí; Orosi Valley; US$19 to US$25

Full day tours combining two of the above; US$38 to US$45

Full day tours to one of the following: Jungle Train with Braulio Carrillo National Park; Arenal Volcano; Barva Volcano; Carara Biological Reserve with Jacó Beach; Cerro de la Muerte; Tapanti National Wildlife Refuge; La Virgen del Socorro; Gulf of Nicoya cruise to Tortuga Island; horse riding; white-water rafting trip on one of the Reventazón, Sarapiquí or Corobicí rivers; trout fishing; US$65

Two-days/one-night river rafting and camping; US$190

Three-days/two-nights at Tortuguero: per person, double occupancy; US$125 to US$325 depending on transport and accommodation

Three-days/two-nights at Monteverde; per person, double occupancy US$200 to US$400

Places to Stay

There are about 100 hotels of all types in San José, but accommodation may be tight during the high season (December to May) and especially in the week before and after Christmas and the week before Easter. If you want to stay in a particular hotel then, you should make reservations – as much as three months in advance for Christmas and Easter.

If travelling in the low (wet) season, discounts may sometimes be offered or arranged. Discounts can also be arranged for longer stays, sometimes of a week, almost always for stays of a month or more. Travellers who would like to use San José as a base for short trips to the surrounding countryside should take advantage of long term discounts. Rates quoted are generally high season unless otherwise stated.

Although there is a large choice of hotels, I find that the accommodation is generally lacklustre, especially downtown. Medium priced hotels, although clean and secure, tend to suffer from musty carpets, street noise and unappealing decor. The most luxurious hotels are good, but not many travellers want to pay US$100 or more for a room. Budget hotel rooms are usually grim and noisy little boxes, but at least they are fairly cheap.

This is a general impression formed after several visits to San José and after traipsing around many hotels – perhaps it's a sign of hotel review burn-out! It does not mean that pleasant accommodation for a reasonable price is impossible to find, but don't expect to encounter scores of quaint and inexpensive hotels in San José.

Many of the mid-priced and all of the top end hotels will accept reservations from outside Costa Rica by phone or mail. Some have US telephone numbers (occasionally toll free). A reservation deposit is normally required. A good travel agent will help you make reservations from home. Local phone numbers and street addresses are given below, and, for those hotels which normally accept reservations from abroad, postal addresses (Apartados) and/or US phone numbers are also given. If making mail reservations, allow several months – letters can be very slow. Phoning or using a travel agent are the best ways to make reservations.

Places to Stay – bottom end

Hotels Travellers on a very tight budget will find accommodation begins at around US$3 for a single, with very few exceptions. One of these exceptions is the *Hotel Nicaragua* (☎ 230292), Avenida 2, 1167, Calle 13, which charges US$2 per person. The small hotel is family run, reasonably clean, friendly and secure. There are only cold water showers and the hotel is often full with Central American travellers. There are several other cheap hotels on the same street.

The *Ticalinda 1* at Avenida 2, 553, Calle 5 & 7, is very popular with foreign budget travellers on the '*gringo*' trail'. It is next door to the La Esmeralda Bar (where mariachis play late into the night); the sign is just a tiny plate on the door. Cramped rooms are US$3/5 single/double and the place is noisy but friendly. For about US$2 you can have a bed in a room with three other people. Laundry facilities are available, but its main attraction is as a place to meet other travellers.

Nearby is the basic but OK *Hotel Avenida 2* at Avenida 2, Calle 9 & 11, which has hot showers and charges US$4 for a double. On the same block is the poor *Pensión Salamanca* at Avenida 2, Calle 9 & 11. The charge is US$3.50 for a single and there are cold showers only.

Another reasonable cheapie is the *Hotel Rialto* (☎ 217456), Calle 2, Avenida 5, which is decent, has hot water and charges US$4 for a double, or US$5 with a private washbasin and toilet. The *Hotel América* (☎ 214116) at Calle 4, Avenida 7, has hot water and is reasonable value for US$5 for a double.

The *Hotel Boruca* (☎ 230016), Calle 14, Avenida 1 & 3, is convenient for buses but somewhat noisy because of them. It is family run, secure, clean and has hot water some of the time. Rooms are small and cost US$3 per person. Nearby is the *Hotel Roma* (☎ 232179), Calle 14, Avenida Central & 1. It is an adequate and secure place charging US$3.50 per person, but there's cold water only.

A less noisy (though not necessarily quiet) choice is the *Hotel Central* (☎ 222377) at Avenida 3, Calle 6 & 8. It has large rooms and the charge is US$3 for a single with communal bath or US$8.25 for a double with private bath and cold water. The *Hotel Astoria* (☎ 212174), Avenida 7, Calle 7 & 9, has been popular for years and is often full, though it's not especially remarkable. It's clean, friendly and has hot water. Rooms are US$4 to US$5.25 per person, depending on quality. Try bargaining in the off season.

The *Hotel Morazán* (☎ 219083), Avenida 3, Calle 11 & 15, is convenient for the Atlantic train station. It has large, clean, bare rooms, and it is secure. When I went there in March (high season) I was quoted US$7/9.50 single/double, communal showers, but a friend who visited in September (low season) was told US$3.50 per person.

Another cheap place is the *Hotel Marlyn* (☎ 333212), Calle 4, Avenida 7 & 9, which charges US$3 for a small single, or US$6 with private bath and (usually) hot water.

The *Hotel Boston* (☎ 210563), Avenida 8, Calle Central & 2, has larger rooms with private baths and hot water for US$6/9.50 single/double. The management is friendly, some rooms are noisy, but inside rooms are reasonably quiet. The *Hotel Asia* (☎ 233893), Calle 11, Avenida Central & 1, charges US$4.75/7.50 single/double in small but clean rooms and has hot water in the communal showers.

The *Pensión Otoya* (☎ 213925), Calle Central, Avenida 5 & 7 is clean, friendly, has long been popular with foreigners and is often full. Despite this, I have just heard that it is up for sale – maybe its popularity will change with new management. Singles are US$4.75, or US$6.75 with private bath and hot water.

The *Hotel Príncipe* (☎ 227983), Avenida 6, Calle Central & 2, is secure and has rooms with private tepid showers for US$4.75/7.50 single/double. The *Hotel Generaleño* (☎ 337877), Avenida 2, Calle 8 and 10, is large, clean, but basic and has cold showers only. Singles/doubles are US$3.50/6 with communal shower, or US$8.25 (one bed, one or two people) and US$11.75 (two beds) with private showers.

The *Pensión Centro Continental* (☎ 331731), Calle Central, Avenida 8 & 10, is a small but clean and friendly hotel. There are kitchen facilities and hot water in the communal showers. Rooms are US$5.50/10 for singles/doubles and US$2.50 per extra person, up to five people.

Hostels There is one youth hostel which is associated with the YHA. This is the *Hostel Toruma* (☎ 244085), Avenida Central, Calle 29 & 31, a little over a km east of downtown. There are bunk beds in segregated dormitories, and hot water is available at times. The charge is US$5 per person for YHA members, US$6 for non-members, although membership is available for US$15. Breakfast is included in the price, and there is an 11 pm curfew, though an exit pass can be arranged. Cheap laundry facilities are available in the afternoons. There is a message board and it is a good place to meet other budget travellers. The hostel is also the headquarters for the network of five Costa Rican

youth hostels and information and reservations for the other four can be made here. The other four are at Rincón de la Vieja National Park, Rara Avis, Arenal and Puntarenas. For Costa Rican Youth Hostel information, write to RECAJ, Apartado 1355, 1002 San José.

An interesting small hostel is the *Peace Center* (☎ 336168), Calle 15, Avenida 6 bis, 1336 (Avenida 6 bis runs between Avenida 6 & 8, west of Calle 15). This centre is operated by Quakers and is good for information and discussion of peace issues. There is a small library and the centre is staffed mainly by volunteers. Accommodation is available in dormitories and private rooms and costs US$5 per person. There are basic kitchen facilities and communal hot showers.

Places to Stay – middle
The *Hotel Musoc* (☎ 229437), Calle 16, Avenida 3 & 5, is a large building which is very convenient for the Coca Cola bus terminal. The hotel is clean, has recently been redecorated and charges US$6.75 for a single with communal bath and US$9.50 for a single with private bath and hot water.

The *Hotel Cocorí* (☎ 330081), Calle 16, Avenida 3, is the best hotel near the Coca Cola bus terminal. Clean rooms with hot water in the private baths are US$9/13 single/double. Similarly priced is the *Hotel Johnson* (☎ 237633), on Calle 8, Avenida Central & 2 (mail to Apartado 6638, San José). There is also hot water in the private showers, and reasonably sized rooms with telephones. This makes it popular with Central Americans in town on business.

The *Hotel Bellavista* (☎ 230095), Avenida Central, Calle 19 & 21, is friendly and clean, and has rooms with private baths and hot water. Older rooms are US$7.50/11.50 single/double, new rooms are US$10.50 per person.

The *Gran Hotel Centroamericano* (☎ 213362), Avenida 2, Calle 6 & 8, has rather small, dark and musty rooms with private bathroom and hot water for US$10 for a single and US$3 more for each extra person, up to six people. It's main attraction is its central location.

The *Petit Hotel* (☎ 330766), Calle 24, Paseo Colón & Avenida 2 (Apartado 1172, Centro Colón, San José), is a clean, pleasant and friendly hotel which allows kitchen privileges on request and has hot showers. Rooms are US$15/27 single/double with private bathroom, US$11 per person with communal bathroom.

The *Hotel Ritz* (☎ 224103, in the USA (305) 271-7829), Calle Central, Avenida 8 & 10, is also pleasant and friendly, and has an American manager and a small English book exchange. They charge US$16.50/21/23.50 single/double/triple with private bathrooms and hot water.

The *Costa Rica Inn* (☎ 225203), Calle 9, Avenida 1 & 3, is also clean and friendly, is centrally located and has hot water, but the rooms are rather small. The inn is popular with North Americans, perhaps because it has a toll-free number in the USA for reservations (☎ 1 (800) 637-0899). Rooms are US$15/19 single/double.

The *Hotel Cacts* (☎ 212928) is a little out of the way at Avenida 3 bis, Calle 28 & 30, but is quiet because of that. Friendly management, clean and spacious rooms, hot water in the private baths, and breakfast is included in the price of US$13/18 single/double, or US$3 less in rooms with communal bathrooms. (Mail to Apartado 379, 1005 San José.)

The *Hotel Galilea* (☎ 336925), Avenida Central, Calle 11 & 13, is clean, pleasant and helpful, and is near several museums. It is popular with biologists and researchers, and students can get a discount. Rooms with private baths and hot water are US$18/22 single/double. Similarly priced, and also clean and quiet, is the *Hotel Fortuna* (☎ 235344), Avenida 6, Calle 2 & 4 (mail to Apartado 7, 1570 San José).

Several hotels charge about US$22/30 single/double with private bathroom and hot water. They seem little better than the ones listed so far, but all are acceptable. The *Hotel Diplomat* (☎ 218133), Calle 6, Avenida Central & 2 (mail to Apartado 6606, 1000 San José) has a good restaurant.

The *Hotel Alameda* (☎ 236333; Apartado 680, 1000 San José), Avenida Central, Calle 12 , also has a restaurant and is quite close to the bus terminals. Similar is the *Hotel Talamanca* (☎ 335033; Apartado 449, 1002, San José), Avenida 2, Calle 8 & 10. It boasts a casino and has a good breakfast restaurant. Similarly priced, but out in the suburbs of San Pedro, on the north side of the University campus, is the *Hotel D'Galah* (☎ 341743; Apartado 85, 2350 San José). Some rooms have kitchen facilities attached.

Other reasonable possibilities in this price range are the *Hotel Plaza* (☎ 225533; Apartado 2019, 1000 San José), Calle 2, Avenida Central & 2; the slightly cheaper *Hotel Doral* (☎ 335069), on Avenida 4, Calle 6 & 8; and the American-run *Hotel Park* (☎ 216944), Avenida 4, Calle 2 & 4.

The *Hotel La Gran Via* (☎ 227737; Apartado 1433, 1000 San José), Avenida Central, Calle 1 & 3, has some rooms with balconies onto the street and quieter inside rooms, some of which are air-con. The cost is US$28/37 for singles/doubles.

The *Hotel Amstel* (☎ 224622, in the USA (305) 532-0726; Apartado 4192, 1000 San José), Avenida 1, Calle 7, has been recommended by travellers, though I feel it isn't much better than other hotels in this price range. Its main attractions are the central location and good management. Most rooms are reasonably sized and cost US$30/37 single/double, or a little more with air-con. The restaurant is popular, and often full (reservations accepted).

The *Hotel Royal Garden* (☎ 570023; Apartado 3493, 1000 San José), Calle Central, Avenida Central & 2, charges US$33/40 for singles/doubles. It has a casino, a good Chinese restaurant, and quiet, pleasant rooms.

A very popular hotel in this price category is the small (and often full) *Hotel Don Carlos* (☎ 216707; Apartado 1593, 1000 San José) at Calle 9, Avenida 7 & 9. The hotel is in a remodelled mansion, each room is different but pleasant, and there is an excellent gift shop. Rates are US$32/39 for singles/doubles including Continental breakfast.

Apartotels Finally there are *apartotels*, which are a cross between an apartment building and a hotel. Rooms come fully furnished, have TV and telephone, private bathroom and a kitchen unit including utensils. They are designed for people who wish to cater for themselves to some extent. Although singles and doubles are always available, rooms are also suitable for families.

Apartotels can be rented by the day (which are the prices I give) but discounts are always available for stays of a week or more. If you do not need to be in the town centre, and do not need restaurant, casino and travel agent facilities in the hotel, then these apartotels provide some of the best value accommodation in San José.

The *Apartotel Lamm* (☎ 214920; Apartado 2729, 1000 San José) is at Calle 15, Avenida 1. It charges US$30/33/37 for single/double/triple rooms and has been recommended as clean and helpful. There are from one to three bedrooms per apartment, so families can be accommodated and daily maid service is provided.

The *Apartotel San José* (☎ 220455; Apartado 5834, 1000 San José), Calle 17, Avenida 2, is in a more modern building and otherwise is similar to the Lamm, but costs a few dollars more per room.

At the other end of downtown is the *Apartotel Castilla* (☎ 222113; Apartado 4699, 1000 San José), Calle 24, Avenida 2 & 4, which charges about US$30/35 for singles/doubles and is also good.

Further away from the centre towards the east is *Apartotel Conquistador* (☎ 253022; Apartado 303, 2050, San Pedro, Costa Rica) in Los Yoses. Also in Los Yoses is the *Apartotel Los Yoses* (☎ 250033; Apartado 1597, 1000 San José). Both have a swimming pool. Apartments vary in size and in the amenities provided. Rates are US$25 to US$35 for a single and US$30 to US$40 double.

Just before Los Yoses is *Apartotel Don Carlos* (☎ 216707; Apartado 1593, 1000 San José) at Calle 29, Avenida Central. Rates are about the same and the place is well run.

Nearby is *Apartments Scotland* (☎ 230833), Avenida 1, Calle 27, which caters mainly to long-stay guests. One-bedroom apartments are US$140 a week or US$330 a month.

All the following places are west of the centre. The *Apartotel Ramgo* (☎ 323823; Apartado 1441, 1000 San José) is at Sabana Sur, a block south of the Sabana Park. Buses for downtown stop nearby. All apartments come with two bedrooms; US$28/36 single/double. Just north of the Sabana Park is *Apartotel Napoleón* (☎ 233252; Apartado 86340, 1000 San José) at Calle 40, Avenida 5. There is a pool and a coffee shop on the premises. Rates are US$34/38 single/double and there are some cheaper rooms without kitchens.

Places to Stay – top end

The *Hotel Ambassador* (☎ 218155, in the USA (800) 344 1212; Apartado 10186, 1000 San José), Paseo Colón, Calle 26 & 28, has large, comfortable rooms and Continental breakfast included in the rates of US$40/45 for single/double rooms and US$113 for top floor suites with good views. Group discounts are available and children under 12 stay free in the same room as parents. The staff are friendly and the hotel is popular.

The strangely named *Hotel Tennis Club* (☎ 321266; Apartado 4964, 1000 San José) on the south-west side of the Sabana Park is the place to stay if you like to keep fit whilst on vacation. There are eight tennis courts, a pool, gym and a sauna. Some of the more expensive rooms have kitchenettes. Rates are US$30 to US$45 single and US$35 to US$50 double.

The *Hotel Torremolinos* (☎ 225266; Apartado 2029, 1000 San José), Calle 40, Avenida 5 bis, also has a pool and sauna, is in a quiet neighbourhood, and has a courtesy bus to downtown. Rates are US$55/60 for a single/double.

About five km west of town just off the freeway to the airport is the *Hotel Irazú* (☎ 324811, in the USA (800) 223-0888, in Canada (800) 663-9582; Apartado 962, 1000 San José). With over 300 rooms, this hotel is reputedly the largest in the country. There is a small shopping mall, tennis, swimming pool and sauna, a casino, discotheque, restaurant, cafeteria and bar. The hotel is popular with charter tour groups escaping the North American winter, and, with the facilities available, some guests don't leave the hotel! But if you do, there is a minibus shuttle to downtown and a daily bus to a beach resort in Jacó. Rates vary depending on air-con and size. Singles are US$45 to US$65, doubles US$55 to US$80. Guests without reservations may be able to arrange a cheaper rate, particularly in the wet season.

The following hotels are in the downtown area. The *Gran Hotel Costa Rica* (☎ 214000, in the USA (800) 327-9408; Apartado 527, 1000 San José), Calle 3, Avenida Central & 2, dates from the 1930s and has a certain old-world charm. The rather small air-con rooms are modern, however, and all have TV. The pavement cafeteria outside the lobby is an attractive and popular place for breakfast, and there is a casino and restaurant on the top floor. Rates are about US$50/60 single/double.

The *Hotel Balmoral* (☎ 225022, in the USA (800) 327-7737, in Canada (800) 237-6067; Apartado 3344, 1000 San José), Avenida Central, Calle 7 & 9, has a casino, and rooms are similar to the Gran Hotel Costa Rica. Another similar downtown possibility is the *Hotel Royal Dutch* (☎ 221414, in the USA (800) 327-9408; Apartado 4258, San José) at Calle 4, Avenida Central & 2. Also, there is the *Hotel Presidente* (☎ 223022; Apartado 2922, 1000 San José) at Avenida Central, Calle 7 & 9.

The *Hotel Europa* (☎ 221222, in the USA (800) 223-6764; Apartado 72, 1000 San José) Calle Central, Avenida 3 & 5, has a pool, is centrally located, and has a good restaurant and service. Spacious air-con rooms cost US$40 to US$57 single and US$53 to US$70 double. The cheaper rooms are on the street; the more expensive ones overlook the inner courtyard and pool and are quieter.

Similarly priced but about 750 metres north of downtown is the new *Hotel Bougainvillea* (☎ 336622; Apartado 69, 2120 Guadaloupe, Costa Rica), Barrio Tournon. There is a decent restaurant, pool, jacuzzi, a spacious feel, and the popular El Pueblo Shopping Centre is nearby.

Next we get into the modern luxury-class hotels with many facilities such as restaurants, shops, pool, gym, sauna, travel agents, etc. These include the *Hotel Corobicí* (☎ 328122, in the USA (800) 367-6046; Apartado 2443, 1000 San José), Calle 42, 200 metres north of the Sabana Park. Rooms are US$85/95 single/double and there is a courtesy shuttle downtown.

Right downtown you'll find the *Aurola Holiday Inn* (☎ 337233, in the USA (800) HOLIDAY; Apartado 7802, 1000 San José), Calle 5, Avenida 5. This new, luxurious, 17 storey building topped with a fancy restaurant is a San José landmark. Rooms range from US$108 to US$128 for a single and from US$119 to US$140 for a double. Suites range from US$147 to US$186 (except for the presidential suite which you can rent for a cool US$453 per night!) Children under 12 stay free in their parents rooms.

A small and exclusive hotel near the Simón Bolívar Zoo is the *Hotel L'Ambiance* (☎231598; Apartado 1040, 2050 San Pedro, San José), Calle 13, Avenida 9 & 11 . The Spanish style house is furnished with antiques and has six rooms and a suite. The emphasis is on service and quiet intimacy – no children. Rooms are US$90/113 single/double and the suite is US$170/226 single/double including breakfast.

Places to Stay – out of town

There are several outlying suburbs with middle to top end hotels. People like to stay here to get out of the hustle and bustle of San José, to be closer to the airport (17 km away), or because of the quiet, rural atmosphere. The hotels are served by local buses, described in the San José Getting Around section.

There are several hotels in San Rafael de Escazú, about seven km west of downtown San José, and in San Antonio de Escazú, about 1½ km to the south of San Rafael. The

Escazú suburb has some elegant residential areas, popular with foreign residents.

The *Apartotel María Alexandra* (☎ 281507; Apartado 3756, 1000 San José), Calle 3, Avenida 23, San Rafael de Escazú, is clean, quiet, and has a restaurant, pool and laundry facilities. Rooms are about US$40 for one, two or three occupants.

The *Posada Pegasus* (☎ 284196; Apartado 370, 1250 Escazú, San José), and the *Mirador Pico Blanco* (☎ 283197; Apartado 900, 1250 Escazú, San José), are both small, friendly, pleasant countryside hotels in Escazú. The Pegasus is smaller and slightly cheaper than Pico Blanco, which charges about US$25/35 for singles/doubles. Both have views of the mountains, and of San José below.

The Tara, (☎ 289651), located in a beautiful mansion in the hills above Escazú, is a new luxury hotel which only recently became fully operational – the rates are apparently higher than other hotels, but with only 20 rooms they aim to provide very personal service and the highest standards of luxury. Obtain more information from Apartado 1459, 1250 Escazú, Costa Rica.

There are four luxury hotels near the Cariari Country Club, about nine km northwest of San José on the way to the airport. The *Hotel Cariari* (☎ 390022, in the USA (800) 344-1212; Apartado 737, 1007 Centro Colón, San José) has exceptional resort facilities (golf, pool, tennis, horse riding, gym, disco, sauna, casino, shopping mall, restaurants). Rooms are US$100 to US$150 depending on facilities, and there's a 25% discount in the wet season.

Nearby is the *Apartotel Villas de Cariari* (☎ 391341; Apartado 849, 1007 Centro Colón, San José). Rates are a little cheaper, but there's no disco, tennis or shopping mall. There is a monthly rate of about US$1000 for golf players. Also for golf players, the *Apartotel Residencias de Golf* (☎ 391020; Apartado 5548, 1000 San José), charges about US$90 per day, or US$1300 per month.

Not far away is the *Hotel Sheraton Herradura* (☎ 390033, in the USA (800) 325-3535; Apartado 7, 1880 San José). Rooms are about US$100/120 for a single/double.

Santo Domingo de Heredia, about six km north of downtown San José, is the second location of the previously mentioned *Hotel Bougainvillea* (☎ 368822; Apartado 69, 2120 Guadalupe, San José). This pleasant country hotel has gardens and orchards, tennis, a pool, and a shuttle bus to San José. Rooms are about US$55/60 single/double.

Places to Eat

Cosmopolitan San José has a wide variety of restaurants – something to satisfy most tastes and budgets. I found Peruvian and Middle Eastern restaurants, as well as the old standbys: Italian, Chinese and French. American chain food restaurants are also popular – though I can't get too excited about them myself. And, of course, there are Tico specialities.

Remember that most restaurants, apart from the very cheapest, add a 10% tax plus a 10% service to your bill. Many of the better restaurants can get quite busy so a telephoned reservation may help avoid a wait. Where I give approximate prices as a guide, bear in mind that anything with shellfish (shrimp, lobster or crab) will be more expensive.

Sodas These luncheonette type snack bars are usually inexpensive and are a good choice for the budget traveller, particularly for breakfast or lunch, when you can have a light meal for US$1 to US$2. Most are rather featureless and certainly not fancy, but are popular with ticos looking for a cheap meal. They cater to students and working people, and hence some tend to close at weekends.

An inexpensive and popular one is the *Soda Central*, Avenida 1, Calle 3 & 5, where the empanadas are good and you can have a gallo pinto with egg for US$1.

The *Soda Coliseo*, Avenida 3, Calle 10 & 12, is clean and quite good. The *Soda La Casita* at Avenida 1, Calle Central & 1, has little booths and is extremely popular with office workers at lunch time.

The cheap *Soda Nini*, Avenida 3, Calle 2 & 4, has both tico and Chinese food. The *Soda Magaly* at Avenida Central, Calle 23, has a good variety of US$1 to US$1.50 meals and is close to the Toruma Youth Hostel. Also close to the hostel is the *Soda Restaurant La Luz* at Avenida Central, Calle 33.

On the north side of Parque Central there is the *Soda Palace* at Avenida 2, Calle 2; and the *Soda La Perla*, Avenida 2, Calle Central. Both are open 24 hours. The Palace is a very popular gathering spot with harsh lights, plenty of action, and musicians wandering in and out at night; meals are about US$3. The Perla is quieter and a little cheaper.

Vegetarian Although vegetarianism isn't very big in Costa Rica, there are several reasonable vegetarian restaurants, most of them fairly inexpensive. One is the *Vishnu* at Calle 3, Avenida Central & 1 (although it may have moved to Calle 14), which has a big set lunch. Another is *Shakti*, Avenida 8, Calle 13, which has been recommended.

For good value lunches only, try *Don Sol* at Avenida 7 bis, Calle 13 & 15, two blocks east of the Jade Museum. The *Soda Yure*, Avenida 2, Calle 3, has also been recommended for vegetarian fare.

Two slightly more upmarket macrobiotic restaurants are *Restaurant La Macrobiótica* at Avenida 1, Calle 11 & 15; and the *La Mazorca*, 100 metres north of the Banco Anglo in San Pedro.

Budget Travellers trying to economise may find San José a somewhat expensive city to eat in. Apart from the *sodas*, here are some suggestions. The *Central Market* at Avenida Central & 1, Calle 6 & 8, has a variety of cheapish eateries inside. Nearby, the *Chicharronera Nacional*, Avenida 1, Calle 10 & 12, has a variety of cheap dishes, many of them fried. The area around the market is not dangerous, but is a little rough and single women may prefer not to go there alone.

The *Restaurant El Campesino*, Calle 7, Avenida 2, is a pleasant place with a homey atmosphere. It serves mainly chicken at about US$1.30 for a quarter, and it's roasted

not fried. The *Restaurant La Vasconia*, Avenida 1, Calle 5, is a cheap but reasonably decent place.

Nearby, next to the Omni Cinema, is the clean *Restaurante Marisquería Omni*, Avenida 1, Calle 3 & 5, where a good set lunch is served from 11.30 am to 1.30 pm for about US$1.25. Good value and with some character is *El Escorial*, Avenida 1, Calle 5 & 7, where meals cost from US$1.25 to US$2.50.

Also good for set lunches is *Restaurant Poás* at Avenida 7, Calle 3 & 5, but realise that the à la carte meals are considerably more expensive. This place used to be a popular cheap *soda* with a budget hotel attached; the hotel has now gone and the *soda* has become a mid-range restaurant with a tico flavour, but the set lunches remain fairly cheap.

Rincón de España at Calle 5, Avenida Central & 2, facing the Gold Museum on the Plaza de la Cultura, offers lunch specials for about US$1.50, but later on in the day becomes a cheap beer bar with a predominantly male clientele. Another cheap possibility is the *Lido Bar* at Calle 2, Avenida 3, which is less of a bar and more a cheap lunch place, at least during the middle of the day. Ticos like to drink (in moderation) and see nothing surprising in eating in a bar.

Most restaurants will offer a *casado*, or cheap meal of the day, for lunch at a price well below eating à la carte. These fixed price meals can cost from just under US$1 in the very cheapest places to US$4 or US$5 in the fancier restaurants, where the meal may be called an *almuerzo ejecutivo*.

Cafés & Coffee Shops These are very popular among Costa Ricans, who seem to have a collective sweet tooth for pastries and cakes. They are often good places for travellers to catch up on journal or letter writing. Prices are not necessarily cheap, but you don't have to buy much and can sit for hours.

A favourite place is the pavement café of the *Gran Hotel Costa Rica* at Calle 3, Avenida 2, where you get a good view of the comings and goings in the Plaza de la

Cultura. Full meals are also served here. In the Plaza de la Cultura itself is the National Theatre, which has an elegant but simple little coffee shop and changing art shows on the walls. Both are well recommended.

I also like *Las Cuartetas* which is a tiny, inexpensive, local coffee shop on Calle 2, Avenida 3 & 5. If you don't have a sweet tooth, ask for one of their tiny but delicious meat or cheese puff pastries to go with your espresso.

There are a few chains worth noting. *Spoons* has three locations: Avenida Central, Calle 5 & 7 downtown; Avenida 2, Calle 45 in Los Yoses; and another in Pavas. They are known for a great selection of pastries and cakes, as well as light lunch items.

Manolo's at Avenida Central, Calle Central & 1, and Avenida Central, Calle 9 & 11, is less exciting but still OK for dessert fans. Ice-cream eaters should look for *Pops* and *Molnpik* for the best ice creams; each chain has several locations in San José and can be found outside the capital.

Chinese Chinese restaurants are found all over the Americas from Alaska to Argentina, and San José has its fair share. Most are good and medium priced; I couldn't find any very cheap ones. Two of the best downtown are the *Restaurante Tin-jo* (☎ 217605) which has Mandarin specialities and the *Restaurante Don Wang* (☎ 336484) which specialises in Taiwanese food. Both are on Calle 11, Avenida 6 & 8. Expect to pay about US$5 to US$8 for a meal.

A highly recommended Chinese restaurant in San Pedro is the *Nueva China* (☎ 244478) 100 metres east of the Banco Popular (most locals and all taxi drivers know it). They have a chef from Hong Kong and the food is authentic – Chinese white wine is available and a dim-sum (a Chinese breakfast buffet with a wide variety of delicious snacks) is served on weekend mornings. For dim-sum downtown, the restaurant in the *Hotel Royal Garden* (☎ 570023) Calle Central, Avenida Central has been recommended. Dim-sum is served

on Sunday mornings, and good Chinese food is available during the rest of the week.

Slightly cheaper Chinese restaurants which have been recommended include the *Restaurant Fulusu* (☎ 237568) Calle 7, Avenida Central & 2; the *Restaurante Kam Wah* (☎ 224714) Avenida 2, Calle 5 & 7; and *Restaurante Kuang Chaou* (☎ 228807) Avenida 2, Calle 9. There are many others.

Spanish My favourite Spanish restaurant is *La Masia de Triquell* (☎ 215073) Avenida 2, Calle 40. The restaurant is in an elegant mansion and the food and service is very good without being snooty. The owner, Señor Francisco Triquell, personally oversees the cooking and often is on hand to help guests choose their meal. The house speciality is Catalonian style cuisine. Meals are US$7 to US$10 for the main course – it is a recommended splurge.

Closer to downtown, there are a number of well-run and recommended Spanish restaurants. *Casino Español* (☎ 229440) Calle 7, Avenida's Central & 1, serves both Spanish and international dishes and has been recommended for its excellent service. Main courses are about US$6 or US$7. Slightly cheaper Spanish food is served at *Goya* (☎ 213887) Avenida 1, Calle 5 & 7, and there's the *Casa España* at Calle Central, Avenida 3 & 5, on the 6th floor of the Banco de San José.

Back in the expensive range (US$8 to US$12 for the main course) is the recommended *La Mallorquina* (☎ 237634) at Paseo Colón, Calle 28 & 30, which serves both Spanish and French food. This restaurant is closed on Sunday.

French There is a surprising number of French restaurants in San José, most of them very expensive (at least by Costa Rican standards), and all recommended by and for lovers of French cuisine. Downtown there's *L'Ile de France* (☎ 224241), Calle 7, Avenida Central & 2. Their daily lunch special is US$10. Cheaper is the *Salón París Bar & Restaurant* at Avenida 3, Calle 1 & 3.

Out along Paseo Colón is the *La Bastilla*

(☎ 554994), Paseo Colón, Calle 22, with excellent main courses starting around US$12. It is another place which is closed on Sunday. *Le Chandelier* (☎ 217947), Paseo Colón, Calle 30, is one of the best in San José, but a full meal will set you back about US$25. There is a cheaper café attached.

Heading east of downtown is the elegant and also expensive *La Petite Provence* (☎ 551559), Avenida Central, Calle 27. It too is closed on Sunday.

Italian One of San José's most popular restaurants is the *Balcón de Europa* (☎ 214841), Avenida Central, Calle 7 & 9. Some people claim it's the best Italian food in town – I found my pasta rather different from what I'm used to, but perhaps I went with the wrong expectations. Meals cost about US$5. Next door is the *Finisterre* which has pizza and cheaper food. There's a cheaper *Europa* around the corner on Calle 7, Avenida Central & 2, under the same management. (The next door *Hotel Presidente* is expanding and these restaurants will eventually move – the *Tico Times* carries advertisements for these restaurants, and so will have the new address when it comes.)

Out on Paseo Colón, you'll find the less expensive *Ana* at Calle 24 & 26, with meals around US$4 and the well recommended *Piccolo Roma* at Calle 24, where meals are about US$5 or US$6. The *La Fontana di Trevi* on Paseo Colón, Calle 28, in the Hotel Ambassador, has a recommended restaurant with Italian specialities from about US$5.

A recommended pizza restaurant is the *San Remo* at Calle 2, Avenida 3 & 5. They also serve other reasonably priced Italian food. There is also a *Pizza Hut* chain; two locations are Calle 4, Avenida Central & 2; and Paseo Colón, Calle 28.

Fast Food These American-style restaurants serve food which is similar in taste and price to what you get in the USA (US$2 to US$3 for a medium sized meal). They are popular among ticos, especially the younger ones.

McDonald's is at Calle 4, Avenida Central & 1, and on the north side of the Plaza de la Cultura at Avenida Central, Calle 3 & 5, and elsewhere. Also on the north side of the Plaza de la Cultura is *Archi's*, a Costa Rican version of American fast food serving both hamburgers and chicken.

Kentucky Fried Chicken (Pollo Kentucky) has two downtown locations: Avenida 2, Calle 6; and Avenida 3, Calle 1 & 3. For some reason, Pollo Kentucky at Paseo Colón, Calle 32 & 34, and in Los Yoses at Avenida Central, Calle 31, have both become local landmarks. Tell a cab driver that you want to go 125 metres north of the Pollo Kentucky on Paseo Colón and you'll be taken there directly and probably charged exactly the same as a local! (This is actually the address of the Machu Pichu restaurant, described further on.)

Other fast food restaurants include *Hardee's*, Calle 1, Avenida Central, for hamburgers; and *Don Taco*, Avenida 1, Calle 2, for instant burritos and tacos.

Steak & Seafood Some of these restaurants are for dedicated carnivores: side salads are usually available but otherwise the meals are very meaty. Many have a good selection of both meat and seafood dishes, whilst others tend to have seafood only.

For mainly meat, *La Hacienda* at Calle 7, Avenidas Central & 2, is quiet and unpretentious, and has good steaks for about US$7 or US$8. Other steak houses are away from the centre. *Los Ranchos* (☎ 327757) on the north side of the Sabana Park, behind the ICE building (most cab drivers know it) is less expensive and recommended. Nearby, and also recommended, is *El Chicote* (☎ 320936), 400 metres west of the ICE building, north of the Sabana Park near Calle 50. Steaks are US$6 or US$7, and some seafood dishes are also available. You can get to the north side of the Sabana Park on the Sabana Estadio bus which goes out along the Paseo Colón.

Out in Escazú, just off the main street, is the well known *El Churrasco Steak House* (289332), which is expensive but recommended. Nearby is *Los Anonos* for barbecued steak, which is also recommended but not as expensive.

Lancers Steak House (☎ 225938) is in the El Pueblo Shopping Centre, about 1½ km north of downtown. Steaks are about US$6 to US$8 and there is a good selection of seafood as well. Also in El Pueblo (which is recommended for a good variety of restaurants, bars and nightspots, as well as shops) is the *Rias Bajas* (☎ 217123) which serves excellent seafood, as well as meat dishes. It is closed on Sundays.

The *Kamakiri Steak House* is a recommended steak and seafood restaurant with two locations, both closed on Sunday. One is on Calle Central, two blocks north of Avenida 11, just across the river (☎ 336966), and the other is in the Centro Comercial Omni at Avenida 1, Calle 3 & 5 (☎ 336204).

A seafood restaurant with a good variety of meat dishes is *Lobster's Inn* (☎ 238954) at Paseo Colón, Calle 24. Main courses are about US$7 to US$10, but lobster is twice that much.

A restaurant specialising in seafood is the moderately priced *La Fuente de Mariscos* (☎ 310631), in the shopping centre next to the Hotel Irazú, a few km north-west of downtown. They have another location in San Pedro, at the Centro Comercial Plaza de Sol (☎ 341931).

Costa Rican As much as anything else, national specialities include steak and seafood, and most of the restaurants in the previous section could be thought of as Costa Rican. There isn't a very strong typical culinary tradition in Costa Rica, but one restaurant does serve what could be considered tico country cooking, and the food is very good. This is the *La Cocina de Leña* (☎ 233704) in the El Pueblo Shopping Centre. The restaurant's name literally means 'the wood stove' and the atmosphere is definitely country kitchen and homey. The tables are small and the menu is printed on a brown paper bag. Dishes include ox tails, corn soup, rice & beans, tamales, and, of course, steak. Meals are medium priced; about US$3 to US$6.

Also try *El Cuartel de la Boca del Monte*, Avenida 1, Calle 21 & 23, which is a coffee house cum restaurant cum art gallery cum bar with some Costa Rican dishes – casually elegant and moderately priced. Eat during the day – it's more of a bar at night. Another possibility is the *Restaurant Poás* (☎ 217802), Avenida 7, Calle 3 & 5, which has 'Rural Night' with Costa Rican country cooking on Wednesdays.

Other There is a host of other international restaurants with food from many countries. One of my favourites is the *Machu Pichu* (☎ 227384), Calle 32, Avenida 1 & 3, 125 metres north of the Pollo Kentucky. They serve authentic Peruvian cuisine, especially seafood, at moderate prices – about US$3 or US$4 gets you a decent meal. Nearby is the *Beirut* (☎ 571808) at Calle 32, Avenida 1, which serves good Middle Eastern food at slightly higher prices. It is closed on Sunday evening and Monday.

Antojitos, Paseo Colón, Calles 24 & 26, serves inexpensive to moderately priced Mexican food, and may have mariachis playing some evenings. *Arirang* (☎ 232838) at Paseo Colón, Calle 38 & 40, serves moderately priced Korean food; about US$4 buys a good meal.

Out in the Cariari Country Club area is the *Sakura* (☎ 390033) in the Hotel Sheraton Herradura. They serve excellent and authentic Japanese food – but it's not cheap. It is closed on Monday.

A recommended downtown restaurant is *Chalet Suizo* (☎ 223118), Avenida 1, Calle 5 & 7, which serves, as you may guess, Swiss dishes such as fondue and a variety of other European dishes. Their US$5 set lunch is very popular, and about US$7 buys you a meal à la carte.

Many of the better hotels have good restaurants. Two hotels in particular have reputations for excellent restaurants; these are the *Hotel Amstel* and the *Hotel Bougainvillea*. The *Hotel Diplomat* serves pretty fancy fixed lunches for moderate prices. See under Places to Stay for more information.

Entertainment

Bars & Discotheques *El Cuartel de la Boca del Monte*, Avenida 1, Calle 21 & 23, is a restaurant by day but at night is transformed into one of the capital's busiest and most popular nightspots for young people. The music is sometimes recorded and sometimes live, but always loud, and it's elbow room only on most nights in the back room where there is a small dance floor. In front it's rather less frenzied but still crowded. It's a good place to meet young ticos.

Many a visitor to San José checks out the well known *La Esmeralda*, Avenida 2, Calle 5 & 7. It's open all day and all night (except Sunday) and is the centre of the city's mariachi tradition. (Mariachis are bands of Mexican street musicians whose members dress elegantly in tight-fitting sequined suits and enormous sombreros.) You can get a meal (US$3 to US$6) any time, but the action begins at night when there are dozens of strolling musicians around.

A few blocks west are the bare fluorescent lights of *Soda Palace*, Avenida 2, Calle 2 – another 24 hour joint. The beers here come with free bocas, and the place is usually crowded with locals and a sprinkling of travellers. It is open to the street and people come to watch the street action, see who comes in, or eat a moderately priced meal (US$3 and up). Musicians wander in later on in the evening; one night about 10 pm some Black ticos wandered in and played a variety of tunes ranging from 'Don't worry, be happy' to Hendrix's 'Hey, Joe', with a good amount of reggae in between. One of their instruments was a bass made from a broom handle attached to a tin tub with a bass string. Practising mariachis, lone guitarists and street urchins wander in and out and it stays pretty lively.

Key Largo, Calle 7, Avenida 3, is a somewhat expensive bar housed in a beautiful mansion built in colonial style. It is busy, popular and fun, and has a casino, live music and dancing. It also has a slightly raffish atmosphere with attractively dressed ladies discreetly working at the world's oldest profession. (Women may prefer not to go there alone, although it's the sort of place where you could take your mother-in-law – I did).

The El Pueblo Shopping Centre has a good variety of restaurants and nightspots – most rather pricey. Wander around on Friday or Saturday night and take your pick; some spots are cheaper than others. The *Bar Tango Che Molinari* is an Argentine bar featuring live tango for a small cover charge. Nearby, *Bar Los Balcones* is a small bar with folk or acoustic musicians and no cover. Other bars feature jazz or reggae; others still are just quiet places to have a drink without any music. There is less selection of live music mid-week, but there's usually something going on. There are several discotheques which charge as much as US$4 to get in – but usually provide at least the first drink free. Three of the better known discos here are the *Cocoloco*, *Infinito* and *La Plaza*.

Discotheques downtown include *El Tunel de Tiempo*, Avenida Central, Calle 7 & 9, with flashing lights and disco music; and the *Dynasty* in the Centro Comercial del Sur, near the Puntarenas railway station, with soul, reggae, calypso, and even rap music. Both these have covers of about US$2. A cheaper place is the *Salsa 54*, Calle 3, Avenida 1 & 3, with Latin music. Slightly more expensive is the *La Torre*, Calle 7, Avenida Central & 1, with a mostly gay clientele and a variety of music.

The *Club Panda*, Paseo Colón, Calle 32 & 34, has disco popular with the younger set, shows surfing videos, and has no cover except when live bands are occasionally featured. In San Pedro, *Club Crocodrilo*, Calle Central opposite the Banco Anglo, is a large bar with dance floor and videos, popular with students from the nearby university. Both these last two serve good hamburgers for around US$3 – the Cocodrilo has a reputation for serving good ones.

If disco isn't your bar scene, there are several alternatives. *Charleston*, Calle 9, Avenida 2 & 4, has almost an English pub decor and plays jazz. Live performances at weekends cost US$2 to get in; at other times the recorded jazz is free.

An American-style bar which tends to be

frequented by Americans and other English-speaking foreigners is *Lucky's Piano Blanco Bar*, Avenida Central, Calle 7 & 9, which has videos of North American sports events and an occasional piano player. Others include *Nashville South*, Calle 5, Avenidas 1 & 3, which has country music; *Tiny's Tropical Bar*, Avenida 2, Calle 9, which was inhabited by middle-aged American tourists on fishing vacations last time I stopped by; and the *Park Hotel Bar*, Avenida 4, Calle 2 & 4.

The *Amstel Hotel Bar*, Calle 7, Avenida 1 & 3, is a quiet place if you're fed up with all the music in other bars. Out on Avenida 2, Calle 28 is *The Shakespeare Bar*, so called because it is next to a couple of small theatres and is the place to go before or after a show. They have a dart board.

An interesting Mexican bar with delicious bocas and great mariachi music is *Bar México*, Avenida 13, Calle 16, next to the Barrio México church. The bar itself is good, although the neighbourhood is a poor one; you may want to take a cab.

A seven-days-a-week, 24-hour downtown bar which has been there for decades and has become something of a local landmark is *Chelles* at Avenida Central, Calle 9. It serves simple medium-priced meals and snacks, and, of course, beer and other drinks, but its main attraction is that it's always open. You never know who may come wandering in to this harshly lit bar. Somewhat more intimate and just around the corner is *Chelle's Taberna*, Calle 9, Avenida Central & 2, which is newer but less bright. Across the street is *Besito's Bar* which is less expensive, has both Western and Costa Rican music on tape, and has several TV sets showing local sports action, especially soccer. There are many other bars in San José; this is just a selection to start with.

Most of the bars mentioned thus far charge about US$1.10 for a beer – US$2 is considered very expensive indeed for a beer in a bar. These bars are generally OK for women to visit. Cheaper beers, at US$0.50 to US$0.75, can be had in many bars in town, but the cheaper bars may not be suitable for women to enter alone. As you start heading west of Calle 5, towards the market area, you'll find frequent bars catering to workmen. Here you'll find cheap beer and bocas in a spit and sawdust, macho atmosphere. Cheaper bars will often advertise their beer prices on signs in the window.

Out along Calle 2 near Avenida 8 is a small red-light district with expensive strip joints.

Theatre Theatres advertise in the local newspapers, including the *Tico Times*. Although many performances are in Spanish, prices are so moderate that you'll probably enjoy yourself even if you don't understand Spanish all that well. A few performances are in English.

The most important theatre is the Teatro Nacional which stages plays, dance, opera, symphony, Latin American music, and has similar cultural events. The season is April to November when the National Symphony Orchestra plays two or three times a week, and there are other events on most days. Tickets start as low as US$1.50. Out of season the schedule is less busy, but expect a performance on average about once every week or two.

The restored 1920s Teatro Melico Salazar has a variety of performances but concentrates on dance. The Teatro La Máscara also has dance performances, as well as alternative theatre. The Teatro Carpa is known for alternative and outdoor theatre. The Teatro Laurence Olivier is a small theatre, coffee shop and gallery where anything from jazz to film to theatre may be performed. Nearby, the Teatro Sala Garbo offers international movies which tend towards the avant garde rather than box-office Hollywood. Teatro Chaplin is known for mime; Teatro del Angel for comedy; Teatro Vargas Calvo for theatre-in-the-round; and the Teatro Eugene O'Neill for performances sponsored by the North American-Costa Rican Cultural Center. There are many other theatres.

Most theatres are not very large, performances are popular, and ticket prices very reasonable. This adds up to sold-out performances, so get tickets as early as possible.

Theatres rarely have performances on Mondays.

The following are some of the most important theatres:

Teatro Bellas Artes
    University of Costa Rica, east side of campus, San Pedro
Teatro Carpa
    Avenida 1, Calle 29 & 33 (☎ 342866)
Teatro Chaplin
    Calle 9, Avenida 1 & 3 (☎ 226491)
Teatro Companía Nacional de Teatro
    Calle 13, Avenida 2 & 4 (☎ 215205)
Teatro de la Aduana
    Calle 25, Avenida 5 & 7 (☎ 234563)
Teatro del Angel
    Avenida Central, Calle 13 & 15 (☎ 228258)
Teatro Eugene O'Neill
    Calle Los Negritos, Barrio Escalante (☎ 250597)
Teatro Laurence Olivier
    Calle 28, Avenida 2 (☎ 231960)
Teatro La Máscara
    Calle 13, Avenida 2 & 6 (☎ 355940)
Teatro Melico Salazar
    Avenida 2, Calle Central & 2 (☎ 214952)
Teatro Nacional
    Avenida 2, Calle 3 & 5 (☎ 211329)
Teatro Sala de la Calle 15
    Avenida 2, Calle 13 & 15 (☎ 226622)
Teatro Sala Garbo
    Avenida 2, Calle 28
Teatro Tiempo
    Calle 13, Avenida Central & 2 (☎ 220792)
Teatro Vargas Calvo
    Avenida Central, Calle 5 & 7 (☎ 221875)

Cinemas Many cinemas show recent films from Hollywood with Spanish sub-titles, and the original English sound track. Occasionally, foreign films are dubbed over in Spanish ('hablado en Español') but this is unusual. Movies are inexpensive – about US$1.50 per performance. Cinemas advertise in the *Tico Times* and in other local newspapers. Some of the best cinemas are:

Bellavista
    Avenida Central, Calle 17 & 19 (☎ 210909)
California
    Calle 23, Avenida 1 (☎ 214738)
Capri 1 & 2
    Avenida Central, Calle 9 (☎ 230264)
Colón 1 & 2
    Paseo Colón, Calle 38 & 40 (☎ 214517)

Magaly
    Avenida Central, Calle 23 (☎ 219597)
Omni
    Calle 3, Avenida Central & 1 (☎ 217903)
Real
    Calle 11, Avenida 6 & 8 (☎ 235972)
Universal
    Paseo Colón, Calle 26 & 28 (☎ 215241)

Casinos & Nightclubs Apart from the casino at Key Largo, gamblers will find casinos in many of the larger and more expensive hotels. Blackjack is the most popular game, but there are others, as well as slot machines.

Many of the more expensive hotels have nightclub shows.

Sport The national sport is soccer. The Costa Rican national team is good, and qualified for the World Cup in 1990. International and national games are played in the Estadio Nacional in the Sabana Park. The soccer season is May to October.

The Sabana Park also has a variety of other sporting facilities. There are tennis courts, volleyball, basketball and baseball areas, jogging paths and an Olympic sized swimming pool, but it costs US$3 to swim there between 12 noon and 2 pm only. Many ticos prefer the excursion to the Ojo de Agua pool (near Alajuela, frequent buses) where swimming costs about US$0.50 for the whole day.

The Cariari Country Club has the only 18 hole golf course in the country. The Costa Rica Country Club in Escazú has a nine hole course. For working out, you can join a local gym for about US$20 a month or use the facilities in the best hotels if you happen to be staying in one. Gyms are listed under Gimnasios in the telephone directory.

Things to Buy

This section deals with stores in San José. If you have the time and the inclination you can often save some money by shopping in the suburb of Moravia, about eight km northeast of downtown, or by taking a day trip to the village of Sarchí, where many of Costa Rica's handicraft items are produced.

A highly recommended souvenir shop is

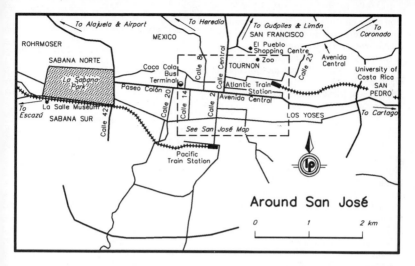

Around San José

0   1   2 km

in the Hotel Don Carlos, Calle 9, Avenida 9. This is not the usual hotel gift store with a limited selection of overpriced gift items for guests with little time to shop around; the public are welcome and both the prices and selection are very good.

Other reasonably priced stores with good selections include the government organised crafts cooperatives such as CANAPI, Calle 11, Avenida 1; and Mercado Nacional de Artesanía, Calle 11, Avenida 2 & 4. Also reasonably priced are Arte Rica, Avenida 2, Calle Central & 2, specialising in folk art; and ANDA, Avenida Central, Calle 5 & 7, specialising in pottery and gourd crafts produced by the few local Indians.

La Casona, Calle Central, Avenida Central & 1, is a complex with a wide selection of items including imports from other Central American countries. Malety, Avenida 1, Calle 1 & 3, specialises in leather goods, especially cases, handbags and wallets.

Some galleries carry top quality work which is excellent but expensive. If you are looking for top quality and are prepared to pay for it, try Suraksa, Calle 5, Avenida 3; Atmosfera, Calle 5, Avenida 1 & 3; Magia, Calle 5, Avenida 1 & 3; or La Galería, Calle

Central, Avenida Central & 1. These stores often have woodwork by North Americans Barry Biesanz and Jay Morrison, two of the best artisans. Their workshops are open to the public. If you want to see more of their work, call Biesanz in Escazú (☎ 281811) or Morrison in Santa Ana (☎ 286697) to arrange a viewing.

The Mercado Central, Avenida Central & 1, Calle 6 & 8, has only a small selection of handicrafts but is the best place to buy fresh coffee beans at a fraction of the price you'll pay at home. If you can't make it to the central market, buy the beans at any supermarket, although they are not as cheap. Also in supermarkets and liquor stores, look for Café Rica, the local liquor which looks and tastes rather like the better known Kahlua.

Getting There & Away

San José is not only the capital and the geographical heart of Costa Rica, it is also the hub of all transport around the country.

Unfortunately, the transport system is rather bewildering to the first time visitor. Most people get around by bus, but there is no central bus terminal. Instead, there are dozens of bus stops and terminals scattered around the city all serving different destinations. There are two railway stations (unconnected) and two airports.

Fortunately, the tourist office does pretty well in keeping up with what goes where and when, so check with them if you get stuck. The inherent friendliness of the Costa Rican people also goes a long way to easing transport difficulties – if you need directions or advice, ask for it.

Air SANSA flies between San José and Golfito (one or two flights daily except Sunday, US$15), Quepos (two flights daily except Sunday, US$8.50), Nosara (Monday, Wednesday, Friday, US$18), Palmar (Monday, Wednesday, Friday, US$12.50), Coto 47 (daily except Sunday, US$15), Tamarindo and Sámara (Monday, Wednesday, Friday, US$18) and Barra Colorado (Tuesday, Thursday, Saturday, US$12). Return flights are later on the same day.

SANSA will check you in at their office downtown and provide transportation to the airport's domestic terminal, which is a few hundred metres to the right of the international terminal. If you have a reservation with SANSA, you must pay the fare in full before it can be confirmed. You should also reconfirm in advance, preferably several times. SANSA is notorious for delayed, cancelled or overbooked flights.

International Airline Offices International carriers which serve Costa Rica or have offices in San José are listed here, with their country of origin in parentheses (where it isn't obvious). Airlines serving Costa Rica directly are marked with an asterisk and also have a desk at the airport:

Aerolíneas Argentinas
    Calle 1, Avenida Central & 1 (☎ 221332)
Aeronica* (Nicaragua)
    Avenida 1, Calle 1 & 3 (☎ 332483)
AeroPeru
    Calle 1, Avenida 5 (☎ 237033)
Air France
    Avenida 1, Calle 4 & 6 (☎ 228811)

Air Panama
    (see COPA)
Alitalia (Italy)
    Calle 1, Avenida Central & 2 (☎ 226009, 226138)
American Airlines* (USA)
    (see Eastern)
Avianca (Colombia)
    (see SAM)
British Airways
    Calle 1, Avenida 5 (☎ 235648)
COPA* (Panama)
    Calle 1, Avenida 5 (☎ 237033)
Eastern* (USA)
    Paseo Colón, Calle 26 & 28 (☎ 225655)
Iberia* (Spain)
    Paseo Colón, Calle 40 (☎ 213311)
KLM* (Holland)
    Calle 1, Avenida Central & 1 (☎ 210922)
Korean Air
    Calle 1, Avenida Central & 1 (☎ 221332)
Lacsa* (Costa Rica)
    Calle 1, Avenida 5 (☎ 310033, 217315)
Mexicana*
    Calle 1, Avenida 2 & 4 (☎ 221711)
Pan Am* (USA)
    Avenida 7, Calle 5 & 7 (218955)
SAHSA* (Honduras)
    Avenida 5, Calle 1 & 3 (☎ 215774)
SAM* (Colombia)
    Avenida 5, Calle 1 & 3 (☎ 333066)
Singapore Airlines
    Avenida 1, Calle 3 & 5 (☎ 553555)
TACA* (El Salvador)
    Calle 1, Avenida 1 & 3 (☎ 221790)
TWA (USA)
    Calle 1, Avenida Central & 1 (☎ 221332)
Varig (Brazil)
    Avenida 5, Calle 3 & 5 (☎ 213087)

Domestic Airline Offices Costa Rica's domestic airline is SANSA. There are also several air taxi companies which provide reasonably priced charters with small (three to nine passenger) aircraft to many airstrips in Costa Rica:

Aviones Taxi Aéreo SA
    Juan Santamaría Airport (☎ 411626)
Saeta
    Tobías Bolaños Airport (☎ 321474)
SANSA
    Calle 24, Paseo Colón & Avenida 1 (☎ 219414)
Taxi Aéreo Centroamericano SA
    Tobías Bolaños Airport (☎ 321317)
Viajes Especial Aéreos
    Tobías Bolaños Airport (☎ 321010)

Top: San José from Jade Museum (RR)
Left: Resplendent quetzal (RL)
Right: Long-tailed manakin (RL)

Top: Gaily painted ox cart wheel, Sarchí (RR)
Bottom: Bull fight, Northern Costa Rica (bulls are never killed) (RR)

Bus Read the general information in the Getting Around chapter about Costa Rican bus travel before you begin taking buses around the country. This section lists the addresses and, where appropriate, phone numbers of the long distance bus companies. Some of them have no more than a bus stop; others have a terminal.

Try to avoid leaving San José on Friday nights and Saturday mornings when the buses are full of josefinos off for the weekend. If you must travel then, book ahead if you can. Buses during Christmas and Easter are very crowded indeed.

The closest San José comes to having a general bus terminal is the Coca Cola terminal, so called after a Coca Cola bottling plant which used to exist on the site many years ago. The Coca Cola terminal is between Calle 16 & 18, north of Avenida 1, and is one of the best known landmarks in San José.

Several companies serve a number of different towns from the Coca Cola terminal. There are a few small signs in the terminal and it seems a little bewildering at first, but just ask someone to show you where your bus is; everyone seems to know where each bus leaves from. Several other companies have buses leaving from within three or four blocks of the Coca Cola terminal, so this is an area to know. It is not in the best part of town, so watch for pickpockets. The area is generally safe, although late at night you might think about taking a taxi rather than walking, particularly if you are a single woman.

To/From Nicaragua & Panama There are two international bus companies with regular services to Managua (Nicaragua) and Panama City. See the Getting There chapter for details of services and what to expect. TICA bus (☎ 218954), Calle 9, Avenida 2 & 4, has buses to Managua on Monday, Wednesday and Friday at 7 am, returning from Managua at 7 am on Tuesday, Thursday and Saturday. The trip takes 11 hours and costs US$8 from San José.

Cheaper but less reliable service to Managua is provided by Sirca (☎ 225541),

Avenida 2, Calle 11. They have buses on Wednesday, Friday and Sunday at 5 am (12 hours, US$6.50). The return trips from Managua leave at 6.30 am on Monday, Wednesday and Friday. Note that fares from Managua (or Panama City) are rarely the same as from San José because of differences in currency regulations.

TICA bus has a daily service to Panama City at 8 pm (20 hours, US$18). This company will also sell you a ticket to David, the first major town in Panama. Another company with buses to David is TRACOPA (☎ 214214), Avenida 18, Calle 4. There are daily directo buses at 7.30 am (nine hours, US$7.50).

To/From Southern Costa Rica TRACOPA also has five daily buses to Ciudad Neily and on to the Panamanian border at Paso Canoas. It is about seven hours to Neily, eight hours to the border. Fares are US$4.75 to Neily directo, or US$4.50 normal. TRACOPA also has two daily buses to Golfito (eight hours, US$4), and a bus to San Vito (five hours directo, US$5; six hours normal, US$3.50).

Buses to Coto Brus, en route to San Vito, also leave four times a day from Empresa Alfaro (☎ 222750), Avenida 5, Calle 14 & 16. Buses to San Isidro de El General are with Transportes Musoc (☎ 230686), under the Hotel Musoc, Calle 16, Avenida 1 & 3, next to the Coca Cola terminal. Fares are US$2.60 for the three hour trip, with eight daily departures.

To/From Meseta Central Buses to Cartago leave several times an hour from the station at Calle 13, Avenida Central & 2, opposite the National Museum. The trip takes almost an hour, depending on traffic, and costs about US$0.40. Some of these buses continue to Turrialba, but more Turrialba buses leave from the station at Avenida 6, Calle 13. The two hour ride costs just under a dollar.

Buses to Heredia leave several times an hour from Calle 1, Avenida 7 & 9; the half hour trip costs about US$0.30.

Buses for Alajuela leave every few minutes from the terminal at Avenida 2,

Calle 12. Most of these buses stop at the international airport. Some buses for Heredia also leave from across the street from here. Note that all of these terminals are closed from about 11 pm to 5 am.

Buses to Grecia (one hour, US$0.40), and on seven km to Sarchí (US$0.50), leave about once an hour from the Coca Cola terminal.

Buses for San Ramón, half way to Puntarenas, leave several times an hour from Calle 16, Avenida 1 & 3, across the street from the Hotel Musoc.

To/From the Pacific Coast Buses for Quepos and Manuel Antonio also leave from the Coca Cola terminal with Transportes Quepos (☎ 235567). Direct buses to Manuel Antonio, with reserved seats, leave at 6 am, 12 noon and 6 pm, and cost US$4.50 for the 3½ hour trip. Slower buses to Quepos leave four times a day and cost US$2.75.

Buses for Puntarenas leave every hour during the day from Calle 12, Avenida 9, with Autobuses del Pacífico (☎ 612158). The two hour trip costs about US$1.50.

To/From the Nicoya Peninsula Buses for the Nicoya Peninsula (and its popular beaches) have to negotiate the Gulf of Nicoya, a formidable body of water. The car ferry from Puntarenas does not normally take buses. Buses either cross the Río Tempisque on the ferry which leaves about every hour, or take the longer route around through Liberia. Thus bus times can vary considerably depending on the route chosen and, if using the ferry, whether you have to spend a long time waiting for it.

Empresa Alfaro (☎ 222750), Avenida 5, Calle 14 & 16, has six daily buses to Nicoya (five hours, US$3), also going to Santa Cruz and Filadelfia. More interestingly, they also have daily buses leaving around the middle of the day for beaches at Sámara and Tamarindo, as well as a bus to Quebrada Honda, Mansión and Hojancha.

From Calle 12, Avenida 7 & 9 (opposite the Puntarenas terminal) is a small office with afternoon buses to Jicaral and the beaches at Bejuco and Islita (five hours, US$5.50).

TRALAPA (☎ 217202), Calle 20, Avenida 3, has daily buses to Flamingo Beach, Junquillal as well as Tamarindo and Nicoya.

The Pulmitan bus station (☎ 221650) at Calle 14, Avenida 1 & 3, has a daily bus to Playa del Coco at 10 am (US$2.75).

These schedules are for the dry season when people go to the beach – during the wet season beach services may be curtailed. Beach resorts are very popular among Costa Ricans and buses tend to be booked up ahead of time. Reserve a seat if possible.

To/From North-West Costa Rica There is no bus terminal for Monteverde, which reflects how isolated this community remains despite the enormous increase in popularity it has experienced in the past decade. Buses to Monteverde currently leave from Calle 12, Avenida 5 & 7, on the east side of the street. (In the past, buses to Monteverde have also left from the northeastern corner of Avenida 9 and Calle 12.) There is no sign, you just have to look for people waiting for a bus and ask them. Although this seems unnervingly casual, a schedule is kept – this is definitely one to check at the tourist office first. The bus company can give you their schedule (☎ 612659). Currently, buses leave at 6.30 am on weekends and 2.30 pm on weekdays for the four hour trip which costs about US$3.50. It is worth getting in line at least half an hour early.

Buses for Cañas leave six times a day from Calle 16, Avenida 1 & 3, opposite the Coca Cola terminal. Cañas buses also leave from TRALAPA (☎ 217202), Calle 20, Avenida 3.

Buses for Liberia (4½ hours, US$2.50) leave eight times a day from Pulmitan (☎ 221650) Calle 14, Avenida 1 & 3.

Buses to the Nicaraguan border at Peñas Blancas, with stops at the entrance to Santa Rosa National Park and La Cruz, leave from CNT (☎ 551932) Calle 16, Avenida 3 & 5. There are three buses daily, and the cost is about US$3 for the five hour trip to the border. CNT also has buses to Upala, a small and remote town in the northern lowlands near the Nicaraguan border.

Buses for Tilarán via Cañas leave three times a day in the afternoon with Autotransportes Tilarán, (☎ 223854), Calle 12, Avenida 9 & 11. The fare is US$2.40 for the 3½ hour ride.

To/From Northern Costa Rica Buses to Ciudad Quesada (two hours, US$1.50) via Zarcero (one hour) leave at least every hour from the Coca Cola terminal. A few buses are express to Ciudad Quesada. (Note that Ciudad Quesada is also known as San Carlos.) From Ciudad Quesada you can take buses west to La Fortuna, the Arenal Volcano, and on to Tilarán, or east towards Puerto Viejo de Sarapiquí and Río Frío).

Direct buses to Puerto Viejo de Sarapiquí (as opposed to Puerto Viejo de Talamanca on the south-eastern Caribbean coast) leave from in front of the Puntarenas bus terminal on Calle 12, Avenida 7 & 9. There are eight buses a day but there is no ticket office; ask locals where the bus stop is. Most of these buses go via Río Frío and Horquetas (for Rara Avis) and return to San José via Varablanca and Heredia; a few do the route in reverse. If going to Puerto Viejo, it makes little difference which way you go, as either way is about US$2.25 and 3½ hours. If going to Horquetas, make sure you go via the Río Frío route or you will get stuck on the bus for 4½ hours instead of 2½. There are also a couple of buses for Puerto Viejo via Heredia leaving at 6 am and 12 noon from the Coca Cola terminal.

To/From the Caribbean Coast In front of the Puntarenas station, near the Puerto Viejo bus stop on Calle 12, Avenida 7 & 9, there is a stop with frequent departures to Guápiles with a few buses continuing to Río Frío. For buses to Siquirres, go to the stop on Calle 12, Avenida 3 & 5, on the east side. There are 10 departures a day and the fare is US$1.50.

Buses for Puerto Limón leave from near the Atlantic train station, at the other end of downtown. The bus stop is on Avenida 3, Calle 19 & 21, with at least hourly departures via Guápiles. It takes 2½ hours and costs US$2 to Limón.

For buses direct to Cahuita, Bribri and Sixaola, Autotransportes MEPE (☎ 210524), Avenida 11, Calle Central & 1, has four departures a day. The fare is US$4.75 to Sixaola (on the Panamanian border) and US$3.75 to Cahuita (four hours). Some MEPE buses will detour to Puerto Viejo de Talamanca en route to Sixaola.

Train The national railroad company, INCOFER (☎ 260011), operates two lines from San José. One provides daily train service to Puntarenas on the Pacific coast and the other provides daily service to Puerto Limón on the Caribbean coast. Both journeys are cheaper and longer than their bus counterparts, but many travellers enjoy taking them simply to enjoy the relaxed pace and scenery. See the Getting Around chapter for full details of these trips and what to expect on Costa Rican trains.

The station for the Puerto Limón train is known as the Atlantic train station and is on Avenida 3, Calles 21 and 23. They have a daily departure for the Caribbean coast at either 9 or 10 am (this changes from year to year – so check with the tourist office or INCOFER). The ride costs less than two dollars and takes about eight hours.

The Pacific electric train station is at Avenida 20, Calle 2. This station serves Puntarenas, about 120 km away, and the journey takes about four hours. Trains leave at 6 am and 3 pm, but check with the station or tourist office for the latest schedule changes. The one way fare is US$1.10. Sit on the left hand side as you go down from San José for the best views.

Getting Around

Downtown San José is very busy and relatively small. I always avoid taking local buses around downtown, finding it easier to walk. The narrow streets, heavy traffic and complicated one-way system often mean that it is quicker to walk than to take the bus. The same applies to driving; if you rent a car, don't drive in downtown – it's a nightmare! If you are in a hurry to get somewhere that is more than a km away, I suggest you hire a taxi.

To/From the Airport There is no airport bus as such but all buses to Alajuela will stop outside the international airport. Alajuela buses leave from Avenida 2, Calle 12 every few minutes and cost about US$0.30, irrespective of whether you go to the airport or Alajuela.

Heading into San José from the airport, you'll find the bus stop outside the international terminal, behind the car rental agencies. During the rush hour, the Alajuela to San José bus may be full when it comes by and you may have to wait for some time. This bus will also drop you off in front of the Cariari Country Club.

There are no buses direct to the local airport at Tobías Bolaños. The nearest bus goes to Pavas from Avenida 1, Calle 16 & 18. From Pavas you could take a taxi or walk.

Airport taxis are orange, and the fare to or from the airport is about US$10.

Bus Local buses are very useful to get you out into the suburbs and surrounding villages, or to the airport. They have set routes and leave regularly from particular bus stops downtown. Buses run from about 5 am to 10 pm and cost from US$0.05 to US$0.30. Buses to Moravia leave from Avenida 3, Calle 3. Buses for Escazú leave from Avenida 6, Calle 12 & 14. Buses for Santa Ana leave from the Coca Cola terminal. Buses from the Sabana Park head into town on Paseo Colón, then go over to Avenida 2 at the San Juan de Dios hospital. They go as far as the Parque Central and then head back to the Sabana Park along Avenida 1 or 3, and then get back on Paseo Colón for the return. Buses are marked Sabana-Cementario or Sabana-Estadio. Buses east for Los Yoses and San Pedro go back and forth along Avenida 2, going over to Avenida Central at Calle 29 outbound.

If you need buses to other suburbs, enquire at the tourist office.

Taxi San José taxis are red, with the exception of airport cabs which are orange. Downtown, meters are supposed to be used but in fact are used less than half the time. Some drivers will prefer you to get out of their cab if you insist on using the meter; others simply don't have one or it doesn't work. Therefore bargaining is a useful skill when riding taxis. Even if you hate bargaining, always ask the fare before you get in to avoid being heavily overcharged at your destination.

I found that most cab drivers will charge foreigners a little more, but not outrageously so. A few will try and gouge you and a few will charge you tico prices straight away.

Techniques for getting the best rates include speaking Spanish, using local landmark addresses rather than street addresses, leaving and arriving from a street intersection rather than an expensive hotel on the same block, and telling the driver his price is too high if it appears that way to you. Short rides downtown should be under US$1; longer rides less than US$2. San José cab drivers are the toughest in Costa Rica; on the other hand they are a lot more friendly than cab drivers in many other countries.

You can hire a taxi and driver for half a day or longer if you want to do some touring around the Meseta Central. Around US$30 to US$40 is reasonable for half a day, depending on how far you want to go. Cabs will take three or four passengers. To hire a cab, either ask your hotel to help arrange it or call one of the numbers listed below. Alternatively, talk to drivers at any cab rank. There are cab stands at the Parque Nacional, Parque Central, near the National Theatre, and in front of several of the better hotels. Taxi drivers are not normally tipped in Costa Rica.

You can have a taxi pick you up if you are going to the airport or have a lot of luggage. The following companies have pick-up services:

Alfaro (☎ 218466)
Co-opeguaria (☎ 231366)
Co-opeirazu (☎ 271211)

Co-opetaxi (☎ 359966)
Co-opetico (☎ 212552)
San Jorge (☎ 213434)
Unidos (☎ 216865)

If you want to get out into some wild country, you could hire a 4WD jeep and driver. Roy Sternberger (☎ 796606) advertises his jeep for hire at US$75 per day plus fuel, driver's meals and overnight expenses. The jeep takes up to six people.

Car Rental There are plenty of car rental agencies if you want to drive yourself, but they are quite expensive, at least by North American standards. I hired a car for part of the time whilst researching this book and had no problems – in fact, I had fun. You should read the section on Road Safety in the Getting Around chapter before venturing onto the roads.

The following agencies have offices at the airport: Ada-Ancla, Avis, Hertz, Santos and Toyota. Others either plan on opening an office or will provide you with a car at the airport if you reserve one. Most companies will let you drop off your car at the airport. You must arrange a time in advance for their representative to be there.

Car rental rates vary about 10% between companies, so shop around. The following agencies are found in San José:

Ada-Ancla
     Avenida 18, Calle 11 & 13 (☎ 337733)
Amigo
     Calle 3, Avenida 13 (☎ 554141)

Avis
     One block east of Datsun, Sabana Norte
     (☎ 329922)
Budget
     Paseo Colón, Calle 30 (☎ 233284)
Dollar
     Avenida 7, Calle Central & 2 (☎ 333339)
Economy
     Sabana Norte (☎ 315410, 329130)
Elegante
     Paseo Colón, Calle 34 (☎ 338605)
El Indio
     Paseo Colón, Calle 40 & 42 (☎ 332157)
Fantasy
     Hotel Irazú (☎ 324811)
Global
     Avenida 7, Calle 7 & 9 (☎ 234056)
Happy
     Avenida 1, Calle 1 & 3 (☎ 333435)
Hertz
     Calle 38, Paseo Colón & Avenida 1 (☎ 235959, 211818)
National
     Calle 36, Avenida 3 & 5 (☎ 334006, 334044)
Nickel
     Calle 24, Paseo Colón (☎ 216964)
Pilot
     Calle 30, Paseo Colón & Avenida 1 (☎ 228724)
Poas
     Paseo Colón, Calle 26 & 28 (☎ 234259)
Rent-a-Auto
     Avenida Central, Calle 7 & 9 (☎ 217166)
Santos
     Avenida 3, Calle 26 & 28 (☎ 217793)
Tico
     Calle 10, Avenida 13 & 15 (☎ 228920)
Toyota
     Paseo Colón, Calle 30 & 32 (☎ 232250)
Tropical
     Avenida Central, Dent Blvd (☎ 342111)

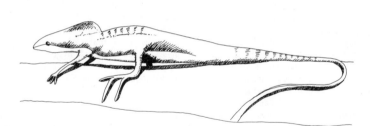

The Central Valley & Highlands

The Central Valley is the popular name for the region around San José in the centre of Costa Rica. It is not really a valley and a more appropriate name would be the 'central plateau' or 'central tableland'. This is, in fact, the translation of the Costa Rican name for the area, La Meseta Central.

This region is both historically and geographically the heart of Costa Rica. To the north and east, the Central Valley is bounded by the mountain range known as the Cordillera Central, which contains several volcanoes including the famous Poás and Irazú. To the south the region is bounded by the north end of the Cordillera de Talamanca and a short mountainous projection called the Fila de Bustamente. Between the Cordilleras Central and Talamanca is the beautiful Reventazón River valley, which gives San José its historical access to the Caribbean. To the west, the plateau falls off into the Pacific lowlands.

This chapter covers the Central Valley (except San José) and, additionally, the upper Reventazón River valley and the volcanoes of the Cordillera Central. Although not geographically part of the Central Valley, these surrounding highlands are most often visited on day trips out of San José.

About 60% of Costa Rica's population lives in the Central Valley. The region's fertile volcanic soil and pleasant climate attracted the first successful Spanish settlers. Before the arrival of the Spaniards, the region was an important agricultural zone inhabited by thousands of Indian farmers, most of whom were wiped out by diseases brought by the Europeans. The first capital city was at Cartago.

Today, four of Costa Rica's seven provinces have fingers of land within the Central Valley, and all four have their political capitals there. Thus we see an unusual situation where there are three provincial capitals within a scant 25 km of San José, which in itself is the capital of San José province. The

others are the cities of Cartago, Alajuela and Heredia, all capitals of provinces of the same name.

Despite their provincial capital status, the cities of the Central Valley do not have a well-developed hotel infrastructure. Most visitors use San José as a base for day trips to the other cities, as well as many of the other attractions of the Central Valley region. As visitors travel throughout the area, they pass through attractive rolling agricultural countryside full of the green shiny-leaved plants bearing the berries that made Costa Rica famous – coffee. There are also many *viveros*, or plant nurseries.

On the way to Poás Volcano, the traveller can see huge areas of hillsides covered with what appears to be a black plastic sheet, rather like a modern environmental sculpture. These are, in fact, the nurseries. Closer inspection reveals that the black plastic is a protective mesh under which a variety of plants are grown for sale to greenhouses.

This chapter is arranged in a roughly west to east sequence around San José.

ALAJUELA

The provincial capital of Alajuela lies about

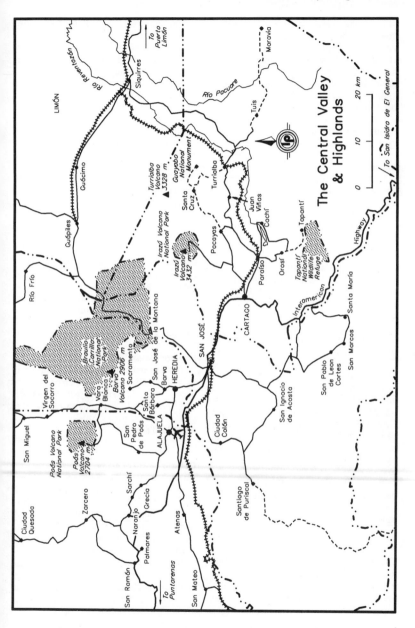

The Central Valley & Highlands

18 km to the north-west of San José as the crow flies. The city is on a gently sloping hill with an altitude of 920 metres on the south-western side of town, rising to 970 metres on the north-eastern side. As such, it is about 200 metres lower than San José and has a slightly warmer climate, thus attracting joséfinos on summer outings.

The city and its immediate suburbs have a population of around 43,000. The Juan Santamaría International Airport, which serves San José, is only 2½ km south-east of Alajuela.

There are three cinemas, all along Avenida Central. Otherwise, there is not entertainment, but the Parque Central is a pleasant place to relax in. Several nearby villages are worth visiting, however, and these are described at the end of the Alajuela section.

Juan Santamaría Museum

Alajuela's main claim to fame is as the birthplace of the national hero, Juan Santamaría, after whom the nearby international airport was named.

Santamaría was a drummer boy who volunteered to torch the building defended by filibuster William Walker in the war of 1856. He is now commemorated by a museum and a park in Alajuela.

The small museum is in what used to be a jail on Calle 2, Avenida 1, at the north-west corner of the pleasant and shady Parque Central. The museum, which contains maps, paintings and historical artefacts related to the war with Walker, is open daily, except Monday, from 10 am to 5 pm; admission is free.

Two blocks south of the Parque Central is the Parque Juan Santamaría where there is a statue of the hero in action, flanked by cannons.

Places to Stay

There are three hotels in Alajuela. The *Hotel Rex* and *Hotel El Real* are both by the bus terminal. They are cheap but not well recommended – 'much street life' as a local euphemistically told me. They would do at a pinch, however. Expect to pay about US$2.50 per person.

The one good hotel in town is the *Hotel Alajuela* (☎ 411241), on Calle 2 just south of the main plaza. Many of the rooms have little kitchenettes attached and the hotel is friendly, clean and well run. Unfortunately, there are only about 30 rooms and it is often full. The rates are US$11.50/16.50 single/double with bath. There are some newer rooms which are about US$4 more expensive. Write to Apartado 110, Alajuela, Costa Rica.

As Alajuela is so close to the airport, people sometimes stay here before or after a flight.

Places to Eat

For reasonably priced food, try the *Kun Wa* Chinese restaurant on Calle 1, south of Avenida Central. There are other cheap restaurants nearby.

Somewhat more expensive, but still reasonable, is the *Bar Restaurant La Jarra* which is upstairs at the corner of Calle 2, Avenida 2. Some of the tables are out on little balconies with views of the Juan Santamaría Park and statue. The ambience is pleasant.

The best and most expensive restaurant in town is up above the Cine Milan on the main plaza. This is *El Cencerro* which translates into 'the cowbell' and so its speciality is, as you can guess, steaks, although they serve other food as well.

Getting There & Away

Buses for Alajuela leave San José from Avenida 2 and Calle 12 several times an hour between 5 am and 10 pm. The return buses from Alajuela leave from the stop at Calle 8, Avenida Central & 1. Behind the bus stop for San José is the Alajuela bus terminal, from where buses to other towns leave.

To get to the airport, either take a San José bus and get off at the airport, or take a taxi. Taxis are available from the Parque Central at any hour of the day or night. The fare is about US$2.

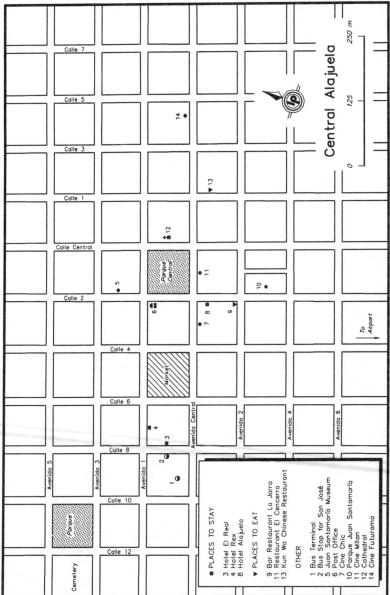

Central Alajuela

PLACES TO STAY
■ 3 Hotel El Real
4 Hotel Rex
8 Hotel Alajuela

PLACES TO EAT
▼ 9 Bar Restaurant La Jarra
11 Restaurant El Cencerro
13 Kun Wa Chinese Restaurant

OTHER
1 Bus Terminal
2 Bus Stop for San José
5 Juan Santamaría Museum
6 Post Office
7 Cine Chic
10 Parque Juan Santamaría
11 Cine Milan
12 Cathedral
14 Cine Futurama

AROUND ALAJUELA
Ojo de Agua
About six km south of Alajuela are the famous Ojo de Agua springs which are a favourite resort for people from both San José and Alajuela. The spring gushes thousands of litres each minute and the water fills swimming pools and an artificial boating lake before being piped down to Puntarenas, for which it is a major water supply. The recreational complex is very crowded with picnicking locals at weekends but is quieter midweek. Entrance to the complex is US$0.50 and there are places to eat.

Getting There & Away Buses leave from the terminal in Alajuela. Buses also leave every hour (more frequently at weekends) from Avenida 1, Calle 18 & 20 in San José.

West to Atenas
West of Alajuela is a road which leads to Atenas, a small village about 25 km away. En route to Atenas you pass Zoo-Ave and La Garita.

Zoo-Ave is about 10 km west of Alajuela and consists of a collection of tropical birds from all over the world, including many Costa Rican specialities displayed in a pleasant park-like setting. The zoo is open daily, except Monday, from 8 am to 3 pm and admission is US$0.50.

A few km beyond Zoo-Ave is **La Garita** where there is a children's amusement park called Bosque Encantado. Also in La Garita is an unusual restaurant which serves every dish you could imagine – as long as it is made from corn (maize). The restaurant is called *La Fiesta del Maíz* and is open from Thursday to Sunday.

The excursion to Ojo de Agua, Zoo-Ave, Bosque Encantado, and finishing at La Fiesta del Maíz is a popular weekend outing by car from San José, but the roads are poorly signed so it would be good to go with a tico friend.

The area is famous for its viveros, or nurseries (plants, not babies!), where local flora is grown and sold for use within Costa Rica.

Getting There & Away Buses go to Atenas from the Coca Cola terminal in San José, but they do not pass Zoo-Ave. To get to Zoo-Ave and La Garita take one of the buses from Alajuela's bus terminal.

North-West to Zarcero
North-west of Alajuela are the villages of Grecia (22 km), Sarchí (29 km), Naranjo (35 km) and Zarcero (52 km). All of these small towns can be reached by buses either from the Coca Cola terminal San José or the bus terminal in Alajuela. They all have colourful churches, typical of the Costa Rican countryside.

Grecia Grecia is an agricultural centre (pineapples, sugarcane) and is known for its red church, something of a local landmark, but otherwise its main importance for the traveller is as a place to change buses to continue to Sarchí (although there are also direct buses there from the Coca Cola terminal in San José).

Sarchí Sarchí is Costa Rica's most famous craft centre, and tour buses and locals stop here to buy crafts, particularly woodwork. It is, of course, commercial but in a charmingly understated Costa Rican way. There is no pressure to buy anything and there is the opportunity to see crafts being made.

A few decades ago, the common form of transport in the countryside was the carreta, gaily painted wooden carts drawn by oxen. Although carretas are rarely seen in use today (I saw two being used in Costa Rica's back-country during my most recent trip) they have become something of a traditional craft form and, as much as anything else, a symbol of agricultural Costa Rica. They are used nowadays to decorate people's gardens; scaled down versions are made for use as indoor tables, sideboards and bars, and miniature models are available for use as indoor sculptures or accent pieces. All sizes come apart and fold down for transport. You can see them being made in several *fábricas de carretas* (cart factories) where the most interesting part of the process is watching local artisans paint the colourful mandala designs onto the carts.

The bright paintwork is also used to decorate wooden trays, plates and other souvenirs. Unpainted woodwork such as salad bowls, kitchen boards, serving dishes, jewellery boxes, letter openers, statuettes and a variety of other utilitarian knick-knacks are also sold. These make inexpensive gifts and souvenirs and prices are as little as half of what you'd pay in San José.

There are also furniture factories in Sarchí. Whilst the elegantly carved headboards and bedsteads, tables and chairs, and sitting room furniture is mainly designed for local sale and use, some travellers buy one or two of the leather and wood rocking chairs which come apart and fold down for transport.

Whatever you do, leave Sarchí to the end of your trip so as not to be encumbered by a bunch of presents whilst you are travelling around the country. And shop around – there are plenty of factories and stores to choose from in Sarchí.

There is no overnight accommodation available in Sarchí, but there are a couple of decent restaurants.

San Ramón From Sarchí, the road continues west to Naranjo where the road divides. You can continue 13 km further west to San Ramón, a pleasant small town about half way between San José and Puntarenas, just of the new main highway joining the capital with the Pacific coast. The town has a couple of inexpensive hotels and restaurants.

Zarcero North of Naranjo, the road climbs for 17 km to Zarcero, a town at over 1700 metres in the western end of the Cordillera Central. The town is famous for its topiary garden in front of the town church. The bushes and shrubs have been cut into a variety of animal and people shapes and the effect is very pretty.

The mountainous countryside in the area is attractive and the climate cool and refreshing. The area is also well known for peach jam and homemade cheese, both of which are for sale in the town.

There are simple restaurants but no hotels in Zarcero.

Getting There & Away The town is reached by bus from the terminal in Alajuela or from the Coca Cola terminal in San José. The trip from San José to Zarcero takes two hours, from Alajuela a little less. A day trip from San José with stops at Alajuela, Sarchí and Zarcero is certainly possible. Buses from Zarcero leave at the red bus stands at the north-west corner of the park (the church plaza with the topiary art).

Northbound buses continue over the Cordillera Central and down to Ciudad Quesada (San Carlos), 35 km away. Southbound buses go to San José every hour; some of them will drop you in Alajuela. Because Zarcero is on the busy San José to Ciudad Quesada run, buses may be full when they come through, especially at weekends.

If you are driving northward through Zarcero on a bus between San José and Ciudad Quesada, look out of the right-hand side for glimpses of the church and its famous topiary work.

POÁS VOLCANO NATIONAL PARK

This 5599 hectare park lies about 37 km north of Alajuela by road and is a popular destination for both locals and visitors alike. It is one of the oldest and best known national parks in Costa Rica.

The centrepiece of the park is the Poás Volcano (2704 metres) which has been active since well before records started in 1828. There have been three major periods of activity, 1888 to 1895, 1903 to 1912 and 1952 to 1954. It appears that the volcano is entering a newly active phase and the park was briefly closed in 1989 after a minor eruption in May of that year sent volcanic ash over a km into the air. At the present time the crater is a bubbling and steaming cauldron but doesn't pose an imminent threat – you should check with either the tourist office or National Parks Service in San José for the current status of the volcano's activity and the park opening hours.

The mountain is composed of composite basalt. The huge crater is 1½ km across and 300 metres deep. Geyser type eruptions take place periodically, with peaceful interludes lasting minutes or weeks depending on the degree of activity within the volcano. Because of toxic sulphuric acid fumes, visitors are prohibited from descending into the crater, but the view down from the top is very impressive. This park is a 'must' for anyone with an interest in seeing what an active volcano looks like.

Apart from Poás itself, there is a dwarf cloud-forest near the crater – the best example of this kind of habitat in the national parks system. Here you can wander around looking at the bromeliads, lichens and mosses clinging to the curiously shaped and twisted trees growing on the volcanic soil. Birds abound, especially hummingbirds such as the fiery-throated and magnificent hummingbirds, which are high altitude specialities of Costa Rica. Other highland specialities to look for include the sooty robin, as well as the resplendent quetzal which has been reported here. A nature trail leads through this cloud forest to another crater nearby (this one extinct), which forms the pretty Botos Lake. There are other walking trails as well.

Information

There is a ranger station and small museum in the park. Current hours are 8 am to 2.30 pm daily except Mondays, but these are subject to change so check in San José before you go. Entrance to the park is about US$1.10 per person. The park is very crowded on Sundays, when there are often slide shows in the museum auditorium, but it is relatively quiet midweek.

The best time to go is in the dry season, especially early in the morning before the clouds roll in and obscure the view. Overnight temperatures can drop below freezing and it may be windy and cold during the day, particularly in the morning, so dress accord-

ingly. Poás receives almost four metres of rain a year, so be prepared for it.

There are well marked trails in the park. It is easy to walk to the active crater lookout for spectacular views; the trails through the cloud forest are somewhat steeper but still not very difficult or long.

Tours

Tours go from San José just about every day, and there are many companies advertising tours. Typically, they cost about US$20 per person and you arrive at the volcano by about 10 am at the earliest. Some tours spend very little time at the crater, so check carefully before you fork out your hard saved cash. I would prefer to be there earlier for the best views, and I suggest either renting a car or hiring a taxi. You could rent a taxi for about US$50 from San José, less from Alajuela.

Places to Stay & Eat

There is no overnight accommodation, and camping is currently prohibited (but has been allowed in the past). Travellers who have been stuck here overnight have been able to sleep on the ground in one of the buildings of the visitor complex.

There is a cafeteria with a limited menu but bringing your own food is a good idea. There are picnicking areas and drinking water.

Getting There & Away

There is supposedly a morning bus leaving at 8.30 am from Alajuela's main square every Sunday but this was not running when I visited recently. There is a very crowded Sunday morning bus leaving San José at 8.30 am from Calle 12, Avenida 2 & 4. The fare is US$2.50.

If you don't want to travel on a busy Sunday, this leaves three options: walk, take a tour or hire a car or taxi. If you walk, you can get local buses part of the way, but they don't run very frequently and you are still left with at least a 10 km walk (uphill all the way) from the nearest village, Poásito. There are one or two buses a day from Alajuela to Poásito and there is nowhere to stay here.

Another possibility is to take one of the two or three buses daily from San José to Puerto Viejo de Sarapiquí via Varablanca and get off at the Poásito turn-off, about 1½ km before Varablanca. From here it is three km to Poásito, or 13 km to the park. You can see that using buses and walking is not an easy way to visit the park, and you'll get there later in the day when it'll probably be clouded over.

Hitch-hiking is a definite possibility but there isn't much traffic. If you arrive late, you'll probably be able to find covered floor space to crash on, if you have a sleeping bag.

A more convenient but also more expensive option is to take one of the buses from the Alajuela bus terminal to the village of San Pedro de Poás. Buses cost US$0.25, take less than an hour, and leave about every hour. From San Pedro de Poás it is roughly 25 km to the volcano. There is a taxi stand by the bus stop in San Pedro de Poás where you can hire a cab to take you up to the volcano for about US$15 to US$20 round trip, allowing about an hour to visit the volcano. If you want to spend longer, you'll have to arrange an extra payment for waiting time. Up to four people could share the cab, which makes it a relatively inexpensive trip if you can find some companions. If you can afford it, this is the best way to go. If you leave San José at dawn, you should be on the volcano within three hours. There is no accommodation at San Pedro de Poás, but there is a decent restaurant where you can get a good lunch.

HEREDIA

This small provincial capital lies about 11 km north of San José. Its downtown population is 26,000; if the suburbs are included there are 65,000 inhabitants. The elevation is 1150 metres above sea level – about the same as San José. The national university is on the east side of town, and there is a sizeable student population which adds to the interest of the town. There is one cinema.

Things to See

The city was founded in 1706 and retains some of its colonial character. The **Parque**

Central is the best place to see the older buildings. To the east of the park is the church of **La Inmaculada Concepción**, built in 1797 and still in use. Its thick-walled squat construction is attractive in an ugly sort of way – rather like Volkswagen Beetles are attractive to many people. The solid shape has withstood the earthquakes which have damaged most of the other buildings in Costa Rica that date to this time.

To the north of the park is a **colonial fortress** simply called 'El Fortín'. The area is a National Historic Site.

The countryside surrounding Heredia is almost completely dedicated to coffee growing. Tour companies in San José sometimes arrange visits to coffee farms (called fincas). The countryside is attractive, has several points of interest and good hotels. See the Around Heredia section for details.

Places to Stay

With San José so close, most travellers stay in the capital. There are quite a few hotels in Heredia, however, probably to cater to the student population of the nearby university. Most hotels give monthly discounts to students.

There are several cheap hotels in downtown Heredia, although most lack hot water unless otherwise indicated. The basic *Hospedaje Herediano*, Calle Central, Avenida 4 & 6, is family run and has an agreeable courtyard. Rooms are US$2.30 per person. The *Hotel Colonial* (☎ 375258), Avenida 4, Calle 4 & 6, is clean and family run and charges US$3 per person.

If those two are full, try the cheap and basic *Hotel El Parque*, Calle 4, Avenida 6 & 8. The *Hotel Verano* (☎ 371616), Calle 4, Avenida 6, charges almost US$6 per person, is clean, but still has cold water in the showers.

The best hotel is several blocks north of downtown. This is the *Hotel Heredia* (☎ 371324), Calle 6, Avenida 3 & 5, which is clean, will change US dollars, and charges US$8.25/14 for singles/doubles with private bath and hot water. Meals are available.

There are a number of middle and top end

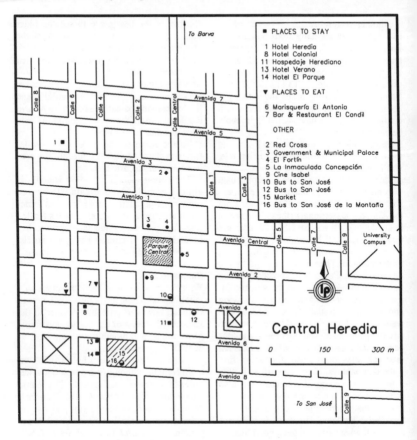

PLACES TO STAY

1 Hotel Heredia
8 Hotel Colonial
11 Hospedaje Herediano
13 Hotel Verano
14 Hotel El Parque

PLACES TO EAT

6 Marisquería El Antonio
7 Bar & Restaurant El Candil

OTHER

2 Red Cross
3 Government & Municipal Palace
4 El Fortín
5 La Inmaculada Concepción
9 Cine Isabel
10 Bus to San José
12 Bus to San José
15 Market
16 Bus to San José de la Montaña

Central Heredia

0   150   300 m

hotels in the countryside surrounding Heredia.

Places to Eat

An inexpensive seafood restaurant is *Marisquería El Antonio* at Avenida 4, Calle 6. The best place I could find was the *Bar & Restaurant El Candil* at Calle 4, Avenida 2 & 4.

There is a *Pizza Hut* where students hang out, and there are also some student bars and cafés near the university; the *El Bulevar* and *La Choza* have been recommended.

Getting There & Away

Buses from San José leave every few minutes from Calle 1, Avenida 7 & 9. Buses from Heredia to San José leave from Calle Central, Avenida 4 or from Avenida 4, Calle Central & 1. The two terminals are less than a block apart. The fare for the half hour ride is about US$0.30.

Buses north for Barva leave from in front of the Cruz Roja (Red Cross) on Calle Central, Avenida 1 & 3. Buses to San José de la Montaña leave every hour from Avenida 8, Calle 2 & 4. Three times a day (currently at 6 am, 12 noon and 3 pm) these buses continue past San José towards Sacramento for access to the Barva Volcano in the Braulio Carrillo National Park. There is no central bus terminal; ask around for other destinations.

AROUND HEREDIA

The small town of **Barva**, 2½ km north of Heredia, is a colonial town which has been declared a historic monument. Although there is no particular building to see, the town as a whole has a pleasant old-world ambience and is fun to stroll around in.

Buses to Barva continue on to **San Pedro de Barva**, a further 3½ km to the north-west. Here there is a coffee research station and small Museo de Café (☎ 371975) explaining everything you always wanted to know about coffee. The museum is four blocks north of the San Pedro church and plaza and is open from Monday to Friday from 7 am to 3 pm and other hours by appointment.

Some buses for San Pedro continue to **Santa Bárbara** and are marked that way. Ask at the bus stop in front of the Cruz Roja.

About one km north of Barva the road forks. The right fork continues to the village of **San José de la Montaña** about five km north of Barva. The village is pleasantly located at about 1550 metres on the south slopes of the Barva Volcano. The higher elevation gives a fresh nip to the air and you should bring some warm clothes, particularly if overnighting in one of the country inns north of the village.

From San José de la Montaña, three buses a day continue towards Sacramento and this is the route to the trails up Barva Volcano, which is part of Braulio Carrillo National Park.

Three km west of Heredia is San Rafael de Heredia from where a road leads about eight km north to **Monte de la Cruz** where there is a restaurant and great views of the mountains and the Central Valley. There is pleasant hiking in the area.

A couple of km before you get to Monte de la Cruz there is the El Castillo Country Club which you can use for US$5 per day. This includes lunch, and use of their pool and

exercise room. There is also an ice-skating rink and go-carts among the attractions.

Places to Stay

Santa Bárbara Just before Santa Bárbara is the *Finca Rosa Blanca* (☎ 399392), one of the most exclusive small country hotels in Costa Rica. It has only five suites, ranging in cost from US$75 to US$150 per night. The most expensive room is surreal: a tower with a 360° view reached by a winding staircase made of a single tree trunk. The bathroom is painted like a tropical rainforest and has water flowing out of an artificial waterfall – not your run-of-the-mill hotel bathroom! Reservations can be made at Apartado 41, 3009 Santa Bárbara, Heredia, Costa Rica.

San José de la Montaña A few km north of San José de la Montaña (and at a higher elevation) are three comfortable country hotels, all known for their attractive settings. Pleasant walks and bird-watching are the main activities. Although three buses a day (from Heredia to Sacramento) come close to the hotels, they will provide you with courtesy pick-up. Alternatively, get a taxi from San José de la Montaña. The hotels are small and sometimes close temporarily midweek if there is no demand, or may be full at weekends with locals, so you should call first to make reservations, get precise directions, or arrange to be picked up.

Cabañas Las Ardillas (☎ 228134) has five cabins each with fireplace and kitchen area and accommodation for four people. There is a restaurant if you don't wish to cater for yourself. Rates per cabin are about US$40; ask about long stay discounts.

The *Cabañas de Montaña Cypresal* (☎ 374466) has 12 rooms, some with cooking facilities, and there's a small swimming pool and a restaurant. Rooms go for US$18/25 single/double. Reservations can be made at Apartado 7891, 1000 San José.

The *Hotel El Pórtico* (☎ 376022) is considered to be the best (though all three are good and recommended). It has 14 heated rooms, a restaurant, sauna and pool. Room rates are US$25/32 single/double. Write to

Apartado 289, 3000 Heredia for reservations.

Monte de la Cruz Between El Castillo and Monte de la Cruz you'll find a recommended small country hotel, the *Hotel Chalet Tirol* (☎ 397070) set at 1800 metres in the foothills of the Cordillera Central. Accommodation is in little alpine style chalets all with heat. There is a good restaurant and pleasant trails into the cloud forest on the grounds and beyond. Rates are about US$30/40 single/double and they will pick you up from San José or the airport. Reservations are recommended – write to Apartado 7812, 1000 San José.

Santo Domingo de Heredia Another good country hotel is the *Bougainvillea Santo Domingo* (☎ 368822) in Santo Domingo de Heredia, about half way between Heredia and San José. It is under the same management as the Hotel Bougainvillea in San José. There are orchards in the extensive grounds, and there is a restaurant, pool and tennis court. Shuttle buses run to San José. Rooms with balconies go for about US$54/62 single/double. Reservations can be made at Apartado 69, 2120 San José.

BRAULIO CARRILLO NATIONAL PARK
This national park is a success story for both conservationists and developers. Until the 1970s, San José's links with the Caribbean coast at Limón were limited to the railway and a slow narrow highway. A fast, paved, modern highway was proposed as an important step in advancing Costa Rica's ability to transport goods, services and people between the capital and the Caribbean coast.

This development was certainly to Costa Rica's economic advantage, but the most feasible route lay through a low pass between Barva and Irazú volcanoes to the north-west of the Central Valley. In the 1970s, this region was virgin rainforest, and conservationists were deeply concerned that the development would lead to accompanying colonisation, logging and loss of habitat.

A compromise was reached by declaring the region a national park and allowing this one single major highway to bisect it. This effectively cuts the region into two smaller preserved areas, but it is considered one national park.

The Braulio Carrillo National Park (named after Costa Rica's third chief of state) was established in 1978. The San José to Guápiles highway was completed in 1987, and 44,099 hectares had been protected from further development. The pristine areas to either side of the highway are large enough to support and protect a great and varied number of plant and animal species, and San José has its much needed modern connection with the Caribbean coast.

The way most people visit the park is simply to drive through it on one of the frequent buses travelling the new highway between San José and Guápiles or Limón. The difference between this highway and other roads in the Central Valley is marked; instead of small villages and large coffee plantations, the panorama is one of rolling hillsides clothed with thick montane rainforest. About 75% of Costa Rica was rainforest in the 1940s; now less than a quarter of the country retains its natural vegetative cover, and it is through parks such as Braulio Carrillo that the biodiversity represented by the remaining rainforest is protected.

The buses travelling the new highway do not stop, and all that the passengers can do is gaze out of the window and admire the thick vegetation covered with epiphytes (air plants) such as bromeliads and mosses. On the steepest roadside slopes there are stands of the distinctive huge-leaved gunnera plants which quickly colonise steep and newly exposed parts of the montane rainforest. The large leaves can protect a person from a sudden tropical downpour – hence the plant's nickname is 'poor folks' umbrella'.

To see the park properly, however, you have to get off the bus and walk around. This will give you the chance to see the incredible variety of orchids, ferns, palms and other plant life, although the lushness of the vegetation makes viewing the many species of tropical animals something of a challenge.

You will certainly hear and see plenty of birds but the mammals are more elusive.

Part of the reason why there is such a huge variety of plant and animal life in Braulio Carrillo is that it encompasses a wide spread of altitudinal zones. Elevations within the park range from the top of the Barva Volcano (2906 metres) to less than 50 metres in the Caribbean lowlands. Five of Holdridge's Life Zones are represented and the differences in elevation create many different habitats.

A visit to the park can consist of anything from a brief stop to see just one habitat to a difficult and adventurous trip of several days, climbing Barva and perhaps the nearby volcano of Cacho Negro (2150 metres) before descending down to the lowlands on foot. The observant naturalist may see Costa Rica's national bird, the resplendent quetzal, as well as umbrella birds, toucans, trogons, guans, eagles and a host of other avifauna. Mammals living in the park include cats such as the jaguar, puma or ocelot, tapirs and sloths, all of which are difficult to see. More likely sightings include peccaries or one of the three species of monkeys present in the park.

Information

There are three routes to the park. One is from the new highway; the second is from the road north of San José de la Montaña towards Sacramento. On both these routes there are ranger stations from where you can get further information. The third route is north-east from San José, via San Vicente de Moravia, Paracito, San Jerónimo and Alto Palma to Bajo Honduras. There used to be a lookout and guard station, and camping was allowed, but this last route has recently been closed because the road is in disrepair. Enquire at the national parks information office in San José for up-to-date information about the status of all these entrance routes.

Information Centre The park entrance on the new highway is less than 20 km northeast of San José. There is a sign, and reportedly a ranger station, but either I was unable to find it or it has closed. Shortly after entering the park, the road goes through a long tunnel (the Tunnel Zurqui) and a park information centre and ranger station is found a couple of km further on the right. Here, you can pay your entrance fee (US$1.20) and get information. Because the road is so new, the infrastructure of the park is not well developed, but being so close to San José by good road, it is expected that more facilities will become available in future.

About 18 km beyond the park entrance, on the left-hand side, there is a parking area and sign saying 'PNBC Sector Carrillo'. From here there is a trail leading steeply down to the Río Patria, about a two hour walk away. Camping is possible there, though there are no facilities.

Near the exit from the park, where the road crosses the Río Sucio, there is an area with picnic ramadas and a circular nature trail. There are various other short hikes you can take from the new road, but they are generally poorly marked.

Climbing Barva Volcano

The entrance via San José de la Montaña is the best way to go if you want to climb Barva Volcano. From the road the track climbs to the summit of Barva, which can be climbed in about four or five hours round trip at a fairly leisurely pace. The trail goes from Paso Llano (Porrosatí) to the summit of Barva and returns to Sacramento if you want to make a round trip of it – about nine km in total from the road. There is a ranger station near Sacramento; check with the information office in San José to see when it may be open. Sometimes the rangers will take you up to the top; it's about four km one way.

The trail up Barva is fairly obvious and there is a sign. If you wish to continue from Barva north into the lowlands, you will find that the trails are not marked and not as obvious. It is possible, however, to follow northbound trails all the way through the park to La Selva near Puerto Viejo de Sarapiquí. A tico who has done it told me that it took him four days and is an adventure only for those people used to roughing it and able to use a map and compass.

The slopes of Barva are one of the best places in the park to see the quetzal. Near the summit there are several lakes. Camping is allowed anywhere you can pitch a tent, but no facilities are provided so you must be self sufficient. There is plenty of water – in fact the park receives between three and six metres of rain per year depending on locality, and there are innumerable lakes, streams, and waterfalls. This means that trails are often very muddy and that you should be prepared for rain at any time of year.

The best time to go is supposedly the 'dry' season (December to April), but it is liable to rain then too, though less than in the other months. If going on a day trip, leave as early as possible as the mornings tend to be clear and the afternoons cloudy. The night temperatures can drop to several degrees below freezing.

Getting There & Away
Via the New Highway There are no buses going to the park. You have to either get one of the buses going through the park along the new highway and get off where you want, or go on a tour. If you take a public bus, you will have to flag one down when you want to leave. The buses are often full and don't want to stop, especially at weekends. Hitchhiking is a possibility, or you could hire a car.

Via San José de la Montaña For the entrance via San José de la Montaña, three buses a day (currently 6 am, 12 noon and 3 pm) leave Heredia for Paso Llano (Porrotosí on most maps) and Sacramento. Ask the driver to set you down at the track leading to the national park and volcano. If you miss the bus, take any of the hourly buses to San José de la Montaña and walk from there – it's about five km to the sign for BCNP – Sector Barva.

Via San Jerónimo de Moravia & Alto Palma There are buses from San José marked San Jerónimo de Moravia, the last village, about 10 km before the park boundary. They leave from Avenida 3, Calle 3 & 5.

MORAVIA
This village is named San Vicente de Moravia or San Vicente on many maps, but is known as Moravia by the local inhabitants. It lies about seven km north-east of San José and is well known for its handicrafts, especially leather. The best known store is the Caballo Blanco on the corner of the spacious and attractive Parque Central. Other good stores nearby include La Rueda and La Tinaja. Shoppers planning a spree should note that most stores are closed on Sundays.

Getting There & Away
There are frequent buses from San José to San Vicente de Moravia. From here it's about 10 km to San Jerónimo for the Alto Palma entrance to Braulio Carrillo; ask about buses or take a taxi.

CORONADO
This is the general name for several villages centered on San Isidro de Coronado, about six km beyond Moravia. About one km before San Isidro de Coronado is San Antonio de Coronado, and close to this is Dulce Nombre de Coronado. The main reason to visit Coronado is to see the snake 'farm' at Instituto Clodomiro Picado at Dulce Nombre.

The institute is run by the University of Costa Rica and has a selection of local poisonous snakes on display. On Friday afternoons visitors can see the snakes being 'milked' for their poison which is then used to make antivenin. On other days of the week the visitor must be content with the opportunity to view the snakes, learn about the serum making process, or buy some serum. The institute is open from 1 to 4 pm on Monday to Friday; entrance is free.

San Isidro de Coronado is at 1383 metres above sea level and is thus 200 metres higher than San José. It is a popular destination during the dry season for joséfinos looking for an escape from the city. There are some simple restaurants but no accommodation.

The village has an annual fiesta on 15 February.

Getting There & Away

Take a bus from Avenida 7, Calle Central & 1. From San Isidro it is one km or so back to the snake institute – ask the bus driver for directions. It is a pleasant downhill walk back to Moravia, about six km away.

CARTAGO

This is the fourth provincial capital of the Central Valley, and the most historic one. The city was founded in 1563 and was the capital of the country until 1823. Unfortunately, major earthquakes in 1841 and 1910 ruined almost all the old buildings and there is not a great deal left to see. Cartago was built at an elevation 1435 metres in the valley between the Cordillera Central and Cordillera de Talamanca and the Irazú Volcano looms nearby. The city itself has a population of 29,000 but the densely settled suburbs and adjoining villages give the canton of Cartago a population of 105,000. The city is 22 km south-east of San José with which it is connected by a good road and frequent buses.

Things to See

The most interesting sights in Cartago itself are churches. The church at Avenida 2, Calle 2, was destroyed by an earthquake in 1910. The ruins were never repaired and the solid walls of the church now house a pretty garden. The ruins are a major landmark of downtown Cartago. It is a pleasant spot to sit on a park bench and watch the people of Cartago go about their business.

The Basilica of Our Lady of the Angels

(La Basílica de Nuestra Señora de los Angeles) East of downtown, at Avenida 2, Calle 16, is the most famous church of the Central Valley, if not all of Costa Rica. The Basilica was destroyed in the 1926 earthquake and rebuilt in Byzantine style. The story goes that a statue of the virgin was discovered on the site on 2 August 1635, and miraculously reappeared on the site after being removed. A shrine was built on the spot, and today the statue, known as La Negrita, is considered a pilgrimage destination and the Virgin associated with the statue is the patron saint of Costa Rica.

La Negrita has miraculous healing powers attributed to her, and pilgrims from all over Central America come to the Basilica to worship every 2 August. There is a procession on foot from San José, 22 km away. Inside the Basilica is a chapel dedicated to La Negrita where gifts from cured pilgrims can be seen. The gifts are mainly metal (including gold) models of parts of the human body which have been miraculously healed.

Around Cartago

There is little else to see in Cartago itself, but a few km out of the city are some interesting sights which can be reached on foot or by local bus. Cartago is also the best point from which to visit the nearby Irazú Volcano National Park, as well as the tourist spots in the Orosí River Valley.

Lankester Gardens This is an orchid garden run by the University of Costa Rica. Originally a private garden run by British orchid enthusiast Charles Lankester, it is now open to the public and is frequently visited by plant lovers. The gardens are about six km east of Cartago. To get there, catch a Paraíso bus and ask the driver to set you down at the turn off for Lankester Gardens. From the turn off it is a further one km on foot to the entrance; there is a sign. A taxi will cost about US$2, or you can walk. Tour buses from San José often stop by the gardens either on the way to the Irazú Volcano or the Orosí River Valley. Hours are 9.30 am to 3.30 pm daily and admission is US$0.60. At half past each hour, free guided tours are given. You can visit the gardens year round, but March and April are the best season for viewing orchids in flower.

After visiting the gardens, you can continue on to Paraíso.

Paraíso Paraíso is eight km east of Cartago. In this village you can eat at the *Bar Restau-*

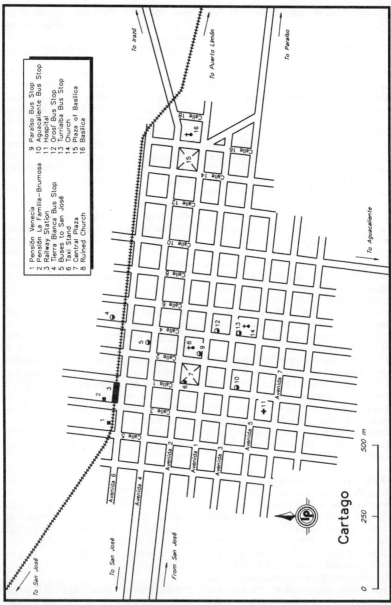

Cartago

1 Pensión Venecia
2 Pensión La Familia—Brumosa
3 Railway Station
4 Tierra Blanca Bus Stop
5 Buses to San José
6 Taxi Stand
7 Central Plaza
8 Ruined Church
9 Paraíso Bus Stop
10 Aguacaliente Bus Stop
11 Hospital
12 Orosí Bus Stop
13 Turrialba Bus Stop
14 Church
15 Plaza of Basilica
16 Basilica

rant Continental which has decent food. From the end of the bus line in Paraíso, walk about 1½ km south of the village to Parque Doña Anacleto. There are well tended gardens, a playground, and picnic areas – closed on Monday. Less than one km further is a viewpoint for the whole of the Orosí River Valley. The view is excellent.

Aguacaliente About five km south of Cartago there are hot springs in the appropriately named village of Aguacaliente. The natural hot springs have been dammed to form a swimming pool, and the area is popular for picnics.

Places to Stay & Eat

Most visitors to Cartago stay in San José because there are no decent hotels. There are a couple of cheap and basic flop houses by the railway station if you are caught in Cartago overnight and are desperate. They are the *Pensión La Familia-Brumosa* and the *Pensión Venecia*. Neither are recommended. I couldn't find anything else.

There are no outstanding restaurants but there are several reasonable places where you can get a meal. Just walk along the main streets of Avenida 2 and Avenida 4 downtown and take your choice. Or take a picnic lunch to one of the scenic spots in the Cartago area.

Getting There & Away

Buses from San José leave several times an hour from Calle 13, Avenida Central & 2. Services run from about 5 am to 11 pm, the journey takes almost an hour depending on the traffic, and the fare is 40 cents. Buses from San José come in on Avenida 2 from the west and head eastwards, stopping every few blocks, until they reach the Basilica, which is the last stop. Buses from Cartago back to San José leave from Avenida 4, Calle 2 & 4.

To continue on to the town of Turrialba, take a bus from the stop in front of the church at the corner of Avenida 3, Calle 4. There are buses every hour, taking about 1½ hours to reach Turrialba and costing US$0.60. Some

of these buses originate in San José, and come through town on Avenida 3. Space may be limited on these buses.

Local destinations are served by a variety of bus stops; if what you need isn't listed here or if the stop has moved, ask locals for directions. For Paraíso (and the turn off for Lankester Gardens), the bus leaves from Avenida 1, Calle 2 & 4. The bus for the Cachí Dam leaves from nearby. For Aguacaliente, the bus leaves from the corner of Calle 1, Avenida 3. For Orosí, the bus leaves from Calle 4 near Avenida 1. All of these buses are cheap and leave at least every hour.

There is a signed bus stop for 'Volcán Irazú' but there is no service there at present. At the same stop there is a sign for Tierra Blanca, which is 18 km before the volcano. Buses leave Cartago at 7 and 9 am for Tierra Blanca from where you could walk or hitch to the volcano. Walkers should remember that the altitude will make the hike a breathlessly difficult one.

There is a taxi rank on the west side of the plaza west of the ruined church. You can hire cabs to take you to any of the local destinations.

IRAZÚ VOLCANO NATIONAL PARK

The centrepiece of this national park is the highest active volcano in Costa Rica, Irazú, at 3432 metres. It is because of eruptions of this and other volcanoes that the soil of the Central Valley is so fertile. Eruptions have been recorded since 1723, when the Governor of the (then) Province of Costa Rica, Diego de la Haya Fernández, reported the event. His name is now given to one of the two main craters at the summit. The last major eruption of Irazú was a memorable one; it occurred on 19 March 1963, the day that US President Kennedy arrived on a state visit. San José, Cartago, and most of the Central Valley were covered with several cm of volcanic ash – it piled up over half a metre deep in places. The agricultural lands to the north-east of the volcano were rendered temporarily uninhabitable due to the rocks and boulders hurled out of the crater. Since that explosive eruption, Irazú's activity has been limited to gently smoking fumaroles which can be observed by the curious visitor.

The national park was established in 1955 to protect 2309 hectares in a roughly circular shape around the volcano. The summit is a bare landscape of volcanic ash and craters. The Principal Crater is 1050 metres in diameter and 300 metres deep whilst the Diego de la Haya Crater is 690 metres in diameter and 100 metres deep. It contains a small lake. There are two smaller craters, one of which contains a lake. There is also a pyroclastic cone. A few low plants are slowly beginning to colonise the landscape – if it wasn't for these you might feel that you were on a different world. A few high-altitude bird species such as the volcano junco hop around. There is a trail about one km in length which takes you from the parking lot right to the edge of the craters.

Below the summit there is a thicker cloud forest vegetation with oak and madroño trees covered with epiphytic plants. The lower you get, the lusher the vegetation. As you emerge from the park boundary, the land is agricultural, with much cattle and dairy farming. About five km below the summit on the left hand side as you descend, there is the *Soda Pastora* which serves basic snacks and early breakfast. About 11 km below the summit on the right hand side is the *Hotel Restaurant Irazú* (☎ 530827) where a double room costs about US$10; there is a basic restaurant and it is cold at night. A little further down is a lookout over Cartago and the Central Valley; San José can be seen in the distance. The first village is called Prussia, and nearby is the **Ricardo Jiménez Oreamuno National Recreation Area** where there is a two km trail leading to a pretty waterfall. There are picnic sites here.

Information

There is a paved road all the way to the summit. At the summit there is a parking lot and a small information centre, open from 9 am to 4 pm. There are no food services or overnight accommodations and no camping facilities. There is a disused observation building at the right-hand side of the end of the road (a few hundred metres past the parking lot) and you could shelter in there if desperate – broken windows, concrete floors, and garbage. A warm sleeping bag would be essential. The entrance fee is about US$1, but during weekdays in the low season, there's often no one there to collect it. There is no gate, so if you drive up to arrive at dawn, as I did, you won't have any problem in getting in.

From the summit, it is possible to see both the Pacific and the Caribbean, but it is rarely clear enough for this to be actually possible. The best chances for a clear view are in the early morning during the dry season (January to April). It tends to be cold and cloudy on the summit, with temperatures ranging from -3°C to 17°C and annual rainfall of 2160 mm. Come prepared with warm and rainproof clothes as well as food.

Getting There & Away

There are no bus services to the national park at this time, though there used to be. You can take an early morning bus from Cartago to Tierra Blanca and walk the remaining 18 or 20 km, but it is hard work at this elevation. You could also hitch, but there isn't much traffic mid-week. Hiring a cab from Cartago is not too expensive if there is a group of you. I was quoted US$30 for the round trip with an hour's waiting time at the summit – the cab will take up to four passengers for this fare.

If you rent a car, you'll find the road is signed occasionally, but not at every turn. Leave Cartago from the north-east corner of the Basilica on Highway 8 which goes all the way to the summit. At road forks, if there is no sign, look for either the more major looking road or avoid signs for highways with numbers other than 8 (you will intersect with highways 233, 230, 227, and 6 on the way up). It is not difficult to find your way.

Tours from San José will take you to Irazú for about US$20 for a half day tour, or about US$40 for a full day combined with visits to Lankester Gardens and the Orosí River Valley.

OROSÍ RIVER VALLEY

This river valley south-east of Cartago is famous for its beautiful views, colonial buildings, hot springs, lake formed by a hydro-electric damming project, and a wildlife refuge. Most people visit the valley by taking a tour from San José or by driving their own car. It is possible to get around by public bus as well.

From Cartago, buses go to the village of **Orosí** south of Paraíso. Buses also go to the **Cachí Lake & Dam** east of Paraíso. The two roads are linked by a gravel road which you can drive in your own car or is used on some tours, but if travelling by public bus, you'll have to do one leg and then backtrack to do the other.

The Cachí bus will drop you off at **Ujarrás**, about seven km east of Paraíso. This village was damaged by the flood of 1833 and abandoned. The waters have since receded and the ruins are a popular tourist sight – the ruined 17th century church is particularly interesting to see.

A short distance above Ujarrás is a good lookout point for the Cachí Lake. On the north shore of the lake, about a half hour on foot east of Ujarrás, is *Charrara*, a government-run tourist complex with swimming pool, a reasonable restaurant, picnic areas, walking paths, and boats for hire on the lake. They are closed on Mondays. The hydroelectric dam itself is at the north-eastern corner of the lake.

The Orosí bus passes the Parque Doña Anacleto and continues past the viewpoint of **El Mirador de Orosí** about 2½ km south of Paraíso. This gives the best views of the entire valley. The bus continues on to the village of Orosí, about six km further south. This is one of the few colonial towns which has survived Costa Rica's frequent earthquakes and boasts an attractive church built in the first half of the 18th century – probably the oldest church still in use in Costa Rica. There is a small religious art museum (☎ 733051, 333298) adjacent to the church; it is open daily except Mondays from 9 am to 12 noon and 1 to 5 pm. There are hot springs and swimming pools on the east side of town.

The Orosí bus usually continues two km south of the village to the *Motel Río* (☎ 733057, 733128) which has a restaurant renowned for its fresh fish meals. The restaurant is open from 8.30 am to 5 pm daily. The motel has a swimming pool and rooms range from about US$10 to US$20 a double, depending on whether or not you have hot water or a private kitchenette. Río Macho is nearby.

TAPANTÍ NATIONAL WILDLIFE REFUGE

This 5090 hectare wildlife refuge is in wild and wet country on the rainforested northern slopes of the Cordillera de Talamanca. Although not a large refuge there are reportedly over 150 rivers within it, which gives an indication of the area's wetness. Waterfalls and trees abound and the wildlife is prolific, though not easy to reach because the terrain is rugged and the trails are few. Nevertheless, Tapantí is a popular destination for dedicated bird-watchers, and the reserve opens at 6 am to accommodate them.

Quetzals are said to nest on the west slopes of the valley in which the park information centre is located. Well over 200 other bird species have been recorded, including eagles and hummingbirds, parrots and toucans, and difficult to see forest floor inhabitants such as tinamous and antbirds. There are plenty of other animals: butterflies, amphibians, reptiles, and mammals. The rare jaguar, ocelot, jaguarundi, and little known oncilla (caucel) tiger cat have been recorded here, but more usual sightings include squirrels, monkeys, raccoons and agoutis. Tapirs are occasionally seen.

Information

The refuge is open from 6 am to 4 pm. There is an information centre near the park entrance. There are a couple of trails leading from here to various attractions, including a picnic area, a swimming hole, and a viewpoint with great views of a waterfall. Fishing is allowed in season (April to October – permit required) but the dry season (January to April) is generally considered the best time to visit the refuge, although you should be prepared with rain gear even then. Camping may be allowed with a permit, although there are no facilities, and I have read an unconfirmed report that the refuge is closed on Thursdays and Fridays, so you should definitely check with the National Wildlife Directorate (☎ 338112) in San José before you go. With advance warning, you may be able to arrange for a ranger to show you around.

Getting There & Away

If you have your own car, you can take a gravel road (passable year round) from Orosí through Río Macho and Purisil to the refuge entrance. Most buses from Cartago to Orosí go as far as Río Macho, from where it is a nine km walk (or hire a taxi). There is a daily early morning bus from Cartago to Orosí going as far as Purisil, from where it is a five km walk. A taxi from Orosí costs about US$4. Some tour companies in San José do guided day trips, eg Costa Rica Expeditions (☎ 570766) which charge US$65 per person.

RÍO REVENTAZÓN

From the north-east end of the Cachí Lake flows one of the more scenic and exciting rivers in Costa Rica, the Reventazón. It tumbles from the lake at 1000 metres above sea level and down the eastern slopes of the mountains to the Caribbean lowlands. It is a favourite river for rafters and kayakers – some sections offer Class III white water, others are relatively flat and placid.

Single and multi-day river trips are offered by several agencies in San José, including Costa Rica Expeditions (☎ 570766), which is the oldest and best known company, Ríos Tropicales (☎ 336455), Horizontes (☎ 222022) and Aventuras Naturales (☎ 253939). A day trip costs about US$65 and includes everything from San José: round-trip bus transportation, a breakfast stop in a country restaurant, all river equipment and life jackets, a delicious gourmet picnic lunch on the river (I had shrimp salad as an appetiser with Costa Rica

Expeditions), and several hours of guided fun on the thrilling white water. Guides all speak English. Because of higher and more constant rainfall on the Caribbean side of the country, it is possible to run this river year round but June and July are considered the best months.

TURRIALBA

This small town is attractively perched on the Caribbean slope of the Cordillera Central at an elevation of 650 metres above sea level. It is on the banks of the Río Turrialba which flows into the Reventazón, four km to the east.

The town used to be the major stopping point on the old highway from San José to Limón but since the opening of the new highway via Guápiles, Turrialba has been bypassed by travellers to the coast and has suffered economically. Nevertheless, it is a pleasant town and makes a good base for several nearby excursions and so tourism, whilst still very low key, is becoming increasingly important.

With the surge of interest in river running during the 1980s, the town has become somewhat of a centre for kayakers and rafters. Turrialba is also an excellent base to visit the nearby agronomical centre (CATIE) and the archaeological site at Guayabo National Monument, as well as for climbing the Turrialba Volcano – all these are described below. The finest views on the jungle train between the capital and the Caribbean coast are between Turrialba and Siquirres.

Turrialba is a minor agricultural centre for the coffee fincas in the highlands around the town and the sugarcane and banana plantations in the lowlands to the east. The population of the town and surrounding district is about 28,600.

Places to Stay – bottom end

There are three basic and inexpensive hotels by the railway station. The best of these is the *Hotel Interamericano* (☎ 560142) which

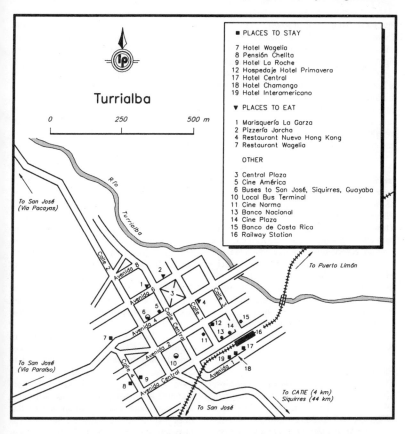

Turrialba

0   250   500 m

To San José
(Via Pacayas)

Río Turrialba

To San José
(Via Paraíso)

To Puerto Limón

To CATIE (4 km)
Siquirres (44 km)

To San José

■ PLACES TO STAY

7 Hotel Wagelia
8 Pensión Chelita
9 Hotel La Roche
12 Hospedaje Hotel Primavera
17 Hotel Central
18 Hotel Chamango
19 Hotel Interamericano

▼ PLACES TO EAT

1 Marisquería La Garza
2 Pizzería Jorcha
4 Restaurant Nuevo Hong Kong
7 Restaurant Wagelia

OTHER

3 Central Plaza
5 Cine América
6 Buses to San José, Siquirres, Guayaba
10 Local Bus Terminal
11 Cine Norma
13 Banco Nacional
14 Cine Plaza
15 Banco de Costa Rica
16 Railway Station

charges US$3.50/6 for singles/doubles or twice that for rooms with private bath and cold water. There is a snack bar on the premises. The other two railway hotels are about the same price but lack private baths.

It's a small town, so any hotel will be within a few blocks of the station. The basic *Hospedaje Hotel Primavera* is OK and charges about the same as the railway hotels. The *Hotel La Roche* (☎ 561624) looks clean and reasonable for US$4.75/8.25, and about US$3 more with private bath. The *Pensión Chelita* (☎ 560214) is another possibility in the bottom end price range.

Places to Stay – middle

The best hotel in town is the *Hotel Wagelia* (☎ 561596) which charges US$17.50/26.50 single/double in rooms with private bath and hot water. Better rooms with air-con and mini-refrigerator are about US$5 more. The hotel is clean and set in an attractively landscaped garden. The restaurant on the premises is one of the best in town. The management will arrange one day Reventazón river running excursions and other local trips.

Places to Stay – out of town

There are two small but pleasant country hotels several km east of Turrialba. About eight km away on the road to Siquirres and Limón is the *Turrialtico* (☎ 561111) which is known for the tico food served in its restaurant. There are a few rooms with private bath and hot water renting for US$17 double (no singles) – reservations are recommended. The hotel is set on a little hill and has great views.

About 11 km away from Turrialba, also on the road to Limón, is the *Pochotel* (☎ 560111), which is a favourite of local river guides. The hotel is above the village of Pavones and there is a sign in the village. There is also a tico-style restaurant here, and a tower with great views. Cabins with private bath and hot water are about US$20 double – again, reservations are recommended.

Both hotels can help arrange nearby excursions or river running trips. If you call them in advance, they will pick you up in Turrialba, or you can get off the Turrialba-Siquirres bus at the appropriate spot.

Other country hotels are found near the Guayabo National Monument and at the Rancho Naturalista, described below.

Places to Eat

The hotels *Wagelia*, *Turrialtico* and *Pochotel* all have good restaurants. Other restaurants where you can have a decent meal for about US$3 to US$5 are *Pizzería Jorcha* for Italian food and *Marisquería La Garza* for seafood. The *Restaurant Nuevo Hong Kong* serves slightly cheaper Chinese food. I have also read good reports of the *Restaurant Kingston* but was unable to find it during my visit.

Getting There & Away

Bus Buses from San José to Turrialba leave from Avenida 6, Calle 13, take about two hours, and cost just under US$1. The route lies through Cartago and then either through Pacayas or through Paraíso and Cervantes to Turrialba. In Cervantes there is a popular country restaurant *La Posada de la Luna* which serves good local food and is especially popular at breakfast with river runners

on their way to the Reventazón or the Pacuare. The restaurant is cluttered with bits and pieces of Costa Rican history, ranging from old guns and swords to household artefacts to archaeological pieces. An interesting place.

There are two main bus terminals in Turrialba. The stop on Avenida 4 near Calle 2 serves San José (you can get off at Cartago) with buses every hour. From this stop you can also go to Siquirres (connecting for Puerto Limón) with buses every two hours. Buses to Guayaba also leave from here – currently the schedule is 1 pm on Monday, 3 pm on Friday and Saturday, and 5 pm on Sunday, but this is liable to change.

The other terminal is between Avenida Central & 2 and Calle Central & 2. This terminal has buses serving the local communities such as La Suiza and Tuís every hour, and Santa Cruz three times every afternoon.

Train The sign at the train station tells us that it is 103.1 km to Limón and 63.6 km to San José. The most attractive section of railroad is between Turrialba and Siquirres on the way to Limón. Buses are available in Siquirres to take you on to Limón more quickly than the train, or to take you back to San José. Currently, the San José-Limón train comes through Turrialba at 12.30 pm and the Limón-San José train passes through at 10 am. There is also a beat up old train that does just the scenic Turrialba-Siquirres run at 6 am daily for US$0.35; the trip takes about three hours. The views of the Reventazón on the right of the tracks are very good. Train times are liable to change so check at the station before you travel.

CATIE

This stands for the Centro Agronómico Tropical de Investigación y Enseñanza, which is known throughout Costa Rica by its acronym of CATIE (which is just as well!) The centre comprises of about 1000 hectares dedicated to tropical agricultural research and education. Agronomists from all over the world recognise CATIE as one of the tropic's most important agricultural stations.

The attractively landscaped grounds of CATIE lie just to the left of the main road to Siquirres, about four km east of Turrialba. Visitors are allowed to walk the grounds and birders enjoy a visit to the small lake on the site where waterbirds such as the purple gallinule are a speciality. Another good birding area is the short but steep trail descending from behind the administration building to the Reventazón.

Those with an interest in tropical agriculture are encouraged to visit the facilities at CATIE. These include one of the most extensive libraries of tropical agriculture literature anywhere in the world, a teaching and research facility with student and faculty accommodation, laboratories, experimental fruit, vegetable, and forest plots, greenhouses, a dairy, a herbarium, and a seed bank. Livestock and seeds suitable for the tropics are available for sale (although these require special permits to be exported). Research interests at CATIE include conservation of crop genetic diversity, high yield/low impact farming techniques for small farms, and development of agricultural strains suitable for tropical environments worldwide.

Although the grounds can be visited without prior arrangement, a tour of the complex should be arranged beforehand, either with one of the tour agencies in San José or direct with CATIE (☎ 566431, 561149). Arrangements to obtain seeds or carry out research at the centre can be made by writing to CATIE, Turrialba, Costa Rica.

GUAYABO NATIONAL MONUMENT

Guayabo lies 20 km north-east of Turrialba and contains the largest and most important archaeological site known in the country. Although interesting, it does not compare with the Mayan and Aztec archaeological sites of Honduras, Belize, Guatemala and Mexico to the north. Nevertheless, excavations have revealed a number of cobbled roads, stone aqueducts, mounds, retaining walls, and petroglyphs which can be examined by the interested visitor. Some pottery and gold artefacts have been found and are exhibited at the National Museum in San José.

Archaeologists are still unclear about the pre-history and significance of the site. It seems to have been inhabited perhaps as far back as 1000 BC and reached the pinnacle of its development around 800 AD when some 10,000 people were thought to have lived in the area. Guayabo is considered an important cultural, religious and political centre, but more precise details remain to be unearthed. The site was abandoned by 1400 AD and the Spanish conquistadors, explorers and settlers leave us with no record of having found the ruins.

The area was rediscovered in the late 19th century by Anastasio Alfaro, a local naturalist and explorer, who began some preliminary excavations and found a few pieces which are now in the National Museum. In 1968, Carlos Aguilar Piedra, an archaeologist with the University of Costa Rica, began the first systematic excavations. As the importance of the site became evident, it was obviously necessary to protect it and it became a National Monument in 1973, with further protection decreed in 1980. The latest round of excavations began in 1989 and are expected to last about five years.

The monument is small, some 218 hectares, and the archaeological site itself is thought to comprise no more than 10% of the total. Well over half of these ruins are yet to be excavated. The remaining 90% of the monument is premontane rainforest. It is important because it protects some of the last remaining rainforest of this type in the province of Cartago, but, because of its small area, there are not many animals to be seen. Those animals there are interesting, however.

Particularly noteworthy among the fauna are the oropendolas which build colonial sack-like nests in the trees of the monument. Other birds include toucans and brown jays – the latter unique among jays in that they have a small, inflatable sac in the chest which causes a popping sound to be heard at the beginning of their loud and raucous calls.

Mammals include squirrels, armadillos and coatis among others.

Information

The archaeological site is being worked upon during the week and is therefore closed to visitors except by special arrangement. On Saturdays and Sundays, the archaeological area is open from 8 am to 4 pm, and park rangers are available to take you around. This is as much to protect the site as to give you a free tour, but it's a good deal anyway!

There is an information centre near the monument entrance where you pay the US$1.10 National Parks admission fee. There is a small interpretive display. There are trails within the monument, picnic areas, latrines and running water. Camping is allowed. You can visit the park midweek if you just want to visit the rainforest, birdwatch, picnic or camp.

Average annual rainfall is about 3500 mm and the best time to go is during the January to April dry season (when it can still rain).

Getting There & Away

There are buses from Turrialba on Fridays, Saturdays, Sundays and Mondays. I have read that there are also buses from Turrialba to Santa Teresita, from where it is a five km walk to Guayabo, but I could not confirm that when I was there. At other times you could try hitchhiking or hire a taxi from Turrialba (about US$10).

Places to Stay

Apart from camping in the monument, visitors can stay in the one country hotel nearby. This is the *Albergue La Calzada* (☎ 513677, 560465), less than one km from the entrance to the monument. It is a small place with a few doubles at US$10 per room, shared bathrooms and hot water. Rooms with private bathrooms are planned. Calling ahead for reservations is recommended. Their restaurant serves good food and is open to the public. The owners are friendly and helpful.

TURRIALBA VOLCANO

This 3328 metre high active volcano is actu-

ally part of the Irazú volcanic massif, but is more remote and difficult to get to than Irazú. The name of the volcano was coined by early Spanish settlers who named it *Torre Alba* or 'white tower' for the plumes of smoke pouring from its summit in early days. The last eruption was in 1866 and today the volcano lies dormant, but it is likely that the tranquil farmlands on Turrialba's fertile soils will again be disturbed by earth shattering explosions sometime in the future.

The summit has three craters, of which the middle one is the largest. This is the only one which still shows signs of activity with fumaroles of steam and sulphur. Below the summit there is a montane rain and cloud forest, dripping with moisture and mosses, full of ferns, bromeliads, and even stands of bamboo.

To climb Turrialba Volcano, take a bus to Santa Cruz from where a 21 km track climbs to the summit. A 4WD vehicle will get you over half way; then you have to walk. It is reported that horses can be hired from the village of Pacayas (half way between Turrialba and Cartago) and there are horse trails to the summit. Guided tours involving foot or horse travel are offered in San José by Tikal Tours (☎ 232811) and Jungle Trails (☎ 553486), among others. A one- day trip costs about US$65. The best time to go is the January to April dry season.

RANCHO NATURALISTA

This 50 hectare ranch is about 20 km southeast of Turrialba near the village of Tuís. The ranch has a small eight room lodge called the *Albergue de Montaña*, which is popular with birders and naturalists. The North American owners are avid birders who have recorded some 300 species of birds within three km of the ranch. Hundreds of species of butterflies are to be found on the grounds as well. The ranch lies at 900 metres above sea level in montane rain and wet forest – there is a trail system. This is a recommended destination for people who would like some quiet days of bird-watching and nature study in a tranquil and undisturbed environment.

Costs are not cheap, but once you decide

to go you'll find almost everything is included. Because the owners wish to maintain a relaxed atmosphere, they ask guests to book for a minimum of three days to enable them leisurely to enjoy and explore their surroundings. Many guests stay for a week. Accommodation is US$65 per person per day (double occupancy) in the wet season (June to November) and US$75 during the rest of the year. Discounts for longer stays are US$390/730 per person, double occupancy for one/two weeks (June to November) or US$450/880 (December to May). Single supplement is a flat US$90 for the first three to seven days, US$10 per day thereafter. The price includes round trip transportation from San José, three home-cooked meals a day, maid and laundry service, guided birding trips, horseback riding, and (with stays of a week or more) a day trip to another area. About the only thing not included are bottled or canned drinks. Rooms are comfortable, most with private bath and hot water. Three rooms share a bath if the lodge is full (maximum occupancy is 16).

Reservations can be made with the owner, John Erb (☎ 398036), Apartado 364, 1002 San José.

RÍO PACUARE

The Pacuare is the next major river valley east of the Reventazón (described earlier in this chapter). It is arguably the most scenic rafting river in Costa Rica and one of the world's classic whitewater experiences. The river plunges down the Caribbean slope through a series of spectacular canyons, clothed in virgin rainforest. The Class IV rapids are exciting and separated by calm stretches which enable you to stare at the near vertical green walls towering hundreds of metres above the river – a magnificent and unique river trip.

The Pacuare does not lend itself to one day trips because it is relatively remote and inaccessible – two and three day trips are done more often, with nights spent camping on the river banks. During the day, stops are made for swimming and exploring some of the beautiful tributaries of the main river. Some of these tributaries arrive at the Pacuare in a plunging cascade from the vertical walls of the canyon, and your raft may pass directly beneath the falls.

The usual agencies in San José do this trip. I went with Costa Rica Expeditions (☎ 570766) which provided excellent service; Ríos Tropicales (☎ 336455), Horizontes (☎ 220222), and Aventuras Naturales (☎ 253939) are other options. The river can be run year round, though June to October are considered the best months. Two-day trips cost about US$220 per person, and three-day trips US$290, with eight passengers. Costs are more per person in smaller groups, but you can sometimes join another group to cut costs.

In 1986, the Pacuare was declared a wild and scenic river and had protected status conferred upon it by the government – the first river to be so protected in Central America. Despite this, the National Electric Company began an 'exploratory feasibility study' for a hydroelectric dam scheduled for approximately the end of the century. It is not clear whether the dam would be successful in generating electricity, but it would certainly ruin the Pacuare River Valley by flooding it, thus destroying the most beautiful tropical river valley in Costa Rica, and one of the most beautiful and unique in the world. Further information about the threat facing the river can be obtained from Friends of the Pacuare, Apartado 6941, 1000 San José, Costa Rica.

North-Western Costa Rica

Costa Rica's central highlands stretch a spectacular arm out to the Nicaraguan border. To the north-west of the Cordillera Central lie two more mountain chains, the Cordillera de Tilarán and the Cordillera de Guanacaste.

The Cordillera de Tilarán is characterised by rolling mountains which used to be covered with cloud forest. The famous Monteverde Cloud Forest Preserve is an important and popular destination for those wishing to see something of this tropical habitat. Separating the Cordillera de Tilarán and Cordillera de Guanacaste is Lake Arenal and the nearby Arenal Volcano, currently the most active volcano in Costa Rica and one of the most active volcanoes in all of the New World.

The Cordillera de Guanacaste is a spectacular string of dormant or gently active volcanoes, two of which are protected in the Rincón de la Vieja National Park. To the west of the Cordillera de Guanacaste, shortly before reaching the Nicaraguan border, is the Santa Elena Peninsula which contains a rare dry tropical forest habitat descending down to remote Pacific beaches. The dry forest and coastline are preserved in the beautiful and historic Santa Rosa National Park which is well worth a visit. All in all, this is a very scenic part of Costa Rica, and, apart from the Monteverde Preserve, one that is not much visited by foreign tourists.

This next section describes the towns, parks, preserves and mountains found along the north-western section of the Interamerican Highway, while the second section deals with a less frequently travelled route on minor roads around the north-east side of the mountains, past the explosive Arenal Volcano, and connecting eventually with the Interamerican Highway at Cañas. If you have the time, consider taking the rougher back route. Otherwise, the well paved Interamerican Highway will speedily take you through this spectacular part of Costa Rica.

Interamerican Highway North

Overland travellers heading from San José to Managua (Nicaragua) usually take buses along the Interamerican Highway. This leaves San José heading west almost to Puntarenas in the Pacific lowlands and then swings north-west to the Nicaraguan border. The highway from the highlands to the lowlands is steep, winding, and often narrow. Because it is a major highway, however, it is heavily used and is plied by large trucks which come hurtling down the steep curves at seemingly breakneck speeds. Whilst truck drivers probably know the road very well, travellers driving rented cars are advised to keep alert on this road. This advice comes from both the Costa Rican authorities and from me – I've driven it a couple of times and found it a little nerve-racking to take a bend and be confronted by a truck trying to pass another on the narrow road.

The lowlands are reached at the village of Esparza where there is a popular roadside

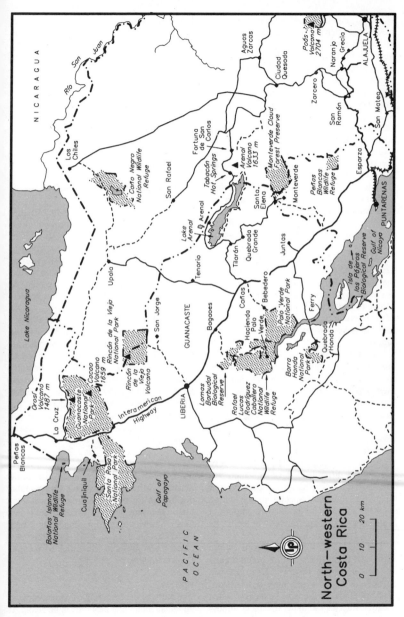

North-western Costa Rica

restaurant and fruit stalls. Tour buses and private cars often stop here for refreshments, but public buses are usually in a hurry to press on. Five km beyond Esparza, and 15 km before Puntarenas, the Interamerican Highway turns north-west and continues through the small town of Cañas and the larger city of Liberia before ending up at the Nicaraguan border. Neither Cañas nor Liberia are particularly important destinations, but the highway provides the best access to the private Monteverde Cloud Forest Preserve and a host of national parks and reserves.

Views from the highway are spectacular, particularly at the northern end. A seat on the right-hand side of the bus as you head north will give excellent views of the magnificent volcanoes in the Cordillera de Guanacaste.

PEÑAS BLANCAS WILDLIFE REFUGE

This 2400 hectare refuge is administered by the National Parks Service. Peñas Blancas lies about six km north-east of the village of Miramar, which itself is eight km north-east of the Interamerican Highway. The Miramar turn-off is six km north of the Puntarenas turn-off.

The refuge clings steeply to a southern arm of the Cordillera de Tilarán. Elevations in this small area range from less than 600 metres to over 1400 metres above sea level. Variation in altitude results in different types of forest, such as tropical dry forest in the lower south-western sections, semi-deciduous dry and moist forests in middle elevations, and premontane forest in the higher northern sections. The terrain is very rugged and difficult to traverse – there are two short trails. The refuge has been created to protect the plant species in the varied habitats and also to protect an important watershed. It is not particularly noted for its animals, however.

The name Peñas Blancas means 'white cliffs' and refers to the diatomaceous deposits found in the reserve. Diatoms are unicellular algae which have a 'skeleton' made of silica. Millions of years ago, when Central America was under the sea, countless dead diatoms sank to the ocean floor and in places built up thick deposits. Diatomaceous rock is similar to a good quality chalk. The whitish deposits are found in the steep walls of some of the river canyons in the refuge.

There are no facilities at the refuge. Camping is allowed, but you must be self-sufficient and in good shape to handle the very demanding terrain. The dry season is the best time to go – I very much doubt if you'll see anyone else there. Further information can be obtained from the National Parks Service in San José.

ISLA DE LOS PÁJAROS BIOLOGICAL RESERVE

This reserve is administered by the National Parks Service, from which permission must be obtained to visit. Isla de los Pájaros (Bird Island) lies less than a km off the coast at Punta Morales, about 15 km north-west of Puntarenas. There are no facilities on the 3.8 hectare islet, which has a small colony of nesting sea birds. The predominant vegetation is wild guava.

With help from the national park authorities, it is possible to charter a boat to visit the island and see the birds, but camping is prohibited and normally landing is limited to researchers working on the birds. Generally speaking, biological reserves administered by the National Parks Service were created to protect flora and fauna, and part of the protection in the more fragile areas consists of not encouraging visitors. This is a case in point.

MONTEVERDE

Monteverde is one of the more interesting places in Costa Rica and is a very popular destination for both foreign and local visitors. There are actually two Monteverdes. One is a small community founded by North American Quakers in 1951; the other is a cloud forest preserve which lies adjacent to the community.

History

The story of the founding of Monteverde is an unusual one that deserves to be retold. It

Top: Chestnut-mandibled toucan (RR)
Left: Tamandua anteater (RL)
Right: Erythrina tree in bloom, Cordillera Central (RR)

Top: Arenal Volcano from Fortuna village at dusk (RR)
Left: Waterfall, Corcovado National Park (RR)
Right: Poás Volcano National Park (RR)

begins in Alabama with four Quakers (a pacifist religious group also known as the 'Friends') being jailed in 1949 for refusing to register for the draft in the USA.

After their release from jail, a group of Quakers began to search for a place to settle where they could live peacefully. After searching for land in Canada, Mexico and Central America, they decided on Costa Rica whose lack of an army and peaceful policies matched their own philosophies. They chose the Monteverde area because of its pleasant climate, fertile land, and because it was far enough away from San José to be (at that time) relatively cheap to buy.

There were 44 original settlers (men, women and children from 11 families) who arrived in Monteverde in 1951. Many flew to San José; they loaded their belongings onto trucks and a few of the pioneering Quakers drove down from Alabama to Monteverde, a journey which took three months. If you think the roads to Monteverde are bad now, imagine what they must have been like four decades ago! The road in 1951 was an ox-cart trail and it took weeks of work to make it barely passable for larger vehicles.

The Quakers bought about 1500 hectares and began dairy farming and cheese production. Early cheese production was about 10 kg per day; today, Monteverde's modern cheese factory produces about 1000 kg of cheese daily and it is sold throughout Costa Rica. The cheese factory is now in the middle of the Monteverde community and can be visited by those interested in the process.

Information

Most hotels will accept US dollars or change small sums of money. There is a bank in Santa Elena.

Santa Elena also has a small clinic in case of medical emergencies.

Responsible Tourism

Monteverde started as a Quaker community founded by peaceful people who wanted to live in a quiet and friendly environment. This has changed drastically in the last decade with the large influx of visitors. There is a

limit to the number of visitors Monteverde can handle before losing its special atmosphere and there is a limit to the number of people who can visit the Preserve without causing too much damage.

Quakers have traditionally been adept at peaceful resolution of problems and they are handling their new status as a tourist attraction with grace and common sense. The income from tourism is important, but preserving their own lifestyle and surroundings is equally, if not more, important to the inhabitants. Monteverde is a special but fragile place – visitors are very welcome but should remember that they are visiting a peaceful community and/or a cloud forest preserve.

Most visitors are delighted with their stay; a few complain incessantly about how muddy the trails are (you have to expect mud in a cloud forest), how boring the nightlife is (Quakers traditionally don't do much night clubbing), or how difficult it is to see the quetzal (this is not a zoo). Monteverde is not for everybody – if clouds and Quakers, cheese and quetzals do not sound like your idea of fun, head for a resort more to your liking.

Things to See

For details on visiting the cloud forest preserve, see the following section.

Tours of the cheese factory, called La Lechería, can be arranged, and cheese and other dairy products can be purchased. Through a huge window behind the cheese store you can watch the workers making the cheeses. Store hours are 7.30 to 3.30 pm daily, except Sunday when it closes at 12.30 pm. Work does not begin until 9 am.

There are a number of art galleries which can be visited. They are all more than just souvenir stores for tourists. A local women's arts and crafts co-operative (CASEM) sells embroidered and hand painted blouses and handmade clothing as well as other souvenirs. Profits benefit the local community.

The Hummingbird Gallery just outside the cloud forest preserve entrance has feeders constantly attracting several species of hummingbirds – great photo opportunities! Inside, slides and photographs by the renowned British wildlife photographer Michael Fogden are on display and for sale.

Sarah Dowell's Art Gallery is in her home up a steep path through pleasant woodlands – her work is bold and distinctive and can be seen in some of the Monteverde hotels as well. There is also a small souvenir shop behind the fuel station.

The Monteverde Conservation League has an office (☎ 612953) and welcomes visitors with serious questions. They operate a trail called Sendero Bajo Tigre, the entrance to which is near the Pensión Quetzal. The trail is open daily from 6 am to 4 pm and there is a day use fee of US$1.10 which benefits the MCL. Children accompanied by adults are free.

Places to Stay

During Christmas and Easter most hotels are booked up months ahead. During the January to April busy season, and also in July, hotels tend to be full often enough that you should telephone before arriving to ensure yourself of a place to stay. You may have to book some weeks in advance for the dates and hotel of your choice. You can write to most of the better hotels c/o MCL, Apartado 10165, 1000 San José.

Places to Stay – bottom end

The cheapest places are in Santa Elena, about five km from the preserve, but most people prefer to stay closer to the preserve. The hotels here are basic but adequate. The *Pensión Santa Elena* (☎ 611151) is clean, has hot water in the communal bathrooms, and has a decent restaurant serving home-cooked food. Lodging is US$3 per person.

The *Pensión Tucán* (☎ 611007) is also clean and has hot water in the shared bathrooms. The charge is US$3.50 per person. Other possibilities in this price range include the *Hotel Imán* (☎ 611255), which has a restaurant attached, and the *Pensión Imán*, which is under the same ownership.

Places to Stay – middle

The recently opened *Pensión Manikin* is about 3½ km from the preserve. The charge in this friendly place is US$6.60 per person, there's hot water in the shared bathrooms, and meals are served for US$4.40 each.

The *Monteverde Inn* (☎ 612756) is almost four km from the preserve. The charge is US$6 per person for bed & breakfast in dormitory style accommodation. Rooms with private bath and full board are US$19 per person. You could ask to camp here.

The *Pensión Flor Mar* (☎ 610909) is run by Marvin Rockwell, one of the original Quakers who was jailed for refusing to sign up for the draft and then spent three months driving down from Alabama. He and his Costa Rican wife Flory (get the name of the hotel?) are very friendly and their little pensión is very pleasant. Rooms with shared bath are US$20 per person; with private bath US$22 per person. This includes all three meals. Horses are available for rent. The hotel is just over two km from the preserve.

The recently opened *Hotel Fonda Vela* (☎ 612551) is the closest to the preserve at just over 1½ km away. The charge is US$15/24 for singles/doubles (communal bathrooms) and US$24/33 for singles/doubles with private bathrooms. Breakfast is US$4, lunch or dinner is US$7, and horses with guide are available for US$7 per hour.

The *Hotel Heliconia* (☎ 611009) is four km away from the preserve and is another family run hotel. Rooms with private bath are US$30, single or double occupancy. Three meals a day cost an extra US$19 per person.

The *Pensión Quetzal* (☎ 610955) is almost three km away from the preserve. It is the oldest hotel in Monteverde and is very popular with birding groups; there is a flower filled garden which attracts plenty of hummingbirds and other species right to the porch. Some rooms are inside the hotel, others are in cabins nearby. Not all rooms have private bathrooms. They have a 'No Smoking' policy in the hotel. Prices vary depending on the room, but all include three

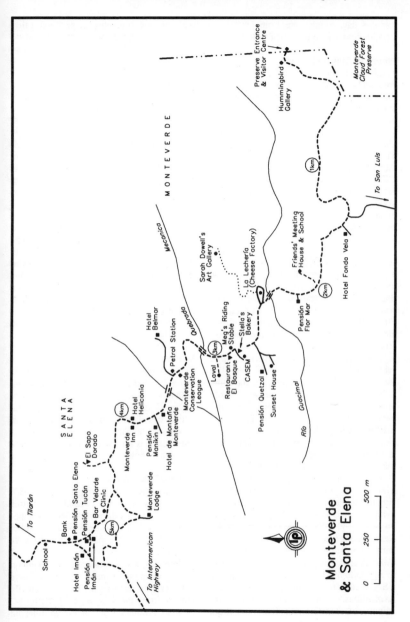

Monteverde & Santa Elena

meals a day. Singles are from US$30 to US$50; doubles are from US$44 to US$60.

Places to Stay – top end

The *Hotel Belmar* (☎ 611001) is a beautiful wooden hotel on a hill, almost four km from the preserve. The road up to the hotel is steep and slippery for the last 300 metres, and cars don't always make it. But once you get there, you are rewarded with superb views of the Gulf of Nicoya when the weather is clear. The hotel is run by a friendly Chilean couple. Attractive rooms (most have balconies) are US$40/45 single/double. Breakfast is US$5, lunch or dinner is US$8, and the food is good. For US$10 you can get a ride to the preserve and be picked up again at a prearranged time.

The *Hotel de Montaña Monteverde* (☎ 611846) has similarly priced rooms and a few suites at about US$70 double. There is a good restaurant, and the spacious gardens are pleasant to walk around in. The hotel is 3½ km from the preserve. This hotel can be reserved in San José (☎ 337078) at Apartado 70, 1001 Plaza Víquez, San José. Both the Belmar and Montaña will provide transport from San José on request.

The brand new *Monteverde Lodge* (☎ 611157) opened for business in 1991. The lodge is five km from the preserve and is the most comfortable hotel in the Monteverde area. The rooms are larger than most, and have forest views. A wildlife observation platform is being built in the forest canopy overlooking a river ravine by the hotel. There is an indoor jacuzzi for guests to soak away the stresses of hiking steep and muddy trails. A walk-in hummingbird aviary is also planned. Rooms are US$54/63/73 for singles/doubles/triples. Excellent meals are available at US$8 for an all you can eat breakfast and US$13 for lunch or dinner. Reservations should be made with Costa Rica Expeditions (☎ 570766, 220333) at Calle Central, Avenida 3, San José, or write to Apartado 6941, 1000 San José. From the USA, mail gets there quicker if sent to CR Expeditions, Dept 235, PO Box 025216, Miami, FL 33102-5216. Complete tours with private transport, expert naturalist guides and all meals and accommodation are also available (US$350 per person, three days/two nights).

Places to Eat

Many people eat in their hotels, most of which provide meals. There are other possibilities, however. The *El Bosque Restaurant* is a very pleasant little place in a rustic setting. Good lunches and dinners are available for about US$4 to US$6. It is open from noon to 9 pm daily, except Wednesday. The restaurant is nearly three km from the preserve. For do-it-yourself picnic lunches, head for the nearby *Stella's Bakery* for delicious home-made bread and rolls, then go to *La Lechería* to pick up some fresh cheese.

The *El Sapo Dorado* (literally 'The Golden Toad') is up a hill about 4½ km from the preserve. There is a patio with views of the Gulf of Nicoya where you can eat good dinners between 7 and 9 pm. After dinner, music and dancing are a possibility. It is closed on Monday and Tuesday.

There are a couple of cheaper places to eat in Santa Elena.

Entertainment

There is not much in the way of nightlife beyond sitting around the hotel and chatting with other visitors about the day's events.

The *El Sapo Dorado* is a bar/restaurant which has dancing in the evenings from Wednesday to Sunday. The *Bar Velarde* in Santa Elena is a bar with loud music, but you can also sit outside.

Getting There & Away

The Monteverde bus company (☎ 612659) can give you current schedules. Buses usually run on six days of the week – sometimes there is no bus on Monday, at other times Friday is the day off, so check in advance.

From San José, buses leave at 2.30 pm on weekdays and 6.30 am on weekends. There is no terminal in San José; the bus currently leaves from the east side of Calle 12, between Avenida 5 & 7, although it has, in the past, left from the north-eastern corner of Avenida 9 & Calle 12. The trip takes about four hours (depending on season and road conditions) and costs about US$3.50.

In Monteverde, the last bus stop is by La Lechería (the cheese factory) about 2½ km before the preserve. Ask to be set down anywhere before there, near the hotel of your choice. At the moment buses return to San José at 6.30 am on weekdays and 3 pm on weekends, but ask at your hotel or call the bus company for current return times. The 3 pm Sunday bus gets full early.

There is also a bus from Puntarenas to Santa Elena. It leaves from the bus stop by the beach, between Calle 2 & 4, at 2.15 pm daily. The bus gets into Santa Elena about 5.30 pm and returns to Puntarenas the next day at 6 am. The bus stop in Santa Elena is by the bank. From Santa Elena, taxis can be hired to the preserve, five km away.

Drivers will find that the highway to Monteverde is in poor condition, and 4WD is often necessary during the rainy season. Many car rental agencies will refuse to rent you an ordinary car during the wet season if you state that you are going to Monteverde. (Ordinary cars are OK in the dry months.)

Take the Interamerican Highway as far as the Río Lagarto bridge (just past Km 149) and here turn right on the steep, winding and scenic dirt road to Santa Elena (32 km) and Monteverde. (There is good bird-watching en route.) It is also possible to drive from Tilarán but the road is worse, especially the last few km before Santa Elena. I know people who have done this in an ordinary rental vehicle in the dry season – they said it was definitely a drive to remember and took much longer than they had expected!

MONTEVERDE CLOUD FOREST PRESERVE

When the Quaker settlers first arrived, they decided to preserve about a third of their property in order to protect the watershed above Monteverde. In 1972, with the help of organisations such as the Nature Conservancy and World Wildlife Fund, about 2000

more hectares were purchased adjoining the already preserved area. This was called the Monteverde Cloud Forest Preserve and became owned and operated by the Tropical Science Center of San José. Gradually, more land was acquired and added to the reserve.

In 1985, the Monteverde Conservation League (MCL) was formed and continues to buy land to expand the reserve. In 1988, the MCL launched the International Children's Rainforest project whereby children and school groups from all over the world raised money to buy and save tropical rainforest adjacent to the preserve. This project does more than ask children to raise money for rainforest preservation – it is an educational programme as well. Recent figures for the Monteverde Cloud Forest Preserve have reached 4000 hectares, and a further 4800 hectares have been designated for the Children's Rainforest.

The most striking aspect of this project is that it is a private enterprise rather than a national park administered by the government. Governments worldwide must begin to count conservation as a key issue for the continued well-being of their citizens, but it is interesting to see what a positive effect ordinary people can have on preserving their environment. This preservation relies partly on donations from the public.

Donations to the preserve or the Children's Rainforest can be sent to: Monteverde Conservation League, Apartado 10165, 1000 San José, Costa Rica

Recently, the Ministry of Natural Resources, Energy and Mines has announced the creation of eight Regional Conservation Units (RCUs) which consolidate protected areas. The RCUs include national parks, national forests, private preserves and farmland which is managed in such a way as to provide buffer zones for more fully protected areas. The RCUs have been dubbed 'megaparks' by local conservationists and will cover about 27% of Costa Rica's territory. The Monteverde Preserve will be included in the Arenal RCU which will cover about 108,000 hectares. This will provide greater protection for Monteverde and the Children's Rainforest.

Information

The information office and gift store at the entrance of the preserve is open daily from 7 am to 4 pm. For some inexplicable reason it is closed on 6 and 7 October. Entrance tickets to the preserve are bought here. Fees are US$5 per day or US$29.50 for a week. Students receive a 40% discount.

You can buy trail guides, bird and mammal lists, maps and obtain other information here.

The walking trails are generally very muddy, and even during the dry season (late December to early May) the cloud forest tends to be dripping. Therefore rainwear and suitable boots are recommended. During the wet season, the trails turn into quagmires, but there are usually fewer visitors. The annual rainfall here is about three metres.

Because of the fragile environment, the preserve will only allow a maximum of 100 people in on any given day. Usually this is no problem, but during Christmas and Easter weeks, it can be full to capacity, so try to avoid these times. In a recent year, the busiest months were January, February, March and July, with over 2000 visitors entering the preserve in each of those months. Conversely, there were less than 1000 monthly visitors during May, June, September, October and November.

Guides

Although you can hike around the preserve without a guide, you'll stand a better chance of seeing a quetzal and other wildlife if you hire a guide. Half day guided hikes can be arranged at the information centre for US$12 per person.

Most hotels will be able to arrange for a local to guide you either within the preserve or in some of the nearby surrounding areas.

The cost of a guide varies depending on how well known or experienced they are, but expect to start at around US$20 for half a day. The best guides will charge about US$50 for half a day. These fees can be split up among a group, however, and so individual costs are not prohibitive. Three well known and highly recommended guides are Gary Diller (☎ 610903) and Richard and Meg Laval (☎ 610952). Meg takes people on horse riding tours; horses cost about US$10 an hour. These guides can all be contacted via the Monteverde Conservation League, Apartado 10165, 1000 San José.

Because of the historical Quaker background, many locals and most guides speak English as well as Spanish.

Things to See

Inside the preserve there are various marked and maintained trails and several shelters where camping is allowed. The bird list includes over 400 species which have been recorded in the area, but the one that most visitors want to see is the resplendent quetzal (described in the Flora & Fauna section of the Facts About the Country chapter). The best time to see the Quetzal is when it is nesting in March and April, but you could get lucky any time of year.

But there is a host of other things to observe. A walk along the Sendero Nuboso (Cloudy Trail) will take you on a two km (one way) interpretive walk through the cloud forest to the Continental Divide. A trail guide describes plants, weather patterns, animal tracks, insects and ecosystems which you see along the way.

One animal which you used to be able to see so often that it became almost a Monteverde mascot was the golden toad. Monteverde was the only place in the world where this exotic little toad occurred. This tiny gold coloured amphibian frequently used to be seen scrambling along the muddy trails of the cloud forest, adding a bright splash to the surroundings. Unfortunately, no one has seen this once common amphibian since the late 1980s, and it is a mystery what happened to it. If you are lucky enough to sight a golden toad, be sure to report it.

Recently, during a conference of herpetologists (scientists who study reptiles and amphibians) from all over the world, it was noted that the same puzzling story was occurring with other frog and toad species all over the world. Amphibians once common were now severely depleted or simply not found at all. The scientists were unable to give a reason for the sudden demise of so many amphibian species in so many different habitats.

One theory is that worldwide air quality has depreciated to the extent that amphibians, who breathe both with primitive lungs and through their perpetually moist skin, were more susceptible to air-borne toxins because of the gas exchange through their skin. Perhaps they are like the canaries miners used in the old days to warn them of toxic air in the mines. When the canary keeled over, it was time for the miners to get out!

Are our dying frogs and toads a symptom of a planet which is becoming too polluted?

When I walked the Sendero Nuboso, the clouds were low over the forest and the gnarled old oak trees, festooned with vines and bromeliads, looked mysterious and slightly forbidding. Palm trees and bamboos bent menacingly over the trail and I felt as if I were walking through a Grimm fairytale – a wicked witch or grinning goblin would not be out of place.

Suddenly the cold, clammy mist was rent by the weirdest metallic BONK!, followed by an eerie high pitched whistle such as I had never heard before. I stopped dead in my tracks.

For a full minute I listened and heard nothing but the sighing of the faintest of breezes and a lone insect circling my ear. Then again, the strange BONK and whistle were repeated, louder, and high overhead. I craned my neck and searched the tree tops with my binoculars.

Finally, after several more extremely loud BONKS and whistles, I spied an odd looking large brown bird with snow white head and shoulders just visible on a high snag.

At first, I thought the bird was eating a lizard or small snake – through my binoculars I could clearly see the worm-like objects hanging from the bill. But then the beak gaped wide open and, instead of a seeing a reptile wriggling away, I heard another BONK and whistle. Finally, I realised that I was watching the aptly named three-wattled bellbird.

The three black, wormy looking wattles hanging from the bill were fully six cm long – about a fifth of the length of the entire bird. The metallic BONK did sound rather bell-like, but it travelled over an incredible distance. It seemed to be flooding the forest with sound, but the bird itself was probably 100 metres away or more, barely visible in the top of the cloud forest.

Places to Stay & Eat

There is a dormitory-style refuge near the park entrance where a bunk costs US$3 per person. These bunks are often used by researchers and may not be available to tourists – contact the Monteverde Cloud Forest Preserve (☎ 612655) or write to the Tropical Science Center (☎ 226241) Apartado 8-3870, 1000 San José for reservations.

There are kitchen facilities, or full board can be provided for US$15 per day if arranged in advance. Camping is allowed a few minutes' walk away from the entrance for a nominal fee. Space is limited and there are no facilities so you should have all your own equipment.

There are two basic refuges on the Continental Divide about two or three hours hike into the preserve, and a third refuge in the lowlands beyond – about a four hour hike. It is possible to sleep in or camp by these shelters. Again, there are no facilities. The information office can tell you which trails to take to get there.

Given the limited accommodation, few visitors actually stay in the reserve itself. The majority of people stay in one of the several hotels, pensións, and lodges in either the Monteverde community or in Santa Elena. The nearest hotel is 1½ km from the entrance; the most distant are in the small town of Santa Elena, about five km from the entrance.

Getting There & Away

The entrance to the preserve is uphill from all the hotels, and there is no public transport. The better hotels can arrange a vehicle to take you up to the preserve, or you can take your own vehicle to the small parking lot by the entrance, or walk.

Many visitors remark that some of the best birding is on the open road leading up to the preserve entrance, especially the final two km.

TEMPISQUE FERRY

About 20 km south of Cañas on the Interamerican Highway is a turn-off to the Tempisque Ferry, 25 km to the west. If you are driving to the Nicoya Peninsula, this will save you about 110 km of driving via Liberia. Some buses from San José to Nicoya and the Nicoya Peninsula beaches come this way – ask about the route in the San José bus offices.

The ferry runs about every 45 or 60 minutes during daylight hours. The crossing takes 20 minutes and costs US$2 per car and US$0.20 for foot passengers. The ferry holds up to 12 cars and you might not be able to get on at peak times, especially Sunday afternoons heading back to the mainland from the Nicoya Peninsula.

CAÑAS

Cañas is a small agricultural centre serving about 21,000 people in the surrounding area. It is a hot little town, 90 metres above sea level in the Guanacaste lowlands and about 180 km from San José along the Interamerican Highway. There is not much to do in Cañas itself, but travellers use it as a base for visits to the nearby Palo Verde National Park and other reserves. Cañas is also the beginning or end point for the Arenal back roads route described later in this chapter.

Places to Stay

There are several basic places. The *Hotel Familiar* on the north-eastern corner of Avenida 3 and Calle Central is the cheapest at US$1.75 per person. There are two basic but adequate hotels on the south-eastern side of the central plaza. They are the *Hotel Guillén* and *Hotel Parque* and they charge US$2.60 per person.

The *Gran Hotel* on the north-western side of the plaza costs US$3 per person. At the south-eastern end of town, by Avenida 2 and Calle 5, you'll find the *Cabinas Corobicí* which is a little more pleasant. The charge here is about US$3 per person. None of these hotels have private baths or hot water.

The best place in Cañas itself is the *Hotel Cañas* (☎ 690039; Apartado 61, Cañas, Guanacaste), Calle 2, Avenida 3. Rooms with private baths cost US$4.50 per person.

You can also stay at the much better *La Pacífica* which is six km north of Cañas.

Places to Eat

There are some decent Chinese restaurants in town. Two of the best are the *Restaurant El Primero* on the central plaza and the *Restaurant Lei Tu* just off the plaza on Avenida 1. Meals are about US$2 to US$4. There are other places nearby.

Getting There & Away

Buses from San José leave six times a day from Calle 16, Avenida 1 & 3, opposite the Coca Cola terminal. There are also buses with TRALAPA at Calle 20, Avenida 3. The trip takes about 3½ hours and costs about US$2.

The bus situation in Cañas is complicated by the recent opening of a new bus terminal and produce market at Calle 1 and Avenida 11. Some buses leave from here and others leave from another part of town. Perhaps, by the time you read this, all buses will be leaving from the new terminal.

Currently, the new terminal has buses to Liberia at 7.30, 9 and 11 am and 3 pm. There are buses to Tilarán seven times a day. There is a daily bus at 11 am to Bebedero (the closest point to Palo Verde National Park).

Buses for San José leave from the Caneria Terminal at Avenida Central and Calle 5. There are six daily buses but the last leaves at 2 pm.

Locals told me that they catch buses to Tilarán or San José as the bus drives along

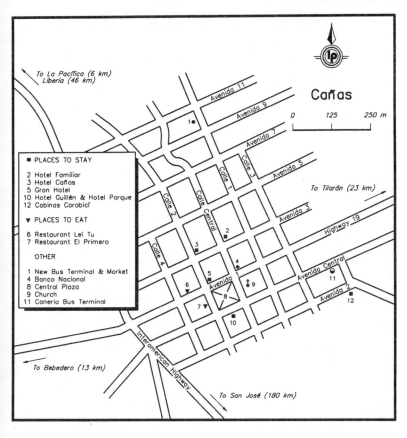

To La Pacífica (6 km)
Liberia (46 km)

Cañas

0   125   250 m

To Tilarán (23 km)

To Bebedero (13 km)

To San José (180 km)

Interamerican Highway

Highway 19

■ PLACES TO STAY

2 Hotel Familiar
3 Hotel Cañas
5 Gran Hotel
10 Hotel Guillén & Hotel Parque
12 Cabinas Corobicí

▼ PLACES TO EAT

6 Restaurant Lei Tu
7 Restaurant El Primero

OTHER

1 New Bus Terminal & Market
4 Banco Nacional
8 Central Plaza
9 Church
11 Cañería Bus Terminal

Avenida 7 on the way out of town. There are bus stops on this avenue between Calle Central & 1. I prefer going to the terminal, but you could wait on Avenida 7.

LA PACÍFICA

La Pacífica is a working hacienda just off the Interamerican Highway about six km north of Cañas. They have about 500 head of cattle, rice paddies, sorghum fields, cashew trees and other crops. The difference between La Pacífica and other farms is that about 400 of its 1300 hectares have been left covered with forest. The owners, to put it in their own words, have attempted an equilibrium between rational exploitation of natural resources and conservation. To a certain extent, this concept has been successful and many species of birds are attracted to the hacienda. Howler monkeys, armadillos and anteaters are among the mammals which can be seen in the forest.

For about two decades, researchers have been coming to the hacienda to monitor the habitats preserved here. In 1986 an Ecological Centre was created at La Pacífica. The aims of the centre are to promote research into agricultural methods which minimise impact on the environment and to provide a working model of a low impact farm for educational purposes. Observation of the flora and fauna is encouraged.

Visitors will find that the entire complex – hacienda, Ecological Centre and forest – is open to inspection on foot or horseback. Bilingual naturalist guides are available for US$25 a half day, and horses can be rented at US$4 per hour. In addition, the National Parks Service has an office here and can give information on visiting Palo Verde, Santa Rosa and Barro Honda national parks and other nearby preserves. Staff can help arrange birding trips, guided visits to the national parks and float trips on the nearby Río Corobicí.

Places to Stay

La Pacífica also has a very pleasant hotel (☎ 690050) with comfortable rooms and cabins with private baths and fans. There is a swimming pool and a highly regarded Swiss run restaurant. The best rooms (with hot water) are US$39/47/55 single/double/triple; other rooms have cold showers and are cheaper. The average temperature here is 27°C so cold showers are not much of a hardship. Reservations can be made at Apartado 8, Cañas 5700, Guanacaste, Costa Rica.

Places to Eat

Travellers with their own transport who do not wish to visit the Ecological Centre can still stop at the tastefully decorated restaurant for the good meals (about US$5 to US$10). If this is too expensive for you, there is also the pleasant restaurant *Rincón Corobicí* which is just past La Pacífica on the banks of the Río Corobicí.

RÍO COROBICÍ

Apart from the La Pacífica, tour companies in San José arrange one-day rafting trips on the Río Corobicí. The emphasis is on wildlife observation rather than exciting whitewater – the river is Class I to II – in other words, pretty flat.

Costa Rica Expeditions in San José has trips involving three hours driving, three hours rafting and three hours return driving with bilingual guides and lunch on the river. Departures are every Saturday and cost US$65 per person. They can also arrange rafting trips on other days and provide overnight tours to La Pacífica with private vehicle and guide. Ríos Tropicales (☎ 336455) also offers Corobicí River trips.

PALO VERDE NATIONAL PARK

The 5704 hectare Palo Verde National Park lies on the north-eastern banks of the mouth of Río Tempisque at the head of the Gulf of Nicoya, some 30 km west of Cañas. Adjoining the national park to the north-west is the 7354 hectare **Rafael Lucas Rodríguez Caballero National Wildlife Refuge** also on the banks of the Tempisque. Just north of the Wildlife Refuge is the 2279 hectare **Lomas Parbudal Biological Reserve**.

The combined protected area of 15,337 hectares is a major bird sanctuary for resident and migrating waterfowl, as well as forest birds. A large number of different habitats is represented, ranging from swamps and marshes to a variety of seasonal forests. The dry season from December to March is very marked and much of the forest dries out. During the wet months, large portions of the area are flooded.

The combined parks and reserves are a magnet for bird-watchers who come to see the large flocks of herons, storks (including the only Costa Rican nesting site of the locally endangered Jabiru Stork), spoonbills, egrets, ibis, grebes and ducks. Inland, birds such as scarlet macaws, great currasows, keel-billed toucans and parrots may be seen. Other possible sightings include crocodiles and iguanas, monkeys and peccaries, and other animals.

It is planned that Palo Verde and the adjoining reserves will be combined with Barro Honda National Park and other reserves in the Nicoya Peninsula to form one of the new 'megaparks' – the Lower Tempisque RCU.

Information

The recommended time for a visit is the dry season because the birds tend to congregate in the remaining lakes and marshes. Trees lose their leaves and the massed flocks of birds become easier to observe. In addition, there are far fewer insects in the dry season and the roads and trails are more passable. Mammals are seen around the waterholes. Binoculars or a spotting scope are highly recommended.

There is a research station run by the Organization of Tropical Studies (OTS). This is called Hacienda Palo Verde but is, confusingly, in the Rafael Lucas Rodríguez Caballero National Wildlife Refuge, and not in Palo Verde National Park. Trails lead from the station into the refuge and there is also an observation tower in the area.

Places to Stay & Eat

Sometimes the research station is full of researchers or students; at other times travellers can stay here for US$35 per day. If you wish to stay overnight at the OTS research station, make arrangements with OTS (☎ 366696), Apartado 676, 2050 San Pedro de Montes de Oca, San José.

Camping is permitted near the Palo Verde National Park Ranger Station, where there are toilets and shower facilities available to campers. If you wish to camp, let the National Parks Service in San José know about it. They can provide you meals with the park rangers if ordered in advance and you may be able to co-ordinate transport with a ranger going into the area. The rangers sometimes take travellers on patrol with them, often by horseback, sometimes by boat around the bird islands of the Río Tempisque. Information can also be obtained from the La Pacífica, who can arrange guided tours. The park has a telephone (☎ 335473).

Getting There & Away

To get there by public transport, take the daily bus from Cañas to Bebedero, from where it is about a 10 km walk to the national park. You can also drive in this way.

Another route is by bus to Bagaces (half way between Cañas and Liberia – take a Liberia bus and get off at Bagaces). From here, hire a taxi or drive and follow signs for the wildlife refuge. The road is supposedly passable year round, but get up-to-date information first because it is a remote region and there are few people to help if you get bogged down. This is the route to the OTS station.

In the dry season only, it is reportedly possible to enter Palo Verde from the Nicoya Peninsula. Take a bus from Nicoya to Puerto Humo on the Río Tempisque. At the port, hire a boat to take you across the river to the national park dock – it shouldn't cost more than a dollar or two. From the dock, it is possible to hike into the national park to your right or the wildlife refuge to your left. The whole area is flooded during the wet season.

LIBERIA

Liberia is Costa Rica's most northerly town of any importance. It is the capital of the province of Guanacaste, but the town and surrounding villages have a combined population of only 28,000. This is an indication of how rural most of Costa Rica is once you leave the Central Valley.

The city is 140 metres above sea level and surrounded by ranches. It is a centre for the cattle industry, and is also a fairly important transportation centre.

From Liberia the Interamerican Highway heads south to Cañas (46 km) and San José (about 220 km). Northbound, the highway reaches the Nicaraguan border at (75Peñas Blancas (75 km). A paved highway to the west is the major road into the Nicoya Peninsula, which is famous for its good beaches, terrible roads and friendly inhabitants. A poor road to the east leads to the Rincón de la Vieja National Park. Liberia is also a good base for visiting the Santa Rosa National Park and the newly created Guanacaste National Park, both to the north.

A monument of a Sabanero (akin to a cowboy) can be seen on the main road into town, and there is a pleasant Central Plaza. There is also a cinema.

Information

There are a number of good hotels, restaurants and bars and the main activities are relaxing in one of them as you plan your next trip to beach or volcano.

Most of the better hotels will accept US dollars and there is also a bank.

The town is busy during the dry season and you should make reservations for the hotel of your choice, particularly at Christmas, Easter and weekends. Conversely, the better hotels give discounts in the wet season.

Tours A travel and tour agency called Guanacaste Tours (☎ 660306) has opened recently. The agency is in the Motel El Bramadero and is run by a friendly English speaking lady, Claudia Fernández de Brenes. They run a variety of day tours using air-con vehicles and bilingual guides. Tours include lunch and cost about US$60 per person – the only drawback is that there is a six person minimum. Sometimes it is possible to hook up with another group. Current offerings include:

Corobicí River float trip (Monday, US$55)
a three beach tour and visit to a 2000 year old Indian cemetery (Tuesday, US$65)
bus and boat to Tamarindo Wildlife Refuge and a visit to Guaitil to see Chorotega Indian ceramics (Wednesday, US$60)
Santa Rosa & Guanacaste national parks with horse riding (Thursday, US$65)
Palo Verde National Park and Tempisque River cruise (Tuesday, Friday, US$65)
Rodeo Fiesta (Saturday, January to April, US$35).

Prices include pick-up and return from hotels in Liberia and major nearby beach hotels. Further information is available from Apartado 55, 5000 Liberia, Guanacaste.

Places to Stay – bottom end

The *Hotel Liberia* just south of the main plaza on Calle Central is basic but adequate. It costs US$3 per person or US$3.50 per person in rooms with private bath (cold water). The *Hotel Oriental* (☎ 662188, 660085) is Chinese run and has a restaurant

attached. It is on Avenida 1, a block off the Interamerican Highway, and is popular with Costa Rican truck drivers and families and is often full. Rooms with private bath are US$3.75 per person.

Other basic hotels charging US$3 or less per person include the *Pensión Margarita* and *Hotel Cortijo* on Avenida Central, Calle 3 & 5; and the *Hotel Rivas* on the corner of the plaza. None of these three look up to much, but are probably OK – try the Margarita first.

Places to Stay – middle

The *Hotel Daisyta* (☎ 660197, 660927) is fairly basic, but has a swimming pool and is family run and friendly. It is on the eastern outskirts of town on Avenida 5 near Calle 13. The charge is about US$6 per person.

The *Motel El Bramadero* (☎ 660371), at the intersection of the Interamerican Highway and the main road into town (Avenida Central), charges US$12/17.50 for singles/doubles with private bath and US$16/24 with air-con. Not all the rooms have hot water. There is a reasonable restaurant and swimming pool. Reservations can be made at Apartado 70, 5000 Liberia, Guanacaste.

The *Hotel La Siesta* (☎ 660678) is on a quiet street – Calle 4, Avenida 4 & 6. The rates are US$18/26/31 for a single/double/triple with bath and air-con. There is a small restaurant/bar and a tiny swimming pool. Reservations should be addressed to Apartado 15, 5000 Liberia, Guanacaste.

The *Hotel Boyeros* (☎ 660995, 660722) is also at the intersection of the Interamerican with the main road into Liberia. Rooms are US$21/29/34 for a single/double/triple with bath and air-con. There is a restaurant, swimming pool, and dancing at weekends. Address reservations to Apartado 85, Liberia, Guanacaste.

The *Hotel El Sitio* (☎ 661211) is on the road to Nicoya, about 300 metres west of the Interamerican Highway. Spacious rooms are US$31 double with private bath or US$37 with air-con. There is a restaurant and pool.

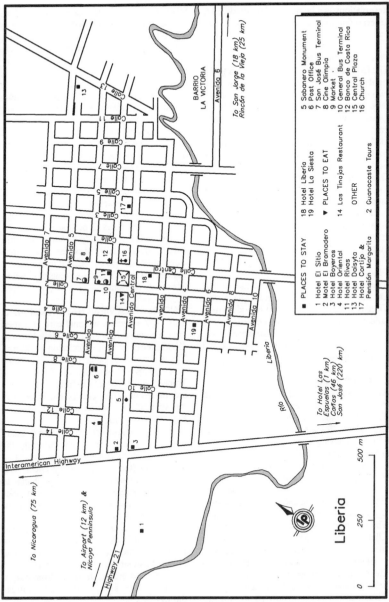

Liberia

PLACES TO STAY
1 Hotel El Sitio
2 Motel El Bramadero
3 Hotel Boyeros
4 Hotel Oriental
11 Hotel Rivas
13 Hotel Daisyta
17 Hotel Cortijo &
Pensión Margarita
18 Hotel Liberia
19 Hotel La Siesta

▼ PLACES TO EAT
14 Las Tinajas Restaurant

OTHER
2 Guanacaste Tours
5 Sabanero Monument
6 Post Office
7 San José Bus Terminal
8 Cine Olimpia
9 Market
10 General Bus Terminal
12 Banco de Costa Rica
15 Central Plaza
16 Church

BARRIO
LA VICTORIA

To San Jorge (18 km)
Rincón de la Vieja (25 km)

To Hotel Las
Espuelas (1 km)
Cañas (46 km)
San José (220 km)

To Nicaragua (75 km)

To Airport (12 km) &
Nicoya Penninsula

Highway 21

Interamerican Highway

Río Liberia

0   250   500 m

Reservations can be made to Apartado 134, Liberia, Guanacaste; or Apartado 471, San José.

Places to Stay – top end

The *Hotel Las Espuelas* (☎ 660144) is to the right (east) of the Interamerican Highway, two km before you get to the main road into Liberia. It is considered the best hotel in Liberia and has pleasant grounds, a pool, restaurant and gift shop. Rooms are US$45/55 for a single/double with private bath and air-con. Reservations can be addressed to Apartado 88, Liberia, Guanacaste. Overnight tours can be arranged to Las Imagénes Biological Station on a working cattle ranch near Rincón de la Vieja National Park.

Note that many hotels (especially the more expensive ones) give substantial discounts in the low (rainy) season.

Places to Eat

The best restaurants are in the better hotels. On the west side of the central plaza, *Las Tinajas* is a good place to sit outside with a cold drink and watch the unenergetic goings on in the plaza. Meals are reasonably priced. There are several Chinese restaurants and *sodas* near the central plaza.

Getting There & Away

There is an airport about 12 km west of town but there are no services currently scheduled. There are plans afoot, however, to turn this into Costa Rica's second international airport, catering especially to the annual influx of North American tourists trying to escape harsh winters by flying to Costa Rica's Pacific beach resorts.

Meanwhile, visitors arrive by bus and car. Buses from San José leave eight times a day from Calle 14, Avenida 1 & 3 (☎ 221650). The 4½ hour ride costs about US$2.50. In Liberia, buses returning to San José leave from the terminal at Calle 2, Avenida 3 & 5.

Buses for other destinations leave from the terminal one block south of the San José terminal and just north of the central plaza. There are two companies servicing Filadelfia, Santa Cruz and Nicoya at least once an hour. There are two or three buses a day to Playas del Coco and two daily buses to Playa Panamá, which are the closest beach resorts to Liberia (see the chapter on the Nicoya Peninsula).

Buses for Peñas Blancas (at the Nicaraguan border) stop at this terminal at 9 am and 12 noon en route from San José, and seats are usually available. There are also slower local buses to Peñas Blancas from here. These are the buses to take if you want to get dropped off at the entrance to Santa Rosa National Park.

There is a taxi stand on the north-west corner of the central plaza. These cabs will take you to the beaches if you can't wait for a bus. They will also take you to Santa Rosa National Park (US$12 per cab) and up the rough road to Rincón de la Vieja National Park (US$30 per cab). Most cab drivers consider four passengers to be their limit. During the wet season, 4WD taxis are used to get to Rincón de la Vieja.

RINCÓN DE LA VIEJA NATIONAL PARK

This 14,083 hectare national park is named after the active Rincón de la Vieja Volcano (1895 metres) which is the main attraction. There are several other peaks in the same volcanic massif, of which the Santa María Volcano is the highest (1916 metres). There are numerous cones, craters and lagoons in the summit area which can be visited on horseback and foot.

Major volcanic activity occurred many times in the late 1960s, but currently the volcano is gently active and does not present any danger (though you should check with the National Parks Service for any change in activity before you go). There are fumaroles and boiling mud pools, steam vents and sulphurous springs to explore.

Thirty two rivers and streams have their sources within the park and thus it is an important water catchment area. It was to protect this that the park was first created in 1974. Forests protect the rivers from evaporation in the dry season and from flooding in the wet season.

Elevations in the park range from less than 600 metres to 1916 metres and the changes in altitude result in the presence of four life zones. Visitors pass through a variety of different habitats as the volcanoes are ascended. Many species of trees are found in the forests. Plants include the country's highest density of Costa Rica's national flower, the *Cattleya skinneri* orchid.

Wildlife

The wildlife of the park is prolific. Almost 300 species of birds have been recorded here, including curassows, quetzals, bellbirds, parrots, toucans, hummingbirds, owls, woodpeckers, tanagers, motmots, doves and eagles – to name just a few.

Insects range from beautiful butterflies to annoying ticks (be especially prepared for ticks in grassy areas such as the meadow in front of the ranger station – long trousers tucked into boots and long sleeved shirts are some protection).

A particularly interesting insect is a highland cicada which burrows into the ground and croaks like a frog, to the bewilderment of naturalists.

Mammals are abundant; deer, armadillos, peccaries, skunks, squirrels, coatimundis and three species of monkeys are frequently seen. Tracks of Baird's tapir are often found around the lagoons near the summit, and you may be lucky enough to catch a glimpse of this large but elusive mammal as it crashes away like a tank through the undergrowth.

Several of the wild cat species have been recorded here, including jaguar, puma, ocelot and margay, but you'll need a large amount of patience and good fortune to observe one of these.

Information

The park is 25 km north-east of Liberia by a poor road that often requires 4WD in the rainy season but is passable in ordinary cars in the dry. Because of its relative remoteness, the park is not heavily visited. Nevertheless, a ranger station exists and there is a trail past various volcanic features to the summit.

Trails

There is a short nature trail through the forests around the Santa María Ranger Station. From the station, a trail leads three km west to sulphurous hot springs with supposed therapeutic properties. You shouldn't soak in them for more than about half an hour without taking a dip in one of the nearby cold springs to cool off.

A further three km of hiking takes you to the boiling mud pools (Las Pailas) where you can carefully scoop out mud to make a rejuvenating (?) face pack. Be careful where you step, however, because the edges of the mudpots are sometimes weak and you could fall through and scald yourself. There is reportedly a locked hut near the mud pools – you could sleep on the porch if there are no National Parks Service personnel to open the hut for you.

From the mud pools, a trail leads north. A fork to the left after about two km leads to Las Hornillas ('the kitchen stoves') which are sulphurous fumaroles about four km from the mud pools. There are waterfalls nearby. Continuing north (instead of taking the left to the fumaroles) takes you to the summit area. The highest point is about nine km beyond the mud pools. (Note that all distances are approximate, as told to me by a park ranger. Other reports give varying distances – allow yourself plenty of time).

Places to Stay

In the Park At the ranger station you can camp, or basic and inexpensive room and board can be arranged.

Camping is allowed in most places but you should be self sufficient and prepared for cold and foggy weather in the highlands – a compass would be very useful if you know how to use one. Beware of ticks in the grassy areas. The wet season is very wet, and there are plenty of mosquitoes then. Dry season camping is much better.

Outside the Park The private *Hacienda Guachipelín* (☎ 660473) is near the southern boundary of the national park. There is a hostel here, the *Albergue de Montaña*, which is operated by the Youth Hostel Association. It offers rustic accommodation in rooms with bunk beds and with communal showers and hot water. There is a simple restaurant. IYHF members can make reservation at the Toruma Youth Hostel in San José. Room and board is US$14 per person; non-members pay about twice as much. Tours with horse and guide are available for US$12 an hour. Multi-day tour packages which include all meals, accommodation, guides and horses are available for about US$130 per person (three days, two nights) or less if there is a group of four or more. Reservations and information can be obtained from Apartado 114, Liberia, Guanacaste.

The *Las Imágenes Biological Station* is on a cattle ranch that has recently opened up to tourism. You can go on tours of the nearby Rincón de la Vieja National Park or ride around the property watching the ranchers at work. About 10% of the property has been left undeveloped and there is plenty of bird life. There are also monkeys, deer, armadillos and other wildlife. Las Imágenes is run by the Hotel Las Espuelas in Liberia; all inquiries and reservations should be made there. Overnight accommodation in rooms with shared baths, plus three meals, are about US$50 a day.

Getting There & Away

To get to the Santa María Ranger Station, drive, walk or take a taxi (US$30) on the road that heads north-east out of Liberia through the Barrio La Victoria suburb. After about 18 km, the road passes the village of San Jorge and then continues as far as the Santa María Ranger Station. This is in an old adobe hacienda where you can spend the night for less than US$1 if you make arrangements with the National Parks Service in advance. There are a couple of old beds or sleep on the wooden floor – bring your own sleeping bag. Mosquito nets or insect repellent are needed in the wet season. Meals can also be arranged for about US$2 or US$3 each, and horses can be hired. Sometimes a ride from Liberia can be arranged when a National Parks Service vehicle is in town. The Santa Rosa National

Park (☎ 695598) maintains daily radio contact with Rincón de la Vieja, or call the radio communications office in San José (☎ 334160).

The Albergue de Montaña is about two km from the mud pools and five km from the hot springs described earlier. You can walk to the lodge from the Santa María Ranger Station, about eight km away, but most visitors take an alternate route from Liberia. Roughly five km north of Liberia on the Interamerican Highway there is a turn-off to the east onto a gravel road to the village of Curubandé, 10 km from the highway. Beyond the village, the road deteriorates. After two km you pass through the signed entrance to the hacienda and continue eight km to the albergue. A little less than one km before you get there, the Río Colorado must be forded for which 4WD is needed. If you have a regular (2WD) car, you can park near the river (in the dry season) and wade and walk the last km. In the wet season, you need 4WD to get this far. If you make arrangements in advance, you can be picked up from Liberia for US$25.R

SANTA ROSA NATIONAL PARK

This national park is one of the oldest (established 1971) and one of the biggest (49,515 hectares) in Costa Rica and has the best developed camping facilities of the nation's parks.

Santa Rosa covers most of the Santa Elena Peninsula which juts out into the Pacific at the far north-western corner of the country. The park is named after the Hacienda Santa Rosa where a historic battle was fought on 20 March 1856 between a hastily assembled amateur army of Costa Ricans and the invading forces of the North American filibuster, William Walker. In fact, it was historical and patriotic reasons which brought about the establishment of this national park in the first place. It was almost a coincidence that the park has also become extremely important to biologists.

Santa Rosa protects the last large stand of tropical dry forest anywhere in Central America, and it also protects some of the largest and most important nesting sites of several species of sea turtles, including endangered ones. Wildlife is often seen, especially during the dry season when animals congregate around the remaining water and the trees lose their leaves. So for historians and biologists, campers and hikers, beach and wilderness lovers, this park is a great attraction.

One of the most innovative features of Santa Rosa National Park is that local people have been involved in preserving and expanding the park. Through a campaign of both education and employment, locals have learnt of the importance of conservation and been able to put it to their own use by working as research assistants, park rangers or other staff, and also by using conservationist techniques to improve their own land use on the surrounding farms and ranches. This attitude of cultural involvement has made the relationship between the national park authorities and the local people one that everybody is benefiting from. It stands as a model for the future integration of preservation and local people's interests in other parts of Costa Rica and in other countries.

The best season is the dry season, when there are fewer biting insects, the roads are more passable, and the animals tend to congregate around waterholes making them easier to see. But this is also the 'busy' season and, particularly at weekends, the park is popular with Costa Ricans wanting to see some of their history. It is less busy midweek, but it's always fairly quiet compared to parks like Poás, nearer to San José. The wet months are when you can observe the sea turtles nesting and often have the park virtually to yourself. The best months for sea turtles are September and October, though you are likely to see some in August, November and December as well.

Orientation

The entrance to Santa Rosa National Park is on the west side of the Interamerican Highway, 37 km north of Liberia and 43 km south of the Nicaraguan border. From the entrance, a seven km paved road leads to the main centre of the park. Here there are administrative offices, scientist's quarters, an information centre, campground, museum and nature trail.

From this complex, a 4WD jeep trail leads down to the coast, 12 km away. About a third of the way down this jeep trail there are two lookout points with views of the ocean. Near the coast, the 4WD road comes to an end, and visitors can continue on foot or horseback. There are several beaches, with camping areas on two of them. There are also other jeep, foot and horse trails which leave the main visitor complex and head out into the tropical dry forest and other habitats.

The Murciélago Sector of the park is a more recent addition which encompasses the wild northern coastline of the Santa Elena Peninsula. The story is that this area was once owned by Nicaraguan dictator Anastasio Somoza – after he was deposed the area became part of the national park. You can't get there from the main body of the park (except perhaps by bushwhacking). The Santa Elena and Murciélago Sectors are still separated by private land which does not yet belong to the National Parks Service, although possession is planned. More funds are needed to pay for the remaining areas, and money sent to the Nature Conservancy or the National Parks Foundation (see the section on conservation in the Facts About the Country chapter) can be earmarked for this.

Information

The park entrance station (just off the Interamerican Highway) is open from 7 am to 5 pm daily. At the entrance booth you pay the US$1.10 park admission, and if you plan on camping, an extra US$0.75. Maps of the park are for sale.

It is seven km from the entrance to the park headquarters (☎ 695598) and campground. There are no buses so you must walk or hitch if you don't have a car. Horses are usually available for hire at the park headquarters (not expensive) and rangers often will allow travellers to accompany them on their rounds of the park.

Museum

The museum is housed in the historic La Casona (the main building of the Santa Rosa Hacienda) around which the battle of 1856 was fought. The battle is described in documents, paintings, maps and diagrams. Apart from antique fire-arms and other weapons, the visitor can see how a typical country kitchen would have been set up in a hacienda over a hundred years ago, and a collection of period antique furniture and tools. A display interpreting the ecological significance and wildlife of the park is also here. Some of the old rooms of La Casona are favourite bat roosts – don't be surprised if you disturb several dozen bats upon entering one of the side rooms. (And don't worry – the bats are completely harmless.)

Wildlife

Outside La Casona is a fine example of the national tree of Costa Rica, the guanacaste *Enterolobium cyclocarpum*. Nearby is a short nature trail with signs interpreting the ecological relationships between the plants, animals and weather patterns of Santa Rosa. Although the nature trail is a short one (a little over one km round trip) you will certainly see a variety of plants and birds and probably, if you move slowly and keep your eyes and ears open, monkeys, snakes, iguanas and other animals.

The wildlife is certainly both varied and prolific. About 260 species of birds have been recorded. A highly visible bird which is common in Santa Rosa and frequently seen and heard around the camp ground is the white-throated magpie jay. This raucous jay is 46 cm long and is unmistakeable with its long crest of manically curled feathers, and white under parts separated from blue upper parts by a narrow black breast-band. The forests contain parrots and parakeets, trogons and tanagers, and as you head down to the coast you will be rewarded by sightings of a variety of coastal birds.

At dusk the flying animals you see probably won't be birds. Bats are very common and about 50 or 60 different species have been identified in Santa Rosa. Other

mammals you have a reasonable chance of seeing include deer, coatimundis, peccaries, armadillos, coyotes, raccoons, three kinds of monkeys and a variety of other species. There are many thousands of insect species, including well over 3000 moths and butterflies. There are many reptiles – lizards, iguanas, snakes, crocodiles and four species of sea turtles.

The olive ridley sea turtle is the most numerous, and during the August to December nesting season, tens of thousands of turtles make their nests on Santa Rosa's beaches. The most popular beach is Nancite, and during September and October especially, it is possible to see as many as 8000 of these 40 kg turtles on the beach at the same time! Nancite beach is strictly protected and restricted, but permission can be obtained from the National Parks Service to see this spectacle.

After nesting has been completed, the olive ridleys range all over the tropical eastern Pacific, from the waters of Mexico to Peru. For more information, see *The Sea Turtles of Santa Rosa National Park* by Stephen E Cornelius (National Parks Foundation, Costa Rica, 1986). This 80 page paperback is beautifully illustrated, written in English, and is available in Costa Rica.

The variety of wildlife reflects the variety of different habitats protected within the boundaries of the park. Apart from the only remaining stand of tropical dry forest in Central America, there is savannah woodland, oak forest, deciduous forest, evergreen forest, riparian forest, mangrove swamps and coastal woodlands.

Research

Santa Rosa is a mecca for scientists, particularly tropical ecologists. Near the park headquarters there is simple accommodation for researchers and students, many of whom spend a great deal of time both studying the ecology of the area and devising means to better protect the remaining tropical forests of Costa Rica.

Tropical ecologist Dr Daniel H Janzen has spent much of his research time in Santa

Rosa, and has been a prime mover in the conservation of not just this national park, but also in the creation of the 'megaparks' system which will make protection of all the national parks more effective. He has been very vocal about how the needs of local people must be addressed in order for conservation to become truly effective on a long term basis.

Janzen has also done much solid research on the tropics and is noted for a plethora of scientific papers. The titles of these range from the whimsical ('How to be a fig'; Annual Review of Ecology & Systematics, 10, 1979) to the matter-of-fact ('Why fruits rot, seeds mold, and meat spoils'; American Naturalist, 111, 1977) to the downright bewildering ('Allelopathy by myrmecophytes: The ant *Azteca* as an allelopathic agent of *Cecropia*'; Ecology, 50, 1969). But perhaps Janzen's strangest claim to fame, among students of ecology at least, is his experiment on tropical seeds where he studied how seed germination was effected by the seeds being eaten and passed through the digestive systems of a variety of animals. Facing a lack of suitable animal volunteers, Janzen systematically ate the seeds himself, then recovered the seeds and tried to germinate them. Tropical ecology can be a messy business!

Places to Stay & Eat

There is a campground at the park headquarters. Facilities are not fancy but do include drinking water, picnic benches, flush toilets and cold water showers. Large fig trees provide shade. The campsites on the coast also have drinking water and latrines, but no showers. If you make arrangements with the National Parks Service in advance, you can eat meals at the park headquarters for about US$11 per day. Otherwise bring your own food – there is none for sale in the park.

Getting There & Away

To get to the park entrance just off the Interamerican Highway by public transport, take any bus between Liberia and the Nicaraguan border and ask the driver to set you down at

the park entrance. The ranger on duty has a timetable of passing buses for when you are ready to leave. There are about seven buses a day heading to the border or to Liberia and San José.

To get to the northern Murciélago Sector of the park, you have to return to the Interamerican Highway and head north for 10 km. Then turn left to the village of Cuajiniquil, eight km away. Buses go here once or twice a day from La Cruz, but it's probably easier to hitch or walk the eight km if you don't have a car. At Cuajiniquil there is a restaurant but no accommodation. Park rangers told me it was a further nine km beyond the village to the Murciélago Ranger Station by poor road – 4WD is advised in the wet season, though you might make it in a high clearance ordinary vehicle if you drive carefully. At the Murciélago Ranger Station you can camp and, if you advise the National Parks Service in advance, eat meals. The dirt road continues beyond the ranger station for about 10 more km, reaching the remote bays and beaches of Bahía Santa Elena and Bahía Playa Blanca. This road may be impassable in the wet season.

GUANACASTE NATIONAL PARK

This is Costa Rica's newest national park and was created on 25 July 1989, Guanacaste Day. The park is adjacent to Santa Rosa National Park, being separated from that park by the Interamerican Highway. Guanacaste National Park is only about five km north-west of the Rincón de la Vieja National Park. Together with a few smaller areas, these three parks comprise the new Guanacaste Regional Conservation Unit (RCU) or 'megapark'.

Guanacaste National Park is much more than a continuation of the dry tropical forest and other lowland habitats found in Santa Rosa. In its lower western reaches, it is an extension of Santa Rosa's habitats, but the terrain soon begins to climb towards two volcanoes, Orosí (1487 metres) and Cacao (1659 metres). Thus it enables animals to range from the coast to the highlands, just as many of them have always done.

Scientists have come to realise that many animal species need a variety of different habitats at different times of year, or at different stages of their life cycles, and if habitats are preserved singly, the animals within may not survive well. If a series of adjoining habitats are preserved, however, survival of many species can be improved. This is one of the main reasons for the formation of the 'megaparks'.

Not all the preserved areas are natural forest. Indeed, large portions of the Guanacaste RCU is ranchland. But researchers have found that if the pasture is carefully managed (and much of this management involves just letting nature take its course) the natural forest will reinstate itself in its old territory. Thus crucial habitats are not just preserved, but in some cases they are also able to expand.

Research Stations

Research is an important aspect of Guanacaste National Park and there are no less than three biological stations within the borders. They are all in good areas for wildlife observation or hiking.

Maritza Biological Station This is the newest station and has a modern laboratory. To get there, turn east off the Interamerican Highway opposite the turn-off for Cuajiniquil (see Santa Rosa National Park). The station is about 13 km east of the highway along a dirt road that is passable to ordinary cars in the dry season, but a 4WD vehicle is advisable in the wet.

From the station there are trails to the summit of Orosí Volcano (about five to six hours). There is also a trail to a site where Indian petroglyphs have been found.

Mengo Biological Station This station is high on the slopes of the Cacao Volcano. The station is reached from the south side of the park. At Potrerillos, about nine km south of the Santa Rosa Park entrance on the Interamerican Highway, head east to the small community of Quebrada Grande. From here, ask about the 4WD road that heads towards

the station, 10 km away. At the end of the road a trail takes you to the station, a further hour on foot. From the station there are trails to the summit of Cacao Volcano and to the Maritza Biological Station.

Pitilla Biological Station This station is a surprise – it lies on the north-east side of the Orosí Volcano in forest more like that found in the Caribbean slope than on the Pacific. Although the Pacific is only 30 km to the west whilst the Caribbean is 180 km to the east, the station is on the eastern side of the continental divide, the rivers flow into the Caribbean, and the climate and vegetation have a Caribbean influence.

To get to the station, turn east off the Interamerican Highway about 10 km north of the Cuajiniquil turn-off, or four km before reaching the small town of La Cruz. Follow the paved eastbound road for about 28 km to the community of Santa Cecilia. From there, ask about the poor dirt road heading 10 km south to the station – you'll probably need 4WD for the last bit. (Don't continue on the unpaved road heading further east – that goes over 50 km further to the small town of Upala.)

Places to Stay & Eat

In the Park Since the creation of the new national park, the biological research stations have become available for tourist accommodation. The stations are all quite rustic with dormitory style accommodation for 30 to 40 people and shared cold water bathrooms. A bed and three meals costs about US$20 a day. Permission to camp near the stations can also be obtained; the fee is about US$0.75 per night. Horses are often available for hire. You should make arrangements with the National Parks Service to stay in the stations. Guanacaste National Park is administered from Santa Rosa Headquarters (☎ 695598) and you can make arrangements either there or in San José. Park personnel in Santa Rosa can arrange transport from the park headquarters to the biological stations for about US$10 to US$15, depending on where you go.

Outside the Park The *Hacienda Los Inocentes* (☎ 669190, 395484) is a working cattle ranch on the north side of Guanacaste National Park. You get there by driving 16 km east of the Interamerican Highway on the paved road to Santa Cecilia. The nearest town with bus service is La Cruz, from which it is about a 20 km taxi ride (about US$10).

The hacienda building itself is a very attractive wooden house converted into a comfortable though not luxurious country lodge. There are 11 bedrooms and four bathrooms, and the food is excellent. Some of the ranch is still forested and there is good bird-watching. Naturalist guides are on hand to take you around the property to see wildlife, which is reported to be quite plentiful, or watch the ranch workers.

Trips into Guanacaste National Park can be arranged, and the Orosí Volcano, about seven km to the south, can be climbed. Naturally, horses are available (by this stage in the chapter, you probably realise that horses are an important way of getting around Costa Rica!). Accommodation with three meals costs about US$50 per day. You can wander around at will, but guided tours are extra. Reservations can be made at Los Inocentes, Apartado 1370, 3000 Heredia, Costa Rica.

Getting There & Away
There is no public transport within the park. See the descriptions of the biological research stations for details on how to get to them if you have your own transport.

BOLAÑOS ISLAND NATIONAL WILDLIFE REFUGE
This 25 hectare island is a national wildlife refuge because brown pelicans, magnificent frigate birds, American oystercatchers and other sea birds nest here. There are about 150 pelican nests on the north end of the island and some 200 frigate bird nests on the southern cliffs. The island is about 80 metres high at its highest point. The refuge is part of the Guanacaste RCU.

The island is in Salinas Bay on the Nicaragua-Costa Rica border. The nearest point on the mainland is Zacate Point, 1½ km away, but there is no road here. The nearest habitation is at Puerto Soley, about five km south-west of La Cruz by road. From Puerto Soley you may be able to hire a boat to take you the four km across the bay to the refuge.

There are no facilities on the island, and you should contact the National Parks Service for permission if you need to land on the island. No permit is necessary for bird-watching from a boat.

LA CRUZ
This is the last settlement of any size before reaching the Nicaraguan border at Peñas Blancas, 19 km further north on the Interamerican Highway. Buses between Liberia and the border can drop you here. Taxis are available to take you to Puerto Soley, Hacienda Los Inocentes and Santa Rosa National Park. There are reportedly two buses a day to Cuajiniquil, in the Murciélago Sector of Santa Rosa.

There are also a couple of hotels in the bottom end price range.

PEÑAS BLANCAS
This is the border with Nicaragua – it is a border post, not a town. There is nowhere to stay.

See the Getting There & Away chapter for full details of crossing the border here in either direction.

Arenal Back Route

The route described here goes from San José in a north-westerly direction through Quesada, Fortuna, Arenal and Tilarán, connecting with the Interamerican Highway at Cañas. From Cañas, you could head north towards Liberia and Nicaragua, or turn south along the Interamerican and thus make a loop trip back to San José. Although this is a less travelled route, you will find adequate bus connections if you are not in too much of a hurry.

CIUDAD QUESADA

The name of this town is often abbreviated to Quesada. To make things even more complicated, the locals know it as San Carlos and local buses often have San Carlos as the destination. This small city lies at 650 metres above sea level on the north-western slopes of the Cordillera Central. The population of Quesada including outlying suburbs is about 27,000.

Roads north and east of the city take the traveller into the Northern Lowlands. Roads to the north-west lead to Fortuna and the spectacular Arenal Volcano, and over the mountains to the Interamerican Highway.

Quesada is not an important tourist destination but does make a convenient place to spend the night if you like to travel slowly and see some of Costa Rica's smaller towns. Quesada's importance is as a centre for the agriculture on the northern slopes of the Cordillera Central and in the San Carlos River plain stretching out north of the city for many km, as far as the Nicaraguan border.

The focal point of Quesada is a large main square with shade trees and benches. Almost everything of importance is either on this square or within a few blocks of it.

Places to Stay – bottom end

The cheapest place is the *Hotel Terminal* which is in the bus terminal, half a block from the plaza. This hotel is very basic and noisy and not particularly recommended.

Budget travellers should stroll along the first two blocks of Calle 2, north of the main plaza. There is a street produce market along here and there are several hotels in the US$3 to US$6 per person price range. These include the hotels *Ugalde, Crystal, Los Fernandos, Los Helechos* and *Axel Alberto*.

Places to Stay – middle

There are two decent hotels on the main plaza, both of which have rooms with private baths and hot water. The *Hotel El Retiro* (☎ 460463) charges about US$8/15 for singles/doubles. The *Hotel La Central* (☎ 460301) has a variety of rooms and prices. Singles range from US$8 to US$12

and doubles from US$15 to US$17, and there is a restaurant.

The comfortable new *Hotel Conquistador* (☎ 460546) is 500 metres south of the plaza on Calle Central. Rooms with private baths are about US$9/16 for singles/doubles.

On the outskirts of town is the *Balneario San Carlos* (☎ 460747) which has cabins with private baths renting for about US$16 for a double. There is a swimming pool and restaurant.

Places to Stay – top end

The *El Tucano Hotel & Country Club* (☎ 461822) is eight km north-east of Quesada on the left hand side of the road leading to Aguas Zarcas – look for the large white gate. Facilities include a good restaurant, swimming pool and sauna, and various sports facilities ranging from tennis courts to miniature golf. Nearby thermal springs are tapped into a small jacuzzi where you can soak away your ills. The thermal waters are said to have medicinal and therapeutic properties. Rooms are about US$45/50/55/60 for from one to four people. Day visitors using the pools are charged about US$2.

Places to Eat

Apart from the hotel restaurants, there are several places to eat within a couple of blocks of the main plaza. One of the better ones is the *Tonjibe* on the plaza itself.

Getting There & Away

Buses from San José leave from the Coca Cola terminal several times a day. The two hour journey costs US$1.50 and is an attractive ride over the western flanks of the Cordillera Central reaching 1850 metres at Laguna, just beyond Zarcero. It then begins the long and pretty descent to Quesada at 650 metres. The bus makes many stops unless you get an express all the way to Quesada.

The bus terminal in Quesada is half a block from the main plaza. Buses return to San José about every hour during the day. Buses to Fortuna (to visit the Arenal Volcano and Lake) take two hours and leave four times a day (currently at 6 and 9.30 am, and

1.30 and 4.30 pm). Buses to Tilarán take about four or five hours and leave at 6.30 am and 3 pm.

There are five buses daily east to Venecia (one hour) and on to Río Frío via Puerto Viejo de Sarapiquí. Buses for Arenal Los Chiles (near the Nicaraguan border) leave seven times a day. There are also buses to other nearby villages throughout the day.

FORTUNA

Officially called La Fortuna de San Carlos, this little village is the nearest town to the spectacular Arenal Volcano. With a population of some 5000, it is about 250 metres above sea level and from the town plaza there are excellent views of the volcano at 1633 metres, only six km away to the west. Because of this, and because of a nearby waterfall, the village has built up a small tourist industry with a handful of small hotels.

There's not much to do in Fortuna. It's a sleepy little town but it's well worth spending a day or two in the area to enjoy the volcano. A pleasant day time excursion can be made to Fortuna Falls.

Fortuna Falls

From the left-hand side of the church as you look at it from the plaza in Fortuna (with Arenal Volcano looming behind the church tower) there is a signed dirt road heading south. The sign reads '5½ km to Fortuna Falls'. The dirt road makes several twists and turns but each one of these is marked. It is a pleasant walk through agricultural countryside. The road is passable with a car during the dry months (January to April) but becomes very muddy in the wet season – a 4WD vehicle could make it.

At the falls there is a small parking area. From here there's a good view of the long ribbon-like falls cascading down the far side of a very steep forested canyon. There's plenty of water, even in the dry season. An extremely steep trail descends down to the base of the falls, but it might be too slippery and muddy in the wet season to be usable, even with hiking boots.

Places to Stay & Eat

There are currently four hotels in Fortuna itself. The *Hotel La Central* (☎ 479004) is basic but clean and the people are helpful. There is a restaurant and US dollars can be exchanged. Rooms are US$3 per person, and the communal showers don't have hot water. For the same price you can stay at *Cabinas Emi* (☎ 479076). The cabins are very basic but do have their own cold water bathrooms. Both these are on the south side of the plaza.

A nicer place is *Cabinas Don Bosco* (☎ 479050) which is two blocks north of the plaza on the road between the plaza and the fuel station. Cabins with private bath are US$11/14/17 for singles/doubles/triples. There is hot water sometimes. A block south of the plaza is the new *Hotel Las Colinas* (☎ 479107) where rooms with private baths and hot water rent for US$11/17/24.

The best place to eat is *El Jardín* opposite the fuel station.

Getting There & Away

Buses arrive and leave from the south side of the plaza. There are four buses daily to and from Ciudad Quesada. It's about a 1½ hour trip.

To continue west through Tabacón and Nuevo Arenal to Tilarán you have to catch the Quesada to Tilarán bus which comes through Fortuna about 8 am and 4.30 pm daily. There are usually spare seats.

If you are coming from the west, you'll find two buses a day from Tilarán to Quesada, and they can drop you off in Fortuna.

TABACÓN HOT SPRINGS

These hot springs are just to the right of the Fortuna to Tilarán road, about 12 km beyond Fortuna. A *balneario*, or bathing resort, has been built here and there is a swimming pool fed by the thermal hot springs. The resort is open from 8 am to 10 pm from Tuesday to Saturday, 8 am to 6 pm on Sunday, and is closed on Monday. There is a US$1 charge for using the pool. There is a reasonably priced bar and restaurant from where you can either watch the bathers bathing or Arenal exploding, depending on where you sit.

The owners are friendly; they allow you to camp on a flat area outside the restaurant. There are no camping facilities except tent or car space. At present there is nowhere to stay, but cabins are being planned. This is a good place to see the exploding volcano, particularly at night.

About two km before you reach Tabacón (coming from Fortuna) there is a new tourist development called La Jungla. There is a restaurant here, and there are trails leading to lakes in the foothills of the volcano (the area is not dangerous). Day use costs US$0.60, overnight use (camping) is US$2.50, bathrooms are available, and cabins are planned.

ARENAL VOLCANO

The best night-time views, of the volcano are to be had from the west side of the volcano looking east at the red lava flows. The degree of activity varies from week to week; sometimes it can be a spectacular display of flowing red hot lava and incandescent rocks flying through the air. At other times the volcano subsides to a gentle glow. It is possible to camp on the west side of the volcano, and there are hot springs and a volcano observatory where you can stay overnight.

The volcano was dormant until 1968 when huge explosions triggered lava flows which killed several dozen people living in the area. Despite this massive eruption, the volcano retained its almost perfect conical shape and with its continuing activity Arenal is everyone's image of a typical volcano. Occasionally, the activity quietens down for a few weeks, but generally Arenal has been producing huge ash columns, massive explosions and glowing red lava flows almost daily since 1968. I visited the volcano first in 1981 and most recently in 1990 and both times it was exploding several times a day.

Every once in a while, perhaps lulled into a sense of false security by a temporary pause in the activity, someone tries to climb up to the crater and peer within. This is probably foolish – climbers have been killed or maimed by explosions. The problem is not so much getting killed (that's a risk the foolhardy insist is their own decision) but risking the lives of Costa Rican rescuers is another matter. (I must admit that I was young and impetuous enough to climb the volcano in 1981 and came close to terminating my climbing career just below the summit. I wouldn't encourage anyone to attempt the climb at this time.)

Arenal Volcano Observatory

This private observatory was established in 1987 on a macadamia nut farm on the south side of Arenal Volcano. Vulcanologists from all over the world have come to study the active volcano, and recently researchers from the Smithsonian Institution of Washington DC were here on an expedition. There is a small lodge here which can be used as a base to explore the nearby countryside. Trips can be made to see recent lava flows from the volcano or to climb Arenal's dormant partner, Chato Volcano which is 1100 metres high and only three km south-east of Arenal Volcano. The macadamia farm can be visited and freshwater fishing on the nearby Lake Arenal can be arranged.

The observatory, lodge and tour services are run by Costa Rica Sun Tours (☎ 553418, 553518; Apartado 1195, 1250 Escazú, Costa Rica) at Avenida 7, Calle 3 & 5, San José. The company is run by the English-speaking Aspinall family.

Things to See

Local guides (with limited English) are available from the lodge for US$15 to climb Chato Volcano or visit lava flows. (There are trails up Chato and a guide is not essential.) You can wander around the macadamia nut farm or through the primary forest which makes up about half of the 250 hectare site. There is good birding as well as good volcano views.

Fishing trips on Lake Arenal are US$50 or US$75 per person for half and full day trips, and there's a two-person minimum. Motor boats, fuel, tackle, lunch and fishing guide are provided. Rainbow bass (locally called *guapote*) weighing up to four kg are reported.

Places to Stay

Because there are only five rooms at the lodge, reservations are essential. Most of the rooms have bunk beds sleeping up to six people; all rooms have private baths with hot water. Rates are US$62.50 for single occupancy, US$42.50 per person for double occupancy, and US$36.25 per person for multiple occupancy; all rates include three meals per day.

Getting There & Away

Transport from San José to the observatory is US$150 one way but the vehicle takes up to eight passengers and the cost is split between the passengers. If you want to make your own way there, you normally need a 4WD vehicle as there are two rivers to ford, though you may get by in a regular car in the dry months. The hearty could take a Quesada to Tilarán bus and then walk.

The entrance to the observatory is marked by a sign reading 'El Parqueo', about four km beyond Tabacón hot springs on the Fortuna to Tilarán road. Turn left off the main road and follow a dirt road for about three km to a fork where there is a large orange sign with Volcán Arenal information. The right fork goes down to Lake Arenal, about two km away; the left fork peters out in the lower slopes of Arenal Volcano (you could camp here, I did); and the road straight ahead follows electrical pylons for about 3½ km to the first river, the Río Agua Caliente. Here, on the left, there is a very simple shelter of logs and earth that looks like it would withstand a major explosion.

The observatory and the Arenal Volcano are separated by the Agua Caliente River valley which acts as a protection against lava flows. On the other side of the river there is a sign indicating 'Macadamia' to the left and 'Tilarán' to the right. (This is an alternate road to Tilarán, rarely used and passable only with 4WD and plenty of time and perseverance). Follow signs for 'Macadamia' to the observatory, about three or four km further.

A second stream, the Danta, is crossed on the way. The observatory entrance is through a gate just past the second river, up the hill and the first left.

ARENAL

This small village, sometimes called Nuevo Arenal, is the only town of any size between Fortuna and Tilarán, and also the only town on Lake Arenal. It is about 39 km from Fortuna and 25 km from Tilarán. Most of the road is narrow and winding, and there is an unpaved section of about eight km which may require 4WD in the wet season, although ordinary cars usually get through.

Lake Arenal is an artificial lake formed by a dam built at the eastern end, which you can see the dam from the road. There are good views over the lake from the road, and sometimes the volcano can be seen smoking quietly at the end of the lake. During the dry season, winds are often strong and steady, and so the lake is considered a good area for sailing and windsurfing.

Arenal village itself has little to offer beyond a fuel station, a couple of stores and a bus stop near the plaza.

Places to Stay

There is reportedly a small *pensión* in Arenal, though I was unable to find it.

A few km off the main road en route to Arenal is the *Arenal Lodge* (☎ 461881), an exclusive small country hotel with pleasant grounds and great views of the volcano. Horse riding and birding are possibilities, but the lodge's main function is to provide fishing excursions on Lake Arenal accompanied by expert fishing guides. Inside the hotel there is a library and billiard room to while away the evenings. Reservations should be made in San José at Apartado 1139, Escazú 1250 (☎ 282588). Rates for comfortable rooms and three meals a day are about US$100 per person; add another US$150 per day for guided fishing.

Roughly 1½ km east of Arenal is the *Lake Arenal Youth Hostel* (☎ 695008). There are four rooms each with bunk beds for four people. Reservations and information should be obtained in San José at the Toruma Youth Hostel (244085). Overnight rates for IYHF members are US$7 including breakfast; non-members pay a little more.

Getting There & Away
Buses to Quesada leave at 8 am and 2 pm and there are five buses daily to Tilarán. There is also a bus leaving at 1.30 pm marked Guatuso. It heads north into the lowlands of Guatuso and the small towns of San Rafael, Caño Negro and Upala, where a few remaining Guatuso Indians live.

TILARÁN
This is a small, quiet market town at 550 metres above sea level near the northern end of the Cordillera de Tilarán; Lake Arenal is the principal attraction, some five km to the north-east of the town. Cattle farming is important in the area and there is a rodeo and fiesta during the last weekend in April. This is very popular and hotels are often full at that time. There is another fiesta on 13 June.

The pleasant climate, rural atmosphere, annual rodeo and proximity of Lake Arenal have brought about the development of a small tourist industry. Fishing, boating, windsurfing and horse riding can be arranged at The Spot (☎ 695711) next to the Cabinas Naralit near the south side of the cathedral. The town cinema is next door.

The local tourist information office publishes a leaflet proclaiming Tilarán as 'the city of broad streets, fertile rains, and healthful winds, in which friendship and progress is cultivated'. I have no quibbles with that.

Tilarán is 23 km by paved road from the Interamerican Highway at Cañas.

Places to Stay – bottom end
The cheapest place is the pretty basic *Hotel Grecia* on the west side of the plaza.

The *Hotel Central* (☎ 695363) is 350 metres south of the principal entrance road into town and has basic but clean rooms at US$2.50 per person, or cabins with private bath at US$4 per person.

The *Cabinas Mary* (☎ 695479, 695470) on the south side of the plaza is good, clean,

pleasant, and has a reasonably priced restaurant attached. Rooms with private bathroom and cold water are US$4/6 single/double. Add US$1 per room for bathrooms with hot water.

Places to Stay – middle
Cabinas El Sueño (☎ 695347) is less than a block away from either the main plaza or the bus terminal. It is very clean, has a restaurant, and is friendly and recommended. Rooms with private bath and warm water are US$7/11.50 single/double.

The *Cabinas Naralit* (☎ 695393) is the best place in town, is associated with The Spot where tourist information and tours are available, and has a cinema next door. Pleasant rooms with private baths and hot water, some with TV, rent for US$17.50/23.50/29.50 for singles/doubles/triples. There is a restaurant and bar attached.

The *Cabinas Puerto San Luis* (☎ 695572) is also in this price range, but is five km north-east of town on the shores of Lake Arenal en route to Tronadora. There are cabins, a restaurant, and boat and horse hire can be arranged.

Getting There & Away
Buses from San José cost US$2.40, take 3½ hours, and leave three times each afternoon with Autotransportes Tilarán at Calle 12, Avenida 9 & 11.

Buses from Tilarán leave from the bus terminal which is half a block from the main plaza as you head away from the cathedral. Buses to San José leave daily at 7 and 7.45 am, and 4.50 pm, but the Sunday afternoon departure is usually sold out by Saturday. Buses between Tilarán and San José go via Cañas and the Interamerican Highway, not via the Quesada/Fortuna/Arenal route. Buses to (Nuevo) Arenal leave at 10 am and 4 pm.

Buses to Quesada (San Carlos) leave at 7 am and 12.30 pm. Buses to Puntarenas leave at 6 am and 1 pm. Buses for a variety of small local towns also leave from this terminal. If you just want to get to Cañas (where the Interamerican Highway is joined), you'll have to take the Puntarenas or San José bus and get off at Cañas.

Although there is a direct road to Monteverde, there is no bus there from Tilarán, though you can get there by car (the direct road is poor; 4WD advised in the wet season). Most people visiting Monteverde go from San José or Puntarenas.

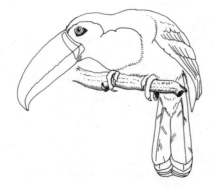

The Northern Lowlands

The traveller heading north from San José, over the volcanic ridges of the Cordillera Central, soon arrives in the flat tropical lowlands stretching from just 40 km north of the capital to the Nicaraguan border and beyond. The northern halves of the provinces of Alajuela and Heredia both contain large tropical plains, called *llanuras*. It is the northern slopes of the central mountains and the two llanuras beyond which are described in this chapter.

The original vegetation of much of the northern lowlands is mixed tropical forest, becoming increasingly evergreen as one heads east to the Caribbean. The climate is generally wet and hot. The dry season is more pronounced in the western part of the northern lowlands, near the slopes of the Cordillera de Guanacaste, but as one moves east towards the Caribbean the dry season tends to be shorter and not entirely dry. Much of the original vegetation has been destroyed and replaced by cattle pasture, which is the main industry of most of the northern lowlands.

In much of the more remote areas near the Nicaraguan border, especially in the Llanura de los Guatusos and the Llanura de San Carlos, the pastureland floods extensively during the wet season, creating vast swamps and lakes. One such area has been protected in the Caño Negro National Wildlife Refuge – one of the more remote and inaccessible of Costa Rica's national refuges and parks. Other swamp areas have been turned to rice cultivation.

The northern lowlands generally have a very low population density, with no large towns, few small towns, rough roads, poor public transport and little in the way of tourist facilities. The one major exception to this is in the north-eastern lowlands around the small town of Puerto Viejo de Sarapiquí, which is well served by public buses. Here there is a number of hotels, and nearby there are several tourist lodges and a biological

station. The Puerto Viejo area is the destination of most visitors wanting to see some of the northern lowlands.

SAN RAFAEL
This small community is locally known as Guatuso. Less than 5000 people inhabit the town and the surrounding district. San Rafael is on the Río Frío, 19 km north-east of the village of Arenal. (This is not the same Río Frío as the one south-east of Puerto Viejo.)

Getting There & Away
There is a daily bus between Arenal and San Rafael. There is also a daily bus from San José en route to Upala.

From San Rafael you can hire a boat in the wet season to take you up the Río Frío to the Caño Negro National Wildlife Refuge. There are poor roads (4WD advised, especially during the wet season) to Upala (about 40 km), and then to Caño Negro and Los Chiles. Except for Upala, San Rafael is the only place which has a gas station, so fill up here.

UPALA

This small town is about 10 km south of the Nicaraguan border in the far north-eastern corner of the northern lowlands. About 9400 people live in Upala and the surrounding district. Dirt roads lead up to and across the border, but these are not official entry points into either Costa Rica or Nicaragua.

Upala is the centre for the cattle and rice industries of the area. A few remaining Guatuso Indians live in the region. It has become increasingly important in recent years, and a paved secondary road from the Interamerican Highway was opened recently, thus allowing daily bus connection with San José. Few travellers go to Upala, however, and those that do are mostly heading to the Caño Negro National Wildlife Refuge. The trip to Upala and on to Caño Negro and Los Chiles is an interesting off-the-beaten-track experience.

Places to Stay

The best place is the *Hotel Upala* (☎ 470169), and there are a few other cheap and basic pensións.

Getting There & Away

Buses from San José leave from Calle 16, Avenida 3 & 5, with CNT (☎ 551932). There is a bus at 3 pm via the Interamerican Highway, taking five to six hours, and a slower bus via Quesada and San Rafael leaving later. Schedules are liable to change during the rainy season, especially on the San Rafael route.

It's also possible to get to Upala by car on the road past Hacienda Los Inocentes and Santa Cecilia (see the chapter on North-Western Costa Rica) or via a road heading north from Bagaces on the Interamerican Highway.

Buses return to San José every day, usually in the mornings. There is also a daily bus during the dry season to Caño Negro, about 35 km east of Upala. The bus may also run during the wet season, depending on road conditions.

CAÑO NEGRO NATIONAL WILDLIFE REFUGE

This 9969 hectare refuge is of interest especially to bird-watchers, who come to see a variety of waterfowl such as anhingas, roseate spoonbills, storks, ducks, herons and the largest Costa Rican colony of the olivaceous cormorant. The refuge is the only place in Costa Rica where the Nicaraguan grackle regularly nests. In addition, pumas, jaguars and tapirs have been recorded here more than in many of the other refuges. It certainly is in a remote and little populated area which is conducive to these rare large mammals. Many smaller mammals have also been reported.

The Río Frío flows through the refuge. During the wet season the river breaks its banks and forms an 800 hectare lake which is best visited by boat for bird-watching. During the dry months of January to April the lake shrinks, and by April has virtually completely disappeared – until the rains in May begin. During the dry season there are some foot and horse trails, but a boat is the only way to go for the rest of the year.

About 1500 people live in the Caño Negro district which is reached by daily bus from Upala.

There is a ranger station where you can sleep and eat meals if arranged in advance with the National Parks Service in San José. Horses and boats can be hired.

LOS CHILES

About 25 km north-east of Caño Negro by poor road is the village of Los Chiles, which is on the Río Frío three or four km before the Nicaraguan border. About 7000 people inhabit the Los Chiles district.

Officially there is a border crossing here, but travellers who are not Nicaraguan or Costa Rican will probably not be allowed through. See the Getting There & Away chapter for full details of the hassles involved with entering or leaving the country via this route.

During the wet season, boats may be hired to take you south along the Río Frío to Los Caños. During the dry season, the road to

Caño Negro is passable by car, but you may need 4WD in the wet. Los Chiles was originally built to service river traffic on the nearby Río San Juan, the south bank of which forms the Nicaragua-Costa Rica border for much of the river's length. A landing strip connected Los Chiles with the rest of the country. Since the construction of a road, there are no scheduled services, although aerotaxis can be hired from San José. During the 1980s, a good all-weather road was built to Quesada, almost 100 km to the south-east, and seven buses a day now connect the two towns.

In the 1980s, Los Chiles was on an important supply route for the Contras, which explains why the Nicaraguan authorities are touchy about the border crossing here. An interesting side effect of the Contra-Sandinista hostilities was that many of the local inhabitants living on or near the Río San Juan left for a safer area. Because fighting in the area was relatively low key compared to, for example, Vietnam, where defoliants and herbicides destroyed much of the countryside, most of the rainforest in the Río San Juan area has been protected from colonisation and preserved. Whilst forests were being cut for pasture in northern Costa Rica, the San Juan area remained free of farmers.

Now, since cessation of hostilities in 1990, the colonists are slowly drifting back. This slow drift will soon become a wave as word gets out that the area is both safe again and untouched. Stories of unexploded mines in the area are stemming the tide of settlement temporarily.

Meanwhile, environmentally aware Costa Rican authorities are working with their Nicaraguan counterparts in an attempt to establish an international park – a national park which spans the border. The proposed name of the park is Si a Paz (literally: Yes to Peace). It is hoped that it will stretch from the Caño Negro Refuge north to Lake Nicaragua and east through a large tract of primary rainforest in south-eastern Nicaragua and along the San Juan to the Caribbean coast, joining up there with the existing Barra del Colorado Refuge. Whether this scheme comes about remains to be seen, but with Costa Rica involved in the project, I have hopes that it will.

Places to Stay

There are a few cheap pensións in Los Chiles. If the proposed Si a Paz International Park becomes a reality, it is likely that more accommodation will become available.

San José to Puerto Viejo

Puerto Viejo can be approached from San José either from the west or the east, and so a round trip can be done without backtracking. The western route, via Varablanca, La Virgen and Chilamate is paved and hence preferred in the rainy season. The eastern route via Río Frío and Horquetas is not yet paved and an ordinary car might not get through in the wet season.

Via the Western Route

The west road is a spectacular one which is a favourite of tour companies. The road leaves San José via Heredia and Barva and continues over a pass in the Cordillera Central between Poás Volcano to the west and Barva Volcano to the east. The steep and winding mountain road climbs to over 2000 metres between the tiny communities of Cartagos and Varablanca.

A couple of km past the highest point, there is a turn-off to Poasito and the Poás Volcano. Then begins a dizzying descent with beautiful views. People on tours or with their own vehicles can stop for photographs or for high and middle elevation bird-watching. Travellers on public buses must be content with window gazing.

About five km north of Varablanca, the Río La Paz is crossed by a bridge on a hairpin bend. On the left side of the bridge is an excellent view of the spectacular Cascada de la Paz (Peace Waterfall). Several other

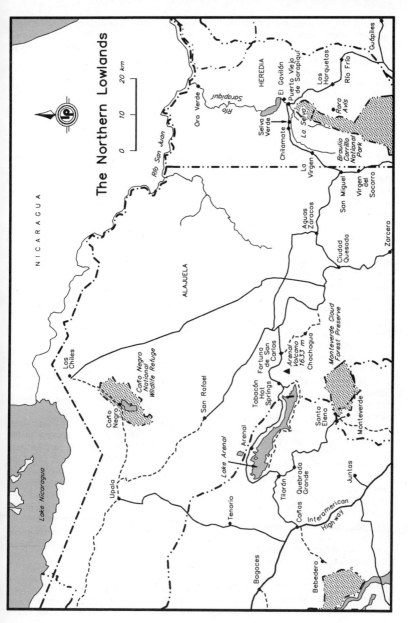

waterfalls may be seen, particularly on the right hand side (heading north) in the La Paz River valley, which soon joins with the Sarapiquí River valley.

About six or seven km beyond the Peace Waterfall there is a turn-off to the right on a dirt road leading to **Colonia Virgen del Socorro**, a small community several km away across the river. This road (which requires 4WD) is famous among birders, who will often spend several hours looking for unusual species along the quiet road with forest, a river, clearings and elevational changes contributing to species diversity in this one spot. The day I went, a friend who had been birding in Costa Rica for over a decade saw his first solitary eagle, a large and uncommon bird which likes remote forested mountainous terrain and is therefore difficult to see. This was a big find. My observations were less unusual but more colourful; the sunbittern – a water bird with a striking sunburst pattern on its spread wings, and the psychedelically coloured red-headed barbet, with a thick greenish-yellow bill, bright red head and eyes, orange breast, black face with little bristles surrounding the beak, green back, yellow belly streaked with green, olive legs and a bluish-white stripe on the neck. The area is certainly a birder's delight.

About seven km north of the Virgen del Socorro turn-off, the road forks at the community of San Miguel. The west bound fork goes to Quesada, about 35 km away by paved road. About 14 km west of San Miguel along this road is the village of **Venecia** where there is a basic pensión.

A few km north of Venecia is the pre-Columbian archaeological site of **Ciudad Cutris** which can be reached by 4WD vehicle or on foot. The site has not been properly excavated, has no tourist facilities, and is on private land. Enquire locally about permission to see the site.

The eastern fork from San Miguel heads for Puerto Viejo to the north-east. After 10 km the road reaches the village of La Virgen (not the same place as Virgen del Socorro mentioned above) which is truly in the northern lowlands. The now flat road goes through mainly agricultural country to **Chilamate** where you can stay at La Selva, a pair of private lodges described below. Puerto Viejo is about six km further on.

Río Sarapiquí Trips Parts of the Sarapiquí are good for river running from May to November. Costa Rica Expeditions (☎ 570766) and Ríos Tropicales (☎ 336455) both run day trips on this Class II to III river for US$65 per person. The trip leaves every Saturday (though other days can be arranged) and involves 3½ hours driving from San José, four hours on the river and 3½ hours back to San José. Lunch and bilingual guides are provided.

Costa Rica Expeditions also arranges guided birding trips to the Virgen del Socorro area for US$65 per person per day.

Via the Eastern Route

After visiting the interesting Puerto Viejo area, you can return to San José via the eastern road. (You can also arrive in Puerto Viejo by the eastern road, reversing this route. Buses go in both directions.)

About four km south-east of Puerto Viejo the road passes the entrance to La Selva Biological Station (described below). About 15 km further is the village of **Horquetas**, from where it is 15 km to the rainforest preservation project and lodge at Rara Avis (also described below).

From Horquetas the road continues about 10 km through banana plantations to the village of **Río Frío** which is an important banana centre. There is a hotel here, the *Cabinas Alohas*, but it appears to be closed. There are a couple of simple restaurants and a bus stop. Buses between San José and Puerto Viejo often stop here for a meal break. You can catch buses several times a day from here to Puerto Viejo, San José or Guápiles. There is also an airstrip to which you can charter flights from San José.

Bananas Everywhere you look in this region you'll see banana plants. Bunches of bananas are often covered with large blue plastic sacks whilst the fruit is still on the tree. The plastic keeps the plants warm

Top: Zarcero church and topiary art in the plaza (RR)
Left: Donald Perry's Automated Web for Canopy Exploration (AWCE), at Rara Avis (RR)
Right: Miskito Indian fishermen unloading crayfish pot, Río San Juan (RR)

Top: Hiking through Monteverde
Cloud Forest Preserve (RR)
Bottom: Orchid at Rara Avis (RR)

Top: Lake Arenal (RR)
Bottom: Leaf-cutter ant at work (RT)

(like in a miniature greenhouse) and also serves to concentrate ethylene gas which is naturally produced by ripening fruit.

Strange looking little tractor trains pull wagons loaded high with the fruit to processing centers. In some plantations, bunches of bananas are hung onto wire contraptions which, when loaded, are pushed by workers into the processing centre. The bananas are washed and sprayed to prevent molding and then shipped off in wooden crates to the coast and the world.

A straight road runs between banana plantations for about 15 km south of Río Frío to the main highway. Turn east for Guápiles and the Caribbean; turn west for San José. This route to San José takes you through the middle of Braulio Carrillo National Park.

PUERTO VIEJO DE SARAPIQUÍ

All the locals simply refer to the town as Puerto Viejo, but I give it its full name here to distinguish it from another popular travellers' destination – Puerto Viejo de Talamanca on the Caribbean coast.

The town is at the confluence of the Río Puerto Viejo and the Río Sarapiquí. About 5500 people live in the Puerto Viejo district, which, despite its ramshackle appearance, has an interesting history. It used to be an important port on the trade route to the Caribbean before the days of roads and railways. Boats plied down the Sarapiquí as far as the Nicaraguan border and then turned east on the Río San Juan to the sea. With the advent of roads and railways, Puerto Viejo has lost its importance as a river port, although adventurous travellers can still sail down the Sarapiquí in motorised dugout canoes.

Today, the region is known for its nearby undisturbed premontane tropical wet forest which extends out from the northern arm of Braulio Carrillo National Park. A biological research station and several forest lodges nearby have made this undisturbed habitat accessible to scientists and travellers.

A few km east of Puerto Viejo is a women's herb cooperative called MUSA. It is a small farm which produces herbs for medicinal, culinary, cosmetic and incense purposes. Products are for sale and visits are

encouraged. Sandra Jimenez will give information about the cooperative.

There is no dry season in this area, but late January to early May is the less wet season. A weather station at La Selva, just outside Puerto Viejo, records about 170 mm of rain in February (the driest month) and close to 500 mm in December, the wettest month. The drier season means fewer insects and less muddy trails, but it's never really dry.

To telephone any of the numbers listed below, call the Puerto Viejo operator (☎ 716901) and ask to be put through to the place you want.

Places to Stay & Eat

There are three cheap and basic hotels in Puerto Viejo itself, all on the one main street so you won't have any difficulty in finding them. The best of these is *Cabinas Restaurant Monteverde* which charges US$4 for a single with a private cold water bath. The restaurant here is popular and reasonable. The cheaper *Restaurant Cabinas La Paz* and *Hotel Santa María* are both OK. There are several inexpensive restaurants, bars and *sodas*.

These hotels are essentially for travellers on a low budget. For the more affluent, staying outside of town at the lodges or biological station described below is suggested.

Getting There & Away

Bus Buses from San José leave eight times a day from a marked bus stop in front of the Puntarenas bus terminal at Calle 12, Avenida 7 & 9. Five or six go via Río Frío and Horquetas; two or three go the other way. Either way, the fare is US$2.25 and the trip takes about 3½ hours. Check with the San José tourist office for the latest schedule, or go to the bus stop and hang around until a bus comes by. The drivers know the schedules. There are also a couple of buses a day from the Coca Cola terminal; recently these were leaving at 6 am and 12 noon via Varablanca.

Returning from Puerto Viejo to San José, there are buses twice daily via Varablanca;

three times a day via Ciudad Quesada; and four times a day via Río Frío.

Taxi There is a taxi sign on the main street. There aren't many taxis but if you wait by the stand one will eventually cruise by. (Conveniently, the bar behind the taxi stand has a serving window to the street, so you can have a beer while you're waiting.) Taxis will take you to the nearby lodges and biological station for US$2 to US$4.

Boat The port is small and not busy. There are a few motorised dugouts available for hire and there is an irregular service (depending on demand) that goes to some ranches and fincas down river – ask around. The people at the El Gavilán Lodge will arrange overnight boat trips to the Río San Juan and the Nicaraguan border.

SELVA VERDE

Selva Verde is in Chilamate, about seven km west of Puerto Viejo. It is a private finca which has been turned into a tourist facility. Well over half of its approximately 200 hectares is forested; the rest contains two lodges in attractively landscaped grounds. There are walking trails through the grounds and into the forest (premontane tropical wet forest); trail maps are available or you can hire a bilingual guide from the lodge. There are plenty of birds and butterflies, and observant visitors may see mammals, frogs and reptiles. The Río Sarapiquí flows close by and boat trips can be arranged.

Near Selva Verde there is a small rainforest preserve called El Bejuco, run by an ex-manager of La Selva Biological Station. There are trails and there is currently no charge for a visit.

Places to Stay & Eat

There are two lodges, both run by Holbrook Travel of the USA. Because of the travel agency connection, the lodges are popular with tour groups from the USA and other countries. The lodge has a useful library for clients, and lectures are sometimes arranged.

If you are a guest, you could take advantage of these bonuses.

Both lodges are rustic looking with thatched roofs and attractive wooden construction. Inside, the rooms are comfortable and fans are provided. The lodges are close to the river and there are pleasant balconies with forest or river views. There is a dining room with buffet style meals. Dining and sleeping areas are screened. The *River Lodge* has spacious rooms with private baths for US$57/96/126 single/double/triple for full board. The slightly smaller *Creek Lodge* has rooms for US$52/84/111 single/double/triple. The Creek Lodge has shared bathrooms, but with almost as many bathrooms as there are bedrooms this does not present an intolerable hardship. Reservations should be made at Selva Verde (☎ 716459), Chilamate, Puerto Viejo de Sarapiquí, Costa Rica. In the USA, reservations can be made at 3540 NW 13th St, Gainesville, FL 32609, USA (☎ (800) 345-7111 in Florida, (800) 451-7111 in the rest of the USA, and (904) 377-7111 elsewhere).

Getting There & Away

Buses en route to Puerto Viejo will drop you off at the entrance – all the drivers know where it is. Taxis in Puerto Viejo can take you to the lodge for about US$3 or US$4. If you make arrangements with Selva Verde, they will provide transport from San José for US$15 per person with a minimum of four passengers.

EL GAVILÁN & ORO VERDE

El Gavilán is a private preserve about four km north-east of Puerto Viejo. Oro Verde is a larger private preserve on the Sarapiquí near the Nicaraguan border, two to three hours by motorised dugout from El Gavilán. Both places have a lodge and are owned and operated by Wolf and Mariamalia Bissinger, a German/Costa Rican couple who also speak fluent English and French. They are very energetic people who love to be on the premises (rather than stuck in the San José office) and enjoy interacting with their guests. Preserving the tropical forests near

Oro Verde is a prime concern. Wolf considers the remote Oro Verde Lodge as his jungle home and loves to accompany guests up there. It's fun to stay at a lodge where the owners are often in enthusiastic evidence.

El Gavilán

El Gavilán is a 180 hectare preserve of which about 80% is forested. The lodge used to be a cattle hacienda and is surrounded by attractive gardens with large trees – great for bird-watching. There is also a variety of tropical fruit harvested for meals. Horses are available for hire and guides will take you into the forest. Or you can wander around at will.

A variety of boat trips are available, ranging from short jaunts down river for a couple of hours to multi-day trips. Wolf is one of the few people I know who takes boats down the Sarapiquí to the San Juan, and obtains permission from the Sandinista authorities to enable tourists to travel down the San Juan. Now, since the election of Violeta Chamorro in Nicaragua and the cessation of Contra-Sandinista hostilities, more people are travelling down the San Juan. It is possible to arrange trips as far as the Barro del Colorado National Wildlife Refuge on the Caribbean coast, continuing to Tortuguero National Park if you wish. The official border between Nicaragua and Costa Rica is the south bank of the San Juan, not the middle of the river, so you are technically travelling in Nicaragua when on the San Juan.

Oro Verde

Oro Verde is a delight. It is a very rustic lodge set in a clearing surrounded by rainforest. The attractive building with its huge cone-shaped thatched roof is only three km from the Nicaraguan border. Although some of the land between Puerto Viejo and Oro Verde remains forested, the majority of the banks of the Sarapiquí have been turned to cattle pasture, with the river being the main highway for the ranchers.

When the Bissingers bought Oro Verde, it came with about 500 hectares of land.

Adjoining property has been added, and now Oro Verde contains about 2500 hectares, of which 80% is forested. Work is going on to expand the boundaries of the Oro Verde preserve to include more of the remaining stands of rainforest at the northern end of the Sarapiquí. Wolf tells me that he expects 4000 hectares near the Oro Verde could be spared from deforestation and he is trying to obtain title to this land.

Sailing down the Sarapiquí is full of surprises. If the water is low, dozens of crocodiles are seen sunning on the banks. If the water is high, river turtles climb out of the river to sun themselves on logs. In trees on the banks, you may see monkeys, iguanas, or maybe a snake draped over a branch. Birds are everywhere.

I was lucky enough to see a sleeping sloth which looked just like a greenish-brown blob on a branch because of the algae which grows in the fur of this lethargic mammal. When my boatman suddenly cut the engine, I turned around to see what was the matter. He grinned and yelled, in his none too good English, 'slow! slow!'. It was obvious that we were going slow, and it took me a while to realise that he was trying to say 'sloth!' How he managed to make out the blob on a branch as a sloth is one of the mysteries of travelling with a sharp-eyed campesino.

It was not until the dugout had gently nosed into the bank beneath the tree, and the sloth raised a languid head to see what was going on, that I finally realised what we were stopping for.

Many of the people working for the Bissingers are local campesinos who speak little or no English. They do have some excellent bilingual guides who know the wildlife, but the campesinos who have been raised in the countryside are often the best spotters of interesting animals, birds and plants. In addition, the policy of hiring locals to work on private preserves is a sensible one – if you tell a parent with children to feed that they can't chop down particular tracts of forest, it is important to offer viable economic alternatives.

The manager of Oro Verde is Romelio Campos, a hard-working local man who can thatch a roof or point out a parrot with equal facility. Señora de Campos presides over the kitchen, and produces the most delicious Costa Rican country cooking I have tasted. Beans and rice, fried bananas, fresh fish, corn tamales, and juicy papayas never tasted as good. Their children love to talk about their lives and are curious about yours. I spent an evening with young Fraiser showing him the coloured plates in my bird guide, whilst he told me the names in Spanish and where the birds could be found in the area. Fraiser and Wolf accompanied a small group of us down the San Juan on a day trip, and Fraiser's young exuberance in pointing out everything from his schoolhouse to an egret roost was very contagious.

On the San Juan, we stopped to visit an old Miskito Indian fisherman named Leandro. He claimed to be 80 years old, but his wizened looking frame had the vitality of a man half his age. From the bulging woven grass bag in the bottom of his fragile dugout, Leandro sold us fresh river lobster to accompany that evening's supper.

Tours

Overnight packages include bus from San José via the Varablanca route (photo stops at waterfalls etc), all meals, guides, accommodation at El Gavilán, a horse ride, a boat trip, and return to San José via the Braulio Carrillo National Park; this package is US$110 per person. For two nights (three days) it is US$150 per person.

For those with less time, a day trip is offered which includes bus from and to San José, lunch at the lodge, and a choice of boat or horse ride. This is US$55 per person. If you prefer to make your own way to El Gavilán, it costs US$25 less. The boat to Oro Verde costs an extra US$30 per person round trip.

Discounts can be arranged if you are a student or researcher, or travelling in a group. If you want to spend more than two nights, or prefer to cook for yourself at Oro Verde, discounts can also be arranged directly with the Bissingers (☎ 237479, 536540) or write to Apartado 445, Zapote 2010, San José, Costa Rica.

Places to Stay & Eat

El Gavilán The *El Gavilán Lodge* has about 10 clean but simple rooms with private bath, and there is electricity.

Oro Verde The *Oro Verde Station* is more spartan. There are four small rooms with communal showers and no electricity – lighting is by kerosene lantern or candles. There are four self contained family cabins with two rooms, private bath and propane stoves for cooking your own food. Both lodges have dining verandahs, and tasty food is served.

Ranchos (small thatched shelters) are available for the adventurous who want to hike or boat into the rainforest around Oro Verde.

Getting There & Away

The bus to Puerto Viejo does not pass by El Gavilán, so you should take a taxi from Puerto Viejo. The fare is about US$3.

LA SELVA BIOLOGICAL STATION

This biological station is the real thing – teeming with research scientists and graduate students using the well equipped laboratories, experimental plots, herbarium, and library to investigate the ecological processes of the rainforest.

La Selva is run by the Organization for Tropical Studies (OTS) which is a consortium founded in 1963 with the purpose of providing leadership in education, research and the wise use of tropical natural resources. Member organisations from the USA, Puerto Rico and Costa Rica include 46 universities and two museums.

Many well known tropical ecologists have received training at La Selva. Twice a year OTS offers an eight week course open mainly to graduate students of ecology. The students visit several of the other OTS sites, but La Selva is the biggest and most frequently used one. Course work is gruelling, with classes, discussions, seminars and field work running from dawn till dusk and beyond on a daily basis. Various other courses and field trips are also offered. There are many long term and ongoing experiments under way at La Selva, and many researchers come here year after year.

Information

The area protected by La Selva is about 1500 hectares of premontane wet tropical rainforest. About 90% of the land has not been disturbed. It is bordered to the south by the 44,000 hectares of the Braulio Carrillo National Park thus affording a large enough area to enable a great diversity of species to live here. Over 400 species of birds have been recorded at La Selva, as well as over 100 species of mammals, and thousands of plants and insects.

You can visit La Selva year round, but with almost 200 mm of rain falling in each of February and March (the driest months) you should be prepared with rainwear or an umbrella. (I find nylon or even Gortex rainwear to be too hot in the tropics, and prefer to keep a collapsible umbrella in my day pack. It keeps my head, glasses and binoculars dry at least – forget about the waist down!)

Insect repellent, a water bottle, clothes which you don't mind being covered in mud, and footwear suitable for muddy trails are also essential. The total annual rainfall is 4100 mm, and temperatures average 24°C but are often higher. The elevation is about 35 metres at the research station and goes up to about 150 metres by the time Braulio Carrillo is reached.

There is a small exhibit room and a gift shop selling books, maps, posters and T-shirts.

Walking Trails

Bird-watching in particular is excellent because of the very well developed trail system at La Selva. A few of the trails have a boardwalk to enable relatively easy access even during the wet season (though watch your footing – those wet boards can get very slick).

Most of the trails are simply dirt tracks which ramble off into the rainforest, but they are marked with posts every 50 metres so that you don't lose your way. The posts are labelled with the distance you have walked. In all, there are 25 maintained trails ranging from 200 metre long boardwalks to difficult, steep and often muddy trails five km long.

The total length of trails is about 50 km. Hikes can combine a variety of different trails so that you can do a round trip loop lasting from one hour to a full day.

The trail guide booklet *Walking La Selva* by R Whittall & B Farnsworth (1989) is available from the OTS. Other booklets about La Selva are also available, including *A Biologist's Handbook* by D B & D A Clark, who are currently co-directors of the station. The handbook describes two nature trails in fascinating detail. Local guides are sometimes available to take you around.

Warnings The well developed trail system tends to lull some visitors into a sense of false security. This is a wilderness area, and you must watch where you step. There are plenty of poisonous snakes. Also watch where you put your hands and where you sit. Many of the plants have very sharp thorns or stingers. Worse still, the large black ant *Paraponera clavata* can reach up to three cm in length, is quite common and delivers a vicious bite.

Places to Stay & Eat

There are simple but comfortable bungalows with four bunks per room, and a limited number of singles and doubles. Bathrooms are communal, but there are plenty of them. There is a dining room serving meals, although researchers and students always have priority. If there is room available, tour groups (especially birding ones) and individual travellers can use the facilities, but reservations must be made in advance. There is usually space available if reservations are made a few weeks (or even a few days) in advance.

The rates are US$70 per person per day for tourists; researchers stay for half price and students (working or studying at La Selva) even less. This is, after all, a research station. Prices include three meals a day, and a maximum of 65 people can stay at La Selva. Beer is available if ordered in advance; other alcohol is not available. Laundry machines are available in the afternoons only. Day visits cost US$15 per person and include use of the trails and lunch.

Reservations should be made with OTS (☎ 366696), Apartado 676, 2050 San Pedro, San José, Costa Rica. José Arturo is the reservations manager.

There is a house near La Selva that you can stay in more cheaply than at the research station itself. If you are interested in following this up, call the Murillo family in San José (☎ 359280).

Getting There & Away

The public bus to Puerto Viejo via the Río Frío and Horquetas route can drop you off at the entrance to La Selva, about three km before Puerto Viejo. From the entrance it is almost a two km walk to the research station. Taxis from Puerto Viejo will take you there for about US$3.

OTS runs buses from San José to La Selva and back on Monday, Wednesday and Friday. The fare is US$10 and reservations should be made when you arrange your visit. Researchers and students have priority.

OTS also runs a van service into Puerto Viejo and back several times a day (except Sunday, when there is only one trip).

RARA AVIS

Rara Avis is a remote private preserve of 1335 hectares of tropical rainforest between 500 and 800 metres in elevation on the northeastern slopes of the Cordillera Central. The land borders the eastern edge of Braulio Carrillo National Park. The rainforest preserve was founded by Amos Bien, an American who came to Costa Rica as a biology student in 1977. As has happened to many biologists who have worked in the tropics, he became fascinated by the incredible complexity of the rainforest ecosystems. But instead of becoming a research biologist bent on discovering more about the rainforest, Amos decided that he wanted to help preserve it. The result is the Rara Avis preserve, in my mind the most interesting tropical rainforest preservation project in Costa Rica.

The logic behind Rara Avis is simple. Tropical rainforests are being destroyed all over the world for one reason only – money. Biologists and conservationists, meteorologists and environmentalists can all provide pressing reasons why the world's rainforests must be protected, but unless economic reality is addressed, destruction of the rainforest will continue. Rara Avis was created with the goal of demonstrating that an intact and preserved rainforest could be just as profitable, if not more so, than one that is logged and turned into cattle pasture, which has been the fate of much of Costa Rica's tropical rainforests.

Certainly, international aid and a national parks scheme go part of the way towards preserving rainforests. But much deforestation occurs in many small operations run by private individuals. It is these individuals for whom Rara Avis is setting an example of what can be done to both preserve and profit from rainforest.

The most obvious solution is ecotourism, and Rara Avis has two lodges, one fairly simple and moderately priced, the other more comfortable and more expensive. But campesinos trying to make a living in the rainforest are rarely going to have the resources to build and run tourist lodges. Rara Avis is unique in Costa Rica in that it is developing other methods of non-destructive profit from the forest, which is a major reason why I believe it is the most interesting and worthwhile private preserve in Costa Rica.

One method is by ecologically sound production and harvest of forest products on a sustained yield basis. This is already a viable option in some parts of the Amazon – for example rubber tapping and brazil nut harvesting both work best in an intact forest rather than in plantations where these plants have been shown to be susceptible to epidemics. Recently, biologists at Rara Avis have rediscovered the dappled understorey palm, *Geonoma epetiolata*, which had been considered extinct in Costa Rica for about half a century. It is an attractive palm with potential as an ornamental house plant. It grows only in deep shade and harvesting just the seeds for growing the plant in nurseries could provide a significant income. It may also be possible to commercially cultivate this plant in the rainforest understorey.

Some philodendron species produce aerial roots which are harvested and used by local artisans and treated to provide wicker. This product can then be woven into baskets, furniture, mats and other utilitarian items. The philodendron is a rainforest plant, and workers at Rara Avis are studying the ecology of the plant to determine what a sustainable harvest size would be, and whether it would be an economically practical crop.

Tree ferns have aerial roots which grow in thick spongy mats. These can be used by florists or horticulturists as supports for epiphytic plants such as orchids. Unfortunately, the excellence of this product has led to it being cut out of the forest in quantities which kill the tree fern. Some countries have now banned the use and import of tree fern roots. However, Guatemala has reported a method of harvesting the roots in sustainable quantities which does not kill the tree ferns and allows for more harvests in the future. Rara Avis is trying to develop production of this product which is abundant in the area.

Another profitable enterprise is paca farming. Pacas, *(Agouti paca,* called *tepezcuintles* in Costa Rica) are large rodents which inhabit the rainforest. Their meat is very tasty and they are considered a delicacy in rural Costa Rica – so much so that illegal poaching has decimated the population of this animal in some areas. Rara Avis suggests that licensed paca farms in enclosures within the rainforest would undermine poaching and provide both income and food for campesinos. (A similar project is being developed in Panama with iguanas.)

Undeniably, there are valuable trees within the rainforest but these comprise less than 10% of the lumber. Clearcutting is an incredibly wasteful procedure. Rara Avis supports the study of how low-impact sustained-yield selective logging procedures could be developed on a rotating basis in appropriate areas with careful management. Whilst low intensity timber removal would initially be more costly and lower yielding than clearcutting, the long term profits would be greater and the rainforest and its trees would remain for future generations.

Straightforward biological research is also a goal at Rara Avis – but with an innovative twist. It is here that biologist Donald Perry built his Automated Web for Canopy Exploration (AWCE). This is a radio controlled ski-lift type machine which is able to travel up, down and along about four hectares of forest canopy. Recent studies have shown that the rainforest canopy is the new frontier of natural history. Until recently, researchers had to be content with examining the canopy through binoculars, trying to peer through the rare gaps in the rainforest. Little did they know that many thousands of new species remained to be discovered in the rainforest canopy. Some species of birds which had been recorded only a handful of times were found to be abundant in the canopy. Many epiphytic plants, mosses, beetles, ants and other insects, frogs, reptiles, fungi, parasites and a host of other creatures spend their entire life cycles in the rainforest tree tops, and were unknown to scientists until exploration of the canopy began recently.

The story of the AWCE can be read in Donald Perry's book *Life Above the Jungle Floor* (1986, Simon & Schuster). Much of the preliminary research for the project was done at the La Selva Biological Station. The final product was built at Rara Avis, and interested visitors can see and sometimes even ride on the machine. This depends on whether it is being used for research, and whether there is a qualified operator available. If you can go on the AWCE, be prepared to sign a lengthy legal waiver in case of any accident. This is, after all, a new and experimental set up, but visitors insist on riding it. It cost me US$25 for a ride, and gave me a completely new perspective of the rainforest.

Other things for visitors to do is take hikes along the trail system at Rara Avis, either alone or accompanied by biologists who work as guides. The bird-watching is excellent, with a list of about 340 species, and growing. Birds seen here but not very common elsewhere include the blue-and-gold tanager, the black-and-yellow tanager, and the snowcap hummingbird (all of which I saw near the lodge) as well as many others. Very common mammals include white-face, spider and howler monkeys, coatimundis, banded anteaters and paca. Peccaries, jaguars, tapirs and sloths are also present in reasonable numbers, but are harder to see. Insects are, of course, abundant and the plants and trees are as varied as anywhere in the tropics. There are reference books available at the lodge.

Rara Avis can be visited year round. The dry season is from January to December inside the lodge. Outside, it rains over 5000 mm every year and there are no dry months, although February to April is slightly less wet. This is definitely rainforest.

A short trail from the lodge leads to La Catarata – a 55 metre high waterfall which cuts an impressive swath through the rainforest. With care, it is possible to take a gloriously refreshing swim at the base of the falls. A perfect end to a day of muddy hiking.

Places to Stay & Eat

El Plastico is at the edge of the preserve, 12 km from Horquetas by very bad road through farmland. Horquetas itself is about 18 km south of Puerto Viejo and 10 km north of Río Frío. A further three km of equally bad (if not worse) road through rainforest brings you to the *Waterfall Lodge*.

El Plastico is a ramshackle building built in 1964 by prisoners from a now defunct jungle penal colony. The prisoners were given pieces of plastic to sleep under – hence the name. The building was abandoned in 1965 and renovated for Rara Avis in 1986. It is available for use by biologists, students and travellers. Accommodation is quite basic – 40 bunk beds in about seven rooms. There are communal showers with hot water on demand, and an open-air dining area with simple but plentiful and tasty food. Accom-

modation is US$45 per person per day, including meals.

Owner Amos Bien is emphatically interested in educating visitors to the rainforest and has an attractive system of discounts for various groups. Working biologists and students groups on courses receive a 50% discount. Costa Rican citizens and residents receive a 30% discount. Anybody wanting an in-depth immersion into the rainforest can stay here for five days or more at a 25% discount; 15 days or more gets a 40% discount. Members of the IYHF who book at the Toruma Lodge in San José also receive substantial savings.

The *Waterfall Lodge* is named after the fall nearby. This is a rustic but comfortable and attractive jungle lodge. Rooms have private showers and hot water, and have balconies overlooking the rainforest. Even when it's pouring outside, you can watch birds from your private balcony. There is a two day minimum stay at the lodge, and prices include meals, guided walks and transport from Las Horquetas. There is no electricity but kerosene lanterns are provided. The open-air dining room serves good and plentiful meals. The rates are US$75 per person per day in single rooms, US$65 per person in doubles and US$55 per person in triples. Another lodge is planned in the future.

There is also a system where you can buy shares in the Rara Avis SA corporation. These cost about US$1200, enable the project to expand and work on rainforest preservation research, and entitle shareholders to several free nights at the lodge each year. Eventually, it is planned to pay dividends to the stockholders.

Reservations are more or less essential. Contact Amos Bien (☎ 530844), Rara Avis; Apartado 8105, 1000 San José, Costa Rica.

Getting There & Away

First get a bus to Horquetas – you are given a schedule when you make your reservation. Here you will be met and transported to Rara Avis. This latter transportation is another major reason why I love Rara Avis. The road is so bad that 4WD won't make it for most of the year. The road climbs from Horquetas at 75 metres to the lodge at 710 metres above sea level. En route two rivers must be forded (there are foot bridges). So what does 'transportation' mean?

A tractor is used to pull a wagon with padded bench seats. The 15 km trip takes three to five hours, and the ride is not a smooth one. Occasionally, the tractor breaks down or the mud is simply too deep (too thick? too sticky? too runny? too disgusting for words?) for the tractor to get through. In which case you walk the rest of the way.

Horses are available if you want to ride or to transport luggage. Take heart – the tractor nearly always gets about nine km of the way up, often makes it to El Plastico (the 12 km mark) and sometimes might even make it to the lodge!

The way to look at it is that getting there is a good introduction to what the rainforest is like – and all just part of the adventure. Many people have suggested to Amos that he fix the road – but I like it just fine the way it is. It makes arriving at Rara Avis just that little bit more special.

The Caribbean Lowlands

The Caribbean and Pacific coasts of Costa Rica are very different. The Pacific coast is indented and irregular, whilst the Caribbean is a smooth sweep of beaches, mangroves and coastal swamp forest. The tidal variation on this smooth coastline is very low. The Pacific has a dry season; the Caribbean is wet year round. About half of the Caribbean coastline is protected by two national parks and two national wildlife refuges, whilst less than 10% of the Pacific is so protected. The most luxurious beach resorts have been developed on the Pacific; the Caribbean coast is visited not simply for a relaxing beach experience but also for wildlife and culture.

The entire Caribbean coast is part of Limón Province which covers 18% of Costa Rica but has only 7% of the population, making it the most sparsely populated province in the country. One third of the province's 210,000 inhabitants are Blacks mainly of Jamaican descent. Most of them live on or near the coast and many speak delightfully archaic English. They add a cultural diversity missing in the rest of Costa Rica. Also, in the southern part of the province, about 5000 Talamanca Indians survive.

Partly because of the low population of the region, and partly because, until the 1949 constitution, Blacks were legally discriminated against, the Caribbean lowlands have been much slower to be developed than the Pacific. There are fewer roads and more areas which can be reached only by boat or light aircraft. Limón province has less than 7% of the country's hotel rooms, whilst the Pacific coastal provinces of Guanacaste and Puntarenas have a combined total of almost 39%. Traditionally, Costa Ricans from the populous Central Valley have vacationed on the Pacific, and even today the Caribbean is not a primary destination for most nationals. This is slowly beginning to change with the opening, in 1987, of the San José-Guápiles-Puerto Limón highway which cut driving time to the coast in half, but traditions die hard.

Foreign travellers, on the other hand, are almost all attracted to the Caribbean, even if it is only to take the famous jungle train ride from San José to the provincial capital at Puerto Limón. At the end of the line there is just a single road heading south along the coast to the Panamanian border. Northbound travellers must rely on boats to take them up the coastal waterway, locally known as *los canales*, through wilderness areas, past remote fishing villages, and on to Nicaragua. Limited access has helped maintain a sense of traditional values in the inhabitants, which makes a Caribbean visit certainly more interesting, if not as luxurious, as a trip to the Pacific beaches.

There are exceptions, of course. Tortuguero and Barra del Colorado both have first class lodges in wilderness areas. But the rest of the Caribbean coast has a gentle, laid back, unhurried feel to it. If a small coastal village with simple accommodation is more to your liking than elaborate tourist developments, I think you'll find what you are looking for right here.

On 22 April 1991 a powerful earthquake

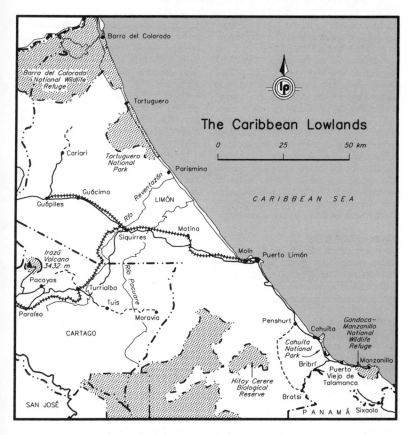

The Caribbean Lowlands

0   25   50 km

CARIBBEAN SEA

measuring 7.4 on the Richter Scale struck Costa Rica killing over 50 people in Costa Rica and about 30 more in neighbouring Panama. Hundreds of people were injured and thousands lost their homes. The epicentre was south of Puerto Limón, which was the city most seriously affected by the disaster.

At time of publication, both roads from San José to Puerto Limón (the old road through Turrialba and the new road through Guápiles) had been badly damaged with at least 17 bridges closed. The railway from the capital to Puerto Limón has also been closed.

Communications between the capital and the Caribbean coast are expected to be severely disrupted for some time. The villages south of Puerto Limón have all been affected by road closures and building damage.

San José to Puerto Limón

GUÁPILES

This town is the transport centre for the Río

Frío banana growing region. A railroad from here goes to Siquirres, where it connects with the main San José to Puerto Limón track and carries bananas to the coast. The 1987 opening of the highway from San José through Guápiles to Puerto Limón has made the town even more important as a banana transporting centre. Certainly, many more people now pass through Guápiles than before, but to what extent this will improve the economy of the town remains to be seen.

The main reason for the traveller to be here is to connect with buses to and from the Río Frío region and on to Puerto Viejo de Sarapiquí in the Northern Lowlands. Also, train enthusiasts can take the passenger train which leaves for Siquirres every morning.

Places to Stay & Eat

The best hotel is the *Ken Wa* near the railway station. Rooms with private bath are about US$8 double. There are a few cheaper hotels.

There are several inexpensive places to eat but no particularly good ones.

Getting There & Away

The bus terminal is two or three blocks from the railway station. Buses to San José (US$1.20) or Puerto Limón (US$1) leave about every hour. Buses to Río Frío leave at 4.30 and 7.30 am and 2 pm (there's no 4.30 am bus on Sundays).

SIQUIRRES

This town is at an important (by Costa Rican standards) railway junction. It is at the end of the scenic Turrialba to Siquirres descent of the San José to Puerto Limón jungle train. This stretch is considered the most scenic part of the jungle train trip.

Beyond Siquirres, the train goes through flat coastal country with banana plantations, coconut groves and rice paddies. Some travellers opt to get off the train at Siquirres and connect with the frequent buses to San José or Puerto Limón. There is also a train service to Guápiles.

Places to Stay & Eat

There are a number of fairly cheap hotels, all

near the railway station. On the street behind the train ticket office you'll find the *Hotel Melissa, Hotel Mireya* and an unnamed *hospedaje*. Some of the rooms have private baths; expect to pay about US$2.50 to US$5 per person.

Opposite the railway station is the town market. With the station behind you, the *Hotel Garza* is on the left hand side and the *Hotel Central* is on the right. Both look OK and in the same price range as above.

Between the market and the bus station look for the *Restaurant Carucy* which looks like the best in town, though it's not very expensive.

Getting There & Away

Bus The bus terminal is two blocks from the railway station, or one block behind and to the right of the market.

Buses leave about every hour to Guápiles (US$0.55), San José (US$1.45) and Puerto Limón (US$0.60).

Train Trains from Puerto Limón en route to San José pass through around 8.30 am; in the opposite direction they pass through at about 3 pm. Trains from Siquirres to Guápiles leave at 3.20 pm. All fares are US$1 or less.

PUERTO LIMÓN

This port is the capital of the province of Limón and many ticos refer to the city as, simply, Limón. The mainly Black population of Limón and the surrounding district is 65,000; thus almost a third of the province's inhabitants live in and around the provincial capital.

Limón is quite lively and busy, as ports tend to be, and sometimes you may hear some coastal music. Generally, though, Limón is not considered a tourist town, although there are good quality hotels and a beach resort at Playa Bonita, four km north of the town centre. Most people just spend a night en route to somewhere else, though you may be stuck here for a couple of days if trying to get to Tortuguero on one of the cheap boats.

Orientation

The streets are very poorly marked. Most streets have no signs, and others have two different street signs on them! Apart from this, the streets and avenues go up one number at a time (Calle 1, Calle 2, etc) as opposed to going up in twos, as they do in San José and most other towns. Most locals get around by city landmarks. Some of the major ones are the market, Radio Casino and the town hall (municipalidad).

Avenida 2 is considered one of the main streets – Parque Vargas, the town hall, the market, the railway station and the San José bus terminal are all on or just off this street.

Information

The Banco Nacional de Costa Rica and other banks will change money, or street moneychangers hang out around the market. Change as much money here as you'll need for your trips on the coast, as exchange facilities are not great elsewhere, though the better places accept cash US dollars or even travellers' cheques.

The post office is at the south-west corner of the market.

For those few arriving at Limón by sea, there is a Migración office on the north side of Parque Vargas. Visa extensions are normally given in San José, just 2½ hours away by bus.

There are at least two cinemas in the downtown area.

Warning People have been mugged in Limón, so stick to the main well lit streets at night. Also watch for pickpockets during the day. These are fairly normal precautions in many port cities – Limón is not especially dangerous.

Parque Vargas

The main attraction is Parque Vargas in the south-eastern corner of town by the waterfront. The park has tall attractive palm and other tropical trees, flowers, birds and sloths hanging out (literally) in the trees. It's not easy to see the sloths, but they are there.

From the park it's a pleasant walk north along the sea wall with views of the rocky headland upon which the city is built.

Beaches

There are no beaches in Limón, but at Playa Bonita, four km north-west of town, there is a sandy beach which is popular for bathing. There are places to eat and picnic areas, and the backdrop of tropical vegetation is attractive.

Uvita Island

Columbus landed at Uvita Island, which can be seen about a km east of Limón. Accordingly, Columbus Day (12 October, locally known as El Día de la Raza) is celebrated with more than the usual enthusiasm. Thousands of visitors, mainly ticos, stream into town for street parades and dancing, music, singing, drinking and general carrying on which goes on for four or five days. Hotels are booked well in advance of this event.

It is possible to hire boats to see Uvita Island, and the better hotels organise tours there. Tours to Tortuguero, Cahuita and other destinations of interest can also be arranged from all the better hotels (as well as in San José).

Other Attractions

Another focal point of the town is the colourful public market.

You might also check out the Ethnography Museum (Museo Etnográfico de Limón) which was being restored when I last looked in.

Places to Stay

Since the opening of the new highway in 1987, hotels all along the Caribbean have been in much greater demand. This is particularly true of weekends during the San José holiday seasons (Christmas, Easter, January, February) and during the Columbus Day celebrations on and around 12 October. You should call in advance if possible during those periods.

Some hotels are beginning to operate two price structures – one for locals and a higher

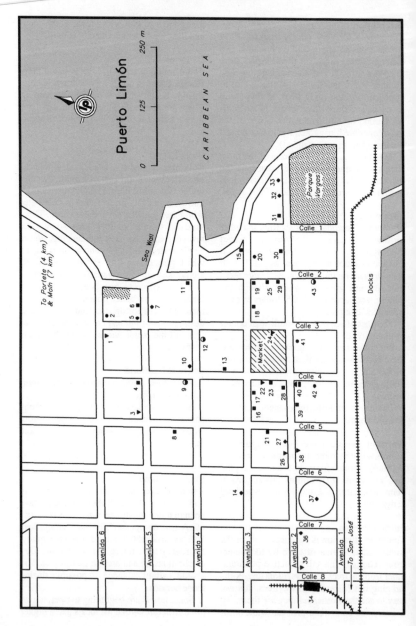

Puerto Limón

CARIBBEAN SEA

0   125   250 m

To Portete (4 km) & Moín (7 km)

Sea Wall

Parque Vargas

Docks

To San José

Calle 1
Calle 2
Calle 3
Calle 4
Calle 5
Calle 6
Calle 7
Calle 8

Avenida 6
Avenida 5
Avenida 4
Avenida 3
Avenida 2
Avenida 1

■ PLACES TO STAY

4	Hotel Ng
6	Hotel Lincoln
8	Hotel Paraiso
11	Hotel Venus
13	Hotel Nuevo Oriental
15	Park Hotel
16	Pensión Los Angeles
17	Hotel Tete
18	Hotel Acon
19	Cariari Hotel
21	Pensión El Sauce
23	Hotel Los Angeles
25	Hotel Palace
28	Hotel Fung
29	Hotel Río
30	Hotel Las Palmeras & Hotel Costa Rica
31	Hotel Caribe
38	Hotel Galaxy
39	Hotel Miami

▼ PLACES TO EAT

1	Restaurant Sien Kong
3	Restaurant Sol de Oro
5	Marisquería Tureski
7	Marisquería La Nueva Casa de Abuela
22	Restaurant Chong Kong
24	Restaurant Doña Toda
26	Soda Restaurant Yans
31	American Bar
38	Palacio Encantador Restaurant
41	Mares Soda Bar/Restaurant

OTHER

2	Gas Station
9	Bus to Moín
10	Radio Casino
12	Bus to Cahuita, Puerto Viejo & Sixaola
14	Cine Atlantic 1
20	Fire Station (Bomberos)
27	Cine Atlantic 2
32	Town Hall (Municipalidad)
33	Migracíon
34	Train Station
35	Bar Estadio
36	Gas Station
37	Baseball Stadium
40	Post Office
41	Banco Nacional de Costa Rica
42	Ethnography Museum
43	Buses to San José

one for visitors. There's not much you can do except go to another hotel if you don't like the price.

Places to Stay – bottom end

The cheapest hotels have little to recommend them except price. The *Hotel Río* seems to be popular with dock workers but looks OK for US$2.40 per person – there are very few single rooms available.

The *Cariari Hotel* has small, basic rooms with no fans for US$3.50 per person and has single rooms; the similar *Pensión El Sauce* has no singles. The *Hotel Galaxy* (☎ 582828) has basic but adequate rooms for US$3.50/6 for a single/double.

The *Hotel Palace* has rooms for US$4 per person with shared communal baths; US$7/10 single double for rooms with private bath. It's in an interesting looking old building around a courtyard with flowers. The *Hotel Fung* charges US$7/9.50 for

singles/doubles with bath and fan. Rooms without private bath are 40% less but are often full.

The *Park Hotel* (☎ 583476) has rooms with private bath starting at US$6.75/8.50 and also has nicer rooms for up to twice as much. This hotel is one of the best in this price category and is often full. Reservations can be made at Apartado 35, Puerto Limón.

The poor *Hotel Lincoln* (☎ 580074) charges US$4.50 per person in airless, dank smelling rooms with private bath. A few rooms have air-con.

The *Hotel Las Palmeras, Hotel Costa Rica* and *Hotel Caribe* all looked fairly cheap, but I suspect night time activity may be rather busy, with rooms being used more than just once a night.

Other cheapish looking hotels to try include the *Pensión Los Angeles, Hotel Paraiso, Hotel Ng* and the *Hotel Nuevo Oriental*.

Places to Stay – middle

The *Hotel Los Angeles* (☎ 582068; Apartado 514, Puerto Limón) is next to the market and has rooms with baths for US$7/$11 single/double and rooms with air-con for another US$1.50. The *Hotel Venus* charges about US$7 per person.

The clean *Hotel Miami* (☎ 580490; Apartado 266, Puerto Limón) charges US$9.50/14 for single/double rooms with private bath and fan; for air-con add US$2.50 per room. There is a cafeteria.

The *Hotel Tete* (☎ 581122; Apartado 401, Puerto Limón) is OK except that the charge is US$11.50/22 single/double with bath for tourists, but barely half that for locals.

The best hotel downtown is the *Hotel Acon* (☎ 581010; Apartado 528, Puerto Limón) which charges US$19/22 for singles/doubles with private bath and air-con. They have a restaurant and dancing at weekends.

There are also some good hotels on the coast just north-west of Limón. If you are driving you can reach them by taking the Moín turn off to the left, about six km before reaching Limón from San José; this avoids

downtown Limón altogether. Just before Moín docks, take a right for Portete and Playa Bonita, and follow the coast road east past the coastal hotels, eventually reaching Limón itself. If you are not driving take the Moín bus, although it is often very crowded; a taxi would be a better way to go.

About two km north-west of downtown, overlooking the rocky coastline, is the *Hotel Las Olas* (☎ 581414; Apartado 701, Puerto Limón). There are two pools and a pleasant sea-view restaurant. If the weather is not hot enough for you, there is a sauna. Some rooms have balconies. Rates are about US$20/$35 single/double with fans; add about US$5 per room for air-con.

About four km out of Limón, by Playa Bonita, is the *Cabinas Cocori* (☎ 582930) which has fairly basic family cabins with four beds and private bath for are about US$25 per cabin.

Places to Stay – top end

The two most luxurious hotels in the area are both near Portete, about five km north-west of downtown Limón.

The *Hotel Matama* (☎ 581123; Apartado

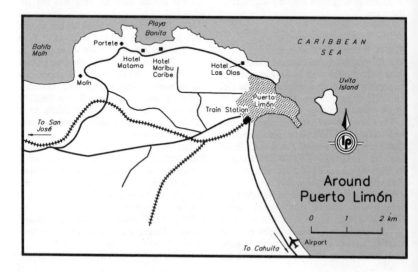

Around
Puerto Limón

686, Puerto Limón) is near Playa Bonita, has a swimming pool, restaurant, gardens, and was refurbished in 1989. Air-con rooms are about US$40/50 single/double – some family rooms sleep up to six people.

The *Hotel Maribu Caribe* (☎ 584543; Apartado 623, Puerto Limón) is a few hundred metres before you reach Playa Bonita from Limón. It is on a small hill which catches ocean breezes and has a good view. There are two pools, a restaurant and air-con throughout. Accommodation is in attractive, private, thatched bungalows and costs US$55/75/85 single/double/triple.

Places to Eat

There are many snack bars and *sodas* around the market – one of the best is *Restaurant Doña Toda* where snacks and simple meals cost up to US$2. There are several cheap bar/restaurants near the market, especially across the street on the west side. One of these is the *Restaurant Chong Kong* with Chinese meals for about US$3. Rather more upmarket, popular and clean is the *Mares Soda Bar/Restaurant* on the south side of the market. It serves a variety of snacks and meals for US$3 to US$5.

Chinese food is often the best bet for inexpensive eating. Two clean places a couple of blocks west of the market are the *Palacio Encantador* and the *Soda Restaurant Yans* – the latter with a small menu but very popular among locals. Meals are about US$2 to US$4. Slightly more expensive Chinese food is available at the clean *Restaurant Sol de Oro*. The best Chinese restaurant is the *Sien Kong*, with meals from US$5 to US$10.

For seafood try the *Marisquería La Nueva Casa de Mi Abuela* which charges about US$3 to US$6 per meal and is quite good. Better, and quite elegant by Limón standards, is the *Marisquería Tureski* where white table cloths and wine glasses greet the prospective diner. Meals here are about US$5 to US$10.

The better hotels have decent restaurants open to the public.

The *American Bar* by Parque Vargas has pricey meals but is a popular hangout for a variety of coastal characters – sailors, ladies of the night, entrepreneurs, boozers and the casually curious.

Getting There & Away

Limón is the transportation hub of the Caribbean coast.

Air The airstrip is about four km south of town, near the coast. Since the opening of the new road in 1987, regular flights are no longer available, although charters from San José can be arranged.

Bus Buses from San José to Limón leave about every hour from near the Atlantic railroad station in the capital. Buses return to San José with two companies, the offices of which are side by side on Calle 2, a block east of the market. Buses with one or the other of the companies leave every hour on the hour, from 5 am to 8 pm. The fare is US$2 for the three hour ride. From the same bus terminal there are buses to Siquirres 13 times a day, and Guápiles eight times a day.

Buses heading south leave from a block north of the market. Currently, buses from Limón to Sixaola leave at 5 and 10 am, and 1 and 4 pm. The buses stop at Cahuita (US$0.70), Puerto Viejo (US$0.90), Bribri (US$1.10) and Sixaola (US$1.60, three hours). The buses are crowded, so try to get a ticket in advance and show up early to get a seat. Advance tickets are only sold for the 10 am and 4 pm departures.

Buses also leave from here to Penshurst and Pandora (Valle la Estrella) six times a day. From Pandora you can go to the Hitoy Cerere Biological Reserve.

Train The 'jungle train' from San José usually arrives after dark. For this reason, local tour agencies recommend taking the train up from Limón rather than down from San José. You could get into trouble wandering around the Limón train station area at night, but there are plenty of taxis available to safely take you into downtown or elsewhere along the coast. If you walk along the reasonably well lit Avenida 2, however, you probably won't have any problem – it's those who arrive at night and wander around in a confused way that are liable to be mugged. It's about one km from the train station to downtown.

Trains to San José leave at 6 am. During the rainy season in the highlands, the train may reach only as far as Turrialba (six hours, US$0.75), where buses meet passengers and transfer them to San José (another 1½ hours, US$0.80). The best views are on the left hand side going up towards San José.

There used to be passenger trains south to Penshurst. Since the opening of the south coastal highway in the 1970s only goods trains use the line.

Boat Limón is the country's major port, and cruise ships occasionally dock here. However, passenger boats are difficult to find and not cheap. Very few people arrive by sea.

Boats to Tortuguero and further north leave from Moín, about seven km north-west of Limón.

Car If you are driving, fill up in Limón because there are no gas stations in Cahuita or Puerto Viejo. There is one in Pandora in the Valle la Estrella. If you plan on doing a lot of driving, consider bringing a spare can of fuel.

Getting Around

Taxi Taxis meet passengers arriving by train from San José and charge about US$1 or less to any downtown hotel. A taxi to Cahuita costs about US$15 to US$20. If you do this at night, make sure you have a hotel reservation in Cahuita.

Taxis to the good hotels around Portete charge about US$3.

The South Caribbean

HITOY CERERE BIOLOGICAL RESERVE

This 9154 hectare reserve is 60 km south of Limón by road, but only half that distance as the vulture glides. Although not far from civilisation, it is one of the most rugged and rarely visited reserves in the country, averaging less than a visitor per week. There is a ranger station but otherwise there are no facilities – no campsites, marked trails or information booths. The reserve lies between about 150 and 1000 metres in elevation on rugged terrain on the south side of the Estrella River valley.

Although few people come here, that is no reason for ignoring it. The reserve sounds like a fascinating place, and being so rarely visited, it offers a great wilderness experience in an area which has been little explored. It has been called the wettest reserve in the parks system – expect almost four metres of rain each year in these dense evergreen forests.

Hiking is permitted but the steep and slippery terrain and dense vegetation make it a possibility only for the most fit and determined hikers. Heavy rainfall and broken terrain combine to produce many beautiful streams, rivers and waterfalls. There are many different plants, birds, mammals and other animals – many of which have not yet been recorded because of the remoteness of the site.

Information

Visitors should call the National Parks Service in San José to make sure that somebody will be at the ranger station when they arrive. Sleeping at the ranger station for a small fee is a possibility if arranged in advance.

Getting There & Away

Take a bus to Valle la Estrella from Limón. This is a cacao growing region with plenty of fincas but not much in the way of places to stay. At the end of the bus line, it is a further 10 km to the reserve along a dirt road. There are jeep-taxis available to drive you there for US$4 or US$5. The drivers are reliable, and will come back to pick you up at a prearranged time. Jeep-taxis from

Cahuita (about 30 km away) will take you to the reserve for about US$25.

RÍO ESTRELLA
About 30 km south of Limón, and about one km north of where the coastal highway crosses the Río Estrella, there is a complex called Aviarios Río Estrella, which offers river trips on the Estrella. These last for several hours, cost US$35 per person including lunch and drinks, and give a look at some of the bird and other wildlife along the Estrella. Guides help identify the birds and binoculars can be borrowed. Reservations can be made at the El Pizote Lodge in Puerto Viejo, or you can just stop on the way if you are driving.

CAHUITA
This is a small village about 43 km south-east of Limón by road. It is known for the attractive beaches nearby, many of which are in the Cahuita National Park which adjoins the village to the south.

Until the 1970s, Cahuita was quite isolated from the rest of Costa Rica. A ride in an old bus on a dirt road, a river crossing by wobbly canoe, and a train ride were required to get to Limón – this journey could take half a day. Now the paved road which links Cahuita to Limón has cut the journey to a 45 minute drive. The 1987 opening of the new road from Limón to San José means that Cahuita is now a little over three hours from the capital by car. Despite this, the area retains much of its remote, provincial and unhurried flavour. Most Costa Ricans still use the Pacific coast for their beach vacations, and there are no luxury hotel developments here. Those hotels which do exist tend to be in high demand at weekends and school holidays (mid December to February, Easter), particularly during the highland dry season (January to May), so travel mid-week if you can.

The approximately 3000 inhabitants of the Cahuita district are predominantly Black and many speak a Creole form of English. This can be confusing at first, because some phrases do not mean the same as other speakers of English are used to. For example 'All right!' means 'Hello!' and 'Okay!' means 'Goodbye!'.

The people are of Jamaican descent and colonised the Costa Rican coast in the middle of the 19th century. They used to subsist mainly by small scale farming and fishing, but tourism is becoming an increasingly important part of the economy. The influx of tourist cash helps improve the standards of living but at a cultural cost. Traditional ways of life slowly become eroded and, inevitably, the local people have some difficulties in adjusting to the new, and sometimes demanding or obnoxious, tourist population. Nevertheless, much of the Creole culture remains for those who look for it, particularly in cooking, music and knowledge of medicinal plants.

Cahuita is expanding as a tourist destination, with more hotels being built and other facilities being developed. But the main street is still made of sand – more suited to horses and clunky wheeled bicycles than the cars and jeeps which tourists drive amidst clouds of choking dust. One local lady told me that the tourists' vehicles were the biggest problem that tourism has caused; she couldn't even hang her laundry out to dry in front of her house because of the dust. This is an example of the clash between 20th century tourism and a 19th century way of life – travellers are urged to enjoy their visit but to try not to impose their own values upon the areas they are visiting.

Information
Telephone Cahuita has only one telephone number: 581515. To call a hotel, call the Cahuita number and ask for the place you want or the extension if you know it. To make outbound calls, go to the public phone office at the Soda Uvita near the plaza.

Warnings Many travellers enjoy their visit to the area – others find that the coastal way of life is not for them. One couple told me that they felt uncomfortable in Cahuita because they met a few young men in a bar who accused them of being racist for not buying them drinks. The couple had also been offered drugs (which they had refused) when walking along the beach. Their hotel room had cockroaches and they'd had to wait an hour in a local restaurant before they were served. They felt as if they were unwelcome outsiders and did not enjoy their stay.

It is true that there are some people living on the coast who try to take advantage of tourists, but this is not generally a major problem. Most travellers find that the relaxed pace, the mainly friendly people, the lack of a highly developed tourist infrastructure, the

cultural diversity, and the attractive environment all contribute to an enjoyable visit. But travellers should beware of rip-offs – keep your hotel room locked, don't leave gear on beaches when swimming, don't walk the beaches alone at night, and be prudent if entering some of the local bars. Beware of drug sellers who may be in cahoots with the police.

I have heard complaints from solo women travellers who feel that some of the local men are too demanding in their romantic advances. Female travellers may feel that

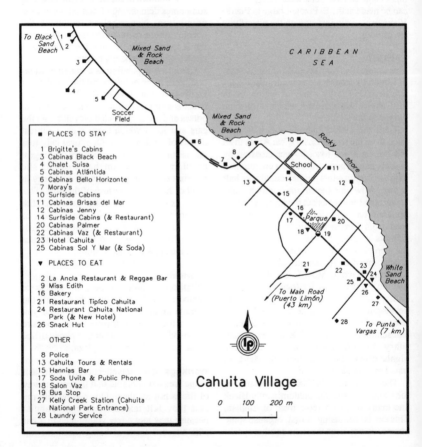

Cahuita Village

PLACES TO STAY

1 Brigitte's Cabins
3 Cabinas Black Beach
4 Chalet Suisa
5 Cabinas Atlántida
6 Cabinas Bello Horizonte
7 Moray's
10 Surfside Cabins
11 Cabinas Brisas del Mar
12 Cabinas Jenny
14 Surfside Cabins (& Restaurant)
20 Cabinas Palmer
22 Cabinas Vaz (& Restaurant)
23 Hotel Cahuita
25 Cabinas Sol Y Mar (& Soda)

PLACES TO EAT

2 La Ancla Restaurant & Reggae Bar
9 Miss Edith
16 Bakery
21 Restaurant Típico Cahuita
24 Restaurant Cahuita National Park (& New Hotel)
26 Snack Hut

OTHER

8 Police
13 Cahuita Tours & Rentals
15 Hannias Bar
17 Soda Uvita & Public Phone
18 Salon Vaz
19 Bus Stop
27 Kelly Creek Station (Cahuita National Park Entrance)
28 Laundry Service

To Black Sand Beach
Mixed Sand & Rock Beach
CARIBBEAN SEA
Soccer Field
Mixed Sand & Rock Beach
Rocky shore
School
Parque
White Sand Beach
To Main Road (Puerto Limón) (43 km)
To Punta Vargas (7 km)

0   100   200 m

travelling with a friend is safer than travelling alone. Some women do travel alone and do have a good time, but not everyone is adept at avoiding unpleasant situations.

Please note that, despite the casual atmosphere both here and in other coastal areas, nude bathing is not accepted. Also, wearing skimpy bathing clothes in the villages is frowned upon. Wearing a T-shirt and shorts is appreciated.

Beaches

There are three nearby beaches within walking distance. At the north-west end of Cahuita there is a long black sand beach with good swimming. Some people think that the black sand beach has better swimming than the white sand beach at the eastern end of town. This beach is in the national park and a trail in the jungle behind the beach leads you to a third beach about six km away. These last two beaches are separated by a rocky headland with a coral reef off it – suitable for snorkelling. This is more fully described in the section on Cahuita National Park.

Tours & Rentals

There are currently two places which rent equipment and arrange tours; Moray's and Cahuita Tours. Other places may open by the time you get there. Both places rent masks & snorkels (US$3.50 per day), fins (US$2.25 per day), bicycles (US$5.50 per day) and binoculars (US$4.50 per day).

Boat trips to the reef in a glass-bottomed boat, with snorkelling opportunities, are US$10 per person for three or four hours. Drinks are provided. Horse riding trips for four or five hours with a guide are US$45 for the first rider, US$27 for each additional person. Snacks and drinks are provided. Guided hiking trips into the local national park areas are US$17 for the first person, US$5.50 for each additional person. Early rides to catch the 6 am Limón to San José train cost US$24 for one person and US$31 for four people in the same vehicle. This includes the price of the train ticket.

Places to Stay – bottom end

Remember that all Cahuita has only one telephone number: 581515. Just the extensions are given below.

One of the least expensive places are the basic but clean *Cabinas Bello Horizonte* which cost US$3.50 per person. *Cabinas Jenny* (☎ 256) has some very basic rooms for US$6 double, as well as some more expensive cabins.

Surfside Cabins (☎ 246) has modern, plain, concrete block rooms, but they are clean, and have a fan and a private bath. Rates are US$6.50/8 for a single/double and are good value, and there is a restaurant on the premises. They have a couple of better cabins a block away, right near the rocky shoreline.

The *Hotel Cahuita* (☎ 201) has some basic old rooms with balconies for about US$8 a double. They also have more expensive cabins. *Moray's* has simple rooms for US$8/9 single/double.

Cabinas Sol y Mar has cabins with private bath and one double and two single beds. The cabins are very close to the national park entrance and there is a restaurant. The rates are US$14 for up to four occupants.

Also in the bottom end price range are *Brigitte's Cabins* and *Chalet Suisa*, the latter having only one cabin for rent, usually by the week or month and therefore usually full.

Places to Stay – middle

Cabinas Palmer (☎ 243) has cheap rooms in the annexe at US$5 per person, and better rooms with baths in the main hotel for US$11 single or double. There are also rooms with kitchenettes for US$16.50 – they'll sleep up to four. The manager is friendly and helpful and they have a little shop selling items such as sun screen, sunglasses and camera film.

The *Hotel Cahuita* (☎ 201) is right next to the national park entrance and has a swimming pool and restaurant. The cheap rooms (mentioned under bottom end) are pretty poor but the modern concrete cabins with private baths are better. Rates range from US$10 for a single increasing at about US$5 per extra person up to US$33 for a cabin for six.

Nearby, a new hotel is being built, which may prove to be better than anything else in town. Maybe it'll be open by the time you read this. A block away is the *Cabinas Vaz* (☎ 218) with concrete cabins with private baths renting for US$11 to US$21 for one to five people. There is a restaurant here as well.

Cabinas Jenny (☎ 256) and *Cabinas Brisas del Mar* (☎ 267) are both by the rocky coast just north of the centre of town. Both have cabins with private baths for about US$16 a double.

Out towards the black sand beach at the north-west end of Cahuita is the quiet *Cabinas Atlántida* (☎ 229) set in a pleasant garden. Simple clean rooms with private bath are US$18 for single or double occupancy. Nearby are the clean *Cabinas Black Beach* (☎ 251) consisting of attractive chalets with private bath and balcony. The rooms each have a double bed and a double bunk, so are suitable for families or small groups. Rates are US$19 for a double and US$26 for four occupants. Both these places will serve food if arranged in advance.

Similarly priced, but with inferior rooms, is the *Cahuita Country Club* (☎ 582861). Despite the name, this place is not in Cahuita at all, but by Estero Negro, about 20 km north of Cahuita. If you are driving you can stop in for meals or a snack.

Note that none of the hotels have hot water in the bathrooms – not a real hardship in this tropical environment. The better hotels can help arrange snorkelling or horse riding trips. A new 60 cabin tourist development is being talked about – supposedly it will be built near the black sand beach. I'll believe it when I see it.

Places to Eat

One eatery stands out because it is the best place to eat Caribbean food prepared by friendly local people. It's not a restaurant as much as the front porch of someone's house and the ambience is therefore very homey. With an advance order, *Miss Edith* will prepare the local stew called *rondon*, or 'run down'. This is a mixture of fish, meat and a variety of local vegetables such as peppers, plantains, breadfruit and yams, all gently spiced and boiled in coconut milk for several hours. A variety of other local as well as vegetarian dishes are served, and cooking is to order, so don't expect to get served soon after arriving. Bring a book or a journal to while away the time, or talk to whoever is there. Miss Edith doesn't serve beer; instead a variety of local herb teas and infusions are available. These are credited with having medicinal value. Lemon-grass tea is good for fevers, ginger infusion is good for the stomach, and a variety of other drinks alleviate other ailments.

(It is worth noting that as the local people get older, they traditionally earn a place of respect in the community. This is reflected by their form of address; they are called Miss or Mister, followed by their first name – hence, Miss Edith. You wouldn't refer to a young person in this way.)

There is a small local bakery which makes good breads and cakes; and you can order special items here. Your travelling companion has a birthday? No problem. Ask the friendly baker (whose smile I remember but whose name I forget) and she'll take care of your cake order. Baking is done in the morning and the shop is open from 3 to 9 pm. This is the place to go to pick up rolls or cakes for a beach picnic the next day.

When you get off the beach, stop at the *Snack Hut* by the national park entrance. There's no sign but you'll see the little hut with a bunch of people buying snacks. Hours are erratic – when the food is gone, they close, but the empanadas for sale in the late afternoon are delicious. A couple of blocks from the park entrance is the *Restaurant Típico Cahuita* which is good for seafood.

The *Restaurant Cahuita National Park* is right by the entrance to the national park and is a little pricey, but popular because of its location. The food is quite good and the place tends to be frequented by tourists. Nearby are the *Soda Sol y Mar*, for breakfasts and other meals, and the *Restaurant Vaz*, for meals and drinks. Both are good and attached to the cabinas of the same names.

For drinking, the 'safest' bet is any one of the restaurants mentioned above. Also catering to tourists is *Hannias Bar*. For a little bit of local colour, the *Salon Vaz* is open all day and into the night and is known for its cracking loud games of dominoes. The *La Ancla* restaurant and reggae bar is one of the wilder places in town – but is not dangerous.

Getting There & Away

Buses from San José to Sixaola stop at Cahuita. There are four daily departures with Autotransportes MEPE (☎ 210524) leaving from Avenida 11, Calle Central & 2. The fare is US$3.75 for the four hour ride. Buses return to San José from the crossroads in the middle of Cahuita at 7 and 10 am, and 4 pm.

Buses to Limón (US$0.50) leave from the same intersection at 6.30 and 10 am, 12 noon, and 1.30 and 5 pm.

Buses to Puerto Vargas, Puerto Viejo, Bribri and Sixaola leave from here at 5.50 and 11 am, and 2 pm.

CAHUITA NATIONAL PARK

This small park of 1067 hectares is one of the more frequently visited national parks in Costa Rica. The reasons are simple: easy access and nearby hotels combined with attractive beaches, a coral reef and a coastal rainforest with many easily observed tropical species. They all combine to make this a popular park.

The park is most often entered from the east end of Cahuita village, through the Kelly Creek entrance station and booth. Almost immediately, the visitor sees a two km long white sand beach stretching along a gently curving bay to the east. About the first 500 metres of beach have warning signs about unsafe swimming, but beyond that, waves are gentle and swimming is safe. (But go

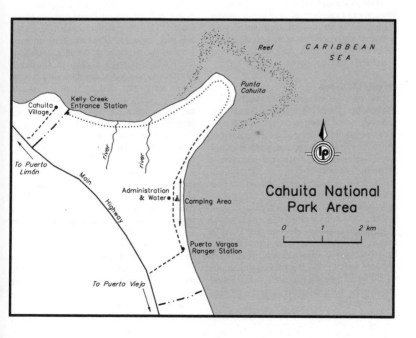

with a friend – it is unwise to leave clothing unattended when you take a dip.)

A rocky headland known as Punta Cahuita (Cahuita Point) separates this beach from the next one, Vargas Beach. At the end of Vargas Beach there is the Puerto Vargas Ranger Station, which is about seven km from Kelly Creek. The two stations are linked by a trail that goes through the coastal jungle behind the beaches and Punta Cahuita. At times, the trail follows the beach; at other times hikers are 100 metres or so away from the sand. A river must be waded near the end of the first beach – the water can be thigh deep at high tide. Various animals and birds are frequently seen, including coatimundis and raccoons, ibises and kingfishers.

Information

The park entrance stations are open daily from 7.30 am to 4 pm and the entry charge is US$1.10. No one stops you from entering the park before or after these hours.

There is not much shade on the beaches so remember to use sunscreen to avoid painful sunburn in the tropical sun. Don't forget your sensitive untanned feet after you take your shoes off on the beach. Also, carry drinking water and insect repellent.

Howler Monkeys

I have a special memory of the trail behind the beaches. I was hiking along it early one morning when I began to notice a distant moaning sound. It seemed as if the wind in the trees was becoming more forceful and I wondered whether a tropical storm was brewing. I decided to continue, and as I did so the noise became louder and eerier. This was definitely unlike any wind I had heard – it sounded more like a baby in pain.

I am not normally afraid of sounds, but the cries began sounding so eerie that I had to reason with myself that there was nothing to be apprehensive about. Finally, after much hesitant walking and frequent examinations of the forest through my binoculars, I found the culprit – a male howler monkey, the first I had ever seen.

At the time, I knew only that their name

related to their vocalisations and I had no idea how weird and unsettling these could be. Only males howl, and to do so they are equipped with a specialised hyoid bone in the throat. Air is passed through this hollow and much enlarged bone, producing the strange and resonant call which can carry up to a km. The hyoid bone contributes to the typically thick necked appearance of the monkeys, which are often seen (or heard) in Cahuita National Park.

The call itself advertises the presence of a troop of monkeys in the area. This means that they can eat their favourite diet of succulent young leaves without being challenged by neighbouring troops. Thus troops remain spaced apart, foraging efficiently and relying on safe howling rather than dangerous fighting to retain their claim to a particular patch of forest.

Coral Reefs

The monkeys and other forest life are not the only wildlife attractions of this national park. About 500 metres off Punta Cahuita is the largest living coral reef in Costa Rica. Corals are tiny colonial filter feeding animals (cnidarians, or, more commonly, coelenterates) which deposit a calcium carbonate skeleton as a substrate for the living colony. These skeletons build up over millenia to form the corals we see. The outside layers of the corals are alive, but, because they are filter feeders, they rely on the circulation of clean water and nutrients over their surface.

Since the opening up of the Caribbean coastal regions in the last couple of decades, a lot of logging has taken place, and the consequent lack of trees on mountainous slopes has led to increased erosion. The loosened soil is washed into gullies, then streams and rivers, and eventually the sea. By the time the coral reef comes into the picture, the eroded soils are no more than minute mud particles – just the right size to clog up the filter feeding cnidarians. The clogged animals die, and the 'living' reef along with them.

It is important to note that the coral reef is not just a bunch of colourful rocks. It is a living habitat, just as a stream, lake, forest, or swamp is a living habitat. Coral reefs provide both a solid surface for animals such as sponges and anemones to grow on, as well as a shelter for a vast community of fish and other organisms such as octopi, crabs, algae, bryozoans and a host of others. Many of these seemingly insignificant species are important links in various food chains. Thus logging can have much greater, and unforeseen, negative effects than simply getting rid of the rainforest.

On a more mundane level, the drier months in the highlands (February to April, when less run off occurs in the rivers, and less silting occurs in the sea) are considered the best months for snorkelling and seeing the reef.

Places to Stay

Camping is permitted at the Vargas Beach, about one km from the Puerto Vargas Ranger Station. There are outdoor showers and pit latrines at the administration centre near the middle of the camping area. There is drinking water, and some sites have picnic tables. The area is rarely crowded, in fact it is often almost empty and most people opt to camp close to the administration centre for greater security – it is safe enough if you don't leave your gear unattended. Easter week and weekends tend to be more crowded, but the campsite is rarely completely full. The daily camping fee is less than US$1. With a vehicle it's possible to drive as far as the campsite via the Puerto Vargas Ranger Station.

Getting There & Away

A good way to do a day hike in the park is to take a Cahuita to Sixaola bus (these leave Cahuita at 5.50 and 11 am) and ask to be put down at the Puerto Vargas park entrance road. A one km walk takes you to the park, and then you can walk the further seven km back to Cahuita.

PUERTO VIEJO DE TALAMANCA

This small village is locally known as Puerto Viejo – I give its full name to avoid confusion with Puerto Viejo de Sarapiquí. In many ways, Puerto Viejo is a more tranquil and lower key version of Cahuita. There is more influence of the local Talamanca Indian culture and there is much less development. Also, Puerto Viejo has the best surfing on this coast, if not the whole country.

The village is 16 km south-east of Cahuita by road, but it can also be reached from Cahuita by walking along the beach. The inhabitants traditionally lived by small time agriculture and fishing, although catering to tourists is now becoming a minor industry. The mixture of Black and Indian culture is very interesting: you can buy Indian handicrafts and listen to reggae or calypso music; take horse rides into local Indian reserves or go fishing with the locals; go surfing and swimming; or hang out with the old-timers and talk. There's plenty to do, but everything is very relaxed. Take your time and you'll discover a beautiful way of life – rush through and you'll end up with a feeling of frustration.

The poor surfing conditions in September and October means that these are the quietest months of the year. It rains year round, but there are often periods of a few dry days during the less wet months of March to May, and September to November. But don't rely on it – it can rain every day for a week during those months as well!

Information

Telephone There are only two public telephones in Puerto Viejo. The Hotel Maritza (☎ 583844) and the Pulpería Manuel León (☎ 580854) allow the public to use their phones. If you need to call someone in Puerto Viejo, can call one of these numbers and ask them to pass a message on. This system works, but is not completely reliable. It should be limited to important calls.

Books Some of the older Black inhabitants of the area told their life stories to Paula Palmer, who collected this wealth of oral history, culture and social anthropology in two books which are available in San José. They are well worth reading. *What Happen:*

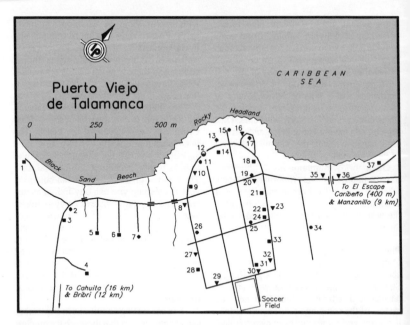

Puerto Viejo de Talamanca

■	PLACES TO STAY		20	Soda Tamara

■ PLACES TO STAY

1   Cabinas Black Sands
3   Mr O'Conner (room for rent)
4   Cabinas Chimuri
5   Cabinas Playa Negra
6   El Pizote Lodge
9   Hotel Ritz
14 Hotel Maritza
18 Cabinas Manuel (& Pulpería)
21 Cabina Anselmo
22 Hotel Puerto Viejo
24 Cabinas
28 Cabinas Kaya
31 Cabinas Recife
33 Cabinas Frederico
35 Stanford's (restaurant, disco, rooms)
37 Cabinas Zoyla

▼ PLACES TO EAT

8   Open air food stand
10 El Zarpe Cantina
16 Jhonny's Place

20 Soda Tamara
23 Miss Dolly (bakery, medicinal plants)
27 Soda La Amistad
29 Julia and Mateo (bakery)
30 Soda Coral
32 Miss Sam (bakery)
35 Stanford's (restaurant, disco, rooms)
36 Restaurant Bambu

OTHER

2   Pulpería Violeta (shop)
7   Antonio's Tropical Paradise
11 Shop
12 Bus Stop
13 School
15 Shop
17 Police
19 Dennise's Beach Shop and Gifts
25 Aldo's Bicycle Rent
26 El Club de La Iguana
28 Jaco's Bicycle Rent
34 Earl Brown (boatman)

A Folk History of Costa Rica's Talamanca Coast, published by Ecodesarrollos, San José, 1977; and *Wa'apin Man*, published by Editorial Costa Rica, 1986. ('What happen' or 'Wa'apin Man' are common forms of greeting among Costa Rican coastal Blacks. North American travellers will have no difficulty in relating this to the 'What's happening' of African-Americans; travellers from other areas may find this greeting somewhat mystifying. 'All right' is probably as good a response as any.)

The pamphlet *Welcome to Coastal Talamanca*, produced by the Comité de Promoción y Conservación de Talamanca (1990), is available in Puerto Viejo and is crammed full of useful information. The committee is concerned with developing the region for tourism without degrading local culture – it meets on Mondays at 6 pm in the Hotel Maritza annexe and welcomes travellers.

Things to See & Do

Indian Reserves There are three reserves in the Caribbean slopes of the Talamanca Mountains: the Talamanca-Bribri, the Talamanca-Cabécar and the KékoLdi Reserves. Together with the nearby national parks and wildlife reserves they are part of the Amistad-Talamanca RCU or 'megapark'. They protect the land against commercial development in a variety of ways. Hunting is prohibited except for Indians hunting for food. Entrance to the reserves is limited to those visitors who receive the necessary permits from the Reserve Associations. Mauricio Salazar in Puerto Viejo has permits to visit the small KékoLdi Reserve; he can give you information about getting permits to visit the others.

The Talamanca-Cabécar Reserve is the most remote and difficult to visit. The Cabécar indigenous group is the most traditional and the least tolerant of visits from Westerners. The Bribri people are more acculturated. Access to the reserves is generally on foot or horseback.

A difficult to find book is *Taking Care of Sibo's Gifts: An Environmental Treatise from Costa Rica's KékoLdi Indigenous Reserve*. 'Sibo' is the word for 'God' in the indigenous language.

Surfing The Brazilian owner of the Hotel Puerto Viejo is a local surfing expert. The waves are best from December to early March, and there is another mini-season for surfing in June and July. From late March to April, and in September and October, the sea is at its calmest.

Surfers tell me that the most exciting surfing is on the famous La Salsa Brava outside the reef in front of Stanford's Restaurant. If you lose it, you're liable to smash yourself and your board on the reef, so this is for experienced surfers.

Tours Mauricio Salazar, a Bribri Indian who owns the Cabinas Chimuri, will take you on horse rides in the local area for $20 per day. Three-day trips into the local Talamanca Indian Reserve cost US$140 per person – local Indian culture is emphasised and accommodation is in Indian huts. It's a physically demanding trip for adventurous travellers. At least a week's warning is needed to arrange this trip with a maximum of six participants. Write to Mauricio Salazar, Puerto Viejo de Talamanca, Limón, Costa Rica.

Fishing, boating and snorkelling trips can be arranged with local boatmen. Earl Brown is the person to talk to – he can take you deep sea fishing.

The new El Pizote Lodge is planning snorkelling and boat trips.

Horse & Bicycle Hire You can rent horses at Antonio's Tropical Paradise. Aldo, behind the Hotel Puerto Viejo, and Jaco at Cabinas Kaya, both rent bicycles for about US$6 for six hours, US$10 for a full day.

Places to Stay

There are a number of places to stay, but none of them are very big. They tend to be full during weekends in the surfing season, and during Christmas and Easter. You should arrive early if you have no reservations. Reservations can be made by writing to the place of choice, Puerto Viejo de Talamanca, Limón, Costa Rica – allow two months.

Places to Stay – bottom end

There is no hot water in Puerto Viejo's hotels. In some of the cheaper hotels, the cold water showers may only work intermittently, but bucket baths are usually available in this case. The majority of hotels will provide either mosquito netting or fans (a breeze fanning the bed will keep mosquitoes away). Check the facilities before getting a room.

Most of the rates below are for one night in the high season. For long stays, or during the low season, discounts can often be arranged.

The *Hotel Puerto Viejo* has 20 double rooms and is the biggest place in town. It is popular with surfers and budget travellers. The bare, basic but clean upstairs rooms are US$4.25 per person; the downstairs rooms are not as good and are a little cheaper. Also popular with surfers is *Cabinas Manuel* (☎ 580854) which has a poor water supply. Single rooms are US$7.75, but there are four beds and you can sleep four people in there for the same price as one.

The *Hotel Maritza* (☎ 583844) charges about US$5/9 single/double in basic rooms in the hotel, and US$17.50 double with bath in better cabins. The *Hotel Ritz* has rooms for US$7, either single or double occupancy.

Cabina Anselmo is one cabin (with a private bath) which sleeps up to four for US$12. *Cabinas Kaya* has two double cabins which rent for US$8 per cabin. *Cabinas Zoyla* has four similarly priced rooms with bath. *Cabinas Frederico* has two units with private bath and a kitchenette – the charge is US$18 for up to six people.

All the above hotels are more or less 'downtown'. A good place to stay about a 20 minute stroll west of Puerto Viejo is *Cabinas Black Sands* owned by a couple of very friendly North Americans, Ken and Diane Kerst. The attractive thatched cabin in the local Bribri Indian style is set in a pleasant garden near the beach. There are three basic rooms each with two beds, and communal

kitchen and bathroom facilities. Rates are US$5/8 single/double or US$20 for all three rooms (six beds).

Places to Stay – middle

Another place out of town that is well worth seeking out is *Cabinas Chimuri* run by Mauricio Salazar who knows as much about the Bribri Indian culture as anyone in Puerto Viejo. There are three simple, attractively thatched, Indian style cabins on stilts renting for US$10 double and one quadruple cabin going for US$18. There are communal kitchen and bathroom facilities. The cabins are set in a small 14 hectare private preserve with trails and good bird-watching possibilities. This is the place to go for trips to the local Indian reserves and to buy indigenous crafts.

Nearby, *Mister O'Conner* has a single room to rent with three beds, a bath and a fan. He charges US$12 for up to three people.

In town, *Cabinas Stanford* has secure rooms with private bath and fans for about US$8 per person. There is dancing at weekends, and things can get a bit noisy then. At the south end of town are the similarly priced but quieter *Cabinas Recife*. About half a km east of Stanford's, on the road to Manzanillo, is *El Escape Caribeño* with one double room with bath and fan renting for US$20 and one quadruple room for US$27.

A new complex being built and expanded on a quiet road just west of town is the *Cabinas Playa Negra* (☎ 561132, 566396). The telephone numbers are in Turrialba, not in Puerto Viejo, but reservations can be made. They have several family style houses with two or three rooms, kitchen, bathroom and TV which rent for US$29 and sleep up to six. They have one bigger house that will sleep up to 12 people and rents for US$35.

Places to Stay – top end

A short way west of town on a quiet back road there is the relatively comfortable *El Pizote Lodge* (☎ 291428 for reservations). This is the fanciest hotel presently operating south of Puerto Limón. The rooms are large and clean, but don't have private baths. That is not a real problem, however, as there are four shared bathrooms for eight rooms. There are also pleasant wooden bungalows with private baths which are more expensive. The lodge is set in a pleasant garden, there are bicycles, horses and snorkelling gear for rent to clients, and boat and snorkelling tours are planned. There is also a restaurant. Rooms are US$20/31/40/45 for one to four occupants; bungalows are US$50/60/65 for two, three or four occupants. Breakfast and dinner costs about US$16 extra per person.

Places to Eat

Two places stand out for breakfasts. The *Soda Coral* has breakfast daily, except Monday, from 7 am to 12 noon. They serve a variety of healthful items such as yoghurt and granola, home-made whole wheat bread, and, of course, the tico speciality – gallo pinto. Eggs and pancakes are also served. On Tuesday, Friday and Saturday evenings from 6.30 to 9.30 pm they serve home-made pizzas. Also good for breakfasts and snacks throughout the day is the *Soda Tamara* – they have coconut bread and cakes.

Stanford's Restaurant Caribe is good for seafood which ranges from US$2 to US$8 depending on how exotic a meal you order. They have a lively disco at weekends. Nearby is the *Restaurant Bambu* which serves tico and Caribbean meals but is better known as a bar. They have dancing and live music on occasion. *Jhonny's Place* has Chinese food (big portions – medium prices), seafood, and a disco/bar as well. *Soda La Amistad* has meals cooked on a wood fire. There is also a restaurant at the *Hotel Maritza*.

If you are economising, check out the open-air food stand at the west end of town. They serve tasty meals most evenings; food is served until it runs out.

Baked goods for picnics are available from a number of local people. *Miss Dolly* sells cakes and breads, and will prepare rundowns and other traditional Caribbean meals if requested a day in advance. Miss Dolly also knows a great deal about local medicinal herbs and will take interested visitors on

plant walks. Other recommended bakers are *Miss Sam, Miss Daisy* and *Julia & Mateo*.

The *El Club de la Iguana* is open from noon, usually at weekends, and has fast food, salads, juices, and is a bar in the evenings. *El Zarpe* is another bar, conveniently located near the bus stop for a drink whilst waiting for the bus.

Getting There & Away

From San José, Autotransportes MEPE (☎ 210524) has four buses a day leaving from Avenida 11, Calle Central & 1. Some of these will drop you off at the intersection five km from Puerto Viejo – check with the bus company. If you don't want to walk the last five km, call the Hotel Maritza or Pulpería Manuel León to arrange for a taxi pick-up. This should be arranged two days in advance.

Alternatively, go to Puerto Limón, where buses leave from a block north of the market at 5 and 10 am, and 1 and 4 pm. It takes about 1½ hours and costs US$0.90 to Puerto Viejo. Buses continue to Bribri and Sixaola from the bus stop marked on the map.

Buses leave Puerto Viejo daily at 6 am, and 1 and 4 pm for Cahuita and Limón; there is no 1 pm Sunday bus. The Sixaola to San José bus may stop at Puerto Viejo.

PUNTA UVA & MANZANILLO

A nine km dirt road heads east from Puerto Viejo along the coast through the small communities of Punta Uva and Manzanillo. The locals mainly use horses and bicycles along this road, though vehicles can get through. There are no buses.

Manzanillo is part of the Gandoca-Manzanillo Refuge.

Places to Stay

Strung out along the road are several places to stay, which offer an even quieter alternative than Puerto Viejo. They are listed here in the order that they are passed as you leave Puerto Viejo.

Cabinas Katty is near the mouth of the Río Cocles, about two km east of Puerto Viejo. There are two rooms with private bath, sleeping up to four people. Each room is about US$10.

There are several places at Playa Chiquita, a small beach about four km east of Puerto Viejo, near Punta Uva. *Cabinas DASA* has a two-bed room with shared bath for US$12/14 single/double, and a four-bed room with private bath for US$18 to US$30 depending on the number of people. They also have a cabin with private bath and kitchenette for up to six people. This costs about US$35 per night, but a two day minimum stay is preferred. Reservations can be made in San José by calling 533431, 204089, or 362631. *Maracú* has two simple cabins with stove and two beds each, and there is a shared bathroom. Rates are about US$7 per person. Reservations can be made by phoning 256215. The nearby *Soda El Aquario* sells meals and snacks.

Further on, there are *Selven's Cabins* with ten basic rooms for US$7 double and a cabin for four people at US$18. There is a restaurant and bar. About six km from Puerto Viejo, on the Punta Uva entrance road, Rodolfo Porras rents out a small house with kitchen for US$24 – it sleeps six.

In Manzanillo, nine km east of Puerto Viejo, there is *Cabinas Maxi* charging about US$5 per person. There is a restaurant, bar and even a disco here at weekends. Several local ladies will prepare traditional Caribbean meals in their homes for travellers – ask around.

GANDOCA-MANZANILLO NATIONAL WILDLIFE REFUGE

This refuge lies on the coast around Manzanillo and continues south-east as far as the Panamanian border. It encompasses 5013 hectares of land plus 4436 hectares of sea. This is the only place in the country apart from Cahuita where there is a living reef. It lies about 200 metres off shore and snorkelling is one of the refuge's attractions.

The land section has several different habitats, not least of which is farmland. The little village of Manzanillo is actually in the reserve. There are also some of the most beautiful beaches on the Caribbean, unspoilt

and separated by rocky headlands. Coconut palms form an attractive tropical backdrop. There is a coastal trail leading 5½ km from Manzanillo to Punta Mono. South of this trail is an unusual 400 hectare swamp containing holillo palms and sajo trees.

Beyond Punta Mono is the only red mangrove swamp in Caribbean Costa Rica, protecting a natural oyster bank. In the nearby Gandoca River estuary there is a spawning ground for the Atlantic tarpon, and cayman and manatees are reported. The endangered Baird's tapir is also found in this wet and densely vegetated terrain. Marine turtles have nested n the beaches at the south end of the refuge.

The variety of vegetation and the remote location attract many tropical birds. The very rare harpy eagle has been recorded here, and other birds to look for include the red-lored parrot, the red-capped manakin and the chestnut-mandibled toucan among hundreds of others. The birding is considered to be very good.

Information

Ask for Florentino Grenald who lives in Manzanillo and acts as the reserve's administrator. He has a local bird list and can recommend guides. A local boatman, Willie Burton, will take you boating and snorkelling from Manzanillo. Horses and guides can be hired.

Places to Stay

Camping is permitted, but there are no organised facilities. People stay in *Cabinas Maxi* in Manzanillo.

BRIBRI

This small village is passed en route from Cahuita to Sixaola. It is the end of the paved coastal road; from Bribri a 34 km gravel road takes the traveller to the Panamanian border.

Bribri is the centre for the local Indian communities in the Talamanca mountains, although there is not much to see here.

The Ministry of Health operates a clinic in Bribri which serves both Puerto Viejo and the surrounding Indian communities. There is a Banco Nacional de Costa Rica here, also serving Puerto Viejo.

Places to Stay
There are a couple of pensións and restaurants in Bribri. Buses sometimes stop for a meal or snack at the *Restaurant King-Giung* which has reasonable Chinese and tico food.

Getting There & Away
Buses leave from Bribri to the village of Shiroles, 17 km away. From here, horse and foot traffic continues on into the Indian reserves.

SIXAOLA
This is the end of the road as far as the Costa Rican Caribbean is concerned. Sixaola is the border town with Panama, but few foreign travellers cross the border here – most overlanders go via Paso Canoas on the Interamerican Highway.

Sixaola is an unattractive little town, with nothing to recommend it except the border crossing itself, which is fairly relaxed. Most of the town is strung out along the main street.

For full details of crossing the border at this point, see the Getting There & Away chapter.

Places to Stay & Eat
There are two *Restaurants Central*, one of which has an extremely basic pensión attached. Other accommodation can be found by asking around, but it is generally unappealing. It's best to get here as early as possible if going to or coming from Panama. There is better accommodation on the Panamanian side.

The best restaurant in Sixaola is the *El Siquerreno*, but it's not always open. There are several other places to eat – when I went through at about 10 o'clock one morning, every restaurant had a bunch of argumentative drunks in it. Maybe it was the day after payday for workers on the local cacao fincas.

Getting There & Away
Direct buses from San José leave four times a day from Avenida 11, Calle Central & 1. If you take the first bus you should be in Sixaola by late morning. Buses return to San José (six hours, US$4.75) at 5 and 8 am, and 2.30 pm. There are also four buses a day to and from Limón.

The North Caribbean

MOÍN
This port is about seven km west of Puerto Limón. The main reason to come here is to take a boat up the canals to Tortuguero National Park and on to Barra del Colorado National Wildlife Refuge. There's really not much reason to stay here.

The canals are so called because they are not all natural. There used to be a series of natural waterways north of Limón as far as Barra del Colorado, but they were not fully connected. In 1974, canals were completed to link the entire system, thus avoiding having to go out to sea when travelling north from Moín. This inland waterway is a much safer way to go than travelling up the coast off shore.

Places to Stay
Try the *Hostal Moín* (☎ 582436) which charges about US$7 for a double room.

Getting There & Away
Bus Buses to Moín leave from Limón several times an hour, starting at 6 am.

Boat The majority of travellers get to the national parks on organised tours with prearranged boat or plane transport. These tours are usually good but not very cheap, although you can pay for just the travel portion and then stay in cheaper accommodation in Tortuguero.

Going independently is more difficult than going on a tour, but it can be done. Several guidebooks recommend calling the harbour authority JAPDEVA about their boats to Tortuguero. When I called them, I was told that they don't operate passenger boats for tourists and directed me to a tour company!

The thing to do is go down to Moín dock early and start asking around. There are passenger and cargo boats, of course (the Tortuguero locals don't take tours to get home), but it takes a little bit of asking around about schedules and availability. Boats periodically break down, schedules change, and priority is given to locals. Some boats are officially cargo only, and it may require a certain amount of pleading to be allowed aboard. The trip to Tortuguero can take from three to eleven hours and fares can be as low as US$3 or as high as US$12 depending on the boat. There are usually boats of one kind or another every couple of days. (Some of them are even JAPDEVA boats!) Currently there are services at 7 am on Thursday, and 8 am on Saturday and Sunday. Getting to the docks before 7 am and asking around persistently will usually get you on a boat within a couple of days.

Paying for the boat-only portion of a tour costs about US$30 per person. Hiring your own boat is also possible – expect to pay about US$150 for a motor boat to Tortuguero.

PARISMINA

This small village is at the mouth of the Parasmina River, about 50 km north-west of Limón, half way between Limón and Tortuguero. You pass by here on the canal boats up to Tortuguero, but most visitors fly in to the local airstrip.

Parismina boasts one of the five best fishing lodges on the Costa Rican Caribbean.

Places to Stay

The *Tarpon Rancho* (☎ 357766, in the USA (800) 531-7232; Apartado 5712, San José; or PO Box 290190, San Antonio, TX 78280, USA) provides everything you need for deep sea fishing for about US$250 per person per day. Record breaking Atlantic tarpon and snook are the fish to go for. Rates include transport from San José, boats and gear in Parismina, accommodation, and meals. The best season is January to May, but August to October is also good. The lodge is closed outside the fishing season.

There's nowhere else to stay.

TORTUGUERO NATIONAL PARK

This 18,946 hectare coastal park is the most important breeding ground for the green sea turtle in all of the Caribbean. There are eight species of marine turtles in the world; six nest in Costa Rica and four in Tortuguero. The many turtles give the national park its name. The Tortuguero nesting population of the green turtle, *Chelonia mydas*, has been continuously monitored since 1955, and is the best studied. Comparatively little is known about other marine turtles.

Information

Humid is the driest word I can think of to describe Tortuguero National Park. With rainfall of from 5000 to 6000 mm throughout the park, it is one of the wettest areas in the country. Rainwear is a must year round; an umbrella is a good idea. There is no dry season, although it does rain less from January to April. Average temperature is 26°C but it is often hotter during the middle of the day. Bring insect repellent – you'll use it!

There are three ranger stations. Two of them, the Agua Fría and Jalova ranger stations, are on a river or canal respectively, can only be reached by boat, and are rarely visited. Most people go to the park headquarters which is at the north end of the national park. It is a few minutes walk away from the village of Tortuguero, which itself is just beyond the park boundary. At the park HQ, there is a small exhibit room and information is available.

From the HQ there is a one km long nature trail, which is maintained, and some other trails in poor condition. You can walk along the beach north for five km (officially outside the park) or south for 30 km. Park rangers will take you on guided walks to see the turtles laying – they leave at 8 pm during the season and cost US$5. Other guided hikes and boat trips can also be arranged through the park HQ.

Top: Fishermen, Puerto Viejo de Talamanca (RR)
Left: Cahuita National Park (RR)
Right: Puerto Viejo de Talamanca (RR)

Top: Cabinas Black Sands (Bri-bri thatched roof), Puerto Viejo de Talamanca (RR)
Bottom: Rafting on the Río Reventazón (RH)

Although the beaches are extensive, they are not suitable for swimming. The surf is very rough, the currents strong, and, if that's not enough to faze you, sharks regularly patrol the waters.

Green Turtles

Scientists now know that anywhere from several hundred to over 3000 female green turtles come to the Tortuguero nesting beach during any given season. The season is July to early October, with the highest numbers nesting in late August. Mating occurs at the beginning of the breeding season, but the fertilised eggs which result from the mating are not laid until the female returns in subsequent seasons.

During a season, an individual female may come ashore as many as seven times to lay eggs, though two or three times is more likely. During the two weeks between layings, the females spend their time in the water close to shore.

About 100 eggs are laid during any one session; these are deposited in a depression in the sand which the female makes with her flippers, and are then covered over for protection.

The incubation period is about two months, after which the hatchlings scramble out of the nest and head for the sea, usually under the cover of darkness. About half of the hatchlings make it to the water; many are preyed upon by birds, coatimundis, dogs and other animals. Once they make it to the sea, they are eaten by fish and other predators, so it it is estimated that less than 1% of eggs eventually become breeding adults.

It is known that females will not lay in successive years, but return every three years on average. During the intervening years, they migrate hundreds of km to feeding grounds elsewhere, often to the Miskito coast of Nicaragua. Tens of thousands of breeding females have been tagged at Tortuguero, and they have never been recovered in other breeding grounds, showing that they always return to the same beach to nest. It is likely that the females return to the beach where they hatched, but it has proved very difficult to tag the new born hatchlings (which weigh only a few grams) and subsequently recover them as breeding females which weigh from 60 kg to over 200 kg. One of the biggest gaps in biologists' understanding of the green turtle life cycle is knowing what happens to the hatchlings during their first year of life after they disappear into the sea. Year old youngsters weighing about 500 grams have been recovered.

Travellers are allowed to visit the nesting beaches and watch the turtles lay their eggs or observe the eggs hatching. However, camera flashes and flashlights may disturb the laying, or attract predators to the hatchlings, so you should check with park rangers or researchers working at the Casa Verde centre for instructions. Often, researchers or park personnel will accompany visitors to the best viewing areas and explain what is going on.

If you are unable to visit during the green turtle breeding season, you can see leatherback turtles from February to July, with a peak in April and May. Hawksbill turtles nest from July to October and loggerhead turtles are also sometimes seen. Stragglers have been observed during every month of the year. Only the green turtle nests in large numbers; the other species tend to arrive singly.

Green turtle meat has long been eaten on the Caribbean coast. In addition, the eggs are considered to have aphrodisiac properties, the shell is used for ornaments and jewellery, and even the skin has a market. In the early and middle parts of this century, the huge nesting colonies of green turtles were harvested so thoroughly that the turtle became endangered.

Since the active protection of the nesting beach in Tortuguero, the green turtle population has recovered to some extent. In other areas, turtles are still harvested, but limits and quotas have been set.

The story of the decline and return of the green turtle and the setting up of turtle conservation projects in the Caribbean is told in two popular books by Archie Carr, a herpetologist who has done much work on turtles and played an important role in getting Tortuguero protected. The books are *The Windward Road*, A A Knopf, New York, 1956, reprinted 1979, Florida State University Press, Gainesville, Florida; and *So Excellent a Fishe*, 1967, Natural History Press, New York. (Yes, fishe is spelt fishe in this book!)

Other Wildlife

Turtles are certainly the most famous attraction at Tortuguero, but they are by no means the only one. The national park offers great wildlife viewing and bird-watching opportunities, both from trails within the park and on guided or paddle-yourself boat trips. All three of the local species of monkeys (howler, spider and white-faced capuchin) are often seen. Sloths, anteaters and kinkajous are also fairly frequently sighted. Manatees are protected but not often seen. Peccaries, tapirs and various members of the cat family have also been recorded, but you have to be really lucky to see them.

The reptiles and amphibians are also of great interest. Apart from the sea turtles, there are seven species of freshwater turtles. Look for them lined up on a log by the river bank, sunning themselves. It seems that as soon as you see them, they see you and, one by one, they plop off the log and into the protective river.

Lizards are often seen; the large basilisk lizard is among the most interesting. The impressively crested males look like little dinosaurs and can reach a metre in length. They have large rear feet with skin flaps on each toe enabling them to run on water, giving them their nickname of Jesus Christ lizard. Younger, smaller individuals can run as far as 20 metres across the surface of the water, but larger adults manage only a few metres. Both the caiman and the crocodile can be seen here.

Snakes are also seen; a friend of mine saw a two metre long fer-de-lance. A variety of colourful little toads and frogs hop around in the rainforest, and the large marine toad is common. This toad can reach 20 cm in length and weigh over a kg. About 60 species of amphibians have been recorded in the park.

Birds

There are over 300 species of birds recorded, ranging from oceanic species such as the magnificent frigate bird and royal tern, to a variety of shore birds such as plovers and sandpipers, to river birds such as kingfishers, jacanas and anhingas, to inland forest species such as hummingbirds and manakins.

Many migrant birds from North America pass through on their way south for the North American winter or north for the North American summer.

The variety of habitats contributes to the diversity of birds. On just one boat ride near Tortuguero I saw six species of herons, including the chestnut-bellied heron which *A Guide to the Birds of Costa Rica* describes as an uncommon to rare resident in humid lowland forests of Caribbean slope.

Places to Stay

You can camp outside the park HQ for US$0.50 – just make sure your tent is waterproof! Drinking water and pit latrines are provided.

Apart from camping, there is nowhere to stay in the park itself. Just outside the north boundary of the park in the village of Tortuguero you can find inexpensive accommodation, food, boats and guides. North of the village there are three comfortable and more expensive jungle lodges between one and four km away (see below).

Getting There & Away

Normally, travellers don't go directly to the park, but to either the village of Tortuguero by public boat, or to one of the lodges by private tour boat. See the Moín section for details of public boats.

There is an airstrip four km north of the park with charter flights to the better lodges. Day trips are offered to Tortuguero from some of the Limón hotels, but these do not give enough time at the park.

TORTUGUERO

The inhabitants of this sleepy little village make most of their living from turtles and the national park. They work in the hotels and tour lodges; they work as park rangers or researchers; they work as guides and boatmen; and a few do a little farming and fishing. Generally speaking, a good balance has been struck between the interests of the local people and the turtles.

Instead of harvesting the turtles, the people exploit them and the accompanying park in non-destructive yet economically satisfactory ways. In the centre of the village is an informative kiosk explaining the natural history, cultural history, geography and climate of the region. The community appears to take some pride in 'its' turtles and national park.

Green Turtle Research Station

This is locally known as 'Casa Verde' (Green House), probably because of its (at one time) greenish paint job rather than because of the green turtles. Green turtle research has been carried out from here since 1954. The station is next to the airstrip, about four km north of Tortuguero.

Activities

Canoeing A house in Tortuguero just north of the entrance to the park has a sign announcing boats for hire. You can paddle yourself in a dugout canoe for about US$1.25 per person per hour, or go with a guide for about US$2.50 per person per hour. Ruben is the name of one guide, Damma is another; he is a bit more expensive but is recommended.

In the village centre, there is a pulpería where you can ask about other guides or boat rentals. Although it is cheaper to paddle your own canoe, it is well worth hiring a guide, at least for a few hours, because you get to see so much more.

Climbing Apart from visiting the waterways of the park and the beaches, a climb can be made of 119 metre high Cerro de Tortuguero, about six km north-east of the village. You

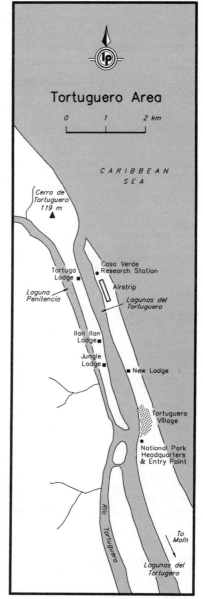

Tortuguero Area

need to hire a boat and guide to get there. Cerro Tortuguero is the highest point right on the coast anywhere north of Limón. There are views of the forest, canals, sea and birds.

Tours

Mitur (☎ 552031, 552262) runs three-day/two-night tours to Tortuguero, staying at the *Ilan Ilan* lodge, across the river from Tortuguero. On the first day, they drive you from San José to Moín, where you board their boat, *Colorado Prince*, for a five to six hour journey through the canals to Tortuguero. The journey itself is part of the adventure – the boat slows down for photographs and a bilingual guide identifies what you see. On the second day, guided walking and boat tours of the area are provided. A night visit to the beach is added during the turtle nesting season. You return by boat and bus on the third day. The cost is US$125 per person, double occupancy, and includes transport by bus and boat, guides, tours, accommodation in rooms with private bathrooms, meals in the lodge, and picnic lunches on the boat. Single occupancy is US$30 extra. There are usually two departures a week; on Tuesday returning Thursday, and on Friday returning Sunday. If there is room available, they will take extra passengers for US$30 one way to or from Tortuguero (you provide your own accommodation). Extra nights can also be arranged. The Mitur office is on Paseo Colón, Calle 20 & 22. Reservations can be made at Apartado 91, 1150 San José, Costa Rica.

Similar tours at similar prices are provided by Cotur (☎ 330155, 336579) using the boats *Miss Caribe* and *Miss América*, and staying in the *Jungle Lodge*, also in rooms with private bath. Reservations can be made at Apartado 26, 1017 San José 2000, Costa Rica.

Costa Rica Expeditions (☎ 570766, 220333) runs the *Tortuga Lodge*, without a doubt the most comfortable and elegant place to stay in Tortuguero. The lodge is on 20 hectares of private grounds, just across from Archie Carr's famous Casa Verde turtle research station. The buildings are in attractively landscaped gardens with a large variety of ornamental tropical trees, palms, shrubs, orchids and other flowers. These attract many birds, so you can bird-watch from the lodge itself. Beyond the gardens, the tropical rainforest begins, and a troop of howler monkeys is usually heard within a few minutes walk of the lodge. The rooms are spacious, screened, and with private baths and fans. The food is plentiful and very well prepared. A radio telephone is available to make connections with anywhere in the world. The staff and guides are good and speak English.

The lodge is famous for both its wildlife tours to the park and beaches, and as a fishing lodge. The head guide and general manager, Eduardo Brown Silva, holds a world fishing record for cubera snapper, and other fishing records for Costa Rica. Tarpon season is from January to June, with 40 kg fish being routinely caught, and fish twice that size having been landed. From July to December is snook season. These average one to five kg, but fish of 24 kg have been caught here. January to May and August to October are the best months. Fishing for other fish is possible: shark, snapper, ray, grouper and jewfish are all caught.

You can get to the lodge by boat, or by flying in to the Tortuguero airstrip nearby. Costa Rica Tours will make all arrangements for the type of tour you want. Current prices are US$51/62/71 for one, two or three people in standard rooms, or US$68/79/95 in deluxe rooms. Large and delicious meals are served and cost US$7.50 for breakfast, US$11.50 for lunch, and US$12.75 for dinner. Boat rental for natural history tours (with motor and guide) costs US$25 per hour and takes up to five people. Night tours of the canals, with a super-powerful searchlight to seek out crocodiles, sleeping animals and night animals on the prowl, cost US$27.50 per person and last about three hours. Boat rental for fishing (with motor, guide and tackle) costs US$35 per hour (two persons per boat). Speed boats from Moín to the lodge cost US$40 per person (three minimum, five maximum, 2½ hours). Slower boats taking four hours cost US$350 for up to 12 passengers. The air fare from San José to Tortuguero in single engined aircraft with five seats is US$69 per person; with a minimum of two people.

Reservations can be made with Costa Rica Expeditions in San José at Calle Central & Avenida 3. From outside Costa Rica, write to Department 235, PO Box 025216, Miami, FL 33102-5216, USA.

Places to Stay & Eat

Tortuguero Village Tortuguero has several cheap places. *Brisas del Mar* (also known as Inez' place) charges US$3 per person in small cabins with shared baths. There is a cheap bar attached, sometimes with dancing or music in the evenings. (This happens when tourists arrive, primarily.) Inez will cook for you on request. *Cabinas Sandia* charges US$4.75/7 single/double with shared bathrooms. If these are full, ask around; you may be able to stay in someone's house.

Restaurants charge about US$3 to US$4 per meal, and it is fairly basic food. Some travellers report that slightly cheaper and better meals are available by asking around and eating in private houses.

Casa Verde At the Casa Verde there are basic dormitory rooms which accommodate 18 people, and camping outside is possible; a rain roof is being built to provide shelter for campers. There are communal kitchen and bathroom facilities, and electricity. The station accommodates researchers and student groups, but is not designed for tourists. Permission to stay and more information is available from the Caribbean Conservation Corporation (☎ 388069), Apartado 6975, 1000 San José, Costa Rica; or from the CCC (☎ (904) 373-6441), PO Box 2866, Gainesville, FL 32602, USA.

Lodges The two lodges across the river from Tortuguero are used by the tour companies, but you could probably stay in one of them

for about US$20/30 for a single/double if they have room.

About a km north of Tortuguero, there is a new lodge under construction – it may be worth checking if you're stuck in town with nowhere else to stay. The luxurious *Tortuga Lodge* about four km north of the village charges US$51/62 single/double.

Getting There & Away

See the Moín section for details of boats from there.

BARRA DEL COLORADO NATIONAL WILDLIFE REFUGE

At 92,000 hectares, Barra del Colorado is the biggest national wildlife refuge in Costa Rica. It is virtually an extension of Tortuguero National Park and the two are combined to form a Regional Conservation Unit.

There are three main differences between Tortuguero and Barra del Colorado: Barra is not famous for its marine turtles (although they are found in the reserve); it is more remote; and is more difficult to visit cheaply.

Despite being a national wildlife refuge, people come here for the sport-fishing rather than for natural history tours. But there are also similarities: Barra receives as much rainfall as Tortuguero, and has much of the same variety of wildlife, and this is best seen from a boat.

The northern border of the refuge is the Río San Juan (the Nicaraguan border). The area was politically sensitive during the 1980s, which contributed somewhat to the isolation of the reserve. Parts of the western half of the reserve are not yet fully explored. Since the relaxing of Sandinista-Contra hostilities in 1990, it has become easier to journey north along the Río Sarapiquí (see Puerto Viejo de Sarapiquí), and east along the San Juan to the reserve. This would be an interesting and unusual trip.

Although the western part of the reserve is little known, that doesn't mean no-one goes there. Infrared satellite photography is showing large amounts of unauthorised logging and road construction at the western boundary of the reserve. Undoubtedly, illegal logging activity is going on within Barra del Colorado, but there are not enough reserve wardens to be able to police the area properly. Recent maps show a dirt road north from Guápiles into the reserve; it's reportedly accessible to motor vehicles.

How long it will be before Barra del Colorado is severely changed and degraded remains to be seen. Meanwhile, it remains mainly the haunt of sport-fishing tourists and a few locals.

Places to Stay

The lodges detailed here operate sport-fishing charters for about US$250 per person per day, including accommodation, transport, meals, boats, tackle and fishing guides. Tarpon from January to May and snook from August to October are the fish of choice.

The *Isla de Pesca* (☎ 215396, 234560) can be reserved at Apartado 8, 4390 San José, Costa Rica; in the USA at Fishing Travel, 2525 Nevada Ave N, Golden Valley, MN 55427.

For the *Casa Mar* (☎ 412820) write to Apartado 825, 1007 Centro Colón, San José, Costa Rica; in the USA to PO Box 787, Islamorada, FL 33036.

The *Río Colorado Lodge* (☎ 328610, 324063; Apartado 5094, 1000 San José) has an office in the Hotel Corobicí in San José; in the USA contact at (800) 243-9777. This lodge offers non-fishing accommodation for about US$80/100 single/double and can arrange boats for wildlife excursions. It is open out of the fishing seasons. They are also planning to resume trips on the Ríos Sarapiquí and San Juan.

There is supposedly cheaper accommodation next to the airport at *Cabinas Tarponland* (☎ 716917), but I have not been able to confirm this. Rooms are reportedly about US$20.

Camping is allowed in the refuge, but there are no facilities. You may be able to find somewhere inexpensive to stay in Barra del Colorado village if you ask around.

Getting There & Away

A few of the boats from Moín to Tortuguero continue to Barra. Boats can be hired in Tortuguero to take you up to Barra for about US$50; they'll take three to five passengers. Most people arrive by air from San José. You can charter a light plane or take one of SANSA's regularly scheduled flights from San José (currently at 6 am on Tuesday, Thursday and Saturday, returning at 6.50 am, US$12 one way).

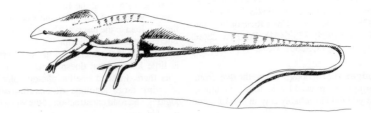

Southern Costa Rica

The southbound Interamerican Highway leaves San José to the east and skirts Cartago before truly heading south. The highway begins to climb steadily, reaching its highest point at over 3300 metres near the sombrely named 3491 metre peak of Cerro de la Muerte (Death Mountain). This area is about 100 km by road south of San José and is often shrouded in mists. The next 30 km stretch is a particularly dangerous section of highway. From the high point, the road drops steeply to San Isidro de El General at 702 metres. San Isidro is the first important town south of Cartago, and is the main entry point for the nearby Chirripó National Park which contains the highest mountains in Costa Rica.

From San Isidro, the Interamerican Highway continues south-east through mainly agricultural lowlands to the Panamanian border, a little over 200 km away. There are no more big towns, but there are several smaller ones which are of interest to those wanting to see some of Costa Rica which is not on the normal tourist trail. From these towns roads lead out to some of the more remote protected areas in the country. These include the magnificent wilderness of Corcovado National Park in the Osa Peninsula, the rarely visited and difficult to get to La Amistad International Park, and the Wilson Botanical Gardens, to name but a few.

From highlands to tropical lowlands, there is a variety of beautiful wilderness parks and preserves – and not many tourists. Slow down and check it out if you can.

SANTA MARÍA & SAN MARCOS

About 50 km south of San José, shortly after the Empalme gas station, a road to the right leads about 10 km to Santa María (de Dota) and on a further six km to San Marcos (de Tarrazú). These small towns are in attractive agricultural countryside on steep mountainous slopes. The people are friendly and the

area is good for walking but there's nothing special to do.

Both towns have two or three hotels in the bottom end price range.

From San Marcos, a 4WD track takes you down to the Pacific coast near Quepos and Manuel Antonio National Park. This is the most direct route from San José, but the road is so bad that only the adventurous with 4WD vehicles attempt it. You could walk it (if you were very fit) in one very long day. It's over 40 km – but at least it's downhill!

Also from San Marcos, you could drive (or perhaps find buses) through a number of other small towns, many of which are named after saints, and get back to San José. I've never visited the area, but I understand it's rural and attractive. This would be a fun trip with a map and a rental vehicle.

Getting There & Away

Buses leave San José three times a day for Santa María – the bus stop is at Calle 21, Avenida 16 bis (☎ 273597), or ask at the tourist office for times. From Santa María you may find onward buses, or you may have to walk or drive yourself.

Southern Costa Rica

SAN GERARDO DE DOTA

This community is nine km off the Inter-american Highway. The turn off is to the right, 80 km south of San José. Take a bus to San Isidro de El General and ask the driver to put you down at the entrance ('la entrada') for San Gerardo. From there it is a nine km walk downhill.

Tours

Costa Rica Expeditions (☎ 570766) has trout fishing tours here in season for US$125 per person (four people minimum). This includes transport from San José (about 2½

hours each way), lunch, fishing gear and a bilingual guide. Four to six hours of fishing can be done.

Places to Stay

You can stay at *Cabinas Chacón* (☎ 711732), a small family run place where the birding is good. Quetzals have been reported here regularly every April and May (the breeding season). The trout fishing in the Río Savegre is also very good. The seasons are May and June for fly fishing, and December to March for lure fishing.

Telephoned reservations are needed to

stay at the Cabinas Chacón. There are hot showers, and rooms cost about US$20 per person, including home-cooked meals. You can drive down there, but will need 4WD to get out again, or you can walk. With a reservation, you can arrange for a member of the Chacón family to pick you up from the Interamerican Highway for about US$12.

CERRO DE LA MUERTE

The mountain overlooking the highest point on the Interamerican Highway got its name before the road was built – but the steep, fog-shrouded highway in the area is known as one of the most dangerous for accidents in Costa Rica. Take care if driving. During the rainy season, landslides may partially or completely block the road. I drove over the pass one dark and misty night in visibility of about three car lengths, speeding along at about 15 km/h – frightening!

This area is the northernmost extent of the páramo habitat – a highland shrub and tussock grass habitat more common in the Andes of Colombia, Ecuador and Peru than in Costa Rica. Nevertheless, here it is – and you can drive through it! Birders look for highland bird species here, such as the sooty robin, volcano junco and two species of silky flycatchers.

Tours

Costa Rica Expeditions has one-day guided birding trips to Cerro de la Muerte for US$65 per person, minimum four people.

Places to Stay

About five km beyond the highest point is the *Hotel Georgina* where buses often stop for a meal and toilet break. Fairly inexpensive rooms are available, simple meals are served, and there is good high-altitude birding nearby.

SAN ISIDRO DE EL GENERAL

Roughly 130 km from San José, San Isidro is the most important town on the southern Interamerican Highway. The town and its surrounding district have a population of 35,000.

The General River valley is important for agriculture, as you can see when descending from the bleak páramos of Cerro de la Muerte through the increasingly lush farming country of the valley. San Isidro is the commercial centre of the coffee fincas, cattle ranches and plant nurseries which dot the mountain slopes. In addition, the town is an important transport hub.

It is a bustling, pleasant and fairly modern town. There really is not much to see or do here, but its position as a gateway to other places is what makes it of interest to the traveller. San José to the north and Panama to the south-east are the most obvious important destinations, of course, but in addition a road to the north-east leads to the village of San Gerardo de Rivas, where the ranger station for Chirripó National Park is found. Another road to the south-west leads to the Pacific coast and beaches at Dominical, which allows a round trip to be made from San José to Dominical and Manuel Antonio National Park without retracing your route. Other minor roads lead into quiet farming country. River-running trips on the nearby General and Chirripó rivers can be arranged in San José, with overnight stops in San Isidro.

Information

You can change money in the bank on the Parque Central, as well as at another bank a block away. The post and telegram office is a block south of the park.

River Running

Ríos Tropicales (☎ 336455) has four-day rafting or kayaking trips on the Río General between June and December – the dry season water levels are too low – and Class III to IV white water can be expected.

Costa Rica Expeditions (☎ 570766) has three and four-day river running trips on the Río Chirripó from mid-June to mid-December. This is a mainly Class IV river.

Trips include round trip transportation from San José, all boating gear including life vests, tents for camping by the side of the river, expert bilingual river guides and all

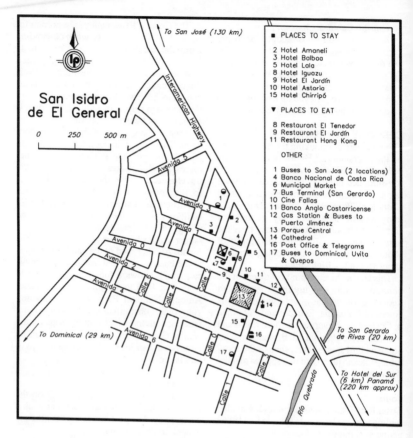

San Isidro
de El General

0   250   500 m

To San José (130 km)

- PLACES TO STAY

  2 Hotel Amaneli
  3 Hotel Balboa
  5 Hotel Lala
  8 Hotel Iguazu
  9 Hotel El Jardín
  10 Hotel Astoria
  15 Hotel Chirripó

▼ PLACES TO EAT

  8 Restaurant El Tenedor
  9 Restaurant El Jardín
  11 Restaurant Hong Kong

  OTHER

  1 Buses to San Jos (2 locations)
  4 Banco Nacional de Costa Rica
  6 Municipal Market
  7 Bus Terminal (San Gerardo)
  10 Cine Fallas
  11 Banco Anglo Costarricense
  12 Gas Station & Buses to
     Puerto Jiménez
  13 Parque Central
  14 Cathedral
  16 Post Office & Telegrams
  17 Buses to Dominical, Uvita
     & Quepos

To Dominical (29 km)

To San Gerardo
de Rivas (20 km)

To Hotel del Sur
(6 km) Panamó
(220 km approx)

meals. Costs depend on the number of people. Sample rates for a four day trip are US$416 per person with eight passengers, and substantially more per person with fewer participants. It is sometimes possible to join other groups if there are not eight of you.

Places to Stay – bottom end

The *Hotel El Jardín* has been recommended by budget travellers for clean, basic rooms and a cheap restaurant. Rooms are US$2.30 per person. The cheapest place in town is the *Hotel Lala* (☎ 710291) which charges US$1.60 per person in basic rooms, or US$4 (one or two people) for a room with a double bed and private cold water shower. It's not bad for the price. The *Hotel Balboa* can also be tried. The *Hotel Astoria* (☎ 710914) has very basic box-like rooms for US$2.25/3 single/double and US$3.50/6.50 with private cold water shower.

The *Hotel Chirripó* (☎ 710529) is modern and quite good for US$4.50/7 single/double or US$7/9.50 in rooms with private bath and hot water.

Places to Stay – middle

The *Hotel Iguazu* (☎ 712571) is new, clean

and secure. Rooms with private bath and hot water are US$6.25/10 single/double. Also good is the *Hotel Amaneli* (☎ 710352) which charges US$5.75 per person in rooms with private bath, hot water and fans.

The best hotel is about seven km southeast of town, on the left side of the Interamerican Highway. This is the *Hotel del Sur* (☎ 710233) with a swimming pool, tennis court and a pleasant restaurant and bar. Rooms with private bath, hot water and fans are US$16/21 single/double. Cabins sleeping up to five people are US$32.

Places to Eat

There are many inexpensive *sodas* downtown. The *Restaurant El Jardín* in the hotel of the same name is cheap and good. The *Restaurant El Tenedor* next to the Hotel Iguazu has a balcony overlooking a busy street and serves meals from US$1 (hamburgers) to US$5; pizzas are a speciality.

The *Restaurant Hong Kong* on the park has been recommended for, predictably, Chinese food. The restaurant at the Hotel del Sur is the best in the area.

Getting There & Away

Buses leave San José from Calle 16, Avenida 1 & 3 (near the Musoc Hotel) about eight times a day for San Isidro. Buses return to San José from Avenida 3, Calle 2 eight times a day. The fare is a little under US$3 and the ride takes three hours.

The bus terminal in San Isidro is next to the municipal market, which is currently being rebuilt and service may be disrupted because of this. If the terminal is closed, the bus leaves from the north-east corner of the park.

Buses for San Gerardo de Rivas (for Chirripó National Park) leave at 5 am and 2 pm and take two hours. Buenos Aires is also served from the bus terminal, with three buses every morning.

Buses leave for the coast at Quepos via Dominical at 7 am and 1.30 pm, and for Uvita at 3 pm. Departures are from Calle 1, Avenida 4 & 6.

Buses to Puerto Jiménez (in the Osa Peninsula) leave from the stop by the gas station on the Interamerican Highway at 6 am and 12 noon. The six hour ride costs US$3.50. Buses heading south along the Interamerican may stop here to pick up passengers.

You can hire a 4WD jeep taxi to San Gerardo de Rivas for US$16. A taxi to the Hotel del Sur is about US$3.

CHIRRIPÓ NATIONAL PARK

This is Costa Rica's main mountain park and, at 50,150 hectares, the nation's largest national park. There are three peaks of over 3800 metres, including Cerro Chirripó itself which, at 3819 metres, is the highest mountain in the country. In fact, of all the Central American countries, only Guatemala has higher mountains. Most of the park lies at over 2000 metres above sea level, and there are hiking trails and simple mountain huts for people wishing to spend a few days hiking at high altitude. I remember when I first visited Chirripó in 1981, I had spent almost a year travelling around tropical Central America and was delighted to find a park where I could get away from the heat for a while!

San Gerardo is at 1300 metres, and so the elevation gain to the top of Chirripó is 2500 metres. That is a lot of climbing. Fortunately, there is an easy-to-follow trail all the way to the top, and no technical climbing is required.

The walk is a fascinating one because it goes through constantly changing scenery, vegetation and wildlife as you ascend. After passing through the pasturelands outside the park, the trail leads through tropical lower montane and then montane rainforests. These are essentially evergreen forests with heavy epiphytic growths in the trees, and thick fern and bamboo understoreys. Emerging above the main canopy (25 to 30 metres) are oak trees reaching 40 or even 50 metres in height.

These highland forests are home to such birds as the flame-throated warbler and buffy tufted-cheek, to name but two. Blue and green frogs and lime coloured caterpillars thickly covered with stinging hairs make their way across the trail, and Baird's tapir lurks in the thick vegetation – though you are much more likely to see squirrels than tapirs. Eventually, the trail climbs out of the rain forests and into the bare and windswept páramo of the mountain tops.

The Chirripó massif is part of the Cordillera de Talamanca which continues to the north-west and south-east. The national park's eastern boundary coincides with the western boundary of the huge and largely inaccessible La Amistad International Park, and thus most of the Talamancan mountains are protected. Chirripó and La Amistad parks, together with some biological reserves and several large Indian reservations, make up the Amistad-Talamanca Regional Conservation Unit.

Information

The dry season (late December to April) is the most popular time to go. During weekends, and especially at Easter, the park is relatively crowded with Costa Rican hiking groups. The mountain refuges may well be full and you should be prepared to camp outside. February and March are the driest months, though it may still rain sometimes. The ranger station in San Gerardo is a good place to ask about weather conditions and get an idea of how many people are in the park.

During the wet season, you are likely to have the park to yourself. I have spent almost two weeks backpacking in the park during the wet season and found that it rarely rained before 1 pm – and I didn't see anybody. A great wilderness experience. But it is as well to remember that as much as 7000 mm of annual rainfall has been recorded in some areas of the park.

At the San Gerardo Ranger Station you can pay the approximately US$1 fee to enter the park and obtain information. If you arrive late it's possible to camp by the ranger station, or stay in one of the cheap and basic rooms at the *Soda Chirripó* by the San Gerardo soccer pitch. If you are driving, you can arrange to leave your vehicle near the ranger station. Park rangers will help you arrange mule hire with the locals – you can

ride the mules, or just have them carry your camping gear. The locals will not normally rent the animals without a local guide to come with you. Expect to pay about US$20 per day for a guide and a pack animal.

The maps available at the ranger station are very sketchy. Good topographical maps from the IGN are available from San José (though huts and trails are not marked). Chirripó lies on the corner of four 1:50,000 scale maps so you need maps 3444 II San Isidro and 3544 III Durika to cover the area from ranger station to the summit of Chirripó itself, and maps 3544 IV Fila Norte and 3444 I Cuerici to cover other peaks in the summit massif.

Climbing Chirripó

From the ranger station it is a 16 km climb to the Chirripó summit area. Allow seven to 14 hours to reach the huts, depending on how fit you are.

There are three huts spaced out along the last hour of the trail – the last one is the best equipped with sleeping platform and wood stove although there is very little dead and down wood available in the páramo and I question that burning it is justified. Rangers will sometimes bring supplies of wood up from the forest by mule, but it's worth having a camping stove. It can freeze at night so have warm clothes and a good sleeping bag. There are caves and possible campsites along the trail if you don't want to go from ranger station to huts in one day.

From the hut it is a further 1½ hours to the summit of Chirripó. Carry water along the trail, particularly during the dry season when there is only one place to get water before the huts. Allow a minimum of two days to climb from the ranger station to the summit and back again, and try and be in San Gerardo by 3.30 pm to catch the last bus returning to San Isidro. Three days would be better.

Almost every visitor to the park climbs the main trail to Chirripó and returns the same way. Some maps show a couple of rarely used, non-maintained wilderness trails leading north and south out of the park, but these are extremely difficult to find and are not recommended.

Other nearby mountains can also be climbed, up fairly obvious trails.

BUENOS AIRES

This small village is 64 km south-east of San Isidro and three km north of the Interamerican Highway. The main reason to stop here is because it is an entry point for the rarely visited La Amistad International Park to the north and Boruca Indian Reserve to the south. The village is in the centre of an important pineapple producing region.

Places to Stay

There is a couple of cheap and basic places to stay in Buenos Aires.

Getting There & Away

Take a bus from San Isidro (three leave every morning) or take any southbound bus on the Interamerican Highway and ask to be put down at the turn-off for Buenos Aires.

LA AMISTAD INTERNATIONAL PARK

This huge park is by far the largest single protected area in Costa Rica. Its 193,929 hectare area is bigger than the two largest national parks (Chirripó and Santa Rosa) and largest national wildlife refuge (Barra del Colorado) combined. It is known as an international park because it continues across the border into Panama, where it is managed separately.

Combined with Chirripó National Park and several indigenous reservations and biological reserves, La Amistad forms the Amistad-Talamanca Regional Conservation Unit. Because of its remoteness and size, the RCU protects a great variety of tropical habitats ranging from rainforest to páramo and so has attracted the attention of biologists, ecologists and conservationists worldwide. In 1982, the area was declared a Biosphere Reserve by UNESCO, and in 1983 was designated a World Heritage site. The complete Biosphere Reserve encompasses approximately 600,000 hectares, well over 10% of Costa Rica's territory.

Conservation International and other agencies are working with the Costa Rican authorities to implement a suitable management plan. This plan must preserve the wildlife and habitat, and develop resources, such as hydroelectricity, without disturbing the ecosystem or the traditional way of life of the Indian groups dwelling within the reserve.

La Amistad International Park has the nation's largest populations of Baird's tapirs, as well as giant anteaters, all six species of neotropical cats – jaguar, puma (or mountain lion), margay, ocelot, tiger cat (or oncilla) and jaguarundi – and many other more common mammals. Within the biosphere reserve as a whole, over 500 bird species have been sighted (more than half of the total in Costa Rica) and 49 of these species exist only within the Reserve. In addition, 115 species of fish and 215 species of reptiles and amphibians have been listed and more are being added regularly. The number of insect species is innumerable. Eight of the nation's 12 Holdridge Life Zones are represented in the park.

The backbone of the park is the Cordillera de Talamanca, which, apart from having the peaks of the Chirripó massif, also has many mountains of over 3000 metres in elevation. The thickly forested northern Caribbean slopes and southern Pacific slopes of the Talamancas are also protected in the park, but it is only on the Pacific side that ranger stations are found. These are on access roads that are outside the actual park boundaries.

Within the park itself, development is almost non-existent, which means backpackers are pretty much left to their own resources. Hiking through steep, thick and wet rainforest is both difficult and lacking in the instant gratification of seeing, say, grizzly bears and North American bison in Yellowstone National Park, or lions and leopards in Kenya's national parks. It is because of the lack of human interference that the shy tropical mammals of Costa Rica are present in relative abundance at La

Amistad – but expect to work hard for a glimpse of them. Bird-watching, on the other hand, will usually be more successful.

Information

There are three park stations currently giving some kind of access to the park, and more are planned. Note that park stations aren't necessarily staffed at all times, but you can camp at any of these places.

It is worth checking with the National Parks Service in San José before you go – they may be able to give more information although the area is so remote that any information tends to be sketchy.

Maps show a dirt road from Buenos Aires heading north for about 10 km to the community of **Ujarrás**, from where a trail is shown heading north-east over a 2200 metre pass in the Cordillera de Talamanca and down towards the Talamanca-Cabécar Indian Reserve on the Caribbean slope. I suspect that this is a poorly maintained trail used almost exclusively by indigenous people, but it might prove to be a way of crossing the park (but don't count on it!).

Getting There & Away

From Buenos Aires there are daily buses at 6.30 am and 12.30 pm to Potrero Grande, a village 34 km south-east of Buenos Aires and eight km east of the Interamerican Highway. From Potrero, it is 12 km by dirt road to the Helechales Park Station on the border of the park. There are no facilities here.

From San Vito there are buses at 3 pm to Santa Elena, a village in the Cotón River valley about 20 km north of San Vito. From Santa Elena, a rough road goes about five km to the community of Aguacaliente, from where it is a 14 km walk to the La Escuadra Park Station. Again, there are no facilities.

From San Vito, there are also buses leaving at 9.30 am and 2 pm for La Lucha and Las Mellizas, about 25 km to the north-east by the Panamanian border. These villages give access to the Las Tablas Park Station, which reportedly has trails nearby, and is the best 'developed'. There are also buses to Las Tablas at 10.30 am and 3 pm.

Jeep taxis (4WD) can usually be hired from the nearest towns to get you to the park stations, but be prepared to do a bit of asking around before finding someone who knows the way. This is a trip only for those adventurers with plenty of time.

BORUCA INDIAN RESERVE

This reserve is centred around the village of Boruca, about 20 km south of Buenos Aires. It is one of the few Indian reserves where visitors are not unwelcome, perhaps because Boruca is only some eight km west of the Interamerican Highway.

The Borucas are known for their carvings, both of balsa wood masks and decorated gourds. The women use pre-Columbian back-strap looms to weave cotton cloth and belts. These can sometimes be bought from the locals. Generally, the people live a simple agricultural life in the surrounding hills. New Year's Eve and 8 February are supposedly important fiesta times.

Places to Stay

There is no hotel as such, but accommodation can be arranged with a local family by asking at the village pulpería.

Getting There & Away

Ask a bus driver to drop you off at the Entrada de Boruca, which is about two km south of Brujo on the Interamerican Highway. From there it is an eight km hike. A school bus from Buenos Aires leaves on school days (March to early December) at 1.30 pm and takes about two hours to Boruca.

If you are simply driving through the area on the Interamerican Highway, you can stop at the community of Curré, a few km south-west of the San Vito turn-off. There is a small crafts co-operative store here, and it sells Boruca work.

PALMAR NORTE & PALMAR SUR

These two places are basically the same town on different sides of the Río Grande de Terraba, which the Interamerican Highway has been following for the last 40 km (if you are southbound). Palmar is about 125 km south of San Isidro and 95 km north-west of the Panamanian border.

The town is important as the centre of the banana growing region of the Valle de Diquís, and as a transportation hub.

The area is also of interest to archaeologists because of the discovery of almost perfect stone spheres up to 1½ metres in diameter. These were made by pre-Columbian Indians and similar spheres have been found on Isla del Caño (now a Biological Reserve) – but exactly who made them and how remains a mystery. Ask in town if you want to see the spheres (esferas de piedra) – they are found in a variety of places including backyards and in banana plantations.

Palmar Norte has a petrol station, and Palmar Sur has the airport.

Places to Stay
There are several cheap and basic hotels, of which the best is the Casa Amarilla in Palmar Norte.

Getting There & Away
Air There are flights from San José with SANSA on Monday, Wednesday and Friday at 11 am (US$12.50), returning at 11.50 am via Coto 47 (US$15).

Road The Interamerican Highway comes through Palmar and buses between more important towns to the north and south can drop you here en route to somewhere else. A side road goes about 14 km to the coastal village of **Sierpe** from where boats can be hired to take you to Corcovado National Park and other points on the coast. There are buses from Palmar Sur.

There is a road from Palmar Norte which goes seven km west to Ciudad Cortés, from where a rough 20 km road goes north-west along the Pacific coast through Coronado as far as Tortuga Abajo. Beyond that a poor track suitable for 4WD jeeps continues 32 km to the coastal village of Dominical. This road may be impassable during the wet months, but plans are afoot to improve it.

GOLFITO
Golfito is on the Golfo Dulce, a large Pacific Ocean gulf just west of Panama. The city is 26 km west of the Interamerican Highway and about 60 km from the Panamanian border by road, although only half that distance in a straight line.

Golfito is the most important port in the far southern part of Costa Rica, although its importance has declined greatly in recent years. From 1938 to 1985 Golfito was the centre of a major banana growing region, and for many years was the headquarters of the United Fruit Company. But a combination of declining foreign markets, rising Costa Rican export taxes, worker unrest, and banana diseases led to the closing of the United complex in 1985. Some of the plantations have since been turned to African palm-oil production, but this hasn't alleviated the high unemployment and economic loss caused by United's departure.

Golfito is still, superficially, two towns strung out along a coastal road with a backdrop of steep thickly forested hills. The southern part of town is where you find the hotels, restaurants and bars. The northern part was the old United headquarters, with large, well ventilated, attractively landscaped, North American-style houses and the airport. Since the United pullout, the northern area has become available for anybody to live in, but most of the houses stand empty because they are too expensive for the average local tico.

In an attempt to boost the economy of the region, Costa Rica has built a new duty-free facility in Golfito. 'Duty free' is a misnomer, because items for sale here are still heavily taxed. Nevertheless, the taxes are substantially lower than elsewhere in Costa Rica, and it is hoped to attract ticos from all over the country into visiting Golfito on shopping sprees for microwave ovens and TV sets.

Meanwhile, Golfito retains a somewhat lost and depressed air. A rusting train engine (No 62444, built in 1940 by the Baldwin

Locomotive Works, Philadelphia, USA) can be seen in town – its decrepitude illustrates the post-United era. Nevertheless, the town is pleasantly situated and visitors often stop by for a day or two en route to somewhere else. There are good surfing and swimming beaches nearby, and the town is surrounded by the Golfito National Wildlife Refuge. Boats and light planes cross the Golfo Dulce to the Osa Peninsula where the Corcovado National Park is found.

Golfito is a well-protected port and a few foreign yachts on oceanic cruises are usually found anchored here. A small tourist and hotel industry is slowly developing to accommodate visitors who want to see some of the interesting surrounding areas.

Places to Stay – bottom end

The cheapest place in town is the *Hotel Delfina* (☎ 750043) which has basic rooms for US$2.50 per person. They also have better rooms with private baths and fan for US$4.50 per person. The best rooms have private bath and air-con, and cost US$10.50, either single or double occupancy.

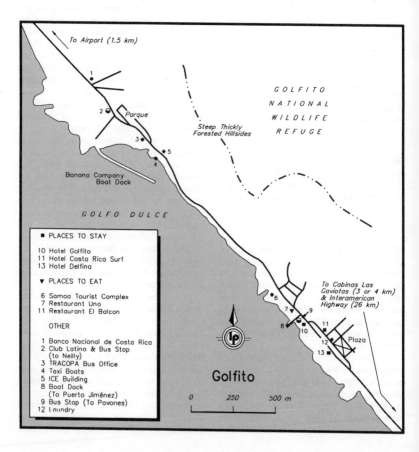

To Airport (1.5 km)

GOLFITO NATIONAL WILDLIFE REFUGE

Steep Thickly Forested Hillsides

Parque

Banana Company Boat Dock

GOLFO DULCE

■ PLACES TO STAY

10 Hotel Golfito
11 Hotel Costa Rica Surf
13 Hotel Delfina

▼ PLACES TO EAT

6 Samoa Tourist Complex
7 Restaurant Uno
11 Restaurant El Balcon

OTHER

1 Banco Nacional de Costa Rica
2 Club Latino & Bus Stop (to Neilly)
3 TRACOPA Bus Office
4 Taxi Boats
5 ICE Building
8 Boat Dock (To Puerto Jiménez)
9 Bus Stop (To Pavones)
12 Laundry

To Cabinas Las Gaviotas (3 or 4 km) & Interamerican Highway (26 km)

Plaza

Golfito

0   250   500 m

Another choice is the *Hotel Golfito* (☎ 750047) which has rooms with private bath and fan for US$6.50, either single or double occupancy. Both hotels are clean and satisfactory.

Places to Stay – middle

The *Hotel Costa Rica Surf* (☎ 750034; Apartado 7, Golfito, Puntarenas, Costa Rica), is the best place in the town centre. It has rooms for US$7/11.50 single/double with private bath and fan, and for US$9/14.50 with air-con. There is a good restaurant attached, and the owners can help arrange local trips.

The *Cabinas Las Gaviotas* (☎ 750062; Apartado 12, Golfito, Puntarenas, Costa Rica), is the best hotel in town. It is actually about four km from the town itself. There are pleasant rooms and some cabins with kitchenettes overlooking the ocean. The restaurant is also the best in town. Rooms with private bath and fan are US$20, and with air-con US$24, either single or double occupancy.

The newly built *Complejo Turistico Samoa* has a restaurant but no rooms – but they are planning on building some. They will be in the middle price range.

Places to Eat

The American-run *Restaurant El Balcon* adjoining the Hotel Costa Rica Surf has a variety of meals ranging from bowls of chili for US$1 to steaks for US$5. Breakfast is also served. The view of the gulf from the balcony is pleasant, and the bar is popular in the afternoon and evenings.

Another good place is the *Restaurant Uno* which has Chinese food for US$2 to US$3. The *Bar Restaurant Samoa* in the Samoa tourist complex has meals for around US$5, a bar and a disco some nights.

Getting There & Away

Air SANSA (☎ in Golfito 750303) flies from San José daily, except Sunday, at 7.45 am returning to San José at 8.45 am. There is a second flight on Tuesday, Thursday and Saturday leaving San José at 1 pm, returning at 2 pm; the fare is US$17. Flights are often fully booked but it's worth getting on the waiting list and showing up at the airport because there are frequent 'no-shows'.

Aeronaves (☎ 750278) has a daily flight (except Sunday) to Puerto Jiménez at 6 am. The flight takes about seven minutes and the fare is US$9. If there are passengers, they may have a second flight at 2 pm. They have single-engined planes taking three passengers (270 kg maximum) available for charter to Puerto Jiménez (US$50) and Sirena in Corcovado National Park (US$140) at any time. Their airport office is open from 6 am to 6 pm daily.

The airport is almost four km north of the town centre.

Bus TRACOPA (☎ 214214) has two buses a day from San José to Golfito (eight hours, US$4). The buses leave from Avenida 18, Calle 4. Return buses from Golfito leave at 5 and 10 am daily, except Sunday when the second bus leaves at 1.30 pm. Fares are US$4.75 to San José and US$3.50 to San Isidro. TRACOPA's office hours in Golfito are 6 to 11.30 am and 1.30 to 4 pm from Monday to Saturday, and 7 to 11 am on Sunday and holidays.

Buses for Ciudad Neily leave every hour from the bus stop outside the Club Latino at the north end of town. They will pick up passengers in town as they pass through for the one hour trip to Neily.

Buses for the surfing area of Pavones leave from the Puerto Jiménez boat dock twice a day. Services may be interrupted during the rainy season – it's a poor road.

Boat The daily passenger boat to Puerto Jiménez leaves at 12.15 pm. It takes 1½ hours and costs US$1.75.

Getting Around

Bus City buses go up and down the main road of Golfito for about US$0.15 per ride. They get within a km of the airport, but don't usually get all the way there.

Taxi Shared (colectivo) taxis go up and down

the main road as far north as the airport and as far south as a little way beyond downtown. The set fare is US$0.60.

A private taxi from downtown to the airport costs about US$2.

Boat Taxi boats leave from the dock opposite the ICE building near the north end of Golfito. Boats are available from 6 am to 5 pm to a variety of destinations. Boats to Cacao and Puntarenitas beaches cost about US$2.50 for up to four passengers (US$0.60 per extra passenger).

Water taxis to Zancudo Beach are about US$29 and take up to six passengers. Other destinations can also be arranged.

AROUND GOLFITO
Cacao Beach
Cacao Beach is opposite Golfito and is a 15 minute boat ride away. You can also get there by walking along a dirt road west and then south from the airport – about 10 km total from downtown Golfito. (This road is motorable most of the time.)

Nearby is Puntarenitas Beach, which can only be reached by boat, has no development, and is supposedly prettier. There is no shade so bring sun protection.

Places to Stay & Eat This beach has accommodation and food available at *Captain Tom's Place*. You can camp or sling a hammock for a few dollars, or stay on his converted boat-hotel for a few dollars more.

Zancudo Beach
This beach, near the mouth of the Río Coto Colorado, about 12 or 15 km south of Golfito, is a popular destination for locals who claim that this is the best swimming beach in the area.

There are mangroves in the area around the river mouth.

Places to Stay You can stay at *Los Almendros* (☎ 750515) run by Ray Ventana, who will pick you up from Golfito for US$18 per boat. Pleasant cabins are available for

about US$12 double, and there is a restaurant.

Pavones
A few km further south is the Bahía de Pavón, which is supposed to have some of the best surfing on the Pacific side of the country. The area is known locally as Pavones.

The best season is April to October when the waves are at their biggest and the long left can reportedly give a three minute ride. The best season coincides with the rainy months which makes transport there more difficult.

There are two buses a day from Golfito, and a couple of basic cabins to stay at. Camping is possible.

Sport-Fishing
Golfito is also the pick-up and drop-off point for deep sea fishing at the Golfito Sailfish Rancho which is operated by the same people who run Parismina on the north Caribbean coast.

Information on sailfish sport-fishing is available from PO Box 290190, San Antonio, Texas 78280, USA (☎ (800) 531-7232, (512) 377-0451 in the USA; 357766 in Costa Rica). Expect to pay in the region of US$250 per person a day for food, accommodation, and, of course, sport-fishing. About May to September are the best months for sailfish.

GOLFITO NATIONAL WILDLIFE REFUGE
This small (1309 hectare) refuge was originally created to protect the Golfito watershed. It encompasses most of the steep hills surrounding the town, and whilst the refuge has succeeded in keeping Golfito's water clean and flowing, it has also had the side effect of conserving a number of rare and interesting plant species. These include a species of *Caryodaphnopsis*, which is an Asian genus otherwise unknown in Central America, and *Zamia*, which are cycads. Cycads are 'living fossils' and are among the most primitive plants. They were abundant

before the time of the dinosaurs but only a few species are now extant. *Zamia* are known for the huge, cone-like inflorescences which emerge from the centre of the plant and look rather like a dwarf palm.

Other species of interest include many heliconias, orchids, tree ferns and tropical trees including copal, the kapok tree, the butternut tree and the cow tree, so called for the copious quantities of drinkable white latex which it produces.

The vegetation attracts a variety of birds such as scarlet macaws, and a variety of parrots, toucans, tanagers, trogons and hummingbirds. Peccaries, pacas, raccoons, coatimundis and monkeys are among the mammals which have been sighted here.

Places to Stay

Camping is permitted, but there are no facilities – most people stay in Golfito.

Getting There & Away

About two km south of the town centre, a gravel road heads to the right, past a soccer field, and up to some radio towers (Las Torres), seven km away and 486 metres above sea level. This is a good access road to the refuge (most of the road actually goes through the middle of the preserve). You could take a taxi up first thing in the morning and hike down, birding as you go. There are a few trails leading from the road down to the town, but there is so little traffic on the road itself that you'll probably see more from the cleared road than the overgrown trails.

TISKITA LODGE

This is a private biological reserve and experimental fruit farm on 160 hectares of land at Punta Banco, about 30 km due south of Golfito and 10 km away from the Panamanian border. About 100 hectares are virgin rainforest. Tiskita also has a coastline with tide pools and beaches suitable for swimming.

The lodge is run by Peter Aspinall who was born in Costa Rica. His passion is homesteading and he has an orchard with over 100 varieties of tropical fruits from all over the world. It is planned to export the most suitable of these fruits to San José and abroad. Meanwhile, guests are able to sample dozens of exotic fruits and fruit drinks during their visit to the lodge.

There are trails in the surrounding rainforest, which contains waterfalls and rivers suitable for swimming in. The tide pools have a variety of marine life such as chitons, nudibranchs, bristle and feather worms, starfish, sea urchins, anemones, tunicates, crabs and many shells.

Bird-watchers will find the combination of rainforest, fruit farm and coastline produces a long list of birds. The fruit farm is particularly attractive to frugivorous (fruit-eating) birds such as parrots and toucans, which can be more easily observed in the orchard than the rainforest. Nature trails into the forest help the birder see the more reticent species, and a local checklist is available. This includes such exotic sounding names as yellow-billed cotingas, fiery-billed aracaris, green honeycreepers, and lattice-tailed trogons – to name a few. Monkeys, sloths, agoutis, coatimundis and other mammals are often seen. Of course, insects and plants abound.

Places to Stay

Accommodation is in five simple cabins with private bath and Pacific Ocean views. Electricity is provided by solar and hydro-electric power. There is a lodge with a small library and a dining room serving home cooked food. Up to 18 guests can be accommodated.

Reservations are essential, because the lodge is sometimes full with birding groups and the like. Make reservations with Costa Rica Sun Tours (operated by the Aspinalls), (☎ 553418, 553518; Apartado 1195, 1250 Escazú, Costa Rica.

Daily rates are US$80/113/153 single/double/triple including all meals, fruit drinks, bird checklists, trail maps and snorkelling equipment. Horses can also be hired.

Most people come on a package tour

which includes everything mentioned above plus light aircraft flights from San José to Tiskita, airport transfers, and two guided walks by local naturalists. These packages cost US$440 per person for five days/four nights. Cheaper packages involving SANSA flights to Golfito and 4WD jeep taxi to the lodge cost US$385 per person for the same period. Longer and shorter stays can be arranged. The flight from San José to Tiskita takes about an hour.

Getting There & Away
It is possible to drive to the lodge with a 4WD vehicle, but most people opt to fly to the nearby airstrip. Getting there yourself is rather difficult but can be done by public transport or your own vehicle in the dry season. Ask the Aspinalls for directions.

PUERTO JIMÉNEZ
This small town is almost 20 km away from Golfito by sea, across the Golfo Dulce. It is also linked by about 80 km of poor road with the Interamerican Highway and San José. Puerto Jiménez is the only town of any size on the Osa Peninsula.

Until the 1960s, the Osa Peninsula was one of the remotest parts of Costa Rica, with exuberant rainforests and a great variety of plants and animals. Then logging began, and later gold was discovered, creating a minor gold rush and increased settlement. In the face of this, the Corcovado National Park was created in 1975. Around the park, logging and gold mining go on, but within the park a valuable and unique group of rainforest habitats are preserved.

The gold rush and logging industry, along with the accompanying colonisation, has made Puerto Jiménez a fairly important little town, and because access is now relatively straightforward, there is a burgeoning tourist industry. Ticos come to Puerto Jiménez partly for its slightly frontier atmosphere, and partly for the pleasant beaches nearby. Foreigners tend to come because this is the entry town to the famous Corcovado National Park, and there is a national park

information station here. It is a pleasant and friendly town.

Information
The national park information station (☎ 785036) is open from 8 am to 12 noon, and 1 to 4 pm daily. They have up-to-date information on how to get to the park.

The Banco Central de Costa Rica buys dollars and gold.

Places to Stay & Eat
During Easter week, all the hotels are full. During weekends in the dry season, most hotels are also full. Call ahead to make reservations, or arrive mid-week.

The cheapest place in town is the *Hotel Valentin* which has tiny airless rooms and no fans, but is at least clean. Rooms are US$1.75 per person. The *Pensión Quintero* (☎ 785087) has slightly bigger rooms, is also clean, but still has no fans. Shared bathroom facilities are very basic, and the rates are US$2.50 per person.

The *Cabinas Marcelina* and *Cabinas Brisas del Mar* (☎ 785012) both offer rooms with two beds and private shower for US$6 (single or double occupancy).

The best place is *Cabinas Manglares* (☎ 785002) which is away from the town centre and has a pleasant but simple restaurant attached; the food is good. Rooms with one or two beds and private shower are US$6 per room, and they have some more spacious and comfortable rooms for US$8.25 double or single occupancy. All rooms have fans provided.

In town, the *Restaurant Carolina* is a good place to eat. Near the boat dock the *Restaurant Agua Luna* has seafood and a sea view.

Getting There & Away
Air Aeronaves (☎ 785017) has a daily flight to Golfito at 6 am, and another at 2 pm if there is passenger demand. The fare is US$9 for the seven minute flight. Aeronaves also has SANSA information for connecting with Golfito to San José flights.

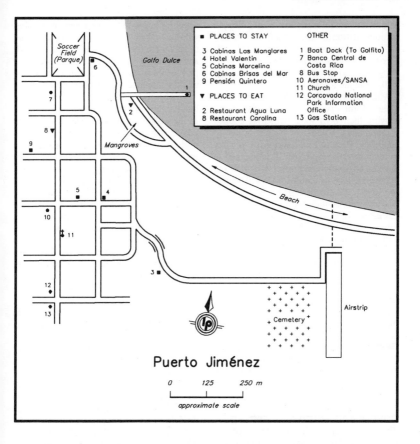

PLACES TO STAY

3 Cabinas Los Manglares
4 Hotel Valentin
5 Cabinas Marcelina
6 Cabinas Brisas del Mar
9 Pensión Quintero

PLACES TO EAT

2 Restaurant Agua Luna
8 Restaurant Carolina

OTHER

1 Boat Dock (To Golfito)
7 Banco Central de Costa Rica
8 Bus Stop
10 Aeronaves/SANSA
11 Church
12 Corcovado National Park Information Office
13 Gas Station

Puerto Jiménez

0   125   250 m

approximate scale

Three-seater aircraft can be chartered into Corcovado National Park for about US$80 to US$100.

Bus TRACOPA buses run here twice a day from San José and San Isidro. There are also buses from Ciudad Neily.

Buses leave from in front of Restaurant Carolina every day for San Isidro at 4 and 11 am (six hours, US$3.50) and for Ciudad Neily at 5.30 am and 2 pm (four hours, US$2.50). A few buses a day go the 14 km to Dos Brazos, where there are gold mines. There are four buses a day to La Palma,

which is an exit/entry point for Corcovado National Park.

Boat The passenger ferry to Golfito leaves daily at 6 am, takes 1½ hours and costs US$1.75.

LA TIERRA DE MILAGROS

This is a 400 hectare private nature preserve and reforestation project at the southern tip of the Osa Peninsula, roughly 20 km south of Puerto Jiménez. It is a new alternative lifestyle project begun by expatriate North Americans in 1990. Volunteers are needed to help with the reforestation work. Simple accommodation is in thatched cabins, and bathroom and cooking facilities are shared. Free time can be spent bird-watching, swimming and hiking on the Pacific coast, and walking in the forest.

Volunteers contribute US$200 per month to their dormitory-style accommodation and provide their own food (which is cooked communally). Volunteers are also asked to contribute three to four hours work per day to the reforestation project. It is planned to develop an ecotourism project with food and accommodation available for US$50 per day (no work). All proceeds go to the preservation and reforestation project.

Further information is available from founder Edith Ingenlath, Tierra de Milagros, Lista de Correos, Puerto Jiménez, Peninsula de Osa, Costa Rica or from PO Box 35203, Siesta Key, Florida 34242, USA (☎ (813) 349-2168).

Places to Stay
Drop-in backpackers can stay for US$7 per night, plus US$3 per meal.

Getting There & Away
You can get there by taxi from Puerto Jiménez; taxi driver Oscar will take you there for about US$10 per person (US$15 minimum).

CORCOVADO NATIONAL PARK
This national park has great biological diversity and has long attracted the attention of tropical ecologists who wish to study the intricate workings of the rainforest. The 41,788 hectare park covers the southwestern corner of the Osa Peninsula and protects at least eight distinct types of habitat. This assemblage is considered both unique and the best remaining Pacific coastal rainforest in Central America.

Because of its remoteness this rainforest remained undisturbed until the 1960s when logging began in the area. The park was established in 1975, but a few years later a small gold rush in the area led to several hundred miners moving into the park. Their activities began silting up rivers, disturbing wildlife and destroying forest. In 1986 the miners were forcibly evicted from the park and now there is an uneasy truce between the park authorities and the miners who are working the lands neighbouring the park.

Whilst it is important to preserve the biodiversity and unique environment found in the park, it is understandable that local people also want to improve their lives. The mining operations within the park were mainly of the gold panning variety, rather than large scale dredging operations, and the miners were often poor people trying to make a living. The Costa Rican authorities, ever mindful of the concepts of peaceful conflict resolution, are trying to work with both conservationists and miners to work out a compromise which allows the people to work without endangering the rainforest protected in the park. It will be interesting to see whether these conflicts will be resolved.

Information
There are five ranger stations. Four of them are at the edges of the park, and the fifth one, the park headquarters at Sirena, is in the middle of the park. There are trails linking these stations, and you can camp at all of them. Sirena offers food and accommodation (if arranged in advance), and meals can be arranged at the other ranger stations. Go to the National Parks Service office in San José to make arrangements, or go to the information office in Puerto Jiménez (allow a few days for arrangements to be made).

Entry to the park is US$0.25.

Wildlife
The wildlife within the park is varied and prolific. Corcovado is home to Costa Rica's largest population of the beautiful scarlet macaw. Many of the other important or endangered rainforest species are protected here; tapirs, five cat species, crocodiles, peccaries, giant anteaters, sloths and monkeys. The rare harpy eagle, which is almost extinct in Costa Rica, may still breed in remote parts of Corcovado. Almost 400 species of birds have been seen here, as well

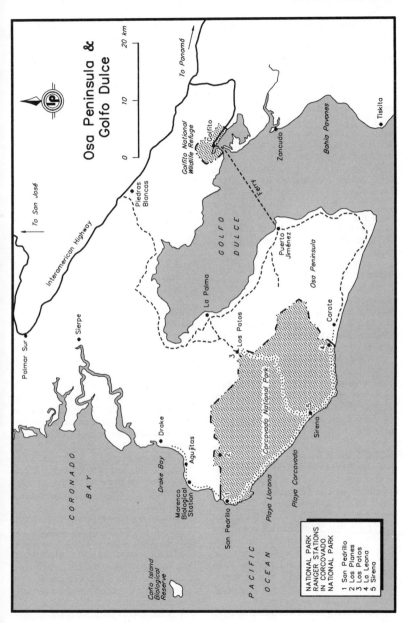

Osa Peninsula &
Golfo Dulce

20 km

10

0

To Panamá

Golfito National
Wildlife Refuge

Golfito

Zancudo

Bahia Pavones

Tiskita

To San José

Interamerican Highway

Piedras
Blancas

GOLFO

DULCE

Puerto
Jiménez

Osa Peninsula

Ferry

Palmar Sur

Sierpe

La Palma

Los Patos

3

Carate

Corcovado National Park

5

Sirena

Drake

Drake Bay

Agujitas

2

Marenco
Biological
Station

San Pedrillo

Playa Llorona

Playa Corcovado

CORONADO

BAY

PACIFIC

OCEAN

Caño Island
Biological
Reserve

NATIONAL PARK
RANGER STATIONS
IN CORCOVADO
NATIONAL PARK

1 San Pedrillo
2 Los Planes
3 Los Patos
4 La Leona
5 Sirena

as about 140 mammals and over 500 species of trees.

Walking Trails

One of the most exciting aspects of Corcovado for visitors is that there are long-distance trails through the park, leading to several ranger stations. Unlike many of Costa Rica's other lowland rainforest parks, backpackers can hike through Corcovado. The trails are primitive, and the hiking is hot, humid and insect ridden, but it can be done. For the traveller wanting to spend a few days hiking through a lowland tropical rainforest, Corcovado is the best choice in Costa Rica.

If you go in the dry season (January to April) you'll have an easier time of it than slogging around in calf-deep mud during the wet season. There are fewer bugs in the dry season, too.

Places to Stay & Eat

It costs about US$0.50 to camp at Sirena, or US$1 to stay at the station. You still need a sleeping bag and insect netting – they provide a breezy attic area with a roof over your head. Meals in Sirena cost about US$10 per day.

Sirena is a research station as well as park headquarters and so accommodation and food is dependent upon how many researchers are staying there. Adventure tour groups also stay there occasionally, so make sure you have reservations if you are not self sufficient.

Getting There & Away

You can take a 4WD taxi from Puerto Jiménez about 40 or 45 km around the southern end of the Osa Peninsula as far as the Carate Beach. A driver named Cyrilo has departures on Thursday and Saturday for US$5 per person. At other times he will take you there for US$50 for the whole jeep. From Carate Beach it is a one or two hour hike to the park station at La Leona. From there it is six to eight hours hike to Sirena, but check that the tides are low – it is a beach hike and high tides can cut you off.

From Sirena, you can hike inland on a trail to Los Patos Ranger Station, six to eight hours away. From there it is four or five hours to La Palma, from where buses go to Puerto Jiménez; the last bus leaves at 2 pm. Alternatively, you can hike north-west from Sirena along the coast to San Pedrillo Ranger Station, eight to 10 hours away. Make sure you check tide tables first. From San Pedrillo you can hike to Marenco Biological Station or Drake Bay (both outside the park and both with good accommodation, see below) in two or three hours.

Note that all these routes can be done in reverse. There are rough shelters built along the trails between ranger stations or you can camp – the Puerto Jiménez Information Centre is your best source of up to date facts.

You can also arrange to fly into either Sirena or Carate with Aeronaves from Golfito or Puerto Jiménez. The National Parks Service also has planes going in – talk to them about it. They take passengers if space is available.

MARENCO BIOLOGICAL STATION

Marenco is about five km north of Corcovado and the closest place to stay to the national park if you want comfortable accommodation. The 500 hectare station is set on a bluff overlooking the Pacific and is a good place for trips to Corcovado, Caño Island Biological Reserve, or simply into the forest surrounding the station. There are four km of trails around Marenco and many of the plant, bird and other animal species seen in Corcovado can be found in the Marenco area. A favourite hike is to the Río Claro which literally cascades through the preserve. There are beautiful swimming holes and waterfalls to reward you at the end of a sweaty hike.

Marenco is a private preserve set up specifically to protect part of the rainforest. As such, the preserve plays an important role as a buffer zone around the Corcovado National Park. Ecologists know that the conservation of a protected area is much enhanced if the region beyond the park boundary is carefully managed. This is the case with Marenco. Not only is the habitat conserved, but employment is provided for local people who work as boatmen, guides and hotel staff. Education and adventurous ecotourism are also important to the people who set up the biological station.

Naturalist guides are on hand to take visitors on excursions to rainforest, beach or islands. In addition, self guiding nature trail booklets are available to those wishing to explore alone. Horses are available for rent. Researchers are encouraged to stay here, and they may add an educational dimension to your trip.

Tours

Most people come on a package deal which includes transport and local tours. A minimum of two nights is required. One of the most complete packages is for five days and four nights, includes chartered flights from San José and return, a day boat trip to Caño Island Biological Reserve, guided day hikes to the Corcovado National Park and Río Claro rainforest, and all accommodation, food, transfers and taxes. This package costs US$630 per person. Cheaper packages with fewer options are available. For information and reservations write to Marenco Biological Station, (☎ 211594), Apartado 4025, 1000 San José.

Places to Stay & Eat

Accommodation is in rustic cabins which are elevated enough to catch the breeze. Each room has a private bathroom and a verandah overlooking the Pacific Ocean. There are four bunks in each room, but double occupancy is possible. A generator runs for a few hours in the evening. Meals are served family style in the dining room, and a small library of reference books is available.

A maximum of 40 people can be accommodated, and the station may well be full during the 'dry' busy months of December to April when advance reservations are needed. During the rest of the year, you can often get in by making a reservation just a day or two in advance. The wettest months are September and October, when the lodge may well be almost empty. Overnight stays

are US$85 per person including meals, but tours are extra.

Getting There & Away

If you are not arriving by plane on a package deal, it is also possible to arrive by boat from Dominical or Uvita.

DRAKE BAY

Drake Bay (pronounced 'dra-cay' by locals) is both 16th century history and natural history. Sir Francis Drake himself supposedly visited the bay in March of 1579, during his global circumnavigation in the *Golden Hind*. The bay is only a few km north of Marenco and the Corcovado National Park, both of which can be visited from here. Caño Island Biological Reserve can also be visited from Drake.

Agujitas is a small village on the bay, with a store and school. There is talk of a road linking Agujitas with Sierpe, thus making Drake accessible by vehicle from San José. I suspect it doesn't yet exist, but there are plans to construct the road – some time. I flew in to the Corcovado airstrip, and was picked up by a launch which took me to the Drake Bay Wilderness Camp – one of the few places to stay on the Bay. You can visit Agujitas and pick up a coke or beer, watch the local kids coming home from the school, and chat with the locals. Most people who visit tend to stay in their lodges, but the locals enjoy talking with travellers, so stop by.

Tours

A variety of packages are available which enable you to go on trips to Caño Island, or deep sea fishing, or hiking in Corcovado. A sample price is US$685 per person for seven days/six nights including a one way charter flight and a return via Palmar Sur, all food, accommodation and taxes, and a variety of local boating and hiking trips. For further information and reservations, write to Apartado 939150, San José, Costa Rica.

Places to Stay

The *Phantom Island Lodge* (☎ 257682) reputedly has scuba diving, deep sea fishing, and guided hiking facilities – but it was closed when I was there. Locals say it opens upon request – write to PO Box 559, Manvel, TX 77578, USA, for information.

The *Drake Bay Wilderness Camp* (☎ 712436 in San José, or directly to the camp by radio telephone 202121) is run by an American, Herb Michaud, and vies with Marenco for the title of best place to stay in the Osa Peninsula. The camp is right on Drake Bay, so you can explore the tide pools or swim in the ocean. Although it lacks the 500 hectare preserve of Marenco, it does have excellent naturalist guides who can take you to see and experience all the local habitats. Horses, snorkelling gear, fishing gear and canoes are available for rent.

The wilderness camp hires friendly local people to work in the lodge, and their kids are often running around which makes the place far from impersonal. Although the place is called a 'wilderness camp', the accommodation ranges from tents to comfortable cabins. The cabins have private solar-heated showers, and several have patios with ocean views. Tasty home-cooked meals are provided in the screened dining room, just a few metres away from the Pacific Ocean. The camp is closed during September and October, when the rains are at their heaviest.

Accommodation prices include three meals a day. Rooms with private shower cost US$55 per person; rooms with shared showers cost US$45 per person; large tents with folding beds and bedding cost US$35 per person – access to bathrooms is nearby. If you arrive with your own tent, you could set it up and arrange a discount – but this is done as a courtesy to travellers rather than a normal option.

Getting There & Away

You can fly in on chartered light planes from San José to the nearby Corcovado airstrip, or you can fly to Palmar Sur and take a boat via Sierpe. This latter option should be arranged with the Wilderness Camp – the Sierpe River mouth is somewhat dangerous and you should go only with an experienced and recommended local boatman.

CAÑO ISLAND BIOLOGICAL RESERVE

This 300 hectare island is roughly 20 km west of Drake Bay. The reserve is of interest to snorkellers, biologists and archaeologists. About 5800 hectares of ocean are designated as part of the reserve.

Snorkellers will find incredibly warm water (about body temperature!) and a good variety of marine life ranging from fish to sea cucumbers. A tropical beach with an attractive rainforest backdrop provides sunbathing (broasting?) opportunities, and a trail leads inland, through an evergreen rainforest, to a ridge at about 110 metres above sea level. Near the top, you can find some of the rock spheres which were made by pre-Columbian Indian people. Although these spheres have been found in several places in southern Costa Rica, archaeologists are still puzzling over their functions. Trees include milk trees (which exude a drinkable white latex), rubber trees, figs and a variety of other tropical species. Birds include coastal and oceanic species as well as rainforest inhabitants.

Places to Stay

Camping is allowed, but you should ask for permission from the National Parks Service first. There are no facilities. The reserve is administered by the Corcovado National Park and there is a ranger station by the landing beach.

Getting There & Away

Most visitors arrive with a tour. These can be arranged with Drake Bay Wilderness Camp or Marenco.

COCOS ISLAND NATIONAL PARK

This island is an isolated one – over 500 km south-west of Costa Rica, in the eastern Pacific. Despite its isolation, Cocos has been known since the early 1500s and was noted on a map drawn by Nicholas Dechiens as far back as 1541. It is extremely wet, with between 6000 and 7000 mm of annual rainfall, and thus attracted the attention of early sailors, pirates and whalers, who frequently stopped for fresh water, and, of course, fresh coconuts. Legend has it that some of the early visitors buried a huge treasure here, but, despite hundreds of treasure hunting expeditions, it has never been found. The heavy rainfall has enabled the island to support thick rainforest which soon covers all signs of digging.

Because of its isolation, Cocos Island has evolved a unique ecosystem which is why it is protected by national park status. Over 70 species of animals (mainly insects) and 70 species of plants are reportedly endemic (occurring nowhere else in the world) and more remain to be discovered. Birdwatchers come to the island to see the colonies of sea birds, many of which nest on Cocos. These include two species of frigate birds, three species of boobies, four species of gulls and six species of storm petrels among the 76 birds listed for the park. Three of the birds are endemic: the Cocos Island cuckoo, Cocos Island finch, and Cocos Island flycatcher. (The Cocos Island finch is part of the group of endemic finches studied in the Galápagos Islands by Darwin – although the Cocos species was not discovered until almost 60 years after Darwin's visit to the Galápagos.) There are two endemic lizard species. The marine life is also varied, with sea turtles, coral reefs and tropical fish in abundance. Snorkelling and diving are possible and pleasurable.

There are no people permanently living on the island, although unsuccessful attempts were made to colonise Cocos in the late 19th and early 20th centuries. After the departure of these people, feral populations of domestic animals began to create a problem and today feral pigs are the greatest threat to the unique species native to the island. The pigs uproot vegetation, causing soil erosion which in turn contributes to sedimentation around the island's coasts and damage to the coral reefs surrounding the island. Feral rats, cats and goats also contribute to the destruction of the natural habitat.

The National Parks Service is aware of the problem, but lack of funding has made it difficult to do anything about it. The island is rugged and heavily forested, with the highest point at Cerro Yglesias (634 metres). As a practical matter, how can you remove a large population of feral pigs from a thickly vegetated and hilly island which is 12 km long and five km wide?

Information
There is a park station and permission is needed from the National Parks Service to visit it. There are some trails, but camping is not allowed. The few visitors who come stay on their boat.

Tours
Ríos Tropicales arranges chartered boat trips to the park. If you want to arrange a trip in advance, contact Okeanos Aggressor (☎ (800) 348-2628, or (504) 385-2416), PO Drawer K, Morgan City, Louisiana 70381, USA. They have 10 day charters leaving every two weeks, except in October, and have space for 19 passengers. Rates are US$2195 per person from San José. Compressed air is provided for divers.

Getting There & Away
The National Parks Service may be able to help with boat charter information.

NEILY
This town, 17 km north-west of the Panamanian border by road, is nicknamed Villa by the locals. It is also sometimes referred to as Ciudad Neily. It is the main centre for the banana and African oil-palm plantations in the Coto Colorado valley to the south of town. At just 50 metres above sea level, it is a hot and humid place, but otherwise pleasant and friendly.

A road goes 31 km north to the attractive little town of San Vito at a cooler 1000 metres. Neily's main importance to the traveller is as a transport hub for southern Costa Rica, with roads and buses to Panama, San Vito, Golfito and Puerto Jiménez, as well as a host of small local agricultural settlements.

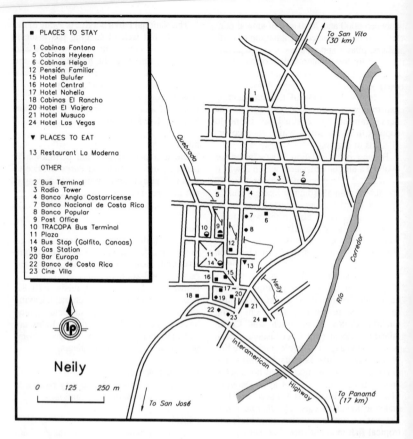

PLACES TO STAY

1 Cabinas Fontana
5 Cabinas Heyleen
6 Cabinas Helga
12 Pensión Familiar
15 Hotel Bulufer
16 Hotel Central
17 Hotel Nohelia
18 Cabinas El Rancho
20 Hotel El Viajero
21 Hotel Musuco
24 Hotel Las Vegas

PLACES TO EAT

13 Restaurant La Moderna

OTHER

2 Bus Terminal
3 Radio Tower
4 Banco Anglo Costarricense
7 Banco Nacional de Costa Rica
8 Banco Popular
9 Post Office
10 TRACOPA Bus Terminal
11 Plaza
14 Bus Stop (Golfito, Canoas)
19 Gas Station
20 Bar Europa
22 Banco de Costa Rica
23 Cine Villa

To San Vito (30 km)

Quebrada

Corredor

Río

Neily

Neily

0   125   250 m

To San José

Interamerican Highway

To Panamá (17 km)

Information

There are a number of banks where you can change money. Operator-assisted telephone calls can be made from the public booths in the Cabinas El Rancho hotel. There is a post office and a cinema.

Places to Stay

There are a number of hotels, all fairly cheap. The cheapest is the basic *Pensión Familiar* which charges about US$2.50 per person. The *Hotel Bulufer* (☎ 753216) and *Cabinas El Rancho* both seem reasonable value at US$3.50 per person in rooms with private

bath and fans. Other places in this price range are the *Hotel Central, Hotel El Viajero, Hotel Las Vegas* and *Hotel Nohelia*.

Cabinas Helga has parking, and clean rooms with private bath and fans for US$6/9 single/double. Similarly priced hotels include *Cabinas Fontana, Cabinas Heyleen* and *Hotel Musuco* – all look clean. The Musuco also has some cheaper rooms with communal baths.

Places to Eat

The *Cabinas El Rancho* has a reasonable restaurant attached. The best place in town is the *Restaurant La Moderna* which has a variety of meals ranging from hamburgers and pizza to chicken and fish. Meals are in the US$2 to US$5 range.

The *Bar Europa* is run by a friendly Belgian woman, Lillian, and is a good place for a drink in the evening. Lillian prepares good European style food if you give her a couple of days notice.

Getting There & Away

Air SANSA has flights from Coto 47 to San José at 12.25 pm on Monday, Wednesday and Friday, and at 12.05 pm on Tuesday, Thursday and Saturday. The flights from San José on Monday, Wednesday and Friday come via Palmar Sur; the other three are direct flights. Coto 47 is about seven km south-west of Neily, and is the closest airport to Panama. Some of the local buses pass near the airport.

Bus TRACOPA buses from San José leave five times a day from Avenida 18, Calle 4. Most of these buses continue on to the Panamanian border at Paso Canoas after stopping at Neily.

In Neily, the TRACOPA bus terminal is on the north side of the Plaza. Direct buses to San José leave five times a day, take seven hours and cost US$5.50. Buses to San Isidro leave four times a day.

The bus terminal at the north-east end of town has buses to many destinations. Buses leave for Paso Canoas 17 times a day and cost US$0.30 for the ride. Buses for Golfito (US$0.55, 1½ hours) leave 15 times a day. Buses for San Vito (US$1.50, 2½ hours) leave at 6 and 11 am, and 1 and 3 pm. Buses for Puerto Jiménez leave at 7 am and 2 pm and take five to six hours. Many local communities are served, including the Fincas 40, Pueblo Nuevo, Piñuelas, Cortes and Zancudo – these services may depend on how much it's been raining.

You can also catch buses to Golfito and Canoas from the bus stop at the south-east corner of the Plaza, although you get a better choice of seats at the terminal.

Taxi Jeep taxis (4WD) are available to take you almost anywhere. From Neily to Paso Canoas costs about US$6l; to Coto 47 the fare is about US$2.50. Taxis between Coto 7 and Paso Canoas cost about US$8.

SAN VITO

With a population of about 10,000, this pleasant town at 980 metres above sea level offers a respite from the heat of the nearby lowlands. The drive up from Neily is a very scenic one, with superb views of the lowlands dropping away as the bus climbs the steep and winding road up the coastal mountain range (called Fila Cruces).

Some buses from Neily go via Cañas Gordas, which is on the Panamanian border but is not an official crossing point – although you can see Panama. There is reportedly a pensión here. The bus continues through Sabalito (which has a gas station and basic hotel) before reaching San Vito. Other buses go more directly, passing the Wilson Botanical Gardens about six km before reaching San Vito.

You can also get to San Vito from San José via the Coto Brus Valley – this route is also scenic and involves crossing the upper Río Terraba by ferry, soon after leaving the Interamerican Highway. (A bridge is planned, but the ferry is more fun if you are not in any hurry.)

San Vito was founded by Italian immigrants in the early 1950s, and today you can still hear Italian spoken in the streets. The most exciting thing to do in San Vito is to eat Italian food in one of the Italian restaurants. San Vito is also a good base for visits to the Wilson Botanical Gardens and to the La Amistad International Park.

Places to Stay

The *Hotel Collina Annex* is clean and charges US$2.30 per person in rooms with shared bath. The *Hotel Tropical* is similarly priced. For US$4.75/7.75 for a single/double you can stay at the *Cabinas Mirlas* (☎ 773054) which is clean, quiet and pleasant with tepid water in the private showers. Windows open onto an orchard. Go down the

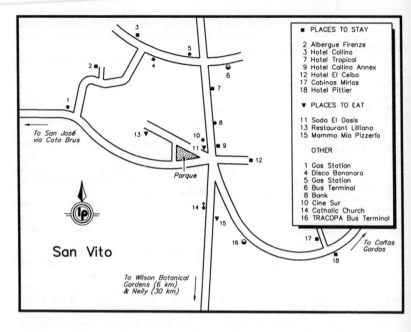

PLACES TO STAY

2 Albergue Firenze
3 Hotel Collina
7 Hotel Tropical
9 Hotel Collina Annex
12 Hotel El Ceibo
17 Cabinas Mirlas
18 Hotel Pittier

PLACES TO EAT

11 Soda El Oasis
13 Restaurant Lilliana
15 Mamma Mia Pizzería

OTHER

1 Gas Station
4 Disco Bananara
5 Gas Station
6 Bus Terminal
8 Bank
10 Cine Sur
14 Catholic Church
16 TRACOPA Bus Terminal

San Vito

Parque

To San José
via Coto Brus

To Cañas
Gordas

To Wilson Botanical
Gardens (6 km)
& Neily (30 km)

drive about 150 metres to the house on the right to ask about these cabins.

Similarly priced hotels are the *Hotel Collina* and *Hotel Pittier* which are both clean and OK. The *Hotel El Ceibo* (☎ 773025) is also good and costs a few cents more. It's reputedly the best in town.

There's also the *Albergue Firenze*, which has a boy scout fleur-de-lis symbol in front of it and is probably an inexpensive place to stay.

Places to Eat

The *Hotel El Ceibo* and the *Hotel Collina* both have OK restaurants. Italian restaurants include the *Restaurant Lilliana* which has pizza, Italian and local food for US$2 to US$4; and the *Mamma Mia Pizzería*, which is another good choice.

The *Soda El Oasis* has cheap snacks. After dinner, check out the *Disco Bananara*, particularly at weekends.

Getting There & Away

TRACOPA has buses to and from San José. In San Vito, the TRACOPA terminal is at the south end of town. They have direct buses to San José at 5 am and 3 pm, and slower buses at 7 and 10 am. They also have buses to San Isidro at 6 am and 1 pm.

The 'downtown' bus terminal (☎ 773010) has buses for many local destinations. Buses to Neily leave at 5.30 and 11 am, and 1.30 pm. For La Amistad International Park, there are buses to Las Mellizas at 9.30 am and 2 pm; to Las Tablas at 10.30 am and 3 pm; and Cotón at 3 pm. Other nearby destinations served include Río Sereno, Los Reyes, La Maravilla, Agua Buena, Cañas Gordas and Los Planos.

WILSON BOTANICAL GARDENS

These gardens are six km south of San Vito. They are very well laid out and many of the plants are labelled. Wandering around the grounds is fun, and the labels turn the walk into a learning adventure. There are many trails, each named for the plants found alongside. Trails include the Heliconia Loop Trail, the Bromeliad Walk, the Tree Fern Hill Trail, the Orchid Walk, Fern Gully and the Bamboo Walk. Most of these trails take 30 minutes to an hour at a very leisurely pace. Other trails are longer, such as the River Trail for which three hours is the suggested time.

The garden was established by Robert and Catherine Wilson in 1963 and became internationally known for its collection. The gardens themselves cover 10 hectares and are surrounded by 145 hectares of natural forest. In 1973, the area came under the auspices of the Organization for Tropical Studies and in 1983 was incorporated into UNESCO's La Amistad Biosphere Reserve.

Today, the well-maintained collection includes over 1000 genera of plants in about 200 families. This attracts both birds and human visitors. As part of OTS, the gardens play a scientific role as a research centre. Species threatened with extinction are preserved here for possible reforestation in the future. Study of conservation, sustainable development, horticulture and agroecology are primary research aims and scientific training and public education are also important aspects of the facilities. Students and researchers stay here and use the greenhouse and laboratory facilities. Members of the public can also be accommodated.

The dry season is January to March, when it is easier to get around the gardens. Nevertheless, the vegetation in the wet months is exuberant with many epiphytic bromeliads, ferns and orchids being sustained by the moisture in the air. Annual rainfall is about 4000 mm and average high temperatures are about 26°C.

Information
The gardens are open daily, except Mondays, from 8 am to 4 pm. Foreign travellers are charged US$3 to get in (a suggested donation) whilst ticos are charged US$0.25 in an attempt to foster interest in plant conservation among locals. A trail map is provided.

The money goes to maintaining the gardens and research facilities.

Places to Stay & Eat
Overnight guests can be accommodated if reservations are made in advance with OTS (☎ 366696), Apartado 676, 2050 San Pedro, San José, Costa Rica. The dry months and July and August are popular with visiting research and student groups, who have priority. Make reservations as far in advance as possible for these months.

Accommodation is in six rooms with four beds each and shared bathrooms with hot water, and there are two double rooms with private baths. Meals and laundry facilities are provided for overnight guests. Rates are US$40 per person per night, including meals. Lunch-only can be arranged for US$15. You can call the gardens direct at 773278 if you are already in San Vito – they may be able to accommodate or feed you if there is space available, although reservations are requested. Also call the gardens direct to arrange guided tours.

About 600 metres before you get to the gardens from San Vito, on the left-hand side, there is the *La Cascada Cabinas & Restaurant*. You can stay here for about US$4 per person in clean simple cabins with cold baths. The restaurant is closed on Tuesdays. Otherwise, stay in San Vito.

Getting There & Away
Buses between San Vito and Neily (and other destinations) pass the entrance to the gardens several times a day. Ask at the bus terminal about the right bus, because some buses to Neily take a different route. A taxi to the gardens costs US$2 to US$3. It is a six km walk from San Vito, mainly uphill, to the gardens (and downhill back!)

PASO CANOAS
This small town is on the Interamerican Highway at the Panamanian border, and is therefore the main land port of entry between Costa Rica and Panama. It is a popular destination for ticos who come here on shopping trips to buy goods more cheaply than in San

José. Therefore hotels are often full with bargain hunters during weekends and holidays, at which time you should go on to Neily, 17 km away. Most of the shops and hotels are on the Costa Rican side.

See the Getting There & Away chapter for full details of the border crossing to or from Panama.

Information

Paso Canoas has a gas station. Moneychangers hang out around the border, and give better rates than banks for exchanging cash US dollars to colones. You can also convert excess colones to dollars, but this exchange is not as good. Try to get rid of as much Costa Rican currency as possible before crossing into Panama. Colones are accepted on the border, but are difficult to get rid of further into Panama. Other currencies are harder to deal with. Travellers' cheques can be negotiated with persistence, but are not as readily accepted as cash. There are banks but they are only open in the mornings from Monday to Friday. The Panamanian currency is the balboa which is on par with and interchangeable with cash US dollars.

Places to Stay & Eat

The *Hotel Miami* is the cheapest place to stay. The *Hotel Palace Sur* next door is better and charges US$3 per person.

The *Cabinas Interamericano* has clean rooms with private bath for about US$4.75 per person. *Cabinas Los Arcos* charges about US$7 per room with private bath and fan. One or two people can sleep in each room. Next door is the *Hospedaje Hortensia* in the same price range.

There are a number of cheap *sodas* where you can eat. One of the better restaurants is in the *Cabinas Interamericano*.

Getting There & Away

Buses from the TRACOPA terminal in San José leave several times a day, but make reservations if travelling on Friday night because the bus is usually full of weekend shoppers. The same applies to buses leaving Paso Canoas on Sundays. Buses leave Paso Canoas for San José at 9 am, and 12.45 and 2.45 pm; the fare is about US$5.25 for the approximately eight hour ride along the Interamerican Highway.

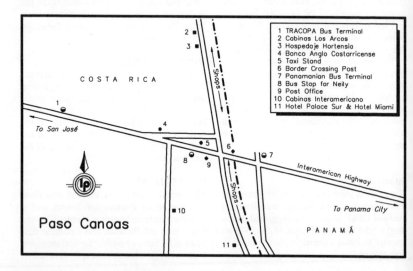

1 TRACOPA Bus Terminal
2 Cabinas Los Arcos
3 Hospedaje Hortensia
4 Banco Anglo Costarricense
5 Taxi Stand
6 Border Crossing Post
7 Panamanian Bus Terminal
8 Bus Stop for Neily
9 Post Office
10 Cabinas Interamericano
11 Hotel Palace Sur & Hotel Miami

COSTA RICA

To San José

Shops

Shops

Interamerican Highway

To Panama City

Paso Canoas

PANAMÁ

Top: Red-lored parrot (RR)
Bottom: Golden toads mating (RL)

Top: Bromeliad in flower, Wilson Botanical Gardens, San Vito (RR)
Bottom: Palm, Wilson Botanical Gardens, San Vito (RR)

Buses for Neily leave about every hour during daylight hours, from less than 100 metres away from the border. If you just miss one and don't want to wait for the next, a taxi will take you the 17 km to Neily for US$6.

The nearest airport to the border is at Coto 47, near Neily.

The Central Pacific Coast

Costa Rica's major Pacific coastal town is Puntarenas, about 110 km west of San José by paved highway. This has traditionally been the town for highlanders to descend to when they wanted to spend a few days by the ocean, but there are now many other popular vacation spots on the Pacific coast south of Puntarenas, These include swimming and surfing beach resorts, sport-fishing towns, well developed and almost undeveloped beaches, a biological reserve and the famous coastal national park at Manuel Antonio.

Generally speaking, the Pacific coast is better developed for tourism than the Caribbean, and if you are looking for some luxury, it is easy to find here. On the other hand, you can also find deserted beaches, wildlife and small coastal villages.

There is a marked wet/dry season along the Pacific coast. The rains begin in April, and from May to November you can expect a lot of precipitation. This eases in December and the dry season continues for the next four months. The dry months coincide with Costa Rican school vacations in January and February, and the biggest holiday of the year at Easter. So the dry season is the high season – wherever you travel on the Pacific coast, expect a lot of visitors and make sure you have hotel reservations at weekends. During Easter week, most beach hotels are booked weeks or months in advance. If you travel during the low (wet) season, you'll see fewer visitors and have little difficulty in booking into hotels. Low season discounts are worth asking about. (The prices given throughout this chapter are the high season rates.)

Average temperatures on the coast, year round, are about 22°C minimum and about 32°C maximum. The dry season is generally a little hotter than the wet.

PUNTARENAS

This city of 36,000 inhabitants is the capital of the province of Puntarenas, which

stretches along the Pacific coast from the Gulf of Nicoya to the Panamanian border.

During the 19th century, in the days before easy access to the Caribbean coast, Puntarenas was Costa Rica's major port. Goods such as coffee were hauled by ox-cart from the highlands down the Pacific slope to Puntarenas, from where they were shipped around the Horn to Europe. A long trip!

After the opening up of the railway to Puerto Limón, Puntarenas became less significant, but still remained the most important port on the Pacific side of the country. Recently, a new port was built at Caldera, about 18 km south-east of Puntarenas by road, and this new facility has become the major Pacific port.

Despite the loss of shipping, Puntarenas remains a bustling town during the dry season, when tourists arrive. During the wet months, however, the city is much quieter.

The geographical setting of the town is an intriguing one. Puntarenas literally means a 'sandy point' or sand spit, and the city is on the end of a sandy peninsula that is almost eight km long, but only 600 metres wide at its widest point (downtown) and less than 100 metres wide in many other parts. The

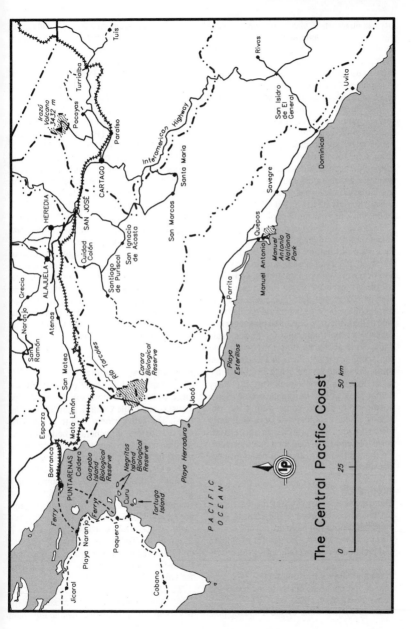

The Central Pacific Coast

city has 60 streets (Calles) from west to east, but has only five Avenidas running north to south at its widest point. Riding into town on the train or bus with the waters of the Pacific lapping up on either side of the road and rails is a memorable experience. Make sure you leave or arrive in daylight hours to see this.

With such a long, narrow street configuration, you are never more than a few minutes walk away from the coast. There are plenty of sandy beaches, but unfortunately they are too polluted for swimming (although the local kids do so). You can walk along the beach, or the aptly named Paseo de los Turistas beach road stretching along the southern coast of town, but if you want to swim, stick to your hotel pool.

Although the town is popular with Costa Rican holiday makers, foreigners tend to look for a destination where they can swim. There are plenty of possibilities in the towns and beaches south of Puntarenas, and many people go there and avoid Puntarenas completely. There are also good beaches and resorts in the Nicoya Peninsula on the other side of the Gulf of Nicoya, and passenger and car ferries leave Puntarenas for the peninsula daily. So if you're heading for Nicoya, you can spend a night or two in Puntarenas en route. Hang out on the beach front with the local tourists, and check out the busy comings and goings during the season. Some people even like to come during the wet season when it is quiet and fresh with daily rain showers. It certainly is the closest coastal town to San José for a quick getaway – although there are plenty of better beaches elsewhere.

Information

There are several banks along the two blocks of Avenida 3 between Calle Central & 3. Puntarenas does not have the normal central plaza or town square. Be careful of thieves and pickpockets, especially along the beach.

Places to Stay – bottom end

One of the cheapest hotels is the basic and rather noisy *Hotel Río* on Calle Central, Avenida 3, just next to the Paquera boat dock. The management is friendly and rooms have fans and communal bathrooms. Rates are US$2.75 per person.

For US$3.50 per person you can stay in the basic but friendly *Pensión Cabezas* on Avenida 1, Calle 2 & 4. There are clean rooms with fans and communal bathrooms. Also in this price range is the *Pensión Chinchilla* on Calle 1, Avenida Central & 2.

The *Hotel Ayi Con* (☎ 610164) on Calle 2, Avenida 1 & 3, charges about US$5 per person. Some rooms have private baths, others don't; some rooms have air-con, others have fans – you get what you pay for. The rooms are pretty basic, but clean.

The Youth Hostel Association in San José (☎ 244085) can make reservations (strongly suggested) for members at the *Cabinas San Isidro* for US$5 per person. San Isidro is a Puntarenas suburb about eight km east of downtown Puntarenas, and there are buses to and from town. The cabinas are near a beach, there are cooking facilities, a restaurant, and a swimming pool. Ask the bus to drop you off at the Monseñor Sanabria Hospital bus stop, from where it's about a 300 metre walk. Rates are more expensive for non-YHA members.

Places to Stay – middle

The *Gran Hotel Imperial* (☎ 610579) is a large old wooden hotel on Paseo de los Turistas and Calle Central, near the bus stations. The better rooms tend to be upstairs, and the doubles are generally better than the smaller singles. Rooms with fans and a communal bath are US$6.65 per person.

The *Gran Hotel Chorotega* (☎ 610998) at Avenida 3, Calle 1, has clean rooms with a private bath and fan for US$8.50/14.50 single/double; rooms with communal baths are about US$3 cheaper. The family run *Cabinas Central* (☎ 611484) on Calle 7, Paseo de los Turistas & Avenida 2, is clean and safe. The rooms are cell-like rather than cabin-like, but have private baths and fans for US$7/12 single/double.

The *Hotel Cayuga* (☎ 610344), on Calle 4, Avenida Central & 1, gets mixed reports. My room with private bath had no hot water

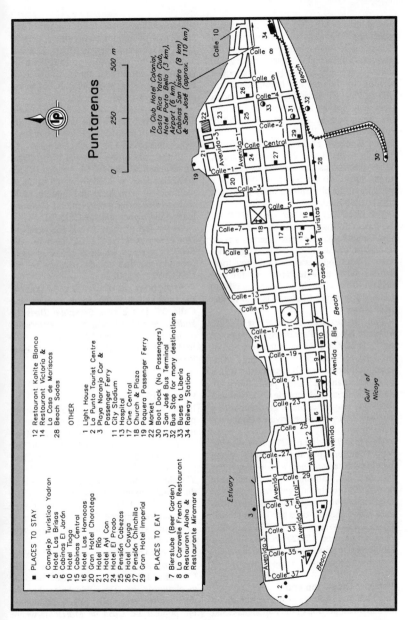

Puntarenas

0   250   500 m

PLACES TO STAY

4 Complejo Turístico Yadran
5 Hotel Las Brisas
6 Cabinas El Jardín
10 Hotel Tioga
15 Cabinas Central
16 Hotel Las Hamacas
20 Gran Hotel Chorotega
21 Hotel Río
23 Hotel Ayi Con
24 Hotel El Prado
25 Pensión Cabezas
26 Hotel Coyoga
27 Pensión Chinchilla
29 Gran Hotel Imperial

PLACES TO EAT

7 Bierstube (Beer Garden)
8 La Caravelle French Restaurant
9 Restaurant Aloha &
   Restaurante Miramare

12 Restaurant Kahite Blanco
14 Restaurant Victoria &
   La Casa de Mariscos
28 Beach Sodas

OTHER

1 Light House
2 La Punta Tourist Centre
3 Playa Naranjo Car &
   Passenger Ferry
11 City Stadium
13 Hospital
17 Cine Central
18 Church & Plaza
19 Paquera Passenger Ferry
22 Market
30 Boat Dock (No Passengers)
31 San José Bus Terminal
32 Bus Stop for many destinations
33 Buses to Liberia
34 Railway Station

To Club Hotel Colonial,
Costa Rica Yacht Club,
Hotel Porto Bello (3 km),
Airport (6 km),
Cabinas San Isidro (8 km)
& San José (approx. 110 km)

Estuary

Gulf of Nicoya

Beach

but did have a very efficient air-con system, which was a relief in the hot temperatures. The rooms are uninspiring but clean and the restaurant attached to the hotel is quite good, although not very cheap. There is a locked parking lot behind the hotel. Rates are US$11.30/21.30 for a single/double – not a great deal, but not bad either. Reservations can be made at Apartado 306, 5400 Puntarenas, Costa Rica.

The *Cabinas El Jorón* (☎ 610467) on Avenida 4 bis, Calle 25, has both small, rather dark rooms and roomier cabins. The rooms have private baths, air-con and a refrigerator (locally called a 'refri'), and cost US$18 for a double.

The *Hotel Las Hamacas* (☎ 610398), on the Paseo de los Turistas, Calle 5 & 7, is popular with younger ticos. There is a pool, restaurant, disco and bar, so it can get a bit noisy if your room is close to the revelries. Rooms with private bath and fan are US$17.30 for a double, with air-con US$20 double. The *Hotel El Prado* is also in this price range.

The *Hotel Las Brisas* (☎ 612120; Apartado 83, 5400 Puntarenas) on Paseo de los Turistas, Calle 31, near the very end of the point of Puntarenas, is a recently renovated, quiet, clean and pleasant hotel with a good restaurant and small pool. Rates are US$22/30 for a single/double at the back and US$34/44 single/double at the front with a sea view. All rooms have private bath and hot water.

The *Hotel Tioga* (☎ 610271; Apartado 96, 5400 Puntarenas) is the best hotel in the middle price range. There's 46 rooms, but as it's often full, call ahead. All rooms have air-con and private bath with hot water. The more expensive rooms have balconies with a sea view; cheaper ones are inside around the pool. Rates range from US$21 to US$32 for a single, and US$27 to US$40 for a double, and this includes breakfast in the 4th floor dining room with ocean view.

Places to Stay – top end

There are three hotels in Cocal, a suburb on the narrowest portion of the Puntarenas sand

spit, about three km east of downtown. They are all next to one another between Calles 68 & 74, just north of Avenida Alberto Echandi Montero, the eastward prolongation of Avenida Central. All three hotels have mooring facilities, pools, air-con, hot water, restaurants and clean, pleasant rooms.

The cheapest of the three is the *Club Hotel Colonial* (☎ 611833; Apartado 368, 5400 Puntarenas or telephone 291931 in San José) which charges US$33/42 single/double.

To the right of the Colonial is the *Costa Rica Yacht Club* (☎ 610784; Apartado 2530, 1000 San José, ☎ 223818) which caters to members of both local and foreign yacht clubs as well as the general public. Rates are marginally higher than the Colonial.

To the left of those two is the excellent *Hotel Porto Bello* (☎ 611322; Apartado 108, 5400 Puntarenas which is set in pleasant grounds and has rooms with patios for US$42/50 single/double.

At the other end of town near the point of the sand spit at Paseo de los Turistas and Calle 35, is the new *Complejo Turistico Yadran* (☎ 612662) which has comfortable rooms with all the usual facilities, plus TV, for US$60 double. Bicycles are available for hire at US$12 per day.

Places to Eat

Eating in Puntarenas (at least in the cheaper places) tends to be a little more expensive than in other parts of Costa Rica. Many restaurants are along the Paseo de los Turistas and so tend to be tourist oriented and a little more pricey – but not outrageously so. The cheapest food for the impecunious is in the *sodas* around the market area, by the Paquera boat dock. There are also several inexpensive Chinese restaurants within a block or two of the intersection of Calle Central and Avenida Central.

There is a row of fairly cheap *sodas* on the beach by the Paseo de los Turistas, Calle Central and 3. They serve snacks and non-alcoholic drinks. Three blocks to the east there are two reasonably priced restaurants, the popular *La Casa de Mariscos*, where

English is spoken, and the *Restaurant Victoria*, which serves Chinese food and seafood.

Just west of the Hotel Tioga are four international restaurants to choose from. The *Restaurant Aloha* is one of the better ones in town and has meals in the US$5 to US$10 range. The *Restaurante Miramare* (☎ 610066) next door serves good seafood cooked Italian style. Half a block further is the *La Caravelle* French restaurant with meals in the US$4 to US$8 price range; it is closed on Mondays. Just beyond is a German style beer garden, the *Bierstube* (☎ 610330). Apart from beer, it has a variety of snacks and light meals.

On the north side of town, at Avenida 1 and Calle 19, is the *Restaurant Kahite Blanco* (☎ 612093) which is a rambling restaurant popular with the locals. It serves good seafood in the US$3 to US$6 range. They have music and dancing at weekends.

Most of the better hotels have decent restaurants.

Getting There & Away

Air There are no regularly scheduled flights here, but you can charter a plane to the Chacarita airstrip, six or seven km east of downtown Puntarenas.

Bus The drive from San José takes less than two hours and costs about US$1.50. Buses leave frequently from Calle 12, Avenida 9. From Puntarenas, buses for San José leave frequently from the terminal on Calle 2, just north of the Paseo de los Turistas.

Across the Paseo from the San José bus terminal is a covered bus stop right by the ocean, from where buses leave to many nearby destinations. There are 10 buses daily to Miramar (near the Peñas Blancas Wildlife Refuge), five daily to Liberia, and buses inland to Esparza every hour or so. Buses to communities on the coast north of Puntarenas include a 1 pm bus to Pitahaya, a 12.15 pm bus to Chomes, and buses to Costa de Pajaro at 10.45 am and 4.30 pm.

Other buses include the 11.30 am and 4.30 pm departures for Tilarán, a bus to Guácimal at 1 pm, and a bus for Santa Elena (near

Monteverde) at 2.15 pm. Buses to Quepos (which could drop you at Jacó) leave at 5 am and 2.30 pm.

Buses for the port of Caldera (also going past Doña Ana Beach and Mata Limón) leave from the market about every hour and head out of town along Avenida Central.

There is also a bus stop for Liberia at Calle 4, Avenida Central.

Train The train station is at the eastern end of downtown. There are daily departures for San José at 6 am and 3 pm. The four hour trip costs US$1.10.

Boat There are two ferry terminals. The Playa Naranjo terminal (☎ 611069) at the north-west end of town has a car/passenger ferry which does the 1½ hour trip to Playa Naranjo, on the Nicoya Peninsula west of Puntarenas. There are departures at 7 am and 4 pm daily and at 11 am on Thursday, Saturday and Sunday. The fare is US$0.85 for adults, half fare for children, and US$6 for cars. There is rarely any problem with getting a passenger ticket, but cars may be turned away so try to get in line a couple of hours early. (Note that if you want to continue from Playa Naranjo without a car, the only buses meeting the ferry go to Nicoya.)

The Paquera ferry terminal at the dock behind the market has passenger boats only. There are daily departures at 6 am and 3 pm for the village of Paquera, a 1½ hour ride away to the south-east across the Gulf of Nicoya. The fare is US$1.20 per person. En route, the ferry passes near the Guayabo Island Biological Reserve, which is known for its sea bird colonies. Buses heading further south into the Nicoya Peninsula meet the ferries in Paquera.

On Sunday a ferry leaves from by the Paquera ferry terminal at 9 am for Isla San Lucas, returning at 3 pm. The island is a prison, and you can visit the prisoners and buy their handicrafts to give them pocket money. The prisoners enjoy meeting other people and are reasonably pleasant. If you want to do this, bear in mind that the prisoners' families will also be visiting the island, the boat will be very crowded, and you should get there at least an hour early to find a seat. Single female visitors should not go without an escort – the prisoners rarely get to see single women and can be overly 'friendly'. There are good beaches on the island, but don't miss the boat back!

You can charter boats to the above destinations, and others throughout the Gulf of Nicoya. Small boats holding up to six passengers are available from Taximar (☎ 611143, 610331) for US$20 to US$40 per hour, depending on the size and type of boat. The offices are in the Hotel Río building, near the Paquera boat dock.

Taxi Bus lines can be very long during dry season weekends. A taxi back to San José costs about US$80. You can also get taxis to take you south to other beach destinations.

Getting Around
Buses marked 'Ferry' run up Avenida Central and go to the Playa Naranjo terminal, two km from downtown. The taxi fare from the San José bus terminal to the ferry terminal is about US$2.

ESPARZA
This small town is about 20 km inland from Puntarenas, and the two are linked by hourly buses. It is a clean and pleasant town, with a few inexpensive hotels which can provide an alternative to Puntarenas. These include the *Pensión Cordoba* and *Pensión Fanny* (☎ 635158) which charge about US$3 or US$4 per person, and the more expensive *Hotel Castanuelas* (☎ 635105) which has rooms with private baths, some with air-con.

TORTUGA ISLAND
This is actually two uninhabited islands off the coast of the Nicoya Peninsula near Paquera. There are beautiful beaches for snorkelling and swimming.

Tours
The islands can be reached by daily boat tours from Puntarenas. Tours from San José cost US$65 per person and include continental breakfast in San José, a private bus to Puntarenas, boat trip to the islands, delicious picnic lunch and cocktails on the deserted beaches, time for swimming, snorkelling and sunbathing, and transport back to San José. The fare from Puntarenas is marginally cheaper. Two island biological reserves, famous for their sea bird colonies, are passed en route.

Although this trip is not cheap, the yacht *Calypso* (☎ 333617 or 553022 in San José; 610585 in Puntarenas) has built up a reputation for excellence in food and service for this trip and has many repeat customers. Reservations can be made at Apartado 6941, 1000 San José. *Calypso* has been operating since the mid 1970s and there are now other companies which also do the trip. These include Bay Island Cruises (☎ 312898) and Fantasy Cruises (☎ 550791, 610697). Better hotels in Puntarenas and San José, and travel agents in San José, can book this cruise for you.

GUAYABO & NEGRITOS ISLANDS BIOLOGICAL RESERVES
These two islands in the Gulf of Nicoya are well known sea bird sanctuaries, and so are protected, with no land visitors allowed except researchers with permission from the National Parks Service. The reserves can be visited by boat however, and you can observe many of the sea birds from the boats. The Paqueras ferry is the cheapest way to get fairly close, and the Tortuga Island trips and chartered boats are another way to go.

Guayabo Island is a 6.8 hectare cliff-bound, rocky islet about eight km south-west of Puntarenas, and two km south-east of Isla San Lucas. There is very little vegetation. Costa Rica's largest nesting colony of brown pelicans (60 pairs) is found here, and the peregrine falcon overwinters on the island. Both Guayabo and Negritos have magnificent frigate bird and brown booby colonies.

The Negritos Islands are two islands 16 km south of Puntarenas, with a combined size of 80 hectares. Although they are only a few hundred metres from the Nicoya Peninsula, both these biological reserves are more frequently visited with boats from Puntarenas, though you may be able to find someone from Paquera to take you out in a boat. Negritos Islands are covered with more vegetation than Guayabo, and frangipani, gumbo limbo and spiny cedar have been reported as the dominant trees.

DOÑA ANA BEACH
This is the first clean beach south of Puntarenas, and is about 12 km away from downtown. There are actually two beaches a few hundred metres from one another: Boca Barranca and Doña Ana. Surfing is reportedly good at both beaches. The Doña Ana beach has been developed for tourism – there is a sign on the coastal highway south of Puntarenas but it's not easy to see. The *Soda Doña Ana* is by the turn-off. At the beach entrance there is a parking lot. Daily use fee for the beach is US$0.40 for adults, half that for children. There are snack bars, picnic ramadas and changing areas.

Places to Stay
On the left of the coastal highway, just before reaching Doña Ana, is the *Hotel Río Mar* (☎ 630158) which has rooms with private bath for about US$10 per person.

Getting There & Away
You can get to this area from Puntarenas on buses heading for Caldera.

MATA LIMÓN
This is an old beach resort which has long been popular with locals from Puntarenas as well as highlanders. It is near the new port of Caldera, and buses from Puntarenas to Caldera will get you to Mata Limón. There is also a train station and any of the Puntarenas to San José trains can put you down here.

The resort is around a mangrove lagoon which is good for bird-watching. The village is divided into two by a river, with the railway station on the north side.

Places to Stay
Two of the better hotels are the *Manglares*

(☎ 634010), near the train station, and the *Casablanca* (☎ 222921) nearby. Both have rooms with private bath for about US$8/14 single/double.

South of the river there are several cheaper hotels.

CARARA BIOLOGICAL RESERVE
This 4700 hectare reserve is at the mouth of the Río Tarcoles, about 57 km south-east of Puntarenas by road. The reserve is surrounded by pasture and agricultural land, and forms an oasis for wildlife from a large surrounding area. It is the northernmost tropical wet forest on the Pacific coast, and is known for its abundant birds and diverse plants. There are also archaeological remains which you can see with a guide – but they are not very exciting ruins.

If driving from Puntarenas or San José, pull over to the left immediately after crossing the Río Tarcoles bridge. Carefully scan the river, particularly the muddy banks, and you will often be rewarded with a view of basking crocodiles. Binoculars help a great deal. A variety of water birds may also be seen – herons, spoonbills, storks and anhingas. Half a km further south on the left hand side is a locked gate where you can park your car and walk in to the reserve. A further 2¼ km brings you to the Carara Reserve administration building which is open from 8 am to 12 noon, and 1 to 4 pm. There are bathrooms, picnic tables and a short nature trail. You can get information here and pay the US$1.20 fee to enter the reserve.

A variety of forest birds inhabit the reserve, but can be difficult to see without an experienced guide. The most exciting bird for many visitors is the brilliantly patterned scarlet macaw which is seen here, especially in June and July. Other birds to watch for include guans, trogons, toucans, motmots and many other forest species. Monkeys, squirrels, sloths and agoutis are among the more common mammals present.

The dry season from December to April is the easiest time to go – though the animals arc still there in the wet months! Rainfall is almost 3000 mm annually, which is less than the rainforests further south. Carara is in a transition zone between the wet and dry tropical forests, and hence is of great interest to biologists. It is fairly hot, with average temperatures of 25°C to 28°C – but it is cooler within the rainforest. Make sure you have insect repellent. An umbrella is important in the wet season – and occasionally in the dry months.

Tours
If you are not experienced at watching for wildlife in the rainforest, you will have difficulty in seeing very much. Going on a tour with a guide is expensive, but worthwhile if you want to see a reasonable number of different species. Geotur (☎ 341867) and Costa Rica Expeditions (☎ 570766) both have day tours to Carara from San José for US$65 per person. It takes about 2½ hours to drive down from San José.

Places to Stay
Camping is not allowed and there is nowhere to stay in the reserve, so most people come on day trips. There is simple accommodation available at Playa Tarcoles, two or three km from the reserve. There is a gravel beach here which is good for watching shorebirds.

Getting There & Away
There are no buses to Carara, but you can get off any bus bound for Jacó, Quepos or Manuel Antonio. This may be a bit problematical at weekends when buses are full – so go midweek.

Many of the remoter parts of the Pacific coast are best visited by car.

PLAYA HERRADURA
Herradura is on the coastal highway about 10 km south of Carara. A turn-off here leads three km west to Playa Herradura – a quiet, sheltered, palm-fringed, black-sand beach. There are simple restaurants, cabins and places to camp – either come by car or walk the three km from the highway.

Places to Stay
Development is minimal. At the point where

the road reaches the beach is a campsite with bathrooms available. The cost is US$1.75 per person.

Nearby is the *Cabinas Herradura* (☎ 455775, 643181) which charge US$26 for cabins which sleep six people, but may charge more during dry season weekends.

JACÓ
Jacó Beach is the first developed beach resort on the Pacific coast as you head south, and is the closest resort to San José. It is popular and crowded by Costa Rican standards – though it will seem relatively quiet to many visitors who may be used to shoulder to shoulder sunbathing on their own crowded beaches. The turn-off from the coastal highway for Jacó is just five km beyond Herradura, so you have the choice of beaches. Jacó Beach is about two km off the coastal highway. The beach itself is about three km long, and hotels and restaurants are scattered along the road running behind it.

Jacó has something of a reputation as a 'party beach' – especially during the dry season – but it is pretty sedate compared to some of the North American 'party beaches' like Daytona Beach in Florida. Nevertheless, it is popular with young people and the beaches are reasonably clean and swimming is possible, though you should be careful of rip currents.

Jacó is also something of a surfers' hangout, although Jacó Beach itself does not offer the best surfing. To get better surfing, head out to Tivives and Boca Barranca on the way back to Puntarenas, or to Hermosa, Esterillos and Bejuco south of town. You need either a rental car or a taxi to get to most of these places easily.

Information
The Banco Nacional de Costa Rica (☎ 643072) changes money. There are a number of stores where you can buy your own food and several souvenir shops where you can spend the money you saved by buying your own food.

Ferretería Macho e Hijos (☎ 643036) is a hardware shop and has bicycle rentals. Bicycles can also be hired from the store next door to the Hotel El Jardín for about US$1.75 per hour or US$6 per day. Some hotels also rent bikes.

Cars can be rented from Fantasy Rent-a-Car at the Hotel Jacó Beach.

Fishing and tour boats (☎ 643002, 643067) can be hired from near the bus stop at the town entrance.

Places to Stay

Reservations are strongly recommended during the dry season, and definitely required during Easter week and most weekends. There are plenty of places to stay – but few in the bottom end price range. Low season discounts are available in most hotels, as are surfers' discounts – the latter probably because surfers tend to stay for days or even weeks. If you plan on a lengthy stay (surfer or not) ask for a discount. The rates given here are full high season rates, but discounts could be as high as 40% to 50% if you're staying for several nights in the low season.

Jacó Beach is a growing resort – you can expect more hotels to open in the future.

Places to Stay – bottom end

Cabinas Alice (☎ 643061), across from the Red Cross building, has basic rooms with private bath for US$14 double. Nearby, the *Cabinas Andrea* is similarly priced. The *Cabinas Naranjal* (☎ 643006) near the south-east end of the beach is also in the same price range.

Cabinas Heredia (☎ 643171, 633131; Apartado 8, Jacó, Puntarenas) has basic but clean rooms with private showers and fans for about US$7.75 per person, and there is a restaurant attached. The friendly, North American owned *Cabinas Las Brisas* (☎ 643074, 643087) has rooms with a double and single bed which cost from US$13 to US$26 per room. The cheaper ones are very basic with no fans, but are clean, and the beachfront location is pleasant.

Cabinas Garabito charges US$11.75/16 single/double in clean rooms with private bath and fans.

If you have a tent you could try *Camping El Hicaco* (☎ 643004) which has a bathroom and tent space for about US$2 per person. Ask around for other tent spaces.

Places to Stay – middle

Cabinas Los Ranchos (☎ 643156), run by Charlotte Dean, is very popular with English speaking visitors who often rent rooms on a long term basis. There are many repeat clients. Rooms are quiet and have fans, refrigerator, stove and private bath with warm water for about US$10 per person – an excellent deal if you can get in. Also in this price range is *Cabinas Antonio* (☎ 643043) which has clean and reasonably quiet rooms with private bath and fans.

Cabinas Las Palmas (☎ 643005; Apartado 5, Jacó, Puntarenas) is set in a pleasant garden and has rooms with private bath and fans for US$23 for a double. They also have some new cabins with kitchenettes attached, but these are more expensive. *Cabinas Zabamar* (☎ 643174) has a pool, and the pleasant rooms with private bath, fan and refrigerator rent for US$23.50/29.50 single/double.

The *Hotel El Jardín* (☎ 643050) has a pool, green areas and a good restaurant serving French cuisine. Rooms have fans and private baths with hot water. Rates are US$25/33.50 single/double.

Villas Miramar (☎ 643003) has quiet and pleasant apartments with kitchenettes, private bath with hot water, and one or two bedrooms, each with a double and a single bed. Rates for apartments with one bedroom are US$37.50, with two bedrooms US$53.

The recommended *Hotel Cocal* (☎ 643067) is also in this price range, and German, English and Spanish is spoken. There are two pools and a restaurant and the pleasant rooms have hot water in the private baths. Reservations can be made through the Hotel Galilea in San José. Also in this price range is *Apartamentos El Mar* (☎ 643165) which has a pool and spacious apartments with kitchenettes and private bathrooms.

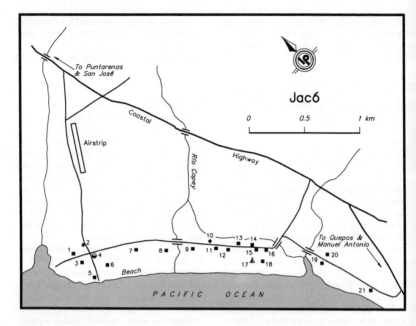

1 Cabinas Antonio
2 Foxy's Disco
3 Cabinas Garabito & Las Palmas
4 Bus Stop
5 Hotel El Jardín
6 Hotel Jacó Beach
7 Cabinas Heredia
8 Tangerí Chalets
9 Cabinas Los Ranchos
10 Area of Stores; Rental Gear; Bus Stop ("Downtown")
11 Cabinas Zabamar & Villas Miramar
12 Hotel Cocal
13 Hotel Las Gaviotas
14 Red Cross Post & Cabinas Andrea
15 Cabinas Alice
16 Apartamentos El Mar & Casas de Playa Mar Sol
17 Camping El Hicaco
18 Cabinas Las Brisas
19 Hotel Jacofiesta
20 Cabinas Naranjal
21 Hotel Marparaiso

Places to Stay – top end

The *Hotel Las Gaviotas* (☎ 643092) is an attractive place and has clean rooms with kitchenette attached, and there is a pool. Rates are about US$32/46 for a single/double.

The *Hotel Jacó Beach* (☎ 643032, 643064) is by far the biggest hotel in Jacó, with over 100 rooms. It is connected with the Hotel Irazú in San José and many Canadian charter groups stay here. This is a full beach resort, with bicycle, surfboard, kayak, boat and car rentals. There is a restaurant (with limited menu), disco, swimming pools and sunbathing areas. Rooms are air-con and come with private bath and hot water. Rates are US$55 for a double, including breakfast. Reservations can be made through the Hotel Irazú in San José.

The *Tangerí Chalets* (☎ 643001, 420977; Apartado 622, 4050 Alajuela) has spacious chalets with three bedrooms and kitchen. There is a swimming pool and snack bar.

They prefer long term guests, and rates per chalet are US$65 midweek and US$80 at weekends.

Other places in this price range which have rooms with kitchenettes include the *Hotel Marparaiso* (☎ 643025), Apartado 24, Jacó, Puntarenas; *Casas de Playa Mar Sol* (☎ 643008); and *Hotel Jacofiesta* (☎ 643147), Apartado 38, Jacó, Puntarenas. All these places have pools.

Places to Eat

Many of the better hotels have restaurants open to the public. The French restaurant at the *Hotel El Jardín* is considered one of the better ones.

There are plenty of *sodas* and restaurants in town – none of them are particularly outstanding but most are satisfactory. The best place is usually where your (newfound) friends are eating – it's probably as good as any.

Entertainment

For dancing at weekends there is *Disco La Central* (☎ 643076) in the middle of town and *Foxy's Disco* near the bus stop. The *Hotel Jacó Beach* also has a disco.

Getting There & Away

There are direct buses with Transportes Jacó (☎ 415890) from the Coca Cola terminal in San José, leaving at 7.30 am and 3.30 pm daily. The journey takes about three hours and costs about US$2.50. Buses between either San José or Puntarenas and Quepos or Manuel Antonio could drop you off at the entrance to Jacó Beach. Buses tend to be full at weekends – get to the terminal as early as possible.

Buses leave from Jacó for San José at 5 am and 3 pm daily. Departures for Puntarenas are at 6 am and 4 pm. There is a bus stop near the north end of town – tickets are sold here on Friday, Saturday and Sunday. There is also a bus 'terminal' next to the Marisquería La Ostra in 'downtown' Jacó.

If you get stuck in Jacó and can't get a bus out at weekends, try Taxi Jacó (☎ 643009) or Taxi 30-30 (☎ 643030). A rough estimate of the fare to Puntarenas is US$50, twice that to San José.

If you are staying at the Hotel Jacó Beach you can take advantage of their shuttle bus to the Hotel Irazú in San José.

Light aircraft can be chartered to the airstrip at the north end of town.

JACÓ TO QUEPOS

The paved coastal highway continues southeast from Jacó to Quepos, 70 km away. The road parallels the Pacific coastline, but only comes down to it a few times. There are a few good beaches (some with good surf) on this route, which are rather off the beaten track and most easily visited by car, though you could get off buses to Quepos or Manuel Antonio and walk down to the beach.

The first beach is **Playa Hermosa** about five km south of Jacó. This beach stretches for about 10 km and is for expert surfers – there is an annual contest here in August.

Esterillos Oeste and **Esterillos Este** are about 22 and 30 km respectively south-east of Jacó. Between the two, the Esterillo Beach stretches for several deserted km. At Esterillos Este is the recommended and good *Hotel El Delfín* (☎ 711640; Apartado 2260, 1000 San José). Rooms with private bath (hot water) and balcony with sea views are in the top end price range. There is a restaurant and pool. There is also cheaper accommodation in Esterillos.

Infrequently visited beaches beyond Esterillos include **Bejuco** and **Palma**, both reached by short side roads from the coastal highway. Parrita, on the river of the same name and 44 km from Jacó, has a couple of basic hotels. The coastal road is now inland and continues so until Quepos. For the last section, the road is unpaved but is passable in all weathers with normal cars. African oil-palm plantations stretch for several km before Quepos is reached.

QUEPOS

This town gets its name from the Quepoa Indian tribe, a sub-group of the Borucas, who inhabited the area at the time of the conquest.

The Quepoa people declined because of diseases brought by the Europeans, internecine warfare with other Indian groups, and being sold as slaves. By the end of the 19th century, there were no pure-blooded Quepoa left, and the area began to be colonised by farmers from the highlands.

Quepos first came to prominence as a banana exporting port. Its importance has declined appreciably in recent decades because of disease which has severely reduced banana crops. African oil-palm has replaced bananas as the major local crop, but, as it is processed into oils used in cosmetics, machine oils and lard, the finished product is much less bulky than bananas. Consequently Quepos has not been able to recover as a major shipping port. Instead, it has become important as a sport-fishing centre and also as the nearest town to the Manuel Antonio National Park, which is only seven km away and one of the most visited national parks in Costa Rica. There are regularly scheduled flights from San José, as well as buses, and the tourist industry has enabled Quepos to find a new economic niche for itself. The population of the town and the surrounding district (including Manuel Antonio) is 11,500.

Information

The La Buena Nota (☎ 770345) store at the entrance to town sells beach supplies and acts as an information centre for tourists. They were planning to move to near the Manuel Antonio Beach.

Next to the Buena Nota is the Elegant Rent-a-Car (☎ 770115) office – I suggest you arrange car rentals in advance in San José to pick up cars here, as they are in short supply. There are offices of sport-fishing companies on this block.

The Banco Nacional de Costa Rica (☎ 770144) changes US dollars, and is extremely air-con – a cool wait. The post office is on the north side of the soccer field at the east end of town.

The annual Fiesta del Mar (Sea Festival) takes place near the end of January with processions, street dancing and general revelry.

Tours

SANSA (☎ 226561 for tours) has a tour package to Manuel Antonio which includes round-trip air transport from San José, bus to Manuel Antonio, one night's accommodation at a hotel within a few minutes walk of the park (ask SANSA which hotel!) and two lunches and one breakfast. The cost is US$47 per person (minimum two people in one room). Longer stays are US$75 per person for two nights and US$102 per person for three nights, including extra meals. There are no flights on Sundays.

Places to Stay

Hotels tend to be full during weekends in the dry season. Hotels are generally cheaper here than on the way to and at Manuel Antonio. You can get wet season discounts.

Places to Stay – bottom end

The *Hotel Luna* charges US$3 per person in basic rooms with private baths. Only some of the larger rooms have fans – otherwise it's only a bed and a shower. The *Hotel Linda Vista* has basic rooms for US$7 double and some rooms with private baths for a little more, but there are no singles. The rooms are reasonably clean but noisy.

The *Hotel Mar y Luna* (☎ 770394) is reasonably clean and has basic single rooms for US$3.50. Double rooms have private baths and fans and cost US$8.25. Also in this price range is the *Hospedaje Familiar La Macha* (☎ 770216). Other very basic and cheap hotels you could try are the *Hotel America, Hotel Dan Gun* and *Hotel Majestic.*

Places to Stay – middle

The *Hotel Ramus* (☎ 770245) has rooms with private bath and fan for US$4.70 to US$6.50 per person, depending on the day of the week (weekends are more). The *Hotel Malinche* (☎ 770093) is quite good and has rooms with private bath and fan for US$5.90 per person.

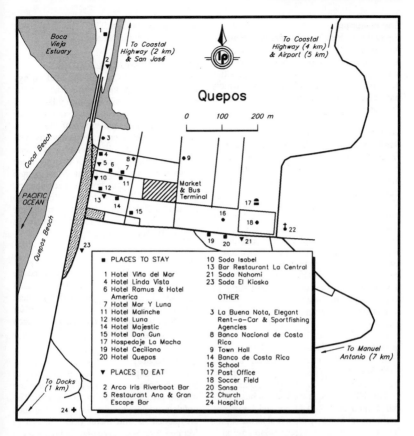

Quepos

0   100   200 m

PLACES TO STAY
1 Hotel Viña del Mar
4 Hotel Linda Vista
6 Hotel Ramus & Hotel America
7 Hotel Mar Y Luna
11 Hotel Malinche
12 Hotel Luna
14 Hotel Majestic
15 Hotel Dan Gun
17 Hospedaje La Macha
19 Hotel Ceciliano
20 Hotel Quepos

▼ **PLACES TO EAT**

2 Arco Iris Riverboat Bar
5 Restaurant Ana & Gran Escape Bar
10 Soda Isabel
13 Bar Restaurant La Central
21 Soda Nahomi
23 Soda El Kiosko

OTHER

3 La Buena Nota, Elegant Rent-a-Car & Sportfishing Agencies
8 Banco Nacional de Costa Rica
9 Town Hall
14 Banco de Costa Rica
16 School
17 Post Office
18 Soccer Field
20 Sansa
22 Church
24 Hospital

The *Hotel Quepos* (☎ 770274; Apartado 79, Quepos, Puntarenas) above the SANSA office is good but often full. Rooms with communal bath are US$5.75 per person; rooms with private baths US$7 per person.

The pleasant, quiet and family run *Hotel Ceciliano* (☎ 770192) has clean rooms with shared baths for US$9.50/14 single/double and rooms with private bath for US$14/16.50 single/double. The *Hotel Viña del Mar* (☎ 770070; Apartado 5527, San José; tel 233334) is at the entrance to town and has clean, spacious, wooden rooms with private bath and fan for US$9 per person.

Places to Eat

The *Soda El Kiosko* at the south end of town has a menu in English and tries to attract foreign tourists – they have simple but good food. Good snacks are available at the *Soda Nahomi* at the east end of town on the way out to Manuel Antonio beach.

In the centre of town, there are several reasonable places, of which the *Restaurant Ana* is one of the cheapest for set casados. The *Bar Restaurant La Central* is also inexpensive and the *Soda Isabel* is a little less cheap but still good value.

Entertainment

For nightlife, the *Gran Escape Bar* is popular with sport-fishing visitors and other tourists and is one of the more lively bars. They also serve good food. Also worth checking is the *Arco Iris Riverboat Bar* (☎ 770449) which has dancing at weekends, and they serve food as well.

Getting There & Away

Air SANSA has regularly scheduled flights from San José at 9.50 am daily except Sunday. During the dry season they also have afternoon flights at 3 pm on Tuesday, Thursday and Saturday, and 3.50 pm on Monday, Wednesday and Friday. The flight takes 20 minutes, costs US$9, and returns for San José 20 minutes after arriving in Quepos. Make reservations and pay for your ticket well in advance to ensure a confirmed reservation. Reconfirm your flight as often as you can. Flights are nearly always full and with a waiting list – get to the airport early to avoid losing your reservation.

It is also possible to charter light planes to Quepos.

Bus Buses leave San José several times a day from the Coca Cola terminal. Direct buses go to Manuel Antonio (3½ hours), and there are regular services to Quepos (five hours).

The ticket office in the Quepos bus terminal is open from 7 to 11 am and 1 to 5 pm daily except Sunday, when it closes at 4 pm. There are regular services to San José at 7 and 10 am, and 2 and 4 pm daily (US$2.75). Direct buses leave three or four times a day (US$4.50) from Manuel Antonio and pick up passengers in Quepos before continuing directly to San José. There are six daily buses to Parrita.

Buses to Puntarenas leave daily at 4.30 am and 3 pm; to San Isidro at 5 am and 1.30 pm; to Hatillo (near Dominical) at 9.30 pm and 4 pm; and to various local communities in the agricultural country surrounding Quepos.

Buses for Manuel Antonio leave every couple of hours; departures are at 5.40, 8 and 10.30 am, and 12.30, 3 and 5 pm; the fare is about US$0.30.

Taxi Quepos Taxi (☎ 770277) will take you to Manuel Antonio for about US$3.

QUEPOS TO MANUEL ANTONIO

From the port of Quepos, the road swings inland for seven km before reaching the beaches of Manuel Antonio village and national park. The road goes over a series of hills with picturesque views of the ocean. Along this road, every hilltop view has been commandeered by a hotel which lists 'ocean views' as a major attraction. Certainly, these views are often magnificent. Most people staying in these pricey hotels expect, and get, good services. These hotels are generally so pleasant and comfortable that spending the whole day there is an attractive alternative to visiting the national park.

Tours

A rough dirt road to the right, just beyond the Restaurant Barba Roja, leads down to Punta Quepos Trail Rides (☎ 770566) where horses and guides can be hired. They offer half-day riding tours with lunch on the beach and 'polilingual naturalist guide'.

Places to Stay

The first couple of hotels on the road to Manuel Antonio after leaving Quepos are middle priced; the rest are all top end. The hotels are listed here in the order that they are passed as you travel from Quepos to Manuel Antonio. I give high and dry season prices (mid December to mid April). Substantial discounts (40% or even 50% is not unusual) are available in the wet season. Reservations are a must for weekends and often mid-week in the dry months.

Many of these hotels (even the most expensive ones) will not accept credit cards or personal cheques, so you need cash or travellers' cheques. Ask about this when calling for reservations. Most of these places are small and intimate – few have more than a dozen rooms and many have only eight or less.

The Manuel Antonio area is experiencing a tourist boom, and many of these hotels were built or opened in the late 1980s. More will probably open in the 1990s.

Places to Stay – middle

Cabinas Pedro Miguel (☎ 770035) is up the hill out of Quepos, about one km out of town on the right. It has fairly basic rooms at US$13 for a double with bath, or cabins with kitchenettes for US$23.50 which will sleep up to three people. The place is family run and friendly, and they'll cook for you. Almost opposite the entrance to these cabinas, on the left side of the road, is the *Hotel Plinio* (☎ 770055; Apartado 71, Quepos, Puntarenas). There are six rooms and the charge is US$26/33 single/double with private bath, including breakfast. The people are friendly, the food is good and guests tend to be young and international.

Places to Stay – top end

The new Canadian-run *Hotel Lirio* (☎ 770403; Apartado 123, Quepos, Puntarenas), is about three km from Quepos on the left. There are four rooms with queen-sized beds, private showers, hot water and ceiling fans. Rates are US$65 per room, including breakfast, and there is a small pool. Opposite the Lirio is the cheaper *Hotel Las Charrucas* (☎ 770409).

With about 21 rooms, the *Hotel Divisimar* (☎ 770371; Apartado 82, Quepos, Puntarenas; or Apartado 7857, 1000, San José), is one of the bigger hotels. The staff are helpful and rent mountain bikes, surfboards and sea kayaks. There is a pool, restaurant and a good hot water supply in the private bathrooms. Rates are US$45 for a double with fan, and US$55 double with air-con. Across the street is the *Hotel Casablanca* (☎ 770055; Apartado 184, Quepos, Puntarenas), which is in the same price range.

Nearby is the region's most exclusive hotel, the 10 room *Hotel La Mariposa* (☎ 770355, 770456; Apartado 4, Quepos, Puntarenas). Reservations can also be made in the USA at (800) 223-6510 or (212) 832-2277. Rates are US$120/160 for a single/double including breakfast and

dinner, and children are not allowed. Rooms are very comfortable, all with excellent views from the balconies, and the food and service is reportedly commensurate with the rates. Non-guests can use the pool for a modest fee, and the good restaurant is open to the public.

In the same area is the *Hotel Byblos* (☎ 770411; Apartado 15, Quepos, Puntarenas). It's about four km from Quepos, on the left. There are eight rooms accommodating up to three people each, and the rates are US$75 with fan, US$86 with air-con. There is a pool, jacuzzi and a restaurant with a good reputation.

A little way beyond the Byblos, and back from the road on the left, is the *El Colibrí* (☎ 770432; Apartado 94, Quepos, Puntarenas). Colibrí means 'hummingbird', and there are certainly plenty of these in the pleasant gardens in which the eight cabins are set. The cabins have hot water, kitchenette with refrigerator and stove, and fans. Rates are US$40/50 for a single/double, and pre-teen children are not allowed.

The next hotel on the left, a few hundred metres away, is *La Quinta* (☎ 770434; Apartado 76, Quepos, Puntarenas). There are five spacious three-bedded cabins set in pleasant and quiet gardens. Cabins have balconies, views, fans, and some have kitchenettes. There is a small pool. Rates are US$50 for a double, or US$60 for a double with kitchenette.

The *Hotel Arboleda* (☎ 770414, in San José 351169; Apartado 55, Quepos, Puntarenas) is the biggest hotel in the area. There are about 35 stone cabins, some near the beach and others lined up on a hillside. Some cabins have fans, other have air-con, while a few lack hot water. The rates are about US$40/50 for a single/double. The hotel also has a pool and restaurant. Nearby is the *Costa Verde* (☎ 770564) which has a variety of apartments and condominiums, most with kitchenettes and balconies. They sleep from two to five people and rates are US$40 to US$80 per room. This place is popular with tico families.

On the final hill before reaching Manuel

Antonio, about 6½ km from Quepos, on the left, is the *Hotel Karahé* (☎ 770170; Apartado 100, Quepos, Puntarenas). This is the last hotel on the road before reaching Manuel Antonio, and you could easily walk to the national park from here in about 20 or 30 leisurely minutes. There are 10 cabins which have good views, but require a lot of step climbing to reach. The cabins sleep up to three, have hot water and refrigerators, but are rather bare looking. There is a pool and a decent restaurant. The rates are US$55 per cabin.

There is more accommodation in Manuel Antonio village, all of it cheaper.

Places to Stay – houses

For people who want to stay for at least a week or more, it is possible to rent a house and cater for yourself. The Biesanz family (☎ 281811, 491507) have a house on a beach north of the national park. You need 4WD to get there, or otherwise walk. The owner of La Buena Nota (☎ 770345) has a house near the Hotel Mariposa. The people at the Vela Bar (☎ 770413) in Manuel Antonio also have a house to rent. Ask around about others.

These houses are generally comfortable and fully equipped, and you can expect to pay between US$200 and US$400 a week.

Places to Eat

Many of the hotels mentioned above have good restaurants open to the public – the *La Mariposa, Byblos, Plinio* and *Arboleda* hotels have all been recommended. The Plinio serves excellent Italian and German food, Byblos specialises in French, Arboleda is a Uruguayan steak house, and La Mariposa is international. All are pricey by Costa Rican standards – the Plinio is the least expensive.

Another good place is the *Restaurant Barba Roja* (☎ 770331), opposite the Hotel Divisimar. The name means 'red beard', and the place has well prepared North American food (hamburgers, sandwiches, Mexican, steak and seafood) and there is a great view. They also advertise boat charters. *Bahías*

Bar & Restaurant (☎ 770409) serves exotic drinks and seafood. Both places are popular. None of the restaurants along the road to Manuel Antonio are particularly cheap.

Getting There & Away

Many visitors get here by private or rented car, which enables them to drive the few km to Manuel Antonio. Others rely on the Quepos taxi service, catch the bus which comes by about six times a day, walk or hitch-hike down to the park.

MANUEL ANTONIO

The small village at the entrance to the national park has a number of less expensive hotels and restaurants and is popular with younger international travellers. The same advice regarding hotel reservations during the high season applies here – the village is packed during Easter week, and few rooms are available at weekends.

There is a good beach (Playa Espadilla) but swimmers are warned to beware of rip currents. The town is generally safe, but swimmers should never leave belongings unattended on the beach here, or in the national park beaches. Make sure your hotel room is securely locked when you are out, even briefly.

Places to Stay – bottom end

The cheapest place is *Grano de Oro* (☎ 770578), which has very basic rooms, without fans, for US$3 per person. They don't like to take reservations over the phone. A better bet is the self styled youth hostel *Costa Linda* (☎ 770304) which is not affiliated with the Costa Rican Youth Hostel system, but is affiliated with the Ticalinda budget travellers' hotel in San José. The charge is US$4 per person in basic stuffy rooms, or US$30 for a cabin sleeping six, and including a private bath and kitchenette.

The *Cabinas Manuel Antonio* (☎ 770212), which is opposite the more expensive hotel of the same name, has small basic rooms at US$5 per person, and bigger beach front rooms sleeping up to four for

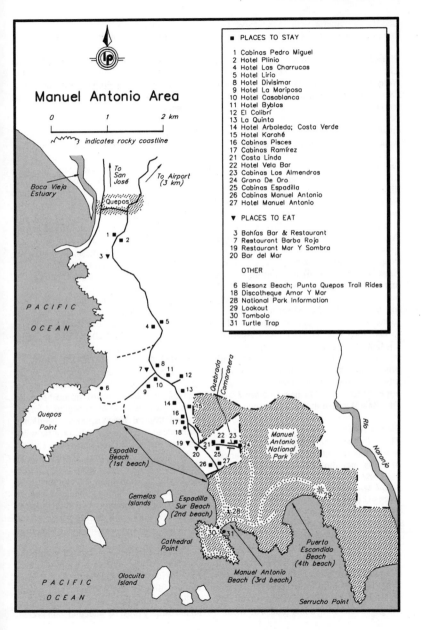

Manuel Antonio Area

0   1   2 km

~~~~ indicates rocky coastline

■ PLACES TO STAY

1 Cabinas Pedro Miguel
2 Hotel Plinio
4 Hotel Las Charrucas
5 Hotel Lirio
8 Hotel Divisimar
9 Hotel La Mariposa
10 Hotel Casablanca
11 Hotel Byblos
12 El Colibrí
13 La Quinta
14 Hotel Arboleda; Costa Verde
15 Hotel Karahé
16 Cabinas Pisces
17 Cabinas Ramírez
21 Costa Linda
22 Hotel Vela Bar
23 Cabinas Los Almendros
24 Grano De Oro
25 Cabinas Espadilla
26 Cabinas Manuel Antonio
27 Hotel Manuel Antonio

▼ PLACES TO EAT

3 Bahías Bar & Restaurant
7 Restaurant Barba Roja
19 Restaurant Mar Y Sombra
20 Bar del Mar

OTHER

6 Biesanz Beach; Punta Quepos Trail Rides
18 Discotheque Amor Y Mar
28 National Park Information
29 Lookout
30 Tombolo
31 Turtle Trap

To San José

To Airport (3 km)

Boca Vieja Estuary

Quepos

PACIFIC OCEAN

Quepos Point

Quebrada Camaronera

Manuel Antonio National Park

Río Naranjo

Espadilla Beach (1st beach)

Gemelas Islands

Espadilla Sur Beach (2nd beach)

Cathedral Point

Olocuita Island

Puerto Escondido Beach (4th beach)

PACIFIC OCEAN

Manuel Antonio Beach (3rd beach)

Serrucho Point

US$16. A pulpería with inexpensive soft drinks and beer is attached.

Places to Stay – middle

The nearest place to the park entrance is the *Hotel Manuel Antonio* (☎ 770290; Apartado 88, Quepos, Puntarenas). Rooms are US$16 for single or double occupancy, and US$2 per extra person (up to four). The rooms are small but clean, with private bath and cold water, and there is a restaurant attached.

The friendly *Cabinas Ramírez* (☎ 770510) has rooms sleeping three people for US$16. During the high season it may be difficult to get cheaper single or double rates. Rooms have fans and private baths (cold water), but seem rather dank.

The *Cabinas Los Almendros* (☎ 770225; Apartado 68, Quepos, Puntarenas) has large, quiet and pleasant rooms sleeping three people for US$27 per room. The *Cabinas Espadilla* (☎ 770416) has helpful owners and spacious clean rooms with private bath and fan. Rooms with kitchenette and sleeping up to four cost US$33; some cheaper rooms without kitchenette are also available.

The *Hotel Vela Bar* (☎ 770413; Apartado 13, Quepos, Puntarenas) has large pleasant rooms for US$20/30 for a single/double with private bath; rooms with air-con cost US$10 more. The owners are pleasant and run a popular restaurant. The new *Cabinas Pisces* (☎ 770046) is also in this price range.

Places to Eat

The *Vela Bar* is the best and priciest restaurant in Manuel Antonio. They serve a variety of meals, including a few vegetarian plates, for US$6 to US$12. The restaurant at the *Hotel Manuel Antonio* is a little cheaper (US$5 to US$8) and also popular. The *Costa Linda* hostel serves good and reasonably priced breakfasts with yoghurt, pancakes and gallo pinto available.

The *Restaurant Mar y Sombra* (☎ 770003) is popular and serves seafood. It has a reputation as one of the cheapest places to eat in town, but I found most meals were about US$4 or US$5. People on a tight budget should bring some food with them.

Entertainment

The *Discotheque Amor y Mar* (☎ 770510) serves fairly cheap meals, if you can stand the invasively loud disco music. As you might expect, there is dancing here at night. The *Bar del Mar* (☎ 770543) is a quiet place for a drink or snack, and they rent surfboards and snorkels.

Getting There & Away

Direct buses from San José leave the Coca Cola terminal at 6 am, 12 noon and 6 pm daily during the dry season; one of these departures may not run in the wet. Return buses leave from near the Hotel Manuel Antonio at 6 am, 12 noon and 5 pm daily, plus 3 pm on Sundays. They will pick you up from in front of your hotel if you are on the road to flag them down, or from the Quepos bus terminal. Buy tickets in advance if possible, particularly at weekends. Try calling 770263 for bus reservations in Manuel Antonio.

Buses for destinations other than San José leave from Quepos. Buses from Manuel Antonio to Quepos leave at about 6, 8.20 and 10.50 am, and 12.50, 3.20 and 5.20 pm daily.

MANUEL ANTONIO NATIONAL PARK

At 682 hectares, Manuel Antonio is by far the smallest park in the national parks system, but it is also one of the most popular ones. This is because of its beautiful forest-backed tropical beaches, rocky headlands with ocean and island views, prolific wildlife, and maintained trail network.

Fortunately, Manuel Antonio was declared a national park back in 1972, thus preserving it from hotel development and encroachment. Although the park can be busy during dry season weekends, it quietens down midweek, and during rainy season weekdays you can have the place well-nigh to yourself.

Vehicular traffic is prohibited within the park and arriving on foot is a minor adventure in itself. The Quebrada Camaronera estuary divides the southern end of the village from the park and there is no bridge, so the estuary must be waded to gain access.

The water may be ankle deep at low tide and thigh deep at high tide (spring tides in the rainy season have been known to be chest high!), so prepare yourself to get at least a little wet.

Once across the estuary, you can follow an obvious trail through forest to an isthmus separating Espadilla Sur and Manuel Antonio beaches. This isthmus is called a *tombolo* and was formed by the accumulation of sedimentary material between the mainland and the peninsula beyond, which was once an island. If you walk along Espadilla Sur Beach, you will find a small mangrove area. The isthmus widens out into a rocky peninsula, with forest in the centre. A trail leads around the peninsula to Cathedral Point from where there are good views of the Pacific Ocean and various rocky islets. These are bird reserves and form part of the national park. Brown boobies and pelicans are among the sea birds which nest on these islands.

You can continue around the peninsula to Manuel Antonio Beach, or you can avoid the peninsula altogether and hike across the isthmus to this beach. At the western end of the beach, during low tide, you can see a semicircle of rocks which archaeologists believe were placed there by pre-Columbian Indians, and which functioned as a turtle trap. The beach itself is an attractive one of white sand, and is popular for bathing. It is protected and safer than the Espadilla beaches.

Beyond Manuel Antonio beach, the trail divides. The lower trail is steep and slippery during the wet months, and leads to the quiet and aptly named Puerto Escondido ('hidden port') Beach. This beach can be more or less completely covered by high tides, so don't get cut off. The upper trail climbs up to a bluff overlooking Puerto Escondido and Serrucho Point beyond – a nice view. I have a map showing a trail continuing from here to the Playita Beach, but it seems that it is now closed; check with park rangers.

There is also a trail leading from past the Cabinas Los Almendros and into the park, finally coming out at the Manuel Antonio Beach. This trail used to go through private property and may not be open to the public, so check before you go, and respect property rights.

Monkeys abound in the park, and it is difficult to spend a day walking around without seeing some. White-faced monkeys are the most common, but the rarer squirrel monkeys are also present and howler monkeys may be seen. Sloths, agoutis, peccaries, armadillos, coatimundis and raccoons are also seen quite regularly. Over 350 species of birds are reported for the park, and a variety of lizards, snakes, iguanas and other animals may be observed. All of the trails within the park are good for animal watching – ask the rangers where the most interesting recent sightings have occurred. There is a small coral reef off Manuel Antonio beach, but the water is rather cloudy and the visibility limited. Despite this, snorkellers can see a variety of fish as well as marine creatures like crabs and corals, sponges and sea snails, and many others.

Immediately inland from the beaches is an evergreen littoral forest. This contains many different species of trees, bushes and other plants. A common one to watch out for is the manzanillo (little apple) tree, *Hippomane mancinella* – this tree has fruits that look like little crab apples and which are poisonous. The sap exuded by the bark and leaves is also toxic, and causes the skin to itch and burn, so give the manzanillo a wide berth. There are warning signs prominently displayed by examples of this tree near the park entrance.

Information

There is a visitor information centre just before Manuel Antonio Beach. Drinking water is available at the information centre and there are toilets nearby. The park is officially open from 7 am to 4 pm, and guards come round in the evening to make sure that nobody is camping. It used to be possible to camp, but heavy user pressure has caused the closure of the campsite and visitors have to stay outside the park.

The beaches are often numbered – most people call Espadilla Beach (outside the park) first beach, Espadillo Sur is second beach, Manuel Antonio is third beach, Puerto Escondido is fourth beach, and Playita is fifth beach. Some people begin counting at Espadilla Sur, which is the first beach actually in the park, and so it can be a bit confusing trying to figure out which beach people may be talking about.

Average daily temperatures are 27°C and average annual rainfall is 3800 mm. The dry season is not entirely dry, merely less wet, and so you should be prepared for rain then too (although it can also be dry for days on end). Make sure you carry plenty of drinking water and sun protection when visiting the park. Insect repellent is also an excellent idea.

Entrance into the park is US$1.10 per day.

DOMINICAL

It is not possible to continue further south along the coast from Manuel Antonio. You have to backtrack to Quepos, and from there head to the coastal highway. It is 42 km from Quepos to the next village of any size, Dominical. The road is gravel and easily passable in the dry season, but requires some care to negotiate with an ordinary car in the wet. En route, the coastal highway goes through km after km of African oil-palm plantations, with identical looking settlements along the way. These are minor centres for the palm-oil extracting process. Each settlement has a grassy village square, institutional looking housing, a store, church, bar and, somewhat strangely, an Alcoholics Anonymous chapter. Three beaches maybe worth a look if you are a beach lover; Playa Savegre, Matapalo and Barú. There are no noteworthy facilities at these.

Dominical is at the mouth of the Río Barú. There is now a bridge across the mouth of the river, but roads paralleling both banks for almost four km inland attest to the bridge's recent construction. Dominical is on the south-east side of the river mouth. From here, a steep but paved road climbs 29 km inland to San Isidro de El General. Thus, if you can negotiate the somewhat rough

Quepos to Dominical road, a round trip from San José to Quepos, Dominical, San Isidro and back to San José is quite possible, and indeed, makes a good excursion. There are plans to pave the Quepos to Dominical section, but as of the early 1990s this seems to be some years from completion.

The Dominical Beach is a long one, and has a reputation for strong rip currents so exercise extra caution.

Places to Stay & Eat

There are two basic places near the beach in Dominical. *Cabinas El Coca* charges US$4.70/8.25 for a single/double. *Cabinas Nayarit* (☎ 771878) charges US$11.75 in rooms with private bath and fan, and up to three people can sleep in a room.

About one km south of town is the *Cabinas Costa Brava* which charges US$11.75 for rooms similar to the Nayarit. The *Costa Brava* has a simple restaurant; there is also a restaurant/bar in town. It's all pretty laid back, slow moving and out of the way.

The *Cabinas Punta Dominical* (☎ 710866 in San Isidro; 255328 in San José) is four km south of the village, built high on a rocky headland named, appropriately enough, Punta Dominical. Isolated and attractive, the cabins are a good place to get away from it all, yet retain a modicum of comfort. Comfortable rooms with fans, private baths with hot water, and a porch to hang a hammock, rent for US$19/27 for a single/double. There are only a few cabins, and reservations are recommended, especially at weekends. The cabins overlook a rocky beach; there is a sandy beach near by. There is a restaurant on the premises, and boat trips can be arranged.

Getting There & Away

Buses between Quepos and San Isidro stop in Dominical; you will have to find a taxi to get you to Punta Dominical. Buses between San Isidro and Uvita will drop you off at both Dominical and Punta Dominical, but there is only one bus a day (afternoons from San Isidro; mornings from Uvita – ask locally for expected times of passing through Dominical).

UVITA

This village is 16 km south of Dominical and is the end of the road as far as the central Pacific coast is concerned. A daily bus leaves in the mornings for San Isidro. There is basic accommodation.

Beyond Uvita, a poor dirt road follows the coast as far as Tortuga Abajo, 16 km away. This stretch is suitable for 4WD only, and may be impassable in the wet season. There are several remote beaches along here. Beyond Tortuga Abajo, the road improves and continues 20 km to Ciudad Cortés and seven more km to Palmar Norte.

There are plans to eventually pave this road and connect the central Pacific coast with southern Costa Rica, but it looks like close to the end of the century before this project may be completed. Meanwhile – this is an adventure for drivers of 4WD vehicles, or backpackers who want to walk it. Let me know how it goes!

The Nicoya Peninsula

This peninsula juts south from the north-western corner of Costa Rica, and, at over 100 km in length, is by far the largest in the country. Despite its size, it has few paved roads and most people get around on gravel or dirt roads. Some of Costa Rica's major beach resorts are here, often remote and difficult to get to, and offering beaches and sun rather than villages, culture or wildlife. If all you want to do is swim and sunbathe, then you may enjoy a few days here. Otherwise, you will become bored very quickly.

There are several small and rarely visited wildlife reserves and a national park found in the area, but for the most part, people who come here are looking for beaches to relax on. In 1940 about half of the peninsula was covered with rainforest; this had been mostly cut down by the 1960s. Much of the peninsula has been turned over to cattle raising, which, along with tourism, is the main industry.

The main highway through the peninsula begins at Liberia and follows the centre of the peninsula through the small towns of Filadelfia and Santa Cruz to Nicoya, which is the largest town in the area. (Nevertheless, it is a small town.) From Nicoya, the main road heads east to the Río Tempisque ferry or south-east to Playa Naranjo from where the ferry to Puntarenas leaves twice a day. These roads are good, and, for the most part, paved.

From this main central highway, side roads branch out to a long series of beaches stretching along the Pacific coastline of the peninsula. Almost all of these roads are gravel or dirt and generally are in poor condition. Once you get to the beach area of your choice, you are usually stuck there and cannot continue north or south along the coast for any long distance because there is no paved coastal road. If you have a 4WD vehicle, it's possible to follow the coast (more or less) on the poor dirt roads. In an ordinary car or if you are travelling by bus to

the next set of beaches, you need to back-track to the main central highway and then come back again on another road. Many beaches have a hotel but no village, and bus service may be nonexistent. If there is a small village, the bus service is often limited to one per day.

The beaches at Tamarindo, Nosara and Sámara all have regularly scheduled flights from San José with SANSA. This avoids the difficulties of road travel but limits your visit to just one beach. Some people rent a car (4WD is useful in the dry season and essential in the wet – many car hire companies won't allow you to rent an ordinary car to go to the Nicoya Peninsula in the wet season) but this is an expensive option. If you decide to hire a car, be prepared for a frustrating lack of road signs and gas stations. Fill up whenever you can and ask frequently for directions.

Budget travellers using public buses should allow plenty of time to get around. Hitch-hiking is a definite possibility – given the paucity of public transport, the locals hitch-hike around the peninsula more than in other parts of Costa Rica. If you want to cook for yourself, bring food from inland. Stores

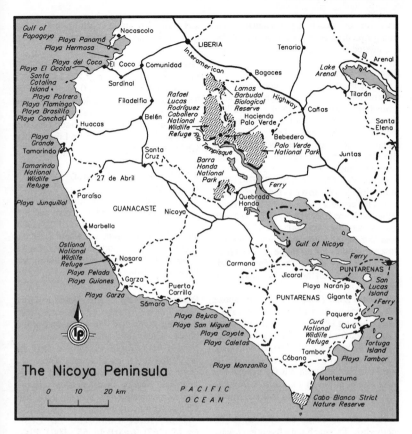

The Nicoya Peninsula

are few and far between on the coast, and the selection is limited and expensive.

What this all means is that most of the Nicoya Peninsula beaches are more suitable for a leisurely visit of several days. If you are looking for a quick overnight getaway from San José, the beaches at Jacó, Manuel Antonio or Cahuita are generally easier to get to and have more of a tourist infrastructure.

As with beach areas throughout the country, you should have reservations during dry season weekends and Easter week. Because of the remote nature of many beaches, reservations are a good idea at any time. Rainy season discounts are also worth asking for.

PLAYA DEL COCO

This beach area is only 35 km west of Liberia and (of the Nicoya Peninsula beaches) the most easily accessible by road from San José. It is attractively set between two rocky headlands. For these reasons there are a number of hotels to choose from, a small village, good bus connections from San José and Liberia, and some nightlife. It is a popular resort for ticos in particular, and foreign travellers to a lesser extent.

However, the beach has a reputation for strong rip currents and is somewhat shabby and littered because of the high visitor use.

Places to Stay & Eat
Camping is possible if you don't mind the construction site and chickens scratching around the palm trees ambiance. Follow signs to the campsite which is about 150 metres from the beach. The place seems secure and there are several bathrooms and showers available. The rates are US$1.10 per person per night.

Cabinas El Coco (☎ 670167, 670110) is to the right as you arrive at the beach and is one of the cheaper hotels. Fairly basic rooms at the back are US$9/12 for a double/triple and at the beachfront are US$11/15 double/triple, all with private bath. There are dozens of rooms but no single prices, at least not during busy weekends. There is a mid-priced restaurant on the premises and a disco next door.

Cabinas Luna Tica (☎ 670127, or annexe 670279) has rooms with private baths and a double bed for US$11.75, with a double and a single bed for US$15.30, and a double and two single beds for US$17.65, all with fans. A triple room with air-con costs US$22. The hotel is near the beach but the annexe has nicer rooms, although it is set back from the beach. The hotel also has an attached restaurant.

The *Cabinas Chale* (☎ 670036) is 100 metres from the beach and a five minute walk from town, to the right as you arrive (there are signs). There are clean rooms for US$19/23 double/triple with private bath, fan and refrigerator. There is a pool, and the staff is friendly.

The best hotel is the *Flor de Itabo* (☎ 670011; Apartado 32, Playa del Coco, Guanacaste) which is almost a km from the beach, on the right hand side as you arrive. There is a restaurant and pool, and the rooms have air-con and hot water. The rates are US$41/48 for a single/double room, and cabins with kitchenettes and refrigerator are US$70. The cabins have one double and two single beds each. The owners are friendly

and will help arrange fishing and diving excursions, and there are horses for rent.

Getting There & Away
Pulmitan has a bus leaving Calle 14, Avenida 1 & 3, San José daily at 10 am (US$2.75). The return leaves Playa del Coco at 9 am daily. Buses to and from Liberia leave three times a day during the dry season (less frequent in the wet). A taxi from Liberia costs US$12 to US$15.

AROUND PLAYA DEL COCO
Playa Hermosa
This gently curving and relatively safe beach is about seven km north of Coco, and it is quieter, cleaner and less crowded. The main 'action' is at the north end where there is a small resort. Aquasport (☎ 670050), near the middle of the beach, rents bicycles, and beach and surfing equipment.

Places to Stay & Eat *Cabinas Playa Hermosa* (☎ 670136) is a quiet North American run hotel near the south end of the beach. Clean and pleasant rooms with private baths (cold water) and fans are US$18/28 for a single/double. There is a good reasonably priced restaurant on the premises. Nearby, there are some cheaper ocean-front restaurants serving fresh fish. Cheaper cabins are available in this vicinity.

The *Hotel Condovac La Costa* (☎ 670267; Apartado 55, 1001 Plaza Víquez, San José) at the north end is a condominium complex with about 100 rooms renting for US$78 double. Rooms have kitchenettes, hot water and air-con. There are tennis courts, a pool, discotheque, restaurant and bar on the grounds, and diving, snorkelling, fishing, kayaking, boating and horse riding can be arranged.

Near Condovac is the new *Hotel Los Corales* (☎ 670255) which has eight rooms. Reservations and rates (expensive) can be obtained from Apartado 50, 2000 San José (☎ 239874).

Aquasport, apart from renting beach gear, has a seafood and steak restaurant.

Getting There & Away One or two buses a day pass Playa Hermosa on their way from Liberia to Playa Panamá. A taxi from Liberia is about US$12 to US$15, and a taxi from Coco is about US$4.

Playa Panamá

This good bathing beach is about three km north of Hermosa, and is the end of the road. There is a basic store, bar and cheap cabinas, and it's possible to camp on the beach. See Playa Hermosa for how to get there.

Nacascolo

This is a pre-Columbian Indian ruin north of Playa Panamá. There isn't a great deal to see, but you can get here by boat across the Bahía Culebra from Playa Panamá. Ask around for someone to take you over. It is possible to camp at Nacascolo, but there are no facilities nor drinking water. Guanacaste Tours in Liberia does trips here, if you're interested in the ruins.

Playa Ocotal

This beach is three km south of Coco by poor road. There are two luxurious resorts here, dedicated to scuba diving and sport-fishing. Both resorts should be booked well in advance.

Places to Stay The *Hotel El Ocotal* (☎ 670230) is on a cliff with great views. Rooms are about US$80 for a double with hot water, air-con and refrigerator. There is a pool, restaurant, tennis court and boating facilities. Dive packages cost about US$500 per person, double occupancy, for four days including two days of boat diving with two tanks each, overnight accommodation and breakfast. Equipment and transportation from San José is included. All gear can be rented, instruction provided and day dives made if you don't want to go on a package. Sport-fishing is available for about US$200 a day. Reservations can be made at Apartado 1, Playa del Coco, Guanacaste; or Apartado 1013, 1002 Paseo de los Estudiantes, San José (☎ 224259). Travel agents in San José also make reservations for Ocotal dive trips.

The *Hotel Bahía Pez Vela* (☎ 670129; Apartado 7758, San José) is a comfortable and attractively located sport-fishing resort which offers complete fishing packages for about US$250 per day.

FILADELFIA

To visit beaches further south than Ocotal, you have to return to the main peninsula highway. En route, you pass through the small town of Filadelfia, 30 km from Liberia. The population of Filadelfia and the surrounding district is 6600.

Five km south of Filadelfia, at the community of Belén, a paved road goes to the right as far as the village of Huacas, about 25 km away. Beyond that, dirt roads continue to the right (north) a few km to a number of different beaches.

Places to Stay

There is an inexpensive hotel here, the *Cabinas Amelia* (☎ 698087) which is three blocks from the central plaza.

Getting There & Away

The bus terminal is half block from the central plaza, and has several buses a day to San José and hourly buses passing through en route to Nicoya or Liberia.

PLAYA BRASILITO

The road from Huacas hits the ocean at the village of Brasilito, which has a few small stores and the cheapest accommodation in the area.

Two or three km south of Brasilito is **Playa Conchal** known for its beach which is made almost entirely of crushed shells. It is possible to camp here – there is no village or facilities. However, a 600 hectare lot has been bought by developers so you can expect hotels in the near future.

Places to Stay

One place is *Cabinas Mi Posada* (☎ 680953), which charges about US$15 for a double. There are cheaper places and camping is possible.

About a km north of Brasilito is the *Hotel*

Las Palmas (☎ 680573), a luxurious hotel with huge air-con rooms and good views. There is a restaurant and swimming pool on the premises. Reservations and rates (expensive) can be obtained from Apartado 10, 5150, Santa Cruz, Guanacaste. They arrange sport-fishing trips.

Getting There & Away
See under Playa Flamingo for details of buses.

PLAYA FLAMINGO
Three or four km north of Brasilito, the road comes to Flamingo, a beautiful white sand beach. It has been developed for fishing and boating and is one of the better known beaches in Costa Rica.

There is no village here, so if you are looking for life beyond the hotels, forget it unless you want to walk a couple of km to Brasilito or Potrero. But if you want comfortable hotels, a pretty beach and boating facilities – and have enough money to pay for them – this is a popular destination.

Places to Stay & Eat
There are no cheap places here.

The *Flamingo Beach Hotel* (☎ 680444; Apartado 692, 4050 Alajuela, Costa Rica) has everything you might want for a beach resort vacation. There are three swimming pools, restaurants and bars, casino, snorkelling, boating, diving and fishing facilities. Car rental is also available. Rates are about US$70/80 for a single/double and suites with kitchenettes are about US$130 double and US$175 for four occupants. Near the hotel is a relatively inexpensive restaurant, *Marie's*, with a variety of snacks and meals.

Getting There & Away
The Flamingo Beach Hotel has a private airstrip, or will pick up SANSA passengers from Tamarindo.

Buses leave Santa Cruz daily at 9 am for Flamingo. TRALAPA buses from Calle 20, Avenida 3 in San José also have daily buses here. The buses can drop you off at Playa Brasilito, and they continue past Flamingo to Playa Potrero.

PLAYA POTRERO
This beach is a couple of km north of Flamingo. There is a small community at Potrero, and this is the end of the bus line. The road continues about four km to **Playa Pan de Azúcar**.

Isla Santa Catalina is a rocky islet 10 km due west of Playa Pan de Azúcar. It is one of the few places in Costa Rica where the bridled tern is known to nest, from late March to September. Bird-watchers could hire a boat from any of the nearby resorts to go and see this bird in season.

Places to Stay
There are hotels on Playa Potrero, two or three km before reaching the village of Potrero. The *Hotel Bahía Flamingo* (☎ 680976; Apartado 45, Santa Cruz, Guanacaste) has cabins with kitchenettes and hot water for about US$60 double. Snorkelling, fishing and boating gear are available for rent, as are bicycles. You can also camp here.

There are reportedly a couple of cheaper places to stay in the Potrero area.

The *Hotel Sugar Beach* (☎ 680959; Apartado 90, Santa Cruz, Guanacaste) is a small, quiet, attractive hotel on Playa Pan de Azúcar. Air-con rooms with private bath and cold water are about US$40 to US$50 for a double. The restaurant is good and has a great view.

PLAYA TAMARINDO
Instead of turning north from Huacas to Brasilito and Flamingo, you can head south to Tamarindo, where there is a small community and large and attractive beach. Both surfing and windsurfing are good, and there is a wildlife refuge nearby. Parts of the beach have rip currents, so make local enquiries before swimming. This beach has better access by public transport than most of the beaches in the area, and so it is a little more developed. But the beach is large enough that you can still find stretches for yourself.

Tamarindo is definitely popular with surfers. Playa Langosta, one km south of Tamarindo, is a favourite and uninhabited surfing beach. Four or five km further south is Playa Avellana, accessible either by walking along the coast or driving inland. This is another good surfing beach with both left and right breaks.

Places to Stay & Eat

There are a few cheap places to stay, of which the *Hotel Doly* (☎ 680174), near the beach, is one of the friendliest. Basic rooms go for about US$4 per person with shared bath, and a little more with private bath. The owner, Doly, will cook meals if you ask. *Cabinas Zullymar* (☎ 264732) is also friendly, and is near a couple of moderately priced restaurants and bars in the village. Clean rooms with private bath and fan rent for US$11/15 for a single/double.

The *Fiesta del Mar* restaurant has been recommended for excellent seafood. *Johann's Bakery* is good for snacks like pastries, croissants, coffee and juices. The bakery is on the right, just as you come into the village.

Just outside the village is *Cabinas Pozo Azul* (☎ 680147) which has air-con rooms with private bath and kitchenette. Rooms are US$20 for a double, larger cabins are US$30 for four people, and there's a pool.

The best hotel is the comfortable *Hotel Tamarindo Diria* (☎ 680652; Apartado 4211, San José; ☎ 330530) which is popular with ticos and is often full during the season, despite having about 60 rooms. Air-con rooms with private bath, hot water and TV cost about US$60/67 for a single/double. The hotel is in pleasant grounds with swimming pools, shaded areas, restaurant, tennis courts and games area. Fishing, diving, water-skiing and boating equipment may be rented. The gift shop sells essentials like sun screen.

Getting There & Away

Air SANSA (☎ 219414) has flights from San José to Tamarindo on Monday, Wednesday and Friday at 1.40 pm during the dry season.

Flights may be less frequent in the wet. The flight takes 35 minutes and costs US$18. Return flights leave 15 minutes after arrival and go on to Sámara to pick up more passengers before returning to San José. The airline office in Tamarindo is at the Diria Hotel.

SANSA package tours (☎ 226501) also has beach vacations which include airport transfers, flights, and two, three or four nights at Cabinas Pozo Azul. The price is about the same as buying the air ticket and hotel room yourself, but you get the airport transfer and convenience at no extra cost – a good deal. Packages including meals are also available at extra cost.

Road TRALAPA buses leave from Calle 20, Avenida 3, San José daily for Tamarindo. Empresa Alfaro at Avenida 5, Calle 14 & 16, San José also has a daily bus. A daily bus leaves Santa Cruz at 7 am for Tamarindo.

A taxi from Santa Cruz should cost about US$12 to US$15. Allow twice that from Liberia.

If you are driving, the better road is from Belén to Huacas and south. It is also possible to drive from Santa Cruz to 27 de Abril on a paved road and then north-west on a dirt road for 15 km to Tamarindo, but this route is rougher.

TAMARINDO NATIONAL WILDLIFE REFUGE

This national wildlife refuge is a bit of a sleeper – it is marked on few maps and not well publicised. Nevertheless, there it is – 420 hectares on the north side of the Río Matapalo estuary just north of Tamarindo village. The main attraction of the refuge is undoubtedly Playa Grande, which is an important nesting site for the leatherback turtle. These turtles are the largest in the world, and adults average an incredible 360 kg each – though specimens in excess of 500 kg are not particularly rare. The nesting season is October to March, and over 100 reptiles may be seen laying their eggs on Playa Grande during the course of a night.

Other things to look for when visiting this reserve are mangrove swamps, caimans, monkeys, otters, crabs and a good variety of birds.

Information

You can visit the reserve any time, but there are no facilities and camping is not allowed. Annual rainfall is almost 2000 mm (rather less than most other parts of coastal Costa Rica) and June to October are the wettest months.

Getting There & Away

The reserve is best visited by boat and people in Tamarindo have boats for hire. Ask around in your hotel and they'll put you in contact with a boat owner.

SANTA CRUZ

This small town is 21 km south of Filadelfia and a possible overnight stop when visiting the peninsula. The population of Santa Cruz and the surrounding district is over 15,000. A paved road leads 14 km west to 27 de Abril from where dirt roads continue to Playa Tamarindo, Playa Junquillal and other beaches. The main peninsula highway heads south-east from Santa Cruz for Nicoya, 20 km away.

The old highway used to go eight km east to Santa Bárbara and then 20 km south to Nicoya, passing **Guaitil** about four km south of Santa Bárbara. This route is now little used, but buses from Santa Cruz go to Guaitil several times a day. Guaitil is known for its pottery which is done in Chorotega Indian style. You can see people making pots outside their houses and there is a pottery cooperative. Ceramics are for sale, and tours to Guaitil are arranged by Guanacaste Tours in Liberia. If you want to go yourself, Santa Cruz is a good base.

There is an annual rodeo and fiesta during the second week in January.

Places to Stay & Eat

The cheapest hotels are the basic and noisy *Pensión Santa Cruz* next to the TRALAPA bus terminal, and the quieter *Pensión Isabel*

(☎ 680173) which is a block away. Both charge about US$3 per person and are OK.

The *Hotel Sharatoga* (☎ 680011; Apartado 345, Santa Cruz, Guanacaste), is half a block away from the TRALAPA terminal. Clean rooms with air-con and private bathrooms rent for US$16/21 single/double.

On the northern outskirts of town, only about six blocks from the centre, is the *Hotel Diria* (☎ 680080, 680402; Apartado 58, Santa Cruz, Guanacaste). It has a pool and restaurant, and air-con rooms with private bath are the same price as the Sharatoga. Both hotels have some kind of entertainment at weekends – live marimba music or recorded dance music are possibilities. If there is a group in one of the hotels, there may be a marimba show mid-week. (Marimbas are wooden xylophones of African origin, although some musicologists claim that the Central American version is of Guatemalan Indian origin.)

Check out *La Fabrica de Tortillas*, on a side street a couple of blocks from the plaza. It looks like a factory, but inside you can get good snacks, bread and tico-style meals as well as tortillas. It's interesting, and the food is tasty and inexpensive.

Getting There & Away

There are two bus terminals. The TRALAPA terminal is on the plaza, and the Alfaro terminal is two blocks south of it. TRALAPA has buses at 5 am to Junquillal, 7 am to Tamarindo and 9 am to Flamingo.

Alfaro has six buses a day from San José to Santa Cruz and on to Nicoya. There are also buses about every hour from Liberia.

PLAYA JUNQUILLAL

This is a wide and wild beach, with high surf, strong rip currents and few people. The beach is two km long and has tide pools and pleasant walking. The local people go surf fishing here.

Junquillal is about mid-way between Tamarindo and Ostional national wildlife refuges and sea turtles nest here, but in smaller numbers than at the refuges. There is no village, but there are a few places to stay.

Places to Stay

You can camp by the *Hotel Playa Junquillal* (☎ 680465) for about US$3 per night, or you can stay in one of their few basic cabins for about US$10 double. You could probably camp almost anywhere along the beach if you had your own food and water.

The *Hotel Antumalal* (☎ 680506; Apartado 49, Santa Cruz, Guanacaste) has 20 attractive cabins with private bath and fans. There is a pool and tennis court, and wild monkeys reportedly visit the grounds. Rates are about US$75/95 for a single/double with meals, rather less without.

The *Hotel Villa Serena* (☎ 680737; Apartado 17, Santa Cruz, Guanacaste) is a small and intimate hotel with seven rooms for lovers and nature lovers. Children are not accepted. The owners are always in residence to ensure everything is satisfactory. There is a small pool, sauna, tennis court, and horses for rent. Spacious rooms with private

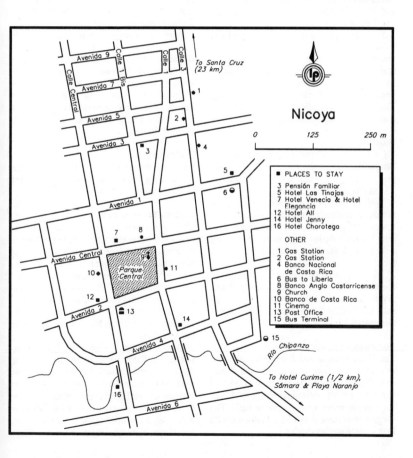

bathroom and patios facing the beach rent for US$100 double including meals. They are usually full during the dry season, so call ahead.

Getting There & Away

TRALAPA, Calle 20, Avenida 3 in San José has a daily bus to Junquillal taking about six hours. There is also a daily TRALAPA bus from Santa Cruz. The bus may go only as far as Paraíso, which is four km by foot or taxi from the beach.

If you are driving, it is about 16 km by paved road from Santa Cruz to 27 de Abril, and about a further 16 km by unpaved road via Paraíso to Junquillal.

From Junquillal, a rough road more or less follows the coast south to the end of the peninsula, but it is in poor shape and 4WD and plenty of time are essential. Expect to have to ford some rivers (especially if it has been raining) and carry spare everything. There are no gas stations on this coastal dirt road, and it carries little traffic.

NICOYA

To visit any of the beaches south of Junquillal, most people return to the main peninsula highway and go through Nicoya, 23 km south of Santa Cruz.

With a population of 22,500 including the surrounding district, it is the most important town on the peninsula. It is a historical place, with a church dating back to the mid-1600s next to a pleasant plaza which is worth a look.

Nicoya is now the commercial centre of the cattle industry as well as the political capital and transportation hub of the peninsula. US dollars can be exchanged at one of the several banks in town.

Places to Stay – bottom end

The *Hotel Venecia* and *Hotel Elegancia* are near the church and both are clean and reasonable value. The Venecia charges US$2.75 per person with communal baths, or US$9 for a triple room with a private bath. The Elegancia charges US$6.50 for a double with bath – there are no singles.

Just across the river at the south end of town is the *Hotel Chorotega* which is quiet and clean. Rooms are US$7 for a double with bath, and the few rooms without bath are cheaper. Other hotels in this price range include the *Pensión Familiar*, which is clean but over a bar and so might be a bit noisy, and the *Hotel Alí*, which seems the least satisfactory.

Places to Stay – middle

The *Hotel Las Tinajas* (☎ 685081) is clean and quite good. Rooms with private bath and fans are US$8/12 for a single/double. The *Hotel Jenny* (☎ 685050) is clean and friendly, and the people can help with bus information. Rooms with private bath (cold water), air-con and TV cost US$12/16 for a single/double. The best place is the *Hotel Curime* (☎ 685238) which is about half a km south of town on the road to Playa Sámara. There is a pool and restaurant, and rooms have air-con, a refrigerator and private bath with cold water. The rates are US$13/26 for a single/double.

Places to Eat

There are three or four Chinese restaurants in the town centre and they are considered the best places to eat.

Getting There & Away

There is a new bus terminal at the south end of Calle 5 in Nicoya from where most buses now leave. There is an antique bus on display here which was the first bus to make the San José to Nicoya run on 11 December 1958.

Both Alfaro and TRALAPA bus companies have several buses a day from San José to Nicoya. There are also buses from the terminal in Liberia to Nicoya about once an hour.

Departures for Liberia leave from Transportes La Pampa which has its office at Avenida 1 and Calle 5, but they may move to the new terminal by the time you are there. Departures for Liberia leave about once an hour; there are six buses a day for San José; four a day for Mansión; and one or two daily for Playa Naranjo, Playa Sámara, Playa

Top: Chirripó National Park, highest in Costa Rica (RR)
Left: Climbing in Chirripó National Park (RR)
Right: Hiking in Corcovado National Park (RR)

Top: Chirripó National Park (RR)
Left: Bromeliad (RR)
Right: Spider (RR)

Nosara, Quebrada Honda, Santa Ana, Copal and various other local towns. The departure for Playa Naranjo is at 5.15 am and 1 pm, connecting with the ferry from Naranjo to Puntarenas.

BARRA HONDA NATIONAL PARK

This 2295 hectare national park is unique in that it was created to protect an area of great geological and speleological interest rather than to conserve a particular habitat. (Speleology is the study and exploration of caves.)

The park lies roughly mid-way between Nicoya and the mouth of the Río Tempisque in a limestone area that has been uplifted into coastal hills over 500 metres in height. A combination of rainfall and erosion has created a series of deep caves, some in excess of 200 metres. There are reported to be over three dozen caves, but only about half of them have been explored and so Barra Honda is of special interest to speleologists looking for something new.

The caves come complete with stalagmites, stalactites and a host of beautiful and (to the non-speleologist) lesser known formations with intriguing names such as fried eggs, organs, soda straws, popcorn, curtains, columns, pearls, flowers and shark's teeth. Cave creatures including bats, sightless salamanders, fish in the streams running through the caves, and a variety of invertebrates live in the underground system. Pre-Columbian human skeletons have also been discovered, although who these people were or how they got into the caves remains a mystery.

None of the caves has easy access to the general public. There are no ladders, lights, walkways, elevators or guided tours available. Barra Honda is the preserve of experienced speleologists arriving with their own ropes and other technical equipment for descending the caves. The 55 metre deep Terciopelo Cave is one of the most beautiful and frequently visited. Visitors require special permits from the National Parks Service to enter most of the other caves. These include: Santa Ana, the deepest, at 249 metres; the Trampa (trap), which has a vertical 52 metre drop; the Nicoya, where human remains were found; and the *Pozo Hediondo* (stink-pot), which has a large bat colony.

Above the ground, the Barra Honda hills have trails and are covered with deciduous vegetation. The top of Cerro Barra Honda boasts a lookout with a good view of the area. There are waterfalls in the rainy reason and animals year-round. Howler and white-faced monkeys, armadillos and coatimundis are seen. Amazonian skunk (also called the striped hog-nosed skunk, *Conepatus semistriatus*) are supposedly frequently sighted.

Information

The dry season is considered to be the only time to go because entrance into the caves is dangerous and discouraged during the rainy months. However, you can come any time to climb the hills, admire the views and observe the wildlife.

There is a ranger station in the south-west corner of the park where basic sketch maps and information may be obtained. About 350 metres beyond the station there is an area with latrines and water where camping is permitted for about US$0.40 per day. Trails from the ranger station lead to the top of Cerro Barra Honda – allow about a half day for the round trip. Rangers will guide you if you call in advance. The message phone number for the park is 690810 (in Cañas).

For cave descents, you should make arrangements with the National Parks Service in San José several days before you go. Rangers used to have caving gear and could take you on a visit to Terciopelo Cave, but their equipment is now old, worn-out and dangerous so you should bring your own. (They may have new equipment by the time you get there – but I wouldn't rely on that.)

Getting There & Away

Getting to the park is somewhat confusing, because a map shows two ways to enter the park. Barra Honda is shaped like an inverted U; at the east end is the village of Quebrada Honda with a dirt road leading north from it into the park. Past reports indicate that there was an administration centre here, but it is now closed and this is no longer the best way to enter the park.

The west arm of the inverted U is the way to the ranger station. If you are driving from the Tempisque ferry, you will see a sign on the right hand side for 'Barra Honda' about 1½ km before you reach the main peninsula highway between Nicoya and Carmona. If you are driving from the peninsula highway, take the turn-off for the Tempisque Ferry and look for the Barra Honda road to your left after 1½ km – there is no sign if you are coming this way. From the turn-off, the road goes four km to the small community of Nacaome, from where a signed dirt road goes a further six km into the park. This road has some steep and rough stretches, and you may require 4WD in the rainy season.

No buses go to the park, but you can get a bus from Nicoya to Nacaome (the bus may be signed Barra Honda) and walk the last six km. There is also a daily bus from Nicoya to the village of Santa Ana, which is two or three km from the ranger station.

RÍO TEMPISQUE FERRY

The car and passenger ferry crossing is 15 km from the main peninsula road. See the description of the Río Tempisque Ferry in the chapter on North-western Costa Rica for more details.

PLAYA NOSARA

This attractive white sand beach is backed by a pocket of luxuriant vegetation which attracts birds and wildlife. The area has not been logged, partly because of the nearby wildlife refuge and partly because of real estate development – an unlikely sounding combination.

There are many houses and condominiums, some of which are lived in year round, and there are others which can be rented by the week or month. The permanent occupants are mainly foreign (especially North American) retirees. The expatriate community is interested in protecting some of the forest, which makes Nosara an attractive area to live in, and so you can see parrots and

toucans, armadillos and monkeys just a few metres away from the beach.

Note that the village and airport of Nosara are four km inland from the beach. Basic food supplies and petrol are available in the village.

The small beaches of Playa Pelada and Playa Guiones, a couple of km south of Playa Nosara, are both attractive and worth visiting if you have a few days.

Places to Stay & Eat

The basic and cheap *Cabinas Chorotega* (☎ 680836) is in the village. Camping is possible on the beach and there are shelters and water. There is reportedly a cheap pensión near the beach.

The usual place to stay is the *Hotel Playa Nosara* (☎ 680495; Apartado 4, 5233, Nosara, Guanacaste). It is attractively located on a hill top south of Playa Nosara. There are beautiful beach views, and there is a pool and restaurant. Rooms have private baths with hot water and fans, and cost about US$30/40 for a single/double.

The *Gilded Iguana Bar & Restaurant* (☎ 680749) has good food but it's not for the budget minded. The are apartments with kitchenettes for rent. The *Condominio Los Flores* (☎ 680696) rents apartments with kitchens and hot water. Expect to pay about US$50 per apartment. If you are interested in long term (minimum one week) rental of a house, try calling 680747. Houses start at about US$200 per week.

Getting There & Away

Air SANSA (☎ 219414) has flights from San José to Nosara on Monday, Wednesday and Friday. Flights leave at 6 am, take 35 minutes, and return from Nosara at 6.50 am; the fare is US$18. Make reservations well in advance during the dry season, and reconfirm frequently.

SANSA package tours (☎ 226561) has two, three and four night visits to Nosara which include ground transfers, air fare, breakfasts and one other daily meal, and overnight stays at the Hotel Playa Nosara. The cost per person, double occupancy, is

US$95 for two nights and an extra US$30 for each extra night.

Road The 35 km dirt road from Nicoya to Nosara is a poor one, and buses are occasionally unable to get through in the wet season. There is a daily bus from Nicoya at 1 pm during the dry season, and at 5 am in the wet season. Buses return to Nicoya at 6 am in the dry months and 12 noon in the wet. The journey lasts two to five hours depending on road conditions.

If you are driving, 4WD is recommended in the wet season. It is also possible to go north to Junquillal and south to Sámara on the coastal road, but this is a very rough road which requires 4WD and is not for people in a hurry.

OSTIONAL NATIONAL WILDLIFE REFUGE

This coastal refuge includes the beaches of Playa Nosara, Playa Ostional, the mouth of the Río Nosara, and the beach-side village of Ostional. The reserve is a narrow strip about eight km long but only a few hundred metres wide. The protected land area is 162 hectares; in addition 587 hectares of adjoining sea are also protected.

The main attraction and reason for creation of the refuge is the annual nesting of the olive ridley sea turtle on the Ostional beach. This beach and the Nancite beach in Santa Rosa National Park are the most important nesting grounds for the olive ridley in Costa Rica (see Santa Rosa National Park for more information). The nesting season lasts from July to November, and tens of thousands of turtles arrive during this period.

Coastal residents used to harvest both eggs and turtles indiscriminately and this made the creation of a protected area essential for the continued wellbeing of the turtles. An imaginative conservation plan has allowed the inhabitants of Ostional to continue to harvest the eggs from early layings. Most turtles return to the beach several times to lay new clutches, and earlier eggs may be trampled or damaged by later layings. Thus

it seems reasonable to allow the locals to harvest the first batches and sell them – they are popular snacks in bars throughout the country.

The turtles tend to arrive in large groups of hundreds or even thousands of individuals – these mass arrivals, or *arribadas*, occur every three or four weeks and last for about a week. However, you can see turtles in lesser numbers almost any night you go during the nesting season. Villagers will guide you to the best places.

The leatherback and Pacific green turtle also nest here in smaller numbers. Apart from the turtles, there are iguanas, crabs, howler monkeys, coatimundis and many birds to be seen. Some of the best birding is at the south-east end of the refuge, near the mouth of the Río Nosara, where there is a small mangrove swamp.

The rocky India Point at the north-west end of the refuge has many tide pools abounding with marine creatures such as sea anemones, sea urchins, starfish, shellfish and fish-fish. Along the beach are thousands of almost transparent ghost crabs, bright red Sally lightfoot crabs and a variety of lizards. The vegetation behind the beach is sparse, and consists mainly of deciduous trees such as frangipani and stands of cacti.

Information

The rainy season is from May to December and the annual rainfall is about 1700 mm. The best time to see the turtles is the rainy season, so be prepared. Average day time temperatures are 28°C. There is no ranger station but the villagers of Ostional are helpful with information and will guide you to the best areas. Ostional has a small store (☎ 680467) where you can get basic food supplies.

Places to Stay

Camping is permitted, but there are no camping facilities. The Ostional store has a few inexpensive cabins for rent.

Getting There & Away

The refuge begins at Playa Nosara, and the

village is about five km north-west of Nosara village. This road is passable, but poor. Reports indicate that the road from Santa Cruz to Junquillal and south along the coast to Ostional is better.

During the dry months, there is a daily bus from Santa Cruz. Public transport is hard to find during the wet season. Many of the better hotels in the region offer tours to Ostional during egg laying periods.

PLAYA GARZA

This small beach is about 11 km south of Nosara along a dirt road. The beach is picturesquely set in a rocky cove with an island at the mouth of the bay.

Places to Stay

There is one good hotel, the *Villagio Guaria Morada* (☎ 680784; Apartado 860, 1007 Centro Colón, San José). There are 30 pleasant cottages, each with private bath, renting for US$65/75 for a single/double. The rooms have no air-con and no fans, but the sea breezes and shady roofs keep them reasonably cool. There is a good restaurant, pool and disco, and horse riding, fishing and snorkelling can be arranged.

PLAYA SÁMARA

This beach is 16 km south-east of Garza and about 35 km south-west of Nicoya. Sámara has a beautiful, gentle, white sand beach which has been called one of the safest and prettiest in Costa Rica. It has gained much popularity in recent years. Former President Oscar Arias has a vacation house near here, as do many other ticos. It is also a favourite beach for tourists, and has an improving bus and air service.

The village has a general store, a discotheque and a couple of basic hotels, restaurants and bars. Local inhabitants (other than retirees!) do a little farming and fishing.

Places to Stay & Eat

The village of Sámara is at the north end of the beach and you can camp near here. The best of the cheap and basic hotels is the *Cabinas Los Almendros* which charges about US$8/12 for single/double rooms with private bath. There is a restaurant attached, and a disco next door.

Cheaper places include the *Cabinas Punta Sámara*, *Hospedaje Yuri* and *Cabinas Milena* – these lack private baths but seem OK for the budget minded. There are other places if you ask around.

The best hotel is at the south end of the beach, a little over a km from the village. This is the *Hotel Las Brisas del Pacífico* (☎ 680876; Apartado 709, 3000 Heredia, Costa Rica). There is a pool, jacuzzi and a good restaurant with a German chef known for his delicious desserts as well as tasty meals. The hotel has a gift shop and sells SANSA airline tickets. Horses, boats, surfboards and diving gear are available for rent. Comfortable and spacious cabins, all with hot water and some with air-con, rent for US$50; single rates are difficult to get during the dry season.

Getting There & Away

Air SANSA (☎ 219414) has flights to Sámara on Monday, Wednesday and Friday. The plane leaves San José at 1.40 pm with an intermediate stop at Tamarindo, arriving at Sámara at 2.45 pm. The return flight is direct to San José and leaves at 3 pm, taking 35 minutes; the fare is US$18. Tickets should be bought well in advance and reconfirmed frequently.

SANSA vacation packages (☎ 226561) offers two, three and four night vacations including airport transfers, flights, accommodation at the Hotel Las Brisas del Pacífico, breakfasts, and one other meal a day. The cost per person, double occupancy, is US$96 for two nights, and an extra US$31 per extra night.

Road Empresa Alfaro in San José has a daily bus to Sámara taking six hours. Buses from Nicoya leave at 8 am and 3 pm, take about two hours and cost US$1.25. During the wet season there is only one bus a day, and it takes longer.

All the roads to Sámara are in poor condition – 4WD is recommended in the wet season.

PLAYA CARRILLO

This beach is four or five km south of Sámara, and is a smaller, quieter version of it. There are a few basic cabinas to stay in. There is also the expensive Hotel Guanamar which is popular as a base for fishing trips.

Places to Stay

The *Guanamar* (☎ 536133; Apartado 1373, 1000 San José) is attractively located on a cliff with good views and ocean breezes. There is a pool and restaurant. Rooms with private bath and fans are about US$180 for a double including all meals, or US$100 for a double without meals. Fishing trips and equipment are not included in the price. There is a private airstrip into which you can charter planes. Diving, boating and horse riding can all be arranged.

SOUTH-WEST PENINSULA BEACHES

It is possible to continue beyond Playa Carrillo, more or less paralleling the coast, to reach the southern tip of the peninsula. It is about 70 km by very rough road from Playa Carrillo to the town of Cóbano – allow about four hours for the trip if you have a 4WD vehicle and encounter no delays. Several rivers have to be forded, including the Río Ora about five km east of Carrillo. This river can be impassable at high tide, even to 4WD jeeps, so check the tides and water levels.

There are various small communities and deserted beaches along this stretch of coast, but accommodation and public transport is minimal. The bus company at Calle 12, Avenida 7 & 9, opposite the Puntarenas bus terminal in San José, has a daily bus which crosses the Gulf of Nicoya on the Puntarenas ferry and continues through the village of **Jicaral** (a couple of basic pensiónes) to **Bejuco** and **Islita**, two villages on the coast about 15 and 30 km respectively south-east of Carrillo. These places may have basic cabinas, but be prepared to camp.

I was unable to discover any other bus services further south along the coast.

Adventurous drivers with 4WD could continue on past Playa San Miguel, Playa Coyote (there's a bar here), Playa Caletas and Playa Manzanillo (camp at any of these places if you are self sufficient) before heading inland to Cóbano, Montezuma and Cabo Blanco. These places are most usually reached by the road which connects with the Puntarenas to Playa Naranjo ferry and follows the south-eastern part of the peninsula.

PLAYA NARANJO

This village is the terminal for the Puntarenas ferry, and the beach is not very exciting. Most ferry passengers continue on to Nicoya, about 70 km to the north-west, or drive further south into the Nicoya Peninsula.

Places to Stay

The *Hotel del Paso* (☎ 612610; Apartado 232, 2120 San José) has clean air-con rooms with private bath for US$17/30 for a single/double, including breakfast. Cheaper rates are available for rooms without air-con or breakfast.

The *Hotel Oasis del Pacífico* (☎ 611555; Apartado 200, Puntarenas) is a resort hotel. Perhaps because the beach is not very good, this place is rarely full. There is a pool, tennis courts and disco, and horses and boats can be rented. The restaurant is good and not too expensive, and the grounds are pleasant. Rooms with fans and private bath cost US$35/45 for a single/double.

Getting There & Away

All transport is geared to the arrival and departure of the ferry. The hotels pick up ferry passengers if they know you are coming – although you could walk as it's not far.

Buses meet the ferry and take passengers to Nicoya, three to four hours away. If you want to go elsewhere, you have to first make your way from Nicoya.

There are two options if you want to head south: either bring your own vehicle across on the ferry, and drive; or take the Puntarenas to Paquera passenger ferry. From Paquera there are buses to the southern part of the peninsula. If you drive, you'll find that the road has some very steep sections – an ordinary passenger vehicle will have difficulty in making some of the grades if it is loaded down with gear and four passengers.

The ferry (☎ 611069 for information) leaves daily at 9 am and 6 pm, plus there is a 2 pm ferry on Thursday, Saturday and Sunday. (The ferry arrives from Puntarenas a short while before these departure times; see under Puntarenas for more details.)

BAHÍA GIGANTE
This bay is about eight km south-east of Playa Naranjo.

Places to Stay
The good *Hotel Bahía Gigante* (☎ 612442; Apartado 1866, San José) has pleasant views of the bay, and large forested grounds where you can hike and bird-watch. Monkeys and other mammals can be seen. Boat trips to the nearby islands can be arranged, and fishing and horse riding is available. There is a restaurant and pool. Spacious rooms with fans and private baths are about US$25 for a double; larger apartments are twice that.

PAQUERA
It is about 20 km by road from Playa Naranjo to Paquera. The village is four km from the Paquera ferry terminal. The passenger ferries operate to Puntarenas at 8 am and 5 pm daily.

A very crowded truck takes passengers into Paquera village, where there are a couple of basic pensiónes. Most travellers take the bus from the ferry terminal to Cóbano (two hours, US$1.25). The bus is very crowded; try to get off the ferry early to get a seat. A taxi to Cóbano costs about US$25; taxis usually meet the ferry.

CURÚ NATIONAL WILDLIFE REFUGE
This small 84 hectare refuge is at the eastern end of the Nicoya Peninsula, about four km south of Paquera village. Despite its small size, a great variety of habitats exists here. There are deciduous and semi-deciduous

forests with large forest trees, mangrove swamps with five different mangrove species, sand beaches fringed by palm trees, and rocky headlands. The forested areas are the haunts of deer, monkeys, agoutis and pacas, and three species of cat have been recorded. Iguanas, crabs, lobsters, chitons, shellfish, sea turtles and other marine creatures are found on the beaches and in the tide pools. The snorkelling and swimming is good. Birders have recorded 115 species of birds, but there are probably more. For such a small place, it has a lot of wildlife.

Information
An intriguing feature of this national wildlife refuge is that it is privately owned. The owners, Señora Julieta Schutz and children (☎ 612392, 616392) can provide tours, rustic accommodation, and home cooked meals if arranged in advance. The Schutzs consider Curú to be a living laboratory for researchers and students (who have priority for the rooms) but travellers are sometimes accommodated. Most of the better hotels in the area will arrange day tours to Curú. The reserve is not signed and is down a dirt road (as is everything in this area!). Call in advance if you want to visit to get directions and make sure the gate is open.

PLAYA TAMBOR
This long dark sand beach is protected by the Bahía Ballena (Whale Bay), the largest bay on the southern peninsula coastline. The calm beach is safe for swimming and whales are sometimes sighted in the bay. It is a tranquil area with three good hotels.

Places to Stay & Eat
Right in the middle of the Whale Bay shoreline is the *Hotel La Hacienda* (☎ 612980; Apartado 398, 2050 San Pedro, San José). The hotel is named after the 7000 hectare hacienda on which it is located. Horses are available for rides around the ranch, and fishing and local tours can be arranged. Most of the nearby wildlife refuges can be visited on day trips for about US$40 per person. There is a pool, tennis court and a decent

restaurant. Rooms with fans and private bath are US$30/40 for a single/double, and cabins sleeping up to six cost US$75. The hacienda has a private airstrip and you can charter planes from San José, or you can arrive by bus. The Paquera to Cóbano bus will drop you off near the hacienda.

At the south end of the beach, in the village of Tambor, is the *Hotel Dos Lagartos* (☎ 611122). It is clean and friendly, and has beach views and a restaurant. Rooms with private bath are US$10/14 for a single/double; rooms with shared bath are less. They can also arrange tours to nearby areas. There are a couple of cheaper basic pensiónes and an inexpensive restaurant in the village.

The *Tango Mar Club* (☎ 612798; Apartado 3877, 1000 San José) is three km south of Tambor village. It is a new beach-front resort complex with a pool, golf course, tennis court and restaurant. The club is built on 50 hectares of property and has some primary forest left. Tours are available, and you can rent 4WD jeeps, boating, fishing and diving gear, and horses. Spacious individual cabins with private bath are US$70 for a double. You can arrive by the Paquera to Cóbano bus, or you can charter a flight and arrange to be picked up at the airstrip.

CÓBANO
This small inland town is the end of the road as far as the bus is concerned. There is a basic pensión, but few people stay here. Taxis meet the bus to take people to the pleasant seaside village of Montezuma, about seven km away. The fare is US$3 to US$4.

MONTEZUMA
This remote little fishing village near the tip of the Nicoya Peninsula has good beaches, friendly residents, and several inexpensive hotels. A half hour stroll takes you to a lovely waterfall with a swimming hole, and there is a beautiful nature reserve a few km away. Montezuma has gained popularity of late with younger gringo travellers who enjoy the laid back atmosphere and affordable prices.

Until recently, there was only one tele-phone in town, at Chico's Bar (☎ 612472). This was the message phone for the whole village – and it sort of worked, some of the time. Now there is a new central phone number, 611122, with extensions to various hotels, houses and restaurants. This new system is expanding.

Places to Stay – bottom end
The cheapest accommodation is your tent – you can camp on a beach reasonably safely, though I wouldn't leave any gear unattended. Mischievous monkeys will remove anything that looks edible or just interesting. There is a shower in the public park behind Chico's Bar.

For better security, you could camp in front of the El Pargo Feliz restaurant. They charge a couple of dollars and allow you to use their bathroom and shower facilities.

Cabinas Karen near the entrance of town, is a white house with a couple of basic rooms. There are communal bathroom and kitchen facilities available. Doña Karen is a well known local (originally from Denmark) who also runs a set of cabins with simple facilities in a private reserve 1½ km outside of town. Along with her late husband Nils, she was responsible for founding the nearby Cabo Blanco Reserve, and she continues to be an avid conservationist. Her private 69 hectare preserve is only open to those staying in one of her four cabins. There is no electricity and bathroom facilities are outside. There is a communal kitchen. Monkeys, birds and other animals abound – it is an opportunity to almost camp in the wild yet still retain a roof over your head and a real bed. Rates are US$5 per person – she doesn't take reservations so you just show up and hope for the best.

The *Hotel Montezuma* (☎ 611122, ext 258) is the biggest hotel, with a couple of dozen rooms. There is a restaurant, and the owners will help with arranging local excursions to reserves. Clean, large rooms with fans and private bathroom cost US$5.50 per person, less in rooms with shared bath. The *Cabinas Mar y Cielo* (☎ 611122, ext 261) are also clean and the charge is about US\$7 per person in rooms with private bath and fan.

Other hotels in this price range include the *Casa Blanca*, next door to Cabinas Karen (in town); and *Hospedaje Alfaro*, with large rooms suitable for families.

Cheaper rooms can be found at the basic but clean and friendly *Cabinas Arenas*, where the charge is about US\$3 per person and there's a small family-run restaurant attached. Another cheap possibility is the *Pensión Lucy*.

Places to Stay – middle

The people who run the *El Sano Banano* restaurant (☎ 611122, ext 272) have a few cabins for rent by the beach. Cabins with one or two bedrooms, private bathroom and kitchen are about US\$30 to US\$40 depending on the size. The owners of this place also rent bicycles.

Montezuma is growing – I would expect more middle range accommodation to open up in the next few years.

Places to Eat

Chico's Bar is the traditional place to go for a beer and a meal – the food is simple, good and not too expensive. Also good is the *El Sano Banano* macrobiotic restaurant which serves yoghurt, juices and sane bananas (*sano* actually means 'healthy', but sane seems like a better transcription!) as well as full vegetarian meals. They have a big-screen TV and show movies about four times a week. *El Pargo Feliz* (the happy red snapper) is good for seafood. Lobsters in season go for about US\$10; fish dishes are less than half that. Out of town a little way, on the road to Cabo Blanco, is the *El Caracol* (the snail) which serves inexpensive casados.

Getting There & Away

The 6 am ferry from Puntarenas connects with the Paquera to Cóbano bus. A taxi from Cóbano will get you to Montezuma (US\$3 to US\$4) in plenty of time for lunch. The 3 pm ferry gets into Montezuma well after dark

– not a good time to be looking for hotels in this sleepy town.

Be in Cóbano by 5.30 am to get the bus connecting with the 8 am ferry to Puntarenas, or take your time and catch the 5 pm ferry. A taxi from Montezuma direct to Paquera costs about US\$25.

CABO BLANCO STRICT NATURE RESERVE

This beautiful reserve encompasses 1172 hectares and includes the entire southern tip of the Nicoya Peninsula. It is about 11 km south of Montezuma by very bad dirt road – 4WD is needed in the rainy season.

The reserve preserves an evergreen forest, a couple of attractive beaches, and a host of birds and animals. There are several km of trails, which are excellent for wildlife observation – often, you'll not see anybody else for hours on end. Monkeys, squirrels, sloths, deer, agoutis and raccoons are among the more common sightings – ocelots and margays have also been recorded, but you'd have to be very lucky to see one of these elusive wild cats. Peccaries and anteaters are also present.

A trail leads from the ranger station to the beaches at the tip of the peninsula. The hike takes a couple of hours and passes through lush forest before emerging at the coast – a great opportunity to see many different kinds of birds, ranging from parrots and trogons in the forest to pelicans and boobies on the coast. You can visit two beaches at the peninsula tip and then return by a different trail. The high point of the reserve is 375 metres, and parts of the trail are steep and strenuous.

The coastal area is known as an important nesting site of the brown booby. Some nest on the mainland, but most are found on Cabo Blanco Island, 1½ km south of the mainland. The island supposedly gains its name (white cape) from the bird-droppings (or guano) encrusting the rocks. It is difficult to get to the island unless you get permission from the National Parks Service and can gain access to a boat. Fishermen in Montezuma may be willing to help you. Other sea birds in the area include brown pelicans, and magnificent frigate birds. The beaches at the tip of the peninsula also abound in the usual marine life – starfish, sea anemones, sea urchins, conchs, lobsters, crabs and tropical fish are a few of the things to look for.

Information

Inside the park is a ranger station where you pay a nominal entrance fee and can obtain a trail map. Officially, the reserve is open from 7 am to 4 pm.

Check with the park rangers about trails and tides. The trail joining the two beaches at the tip of the reserve may be impassable at high tide.

Average annual temperatures are about 27°C and annual rainfall is between 1600 and 2000 mm. The best months to go are December to April – the dry season. One brochure claims that only one mm of rain falls in January, February and March, but I have great difficulty in believing that.

Places to Stay

Camping is not permitted, but it may be possible to obtain a camping permit from the National Parks Service, although there are no camping facilities.

Getting There & Away

If you don't have your own car, you can hire a jeep taxi to take you the 11 km from Montezuma to the park entrance. The trip costs about US$15 (the road is so poor) but you can get about six people into a jeep.

Index

MAPS

TEXT

Where Can You Find Out.........

HOW to get a Laotian visa in Bangkok?

WHERE to go birdwatching in PNG?

WHAT to expect from the police if you're robbed in Peru?

WHEN you can go to see cow races in Australia?

In the Lonely Planet Newsletter!

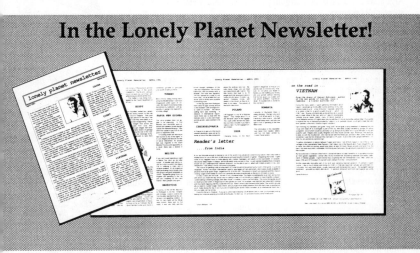

Every issue includes:

- a letter from Lonely Planet founders Tony and Maureen Wheeler

- a letter from an author 'on the road'

- the most entertaining or informative reader's letter we've received

- the latest news on new and forthcoming releases from Lonely Planet

- and all the latest travel news from all over the world

Guides to the Americas

Alaska - a travel survival kit

Jim DuFresne has travelled extensively through Alaska by foot, road, rail, barge and kayak, and tells how to make the most of one of the world's great wilderness areas.

Argentina - a travel survival kit

This guide gives independent travellers all the essential information on Argentina — a land of intriguing cultures, 'wild west' overtones and spectacular scenery.

Baja California - a travel survival kit

For centuries, Mexico's Baja peninsula — with its beautiful coastline, raucous border towns and crumbling Spanish missions — has been a land of escapes and escapades. This book describes how and where to escape in Baja.

Bolivia - a travel survival kit

From lonely villages in the Andes to ancient ruined cities and the spectacular city of La Paz, Bolivia is a magnificent blend of everything that inspires travellers. Discover safe and intriguing travel options in this comprehensive guide.

Brazil - a travel survival kit

From the mad passion of Carnival to the Amazon — home of the richest and most diverse ecosystem on earth — Brazil is a country of mythical proportions. This guide has all the essential travel information.

Canada - a travel survival kit

This comprehensive guidebook has all the facts on the USA's huge neighbour — the Rocky Mountains, Niagara Falls, ultra-modern Toronto, remote villages in Nova Scotia, and much more.

Chile & Easter Island - a travel survival kit

Travel in Chile is easy and safe, with possibilities as varied as the countryside. This guide also gives detailed coverage of Chile's Pacific outpost, mysterious Easter Island.

Colombia - a travel survival kit
Colombia is a land of myths — from the ancient legends of El Dorado to the modern tales of Gabriel Garcia Marquez. The reality is beauty and violence, wealth and poverty, tradition and change. This guide shows how to travel independently and safely in this exotic country.

Ecuador & the Galápagos Islands - a travel survival kit
Ecuador offers a wide variety of travel experiences, from the high cordilleras to the Amazon plains — and 600 miles west, the fascinating Galápagos Islands. Everything you need to know about travelling around this enchanting country.

Hawaii - a travel survival kit
Share in the delights of this island paradise — and avoid its high prices — both on and off the beaten track. Full details on Hawaii's best-known attractions, plus plenty of uncrowded sights and activities.

Mexico - a travel survival kit
A unique blend of Indian and Spanish culture, fascinating history, and hospitable people, make Mexico a travellers' paradise.

Peru - a travel survival kit
The lost city of Machu Picchu, the Andean altiplano and the magnificent Amazon rainforests are just some of Peru's many attractions. All the travel facts you'll need can be found in this comprehensive guide.

South America on a shoestring
This practical guide provides concise information for budget travellers and covers South America from the Darien Gap to Tierra del Fuego. By the author the *New York Times* nominated 'the patron saint of travelers in the third world'.

Also available:
Brazilian phrasebook, *Latin American Spanish* phrasebook and *Quechua* phrasebook.

Lonely Planet Guidebooks

Lonely Planet guidebooks cover every accessible part of Asia as well as Australia, the Pacific, South America, Africa, the Middle East and parts of North America and Europe. There are four series: *travel survival kits*, covering a single country for a range of budgets; *shoestring guides* with compact information for low-budget travel in a major region; *walking guides*; and *phrasebooks*.

Australia & the Pacific
Australia
Bushwalking in Australia
Islands of Australia's Great Barrier Reef
Fiji
Micronesia
New Caledonia
New Zealand
Tramping in New Zealand
Papua New Guinea
Papua New Guinea phrasebook
Rarotonga & the Cook Islands
Samoa
Solomon Islands
Sydney
Tahiti & French Polynesia
Tonga
Vanuatu

South-East Asia
Bali & Lombok
Burma
Burmese phrasebook
Indonesia
Indonesia phrasebook
Malaysia, Singapore & Brunei
Philippines
Pilipino phrasebook
Singapore
South-East Asia on a shoestring
Thailand
Thai phrasebook
Vietnam, Laos & Cambodia

North-East Asia
China
Chinese phrasebook
Hong Kong, Macau & Canton
Japan
Japanese phrasebook
Korea
Korean phrasebook
North-East Asia on a shoestring
Taiwan
Tibet
Tibet phrasebook

West Asia
Trekking in Turkey
Turkey
Turkish phrasebook
West Asia on a shoestring

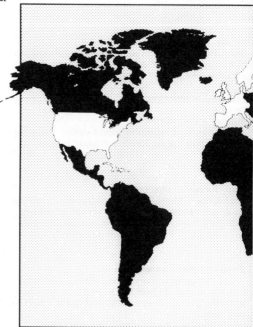

Indian Ocean
Madagascar & Comoros
Maldives & Islands of the East Indian Ocean
Mauritius, Réunion & Seychelles

Mail Order

Lonely Planet guidebooks are distributed worldwide and are sold by good bookshops everywhere. They are also available by mail order from Lonely Planet, so if you have difficulty finding a title please write to us. US and Canadian residents should write to Embarcadero West, 112 Linden St, Oakland CA 94607, USA and residents of other countries to PO Box 617, Hawthorn, Victoria 3122, Australia.

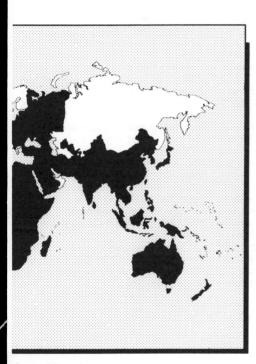

Europe
Eastern Europe on a shoestring
Iceland, Greenland & the Faroe Islands
Trekking in Spain

Indian Subcontinent
Bangladesh
India
Hindi/Urdu phrasebook
Trekking in the Indian Himalaya
Karakoram Highway
Kashmir, Ladakh & Zanskar
Nepal
Trekking in the Nepal Himalaya
Nepal phrasebook
Pakistan
Sri Lanka
Sri Lanka phrasebook

Africa
Africa on a shoestring
Central Africa
East Africa
Kenya
Swahili phrasebook
Morocco, Algeria & Tunisia
Moroccan Arabic phrasebook
West Africa

North America
Alaska
Canada
Hawaii

Mexico
Baja California
Mexico

South America
Argentina
Bolivia
Brazil
Brazilian phrasebook
Chile & Easter Island
Colombia
Ecuador & the Galápagos Islands
Latin American Spanish phrasebook
Peru
Quechua phrasebook
South America on a shoestring

Central America
Costa Rica
La Ruta Maya

Middle East
Egypt & the Sudan
Egyptian Arabic phrasebook
Israel
Jordan & Syria
Yemen

The Lonely Planet Story

Lonely Planet published its first book in 1973 in response to the numerous 'How did you do it?' questions Maureen and Tony Wheeler were asked after driving, bussing, hitching, sailing and railing their way from England to Australia.

Written at a kitchen table and hand collated, trimmed and stapled, *Across Asia on the Cheap* became an instant local bestseller, inspiring thoughts of another book.

Eighteen months in South-East Asia resulted in their second guide, *South-East Asia on a shoestring*, which they put together in a backstreet Chinese hotel in Singapore in 1975. The 'yellow bible' as it quickly became known to backpackers around the world, soon became *the* guide to the region. It has sold well over ½ million copies and is now in its 6th edition, still retaining its familiar yellow cover.

Today there are over 80 Lonely Planet titles – books that have that same adventurous approach to travel as those early guides; books that 'assume you know how to get your luggage off the carousel' as one reviewer put it.

Although Lonely Planet initially specialised in guides to Asia, they now cover most regions of the world, including the Pacific, South America, Africa, the Middle East and Eastern Europe. The list of *walking guides* and *phrasebooks* (for 'unusual' languages such as Quechua, Swahili, Nepalese and Egyptian Arabic) is also growing rapidly.

The emphasis continues to be on travel for independent travellers. Tony and Maureen still travel for several months of each year and play an active part in the writing, updating and quality control of Lonely Planet's guides.

They have been joined by over 50 authors, 40 staff – mainly editors, cartographers, & designers – at our office in Melbourne, Australia, and another 10 at our US office in Oakland, California. Travellers themselves also make a valuable contribution to the guides through the feedback we receive in thousands of letters each year.

The people at Lonely Planet strongly believe that travellers can make a positive contribution to the countries they visit, both through their appreciation of the countries' culture, wildlife and natural features, and through the money they spend. In addition, the company makes a direct contribution to the countries and regions it covers. Since 1986 a percentage of the income from each book has been donated to ventures such as famine relief in Africa; aid projects in India; agricultural projects in Central America; Greenpeace's efforts to halt French nuclear testing in the Pacific and Amnesty International. In 1990 $60,000 was donated to these causes.

Lonely Planet's basic travel philosophy is summed up in Tony Wheeler's comment, 'Don't worry about whether your trip will work out. Just go!'